The Promise of Amida Buddha

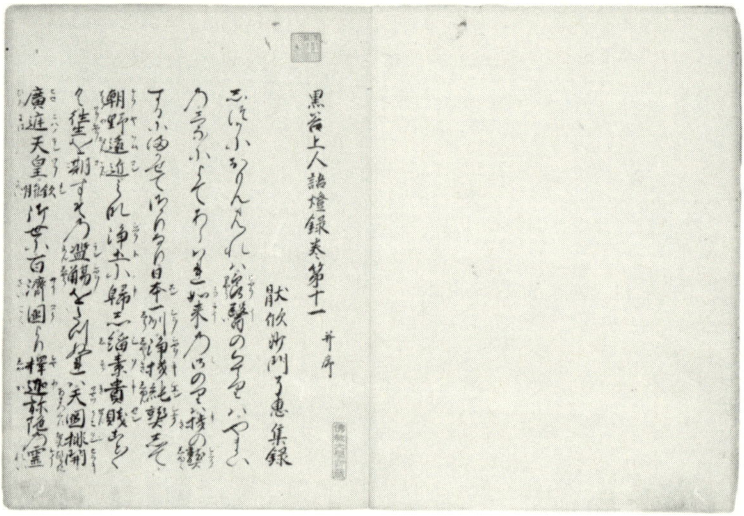

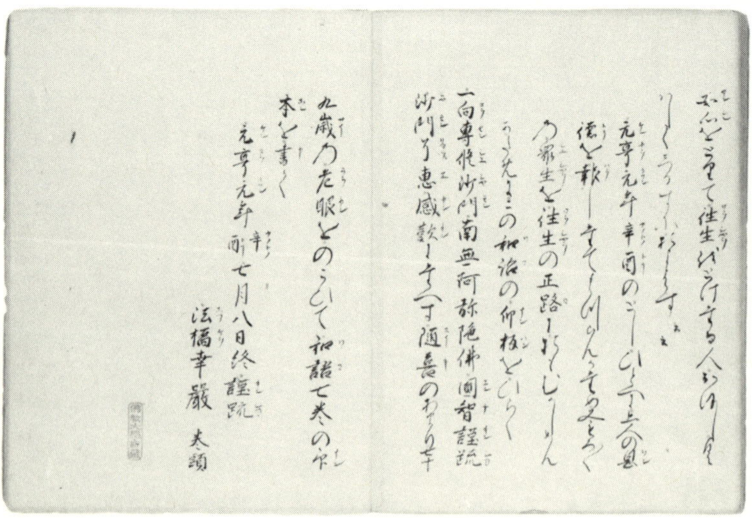

Collected Teachings of Kurodani-shōnin: The Japanese Anthology (Wago Tōroku).
In the collection of Bukkyō University in Kyoto, Japan.

The Promise of Amida Buddha

HŌNEN'S PATH TO BLISS

法然上人和語燈録

Translated by
Jōji Atone & Yōko Hayashi

WISDOM PUBLICATIONS • BOSTON

Wisdom Publications
199 Elm Street
Somerville MA 02144 USA
www.wisdompubs.org

Library of Congress Cataloging-in-Publication Data
Honen, 1133–1212.
[Works. English. 2011]
The promise of Amida Buddha : Hōnen's path to bliss / translated by Jōji Atone & Yōko Hayashi.
p. cm.
Translated from Japanese.
Includes bibliographical references and index.
ISBN 0-86171-696-5 (hardcover : alk. paper)
1. Pure Land Buddhism—Early works to 1800. I. Atone, Joji, 1951– II. Hayashi, Yoko. III. Title.
BQ8649.H662 2011
294.3'926—dc22
2011007533

ISBN 978-0-86171-696-8
eBook ISBN 978-0-86171-693-7
16 15 14 13 12 11
6 5 4 3 2 1

Cover and interior design by Gopa & Ted2, Inc.
Cover image: Hōnen-shōnin (1133–1212). From the Chion-in Temple in Kyōto, Japan.

Wisdom Publications' books are printed on acid-free paper and meet the guidelines for permanence and durability of the Production Guidelines for Book Longevity of the Council on Library Resources.

Printed in the United States of America.

This book was produced with environmental mindfulness. We have elected to print this title on 30% PCW recycled paper. As a result, we have saved the following resources: 28 trees, 9 million BTUs of energy, 2,672 lbs. of greenhouse gases, 12,868 gallons of water, and 781 lbs. of solid waste. For more information, please visit our website, www.wisdompubs.org. This paper is also FSC certified. For more information, please visit www.fscus.org.

Table of Contents

Foreword ix

Preface xi

Introduction 1

The Historical Development of Nembutsu: From Meditation to Recitation 4

An Outline of *Collected Teachings of Hōnen: The Japanese Anthology* 39

A Chronology of Events during the Lifetime of Hōnen 59

PART I: COLLECTED TEACHINGS OF HŌNEN: THE JAPANESE ANTHOLOGY

Prologue 67

1. Commentary on the Three Sutras of Pure Land Buddhism 71
2. The Covenant 92
3. An Outline of the Doctrine for Birth in the Pure Land 93
4. Essential Discourse on Birth in the Pure Land through Nembutsu 118
5. The Significance of the Threefold Devotional Heart 129

6. Instruction in the Seven Articles 134
7. An Outline of Nembutsu 142
8. An Outline of the Essentials of Jōdo Shū 156
9. A Reply to the Lady Kujō 175
10. A Reply to the Nun Holding the Second Rank in the Court of Kamakura 178
11. Dialogue on the Essentials of Nembutsu 185
12. A Reply to Tarō Sanehide in Ōgo 214
13. A Reply to the Lady of Tarō Sanehide in Ōgo 226
14. A Reply to the Lay Priest in Kumagai 234
15. A Reply to the Lay Priest Saburō in Tsunoto 235
16. A Letter to an Eminent Monk in Kuroda 240
17. A Reply to Kōmyō-bō in Ecchū 243
18. A Letter to Nun Shōnyo-bō 246
19. Instruction to Zenshō-bō 253
20. Dialogue on Twelve Topics 255
21. Dialogue on Twelve Issues 263
22. Dialogue on One Hundred Forty-Five Topics 274
23. A Dialogue Between Hōnen-shōnin and Myōhen-sōzu 302
24. The Sayings of Hōnen-shōnin as Stated by His Disciples 304

Part II: First Supplement to Collected Teachings of Hōnen: The Japanese Anthology

25. The Statement Sent to Mount Hiei 323
26. Instruction to a Devotee 346

27. Replies to Saburō in Tsunoto 349

A Reply to Saburō Dated October 18th 349

A Reply to Saburō Dated September 28th 353

A Reply to Saburō Dated April 26th 355

28. Instruction to a Lady 357

PART III: SECOND SUPPLEMENT TO COLLECTED TEACHINGS OF HŌNEN: THE JAPANESE ANTHOLOGY

29. Essentials for Birth in the Pure Land through Nembutsu 361

30. Dialogue on Ten Issues at Tōdai-ji Temple 367

31. Letters 375

A Reply 375

A Letter to Someone 385

A Reply to the Lay Priest Kumagai 386

A Reply on One Occasion 388

32. Admonitions for the Attainment of Birth in the Pure Land 389

Epilogue 403

The Auspicious Dream of the Japanese Anthology 405

Colophon 407

Appendix: The Forty-Eight Vows of Buddha Amitābha 409

Notes 417

Glossary 443

Selected Bibliography 463

Index of Selected Terms 475

Foreword

The Promise of Amida Buddha: Hōnen's Path to Bliss is the first English translation of the Genkō edition of the works of Hōnen-shōnin composed in Japanese. This collection, generally known as the *Japanese Anthology* (*Wago Tōroku*), was compiled by Ryōe Dōkō in 1275. I congratulate Bukkyō University–Los Angeles Extension for introducing this tremendously important work to Western readers.

Traditionally, Buddhist practitioners have attempted to seek inner truth through various types of meditation, such as concentration and insight (*śamatha-vipaśyanā*). These meditative practices are extremely difficult for lay people to pursue, for they were originally designed for monastics and other full-time practitioners. Pure Land Buddhism, in contrast, was designed for the deliverance of the masses. Hōnen (1133–1212), founding master of the Japanese Pure Land school, closely observed human nature, and he became convinced that all mortals are filled with worldly passions and negative karma binding them to the perpetual transmigration of birth and death. He surmised that most people do not have the capacity to awaken through their own efforts. Relying instead on the powerful compassion of Amida Buddha, however, allows people to attain deliverance through birth in his Pure Land. For this reason, Hōnen encouraged busy lay people to rely on Amida Buddha's compassion and recite his name so as to attain birth in the Pure Land.

This publication is significant and timely for Bukkyō University supported me in many ways to accomplish this project. Without their encouragement and help this publication would not have come to fruition.

Joji Atone, Ph. D.

Foreword

The Promise of Amida Buddha: Hōnen's Path to Bliss is the first English translation of the Genkō edition of the works of Hōnen-shōnin composed in Japanese. This collection, generally known as the *Japanese Anthology* (*Wago Tōroku*), was compiled by Ryōe Dōkō in 1275. I congratulate Bukkyō University–Los Angeles Extension for introducing this tremendously important work to Western readers.

Traditionally, Buddhist practitioners have attempted to seek inner truth through various types of meditation, such as concentration and insight (*śamatha-vipaśyanā*). These meditative practices are extremely difficult for lay people to pursue, for they were originally designed for monastics and other full-time practitioners. Pure Land Buddhism, in contrast, was designed for the deliverance of the masses. Hōnen (1133–1212), founding master of the Japanese Pure Land school, closely observed human nature, and he became convinced that all mortals are filled with worldly passions and negative karma binding them to the perpetual transmigration of birth and death. He surmised that most people do not have the capacity to awaken through their own efforts. Relying instead on the powerful compassion of Amida Buddha, however, allows people to attain deliverance through birth in his Pure Land. For this reason, Hōnen encouraged busy lay people to rely on Amida Buddha's compassion and recite his name so as to attain birth in the Pure Land.

This publication is significant and timely for Bukkyō University because its spiritual foundation is based on the teaching of Hōnen-shōnin. We are celebrating the eight-hundred-year memorial anniversary of Hōnen-shōnin this year, and in the following year commemorating the one hundredth anniversary of the founding of Bukkyō University. This precious and arduous work by Jōji Atone and Yōko Hayashi will be cherished by all.

Ryūzen Fukuhara, Litt.D., Former President
Nobuyuki Yamagiwa, Litt.D., President
Bukkyō University, Kyōto, Japan
Twenty-fifth of January, 2011

Preface

The Promise of Amida Buddha: Hōnen's Path to Bliss introduces Hōnen's compassionate and humanistic Pure Land thought to Western readers. Originally composed over eight hundred years ago in Japan, translation of Hōnen's enormous work into straightforward modern English was a challenging task that required more than ten years of effort and investigation. I believe this work will greatly benefit scholars, students, and religious practitioners, as well as the more general audience of those interested in Eastern thought.

I would like to express my sincere gratitude to the professors, friends, and associates who made the completion of this work possible. The late Prof. William R. LaFleur of the University of Pennsylvania, Dr. Alfred H. Bloom of the University of Hawai'i, and Dr. Glenn T. Webb of Pepperdine University gave me valuable suggestions regarding the usage of both Buddhist and Christian terminologies. Dr. Jack D. Van Horn of the College of William and Mary, Dr. Minoru Kiyota of the University of Wisconsin–Madison, and my Japanese teachers gave me special guidance in the importance of critical examination of the subject matter.

In addition, Mrs. Yōko Hayashi, M. Ed., co-translator of this work, provided invaluable expertise, and I am grateful to David Kittelstrom of Wisdom Publications for proficiently editing this work. Finally appreciation goes to my wife Lori Atone, who supported me in many ways to accomplish this project. Without their encouragement and help this publication would not have come to fruition.

Joji Atone, Ph. D.

Introduction

At the rise of the Kamakura period, Hōnen-bō Genkū (1133–1212, hereafter Hōnen or Genkū) established his distinct Pure Land school of Mahāyāna Buddhism called Jōdo Shū in Japan. It was based upon the Pure Land tradition of the Chinese monk Shan-tao (613–81), the systematizer of Chinese Pure Land Buddhism. Hōnen's teachings drew strong resistance from the established Buddhist schools of his time, but today the Pure Land practice descending from Hōnen and from his disciple Shinran (1173–1262) is the most widespread form of Buddhism in Japan.

Buddhism teaches the way to awaken to universal truth in order to realize buddhahood. Buddhist practitioners are traditionally said to pursue over many lifetimes the highest religious states of either an *arhat* (one who has eliminated all worldly passions and attained nirvāṇa) or, in Mahāyāna Buddhism, a *bodhisattva* (one who strives for enlightenment in order to save all suffering beings). Hōnen had followed the Mahāyāna tradition, observed the bodhisattva perfections, and experienced the state of *samādhi*, or tranquility full of insight. But he became dissatisfied with leaving the pursuit of enlightenment to an elite who were able to endure the rigorous discipline of the bodhisattva perfections, and he turned his efforts instead to the deliverance of the populace, who did not have the opportunity or will to engage in longterm austerities or studies. After coming upon the teachings of Shan-tao, Hōnen became convinced that the masses could realize deliverance by merely reciting the sacred name of Buddha Amida (Sanskrit: Amitābha or Amitāyus).

Hōnen taught that all ordinary men, women, and children—even wrongdoers—without distinction as to sex, age, status, or education would be able to be born in the Pure Land through reciting "Homage to Amida Buddha" or *Namu Amida Butsu*. This recitation is called *nembutsu*. Once born in the Pure Land, practitioners could complete the bodhisattva perfections without difficulty, realize enlightenment, and eventually attain buddhahood. Unlike other traditional Buddhist schools, Hōnen's Pure Land Buddhism articulates a posthumous enlightenment: the attainment of birth in the Pure Land presupposes eventual enlightenment there. He encouraged each individual to develop deep faith in Amida Buddha and recite nembutsu continually until his or her last moment.

The consistent theme of Pure Land Buddhism is the acceptance of human fallibility. Both Shan-tao and Hōnen, despite reaching the highest religious states through ascetic exercises, professed to still being common mortals with worldly passions. Those passions had caused their endless rebirths in the six delusive worlds of the cycle of birth and death, or *saṃsāra*, and they were unable to detach from those illusory worlds without relying on the compassionate power of Amida Buddha. The understanding that human nature is weak, ignorant, and karmically burdened is a basic tenet of the Pure Land faith, and this recognition in turn nurtures unshakable faith in the compassion of Amida Buddha. For if one is not able to attain enlightenment through one's own efforts, it becomes essential to rely on the power of a compassionate force greater than oneself. Aspiration for birth in the Pure Land and the recitation of Amida's name are based on a deep understanding of this.

A unique feature of Hōnen's Pure Land Buddhism is the full inclusion of women in the attainment of buddhahood. Like all major religions, Buddhism has a history of discriminating against women. Even though Buddha Śākyamuni preached that there is no distinction between men and women in the fulfillment of the path leading to buddhahood, discrimination arose due to the historical, social, cultural, and racial norms of the time period. In India, 250 precepts were prescribed for a monk but 348 for a nun. In China and Japan, the concepts of the five hindrances for a woman to realize enlightenment and the three types of obedience for a woman were incorporated into Buddhist thought. In Japan, menstruation was regarded as impure and by extension, the whole female body. Against these beliefs, Hōnen stated, "Believe that five recitations of nembutsu destroy the five hindrances for a woman, three recitations of nembutsu eliminate the three types of obedience, and a single utterance of nembutsu will result in one being welcomed by Amida Buddha into the Pure Land at the time of one's death" (in chapter 4 of the present work). Further, Hōnen once said to an infamous woman: "Amida Buddha established the universal vow in order to embrace an undesirable person such as you. Rely implicitly upon his essential vow and never disparage yourself. Once you recite the name of Amida Buddha and rely on the essential vow, birth in the Pure Land will definitely be achieved" (chapter 34 of Shunjō's *Illustrated Biography of Hōnen-shōnin*). Likewise, before the sixteenth century in Japan, it was unusual for women to know how to read Chinese, the language of almost all Buddhist scriptures. That Hōnen composed his teachings in Japanese further accentuates his commitment to women and to the masses more generally.

The recitation of nembutsu is the easiest and simplest form of Buddhist practice. Even a single utterance of nembutsu at the time of death makes it possible for one to be born in the Pure Land. By encouraging even a faint hope for deliverance at the very last moment, the teaching of nembutsu eases one's fear of death. Hōnen said, "In life we should accumulate all the merit of nembutsu so that when death comes, we will be welcomed by Amida Buddha into the Pure Land of Ultimate Bliss. In essence, if we recite nembutsu believing that no matter what comes or goes, there is no anxiety in this life, we will be free from the worry of birth and death."

Before presenting an outline of Hōnen's teachings contained in the present volume, let us look at the historical origins of the central practice of the Jōdo school, the recitation of the name of Amida Buddha.

The Historical Development of Nembutsu: From Meditation to Recitation

Hōnen's greatest religious contribution to the development of Pure Land Buddhism was his espousal of the primacy of *nembutsu*, the act of reciting *Namu Amida Butsu*, "Homage to Amida Buddha." The word *nembutsu* translates the Sanskrit *buddhānusmṛti*, which means "mindfulness of a buddha." Traditionally, it indicates a kind of meditation where one stablizes a mental image of the Buddha's form and qualities. Neither it, nor its Chinese translation, *nien-fo*, connoted any kind of vocal component; both were simply mental functions.

The transformation of nembutsu from mental to vocal was made by Shan-tao in China and Hōnen in Japan, and they defended this dramatic change with the rationale that the recitation of the name of Amida Buddha is not only easy for everyone to perform but also possible to continue throughout life. They cited several key sutras to show that the recitation of nembutsu accords with the compassionate teachings of Buddha Śākyamuni and Amida Buddha. Through the earnest devotion of Shan-tao and Hōnen, the attainment of birth in the Pure Land, and thereby enlightenment (or buddhahood), became possible for the first time for every man, woman, and child.

In the sections below, we will review the historical development of nembutsu from India through China to Japan. In the passages relating to the precursors to the Japanese Pure Land tradition in India and China, Amida is rendered as Amitābha, the well-known Sanskrit version of his name, which means "infinite light."

1. Indian Foundation: Pure Land Texts and Commentaries

The origin of nembutsu is uncertain due to insufficient textual data. The Indians left scant historical records to document its early development. However, the widespread Buddhist practice of taking refuge in the Three Jewels—the Buddha, the Dharma, and the Sangha—may have been a precursor to nembutsu recitation.

In early Buddhism, the recitation of the formula for refuge in the Three Jewels was the initial act in the Buddhist ordination ceremony. In front of the assembly of the Buddhist Sangha, those who desired to become monks or nuns thus invoked: "*Buddhaṃ saraṇaṃ gacchāmi* (I take refuge in the Buddha); *Dhammaṃ saraṇaṃ gacchāmi* (I take refuge in the Dharma); *Saṅghaṃ saraṇaṃ gacchāmi* (I take refuge in the Sangha)." Taking refuge here in the "Buddha" refers to the historical Buddha Śākyamuni, not Buddha Amitābha, but no distinction is reflected in the vocal delivery, and for Buddhists the qualities of enlightenment inhere in all buddhas equally.

Anecdotes in the early Buddhist scriptures describe the relief brought about by invoking the name of Buddha Śākyamuni. Recitation of the name Buddha Amitābha is known to do the same; both were designed for saving people. Perhaps the notion of birth in the Pure Land through reciting the name of Buddha Amitābha arose from this early Buddhist exercise of the vocal praise of Buddha Śākyamuni.

It is said that there are more than two hundred Mahāyāna texts dealing with Buddha Amitābha and his Western Pure Land of Sukhāvatī, or Ultimate Bliss. Very few, however, directly deal with the issue of the recitation of the name of Buddha Amitābha. These include:

1. The *Sutra of the Samādhi of All Buddhas' Presence* (*Pratyutpannasamādhi Sūtra*)
2. The three sutras of Pure Land Buddhism

   a. The *Smaller Sutra* (*Smaller Sukhāvatīvyūha Sūtra*)
   b. The *Larger Sutra* (*Larger Sukhāvatīvyūha Sūtra*)
   c. The *Meditation Sutra* (*Amitāyurdhyāna Sūtra*)
3. Two Indian commentaries
   a. The *Commentary on the Ten Bodhisattva Stages* (*Daśabhūmivibhāṣa Śāstra*) by Nāgārjuna (ca. second century)
   b. The *Treatise on Birth in the Pure Land* (*Sukhāvatīvyūha Upadeśa*) by Vasubandhu (ca. fourth century)

The *Sutra of the Samādhi of All Buddhas' Presence*, translated into Chinese by Lokarakṣa in 179, is considered the oldest of the Pure Land scriptures. It consists of sixteen chapters and describes a method for contemplating Buddha Amitābha: "Buddha Śākyamuni said to Bodhisattva Bhadrapāla: 'If a bodhisattva in this world were to devote himself to being mindful of Buddha Amitābha, he will see him.' Bodhisattva Bhadrapāla asked: 'Through which teaching are we able to achieve birth in the Pure Land of Buddha Amitābha?' Buddha Śākyamuni answered: 'If you wish to be born in the Pure Land and are incessantly mindful of the name of Buddha Amitābha, then you will be born in the Pure Land.'"[1]

Though this text mentions the name of Buddha Amitābha, the phrase "be mindful of the name of Buddha Amitābha" clearly denotes a mental practice, one probably involving visualizing the physical virtues of the Buddha Amitābha. While there is no particular indication of vocal recitation in this work, its significant influence on the later development of Chinese Pure Land Buddhism is undeniable.

The *Smaller Sutra* is the shortest of what are called the three sutras of Pure Land Buddhism. In this text, Buddha Śākyamuni holds a discourse with Śāriputra, one of the ten outstanding disciples of the Buddha, along with 1,250 other disciples, in the monastic residence at Jeta Grove. This text discusses nembutsu in the following three passages:

1. "Those who have been born in that buddhaland all meditate on the Buddha, the Dharma, and the Sangha..."
2. "In those who have heard the exquisite sounds of the trees and nets decorated with precious jewels, there arises naturally the thought of the mindfulness of the Buddha, the Dharma, and the Sangha."
3. "If good men and good women, who upon hearing the teaching of Buddha Amitābha, keep his name in their minds with utmost concentration and without distraction for one day, two days, three days, four days, five days, six days, or seven days, Buddha Amitābha, accompanied by his assembly of holy beings, will appear before them when their lives are at an end. With their minds free from distraction, they will be born in the Pure Land of Ultimate Bliss of Buddha Amitābha."[2]

Both "meditate on the Buddha" in the first passage and "the mindfulness of the Buddha" in the second clearly relate to meditation. The original Sanskrit terms for these two are *buddhamanasikāra* (reflecting on the Buddha) and *buddhānusmṛti* (mindfulness of the Buddha); both are confined to the mental sphere. In the third passage, the statement, "keep the name of Buddha Amitābha" is frequently interpreted as "reciting the name of Buddha Amitābha" by Chinese and Japanese Pure Land masters, including Shan-tao and Hōnen, but its original meaning was a mental act. In short, although the *Smaller Sutra* is one of the core Pure Land texts and teaches the attainment of birth in the Pure Land, vocal nembutsu is not addressed.

The *Larger Sutra* was first translated into Chinese by a Persian monk, An-shih-kao, who came to China in the year 148 and later by Saṅghavarman in the year 252. There were another ten Chinese translations made since then and several more in Tibetan. Voluminous manuscripts, translations, and commentaries also proliferate today, demonstrating how widely the *Larger Sutra* pervaded India, Central Asia, and China.

The *Larger Sutra* has seven principal headings: (1) the practice and enlightenment of Bodhisattva Dharmākara, (2) the glories of the Pure Land, (3) the splendid physical features of Buddha Amitābha, (4) the special virtues of those who have been born in the Pure Land, (5) the practice for attaining birth in the Pure Land, (6) the bodhisattva's praise of the Pure Land, and (7) the defilements of this world of suffering. In the conclusion, Buddha Śākyamuni proclaims to Bodhisattva Maitreya that the *Larger Sutra* alone will remain for another one hundred years after the disappearance of every other teaching of Buddha Śākyamuni in order to lead all remaining sentient beings to deliverance.

The Japanese translation of the *Larger Sutra* employs the term *nembutsu* many times as a translation for the Sanskrit terms *smṛti* (mindfulness), *manasikāra* (reflection), and *citta* (thinking or mind). Note that all three Sanskrit words apply to mental function. One of the features of this text is the set of forty-eight vows made by Buddha Amitābha concerning his Pure Land, and of these, the eighteenth vow is considered the essential one. The essential vow, described in the first fascicle, reads: "If, when I [Buddha Amitābha] am to attain buddhahood, all sentient beings in the ten directions who rejoice in faith with genuine hearts and who wish to be born in my buddha-land are not born there within just ten moments of mindfulness of me, I will not realize enlightenment."

Here, the phrase "ten moments of mindfulness" is important. The original Sanskrit for this is *daśacitta*, literally "ten minds." Some have said that the idea of *daśacitta* derives from the ten types of meditative practices in early Buddhism, ten objects of mindfulness meditation: (1) the Buddha, (2) the Dharma, (3) the Sangha, (4) the vows, (5) generosity or almsgiving, (6) the divine, (7) tranquility, (8) breathing, (9) the body, and (10) death. Of these, numbers 4, 6, and 8—mindfulness of the Buddhist vows, divinity, and breathing—while prominent in early Buddhism, are at odds with the Pure Land approach, which says that nembutsu alone is sufficient. Faced with this, the Chinese Pure Land patriarch T'an-luan (476–542) interpreted the term *daśacitta* in this way: "The term *citta* here does not indicate a span of time but rather mindfulness of Buddha Amitābha... *Daśacitta* does not indicate a specific number but indicates the perfection of mindfulness of Buddha Amitābha." It is still uncertain precisely what the "ten" alludes to in the context of the *Larger Sutra*, but the Sanskrit denotation of the term *citta* as well as T'an-luan's interpretation of the term concurs that it signifies a mental action.

It was Shan-tao who later interpreted *daśacitta* to mean ten recitations. His *Methods of Contemplation on Buddha Amitābha* illustrates this view of the essential vow of the *Larger Sutra* as follows: "If, when I [Buddha Amitābha] am to attain buddhahood, all sentient beings in the ten directions who wish to be born in my buddhaland recite my name at least ten times are not born there through the power of my vow, I will not realize enlightenment." Thus, Shan-tao changed the statement, "just ten moments of mindfulness of Buddha Amitābha" in the *Larger Sutra* to "recite my name at least ten times." This is the crucial interpretation for nembutsu. Following this, Hōnen proclaimed: "*nen* (being mindful) and *shō* (voice) are really one and the same." This transformation of nembutsu from mental to vocal offered by Shan-tao and Hōnen was a key shift for Pure Land Buddhism.

The last of the three sutras of Pure Land Buddhism, the *Amitāyus Meditation Sutra*, or *Meditation Sutra* for short, is a one-fascicle text. Amitāyus, or "Infinite Life," is an exalted manifestation of Buddha Amitābha. There once existed two Chinese translations of this text—one translated by Kālayaśas (383–442) and the other by Dharmamitra (fifth century). While the former work is extant, nothing remains of the latter work, and there are no Tibetan or Sanskrit manuscripts of this sutra, which leaves open the possibility it could be Chinese in origin. This text unfolds the tragic story of Queen Vaidehī and describes sixteen types of meditative practices as a means for achieving birth in the Pure Land. In its conclusion, it states that even the most defiled can attain birth in the Pure Land through reciting the name of Buddha Amitābha. Unlike the *Larger Sutra* or the *Smaller Sutra*, the *Meditation Sutra* twice mentions vocal nembutsu:

1. A virtuous teacher makes practitioners utter *Namu Amida Butsu* with their palms together, and because they invoke the name of Buddha Amitābha, the negative karma binding them to saṃsāra for five billion eons is eliminated.
2. The life of a very ignorant person is about to end. He meets a virtuous teacher who comforts him in various ways, expounding on flawless teachings and urging him to be mindful of Buddha Amitābha. However, he is too tormented by pain to be mindful of Buddha Amitābha. The virtuous teacher then says, "If you cannot be mindful of Buddha Amitābha, say that you take refuge in Buddha Amitābha." With a genuine heart and uninterrupted voice, the ignorant person recites the name of Buddha Amitābha, manifesting ten thoughts. Because he recites the name of Buddha Amitābha in every moment of thought, the negative karma binding him to saṃsāra for eight billion eons is eliminated."[3]

The *Meditation Sutra* further teaches that there are nine grades of aspirants for birth in the Pure Land, and that their birth in the Pure Land depends on their individual potential and depth of practice. There are three classes of birth—low, middling, and high—and these three are further subdivided into three levels each. The first quote above comes from the description of the high level of the low class of birth, and the second quote describes the low level of the low class of birth. Note that the vocal nembutsu is introduced only in the low class and is regarded as the practice performed when a practitioner cannot carry out meditative practices due to a lack of ability or serenity. Based on this, it appears that the recitation of nembutsu was meant for ordinary people and not for the elite.

The doctrine presented in the *Meditation Sutra* is more developed than that in either the *Larger Sutra* or the *Smaller Sutra*, and consequently it is considered the most recent work of the three. In addition, its commitment to Pure Land Buddhism, exemplified by the story of Queen Vaidehī as well as by important Pure Land instructions, including the theory of the threefold devotional heart, made it popular among Chinese Buddhists, particularly after the sixth century. Thus Shan-tao and Hōnen based their Pure Land thought primarily on this *Meditation Sutra*.

In addition to the three sutras of Pure Land Buddhism, the Pure Land thought was greatly furthered in India by two commentaries (*śāstras*): *Commentary on the Ten Bodhisattva Stages* and *Treatise on Birth in the Pure Land*.

Commentary on the Ten Bodhisattva Stages was composed by Nāgārjuna,[4] the forerunner of the Indian Middle Way, or Madhyamaka, school. The commentary focuses on the first two of the ten stages (*bhūmi*) of the bodhisattva practices presented in the *Flower Garland Sutra* (*Avataṃsaka Sūtra*). Chapter 9 of this commentary, entitled "The Easy Practice," is significant because it serves as the basis for the doctrinal foundation of Pure Land Buddhism in India.

Nāgārjuna distinguished between easy and difficult avenues to the state of nonregression (*avinivartanīya*) at the eighth of the ten bodhisattva stages. In the easy practice, a practitioner relies completely, by means of faith, upon the compassionate power of the buddhas; in the difficult practice, a bodhisattva attains nonregression through austerities and the bodhisattva perfections. Nāgārjuna articulated the vocal nembutsu for use in the easy practice as follows:

1. One who listens to the names of various buddhas will receive infinite merit immediately; one who invokes their names will attain the state of nonregression all at once.
2. In accord with the essential vow of Buddha Amitābha, one who is mindful of him and recites his name will immediately attain the stage of perfect enlightenment.[5]

Nāgārjuna here identifies recitation as a viable practice in a context that addresses both listening and reciting. Nevertheless, he undoubtedly portrays the easy practice as a means for the "inferior" and never expressly endorses it as an ideal. Note, too, that citation of the essential vow here signifies that Amitābha worship and recitation practice were already exercised in India prior to Nāgārjuna's time.

The other commentary, *Treatise on Birth in the Pure Land*, is a short discourse on the *Larger Sukhāvatīvyūha Sūtra* attributed to Vasubandhu, the fourth-century master of the Yogācāra school. *Treatise on Birth in the Pure Land*, translated into Chinese by Bodhiruci in 529 and known in Chinese as the *Wang-sheng-lun*, includes both poetry and prose. The verse section enumerates the seventeen merits of the Pure Land, the eight merits of Buddha Amitābha, and the four merits of bodhisattvas. Vasubandhu also presents the *five aspects of contemplation*, that is, the five practices for birth in the Pure Land. They are (1) worshiping Buddha Amitābha, (2) praising his virtues by invoking his name, (3) aspiring for birth in the Pure Land, (4) meditating on the glories of the Pure Land, and (5) dedicating merit to save sentient beings. The second practice may at first appear to mean the vocal nembutsu, but in fact it has a different meaning. "Invoking his name" here refers particularly to praising the twelve different names of Buddha Amitābha presented in the *Larger Sutra*.

Thus, although their teachings were in general too scholastic for the masses, Nāgārjuna and Vasubandhu's commentaries became a bridge between the Mahāyāna bodhisattva and Pure Land ideals, contributing greatly to a transformational stage in Buddhist history. It was on this basis that later Chinese Pure Land masters, concerned about the practicality and accessibility of their religion, adapted the Pure Land tradition to broaden its appeal.

2. Shan-tao and the Development of the Vocal Nembutsu in China

The history of Pure Land Buddhism in China begins with the translation of Mahāyāna texts relating to the Pure Land of Buddha Amitābha. These Pure Land Buddhist texts were taken from India to China through Central Asia; however, complete infiltration of Pure Land Buddhism as an organized unit or school did not happen in

China until later. It was only in the Eastern Chin dynasty (317–420) that Hui-yüan (334–416) of Mount Lu first established a religious group dedicated to worshiping Buddha Amitābha.

Hui-yüan's early training was in Confucian classics and Taoism, but at the age of twenty-one, he, along with his brother, became a pupil of Tao-an (314–85), one of the leading Chinese Buddhist monks. He and Tao-an eventually parted, and Hui-yüan went on to lead a secluded life in Tung-lin Temple on Mount Lu in southern China. There he organized the White Lotus Society, which consisted of 123 monks and lay people, a group thought to be the first organized Buddhist institution in China.

Hui-yüan believed deeply in Pure Land Buddhism, strictly observed the Buddhist precepts, and remained on the mountain until his death. Due to his educational background, he relied heavily on Taoist terminology to express Buddhist concepts.[6]

Hui-yüan derived his notion of nembutsu from the *Sutra of the Samādhi of All Buddhas' Presence*, in which an aspirant realizes wisdom through meditation on Buddha Amitābha. It is uncertain whether Hui-yüan's nembutsu took a vocal or mental form. One may assume, however, that since the *Meditation Sutra*, which first articulated the recitation of the name of Buddha Amitābha, was only translated into Chinese between 424 and 442, it would have been impossible for Hui-yüan to have seen it. If this speculation is correct, his nembutsu was likely based on meditation.

During this period, the most significant event in China regarding the development of Pure Land Buddhism was the translation or retranslation of the three sutras of Pure Land Buddhism. The *Smaller Sutra* was translated into Chinese by Kumārajīva in 402, the *Larger Sutra* by Buddhabhadra in 421, and the *Meditation Sutra* by Kālayaśas between 424 and 442. On the basis of these translations, Pure Land Buddhism was introduced gradually to the Chinese people, particularly in northern China. The situation in southern China, however, was different. A scholastic Buddhism had penetrated southern China, and intellectuals there utilized such Mahāyāna texts as the

Perfection of Wisdom Sutra (*Prajñāpāramitā Sūtra*), the *Nirvāṇa Sutra* (*Mahāparinirvāṇa Sūtra*), the *Vimalakīrti Sutra* (*Vimalakīrtinirdeśa Sūtra*), and the *Lotus Sutra* (*Saddharmapuṇḍarīka Sūtra*).

It was T'an-luan (476–542) who finally systematized Pure Land Buddhism for the Chinese. T'an-luan was born in Yen-mei in Shanhsi Province in 476 and entered religious life at the age of fifteen. He first focused on the Madhyamaka doctrine and then studied the Taoist way to longevity. After receiving Taoist instruction, he met Bodhiruci, a northern Indian monk who arrived in Lo-yang in 508 and was famous for translating Vasubandhu's *Treatise on Birth in the Pure Land*. Bodhiruci presented the *Meditation Sutra* to T'an-luan as the sole teaching for achieving enlightenment. T'an-luan immediately discarded his Taoist texts and became an ardent Pure Land practitioner. His major work, *Commentary on Treatise on Birth in the Pure Land*, a commentary on Vasubandhu's earlier commentary, powerfully shaped Pure Land Buddhism in China.

T'an-luan's view of Pure Land Buddhism was slightly different from that of Hui-yüan on Mount Lu. Hui-yüan emphasized meditation as a means to realize the wisdom of emptiness, while T'an-luan stressed faith in the compassion of Buddha Amitābha to attain birth in the Pure Land. In his commentary, T'an-luan defends this view:

> With respect, I studied the *Commentary on the Ten Bodhisattva Stages* of Bodhisattva Nāgārjuna. It states, "A bodhisattva has two different paths to the state of nonregression; one is the path of the difficult practice and the other is the path of the easy practice." It is very hard to reach nonregression through the difficult practice in the era marked by the five defilements or in the era when Buddha Śākyamuni does not exist... The easy practice to birth in the Pure Land is simply faith in the essential vow of Buddha Amitābha. One can be born in the Pure Land and will immediately become characterized as being in the state of certain attainment of birth in the Pure Land by relying on the power of

> his vow. The certain attainment of birth in the Pure Land leads inexhorably to the state of nonregression. This is as pleasant as voyaging in a ship. The *Treatise*, the ultimate teaching of Mahāyāna Buddhism, is propelled by the winds of nonregression.[7]

T'an-luan employs Nāgārjuna's easy/difficult presentation as his starting point in his *Commentary*, adding his own unique interpretation. There are three basic differences between the theories of these two masters. First, for Nāgārjuna, enlightenment (or attainment of nonregression) through both the easy and difficult practices is realized in this world; for T'an-luan, it is achieved in the Pure Land only. Second, according to Nāgārjuna, enlightenment is possible by praising the names of various buddhas in the ten directions, while T'an-luan emphasizes faith in Buddha Amitābha alone. Third, Nāgārjuna's understanding of Pure Land Buddhism is based on the notion of a Mahāyāna bodhisattva. T'an-luan rejects this and articulates birth in the Pure Land by ordinary believers through faith.

T'an-luan also interprets Vasubandhu's theory of the five aspects of meditation and advocates Nāgārjuna's idea of the *power other than self*, saying, "Any practice pursued by bodhisattvas and celestial beings in the Pure Land is informed by the essential vow of Buddha Amitābha. If these practices were not due to his compassionate power, his forty-eight vows would be meaningless."[8] T'an-luan emphasizes total reliance on the compassionate power of the vow of Buddha Amitābha. He does not value the bodhisattva perfections—in other words, enlightenment through *self-power* (*tzu-li*, *svabala*). To support his *power other than self* (*t'a-li*, *parabala*) theory, he further quotes the eleventh, eighteenth, and thirty-second vows of Buddha Amitābha to prove that one can realize birth in the Pure Land (or the state of nonregression) through faith in Buddha Amitābha.

T'an-luan taught that the three sutras of Pure Land Buddhism were designed for common people, excluding no one, even one who had committed the five grave offenses or the ten transgressions. His strong conviction in saving the masses was remarkable for his time, for until then, it had always been held that enlightenment was effectively unattainable for some—offenders who were destined for hell, there to suffer immeasurable pain for an immeasurable span of time. T'an-luan was the first to portray Buddha Amitābha and the Pure Land as a refuge for all people.

T'an-luan's method relied on faith in Amitābha, but it is unclear how nembutsu was included in this practice. In his *Commentary*, he mentions nembutsu, saying, "If people in the low category of birth hear the name of Buddha Amitābha, which is as pure and beautiful as the jeweled trees, they abandon unwholesome thinking. If they meditate on him, their karmic defilements are eliminated, and immediately they attain birth in the Pure Land."[9] Based on this statement alone, T'an-luan's nembutsu seems to consist of hearing and thinking. At the other points in the *Commentary* no distinction is made between meditation and recitation. For instance, he asserts, "Praising the name of Buddha Amitābha is the same as being mindful of him," and "*Daśacitta* does not indicate a particular number but only the perfection of being mindful of Buddha Amitābha."[10] He clearly considered meditation and praising the name of Buddha Amitābha to be identical. Given his overall emphasis on meditation, however, *nembutsu* to T'an-luan probably meant meditative nembutsu.

Tao-ch'o (562–645) followed the Pure Land tradition of T'an-luan. Tao-ch'o was born in Shan-hsi Province in northern China and entered religious life while still a boy. His studies began with the *Nirvāṇa Sutra*, which elucidates the notion of *buddha nature*, the idea that although the minds of sentient beings are generally considered to be defiled, inherently they are pure, and that buddha nature becomes apparent through the cultivation of purity.

At the age of forty-eight, Tao-ch'o converted to Pure Land Buddhism after seeing the monument memorializing T'an-luan in the environs of Hsüan-c'ung Temple, where T'an-luan had resided. This conversion turned Tao-ch'o away from a belief in reliance on self-power to a belief in reliance on a power other than self. In other words, he saw both the arduousness of the bodhisattva practices and people's weak capacity for attaining enlightenment through those means. He then linked his awareness of this human weakness to a particular understanding of negative karma, the outlook later adopted by Shan-tao and Hōnen.

The political situation in China changed dramatically over Tao-ch'o's lifetime. The frequent wars during the Northern Ch'i (550–57) and Northern Chou (557–81) dynasties threatened many lives with violence, famine, and disease. Emperor Wu (r. 560–78) of the Northern Chou dynasty began to suppress Buddhism as a defensive action against the Buddhist organizations' potentially dangerous accumulation of wealth. Conflict also flared between Buddhism and China's two indigenous religions, Taoism and Confucianism. This "second persecution of Buddhism in China," as it was later called, resulted in widespread destruction of Buddhist monasteries and statues as well as the elimination of many monks and nuns, who were killed or forced to return to lay life. This upheaval and its attendant tragedies critically shaped Tao-ch'o's Pure Land thought. He saw the historical forces at work as a manifestation of the era of the Dharma's decline. Having experienced these tragedies firsthand, Tao-ch'o must have been keenly aware of the mutability of life and thus developed a strong compassion for the populace in their continual suffering.

Tao-ch'o's main work, *Collection of Passages on the Blissful Land*, divides Buddhism into two categories: the holy gate and the Pure Land gate. In the former, a bodhisattva realizes enlightenment through austere self-discipline, while in the latter, an ordinary person attains birth in the Pure Land with ease through the compassion of Buddha Amitābha. Tao-ch'o's idea of nembutsu is expressed in the first fascicle of this text:

> The era in which we sentient beings live is the fourth five-hundred-year period after the death of Buddha Śākyamuni. We must repent of our karmic wrongs, exercise wholesome

> deeds, and recite the name of Buddha Amitābha. If someone meditates on and utters *A-mi-t'o-fo* [Buddha Amitābha] once, the negative karma binding that person to saṃsāra for eight billion more eons is eliminated.[11]

Tao-ch'o alludes to the vocal nembutsu here, although he discusses it in conjunction with meditation. He later clarifies himself stating, "The essence of the *Meditation Sutra* is the samādhi in which a practitioner visualizes the physical features of Buddha Amitābha."[12] Despite this clarification, Tao-ch'o's notion of nembutsu seems to combine both meditation and recitation, and for his own practice, Tao-ch'o was known to have a commitment to recitation. Tao-hsüan's (596–667) *Further Biographies of Eminent Monks* mentions that Tao-ch'o recited *A-mi-t'o-fo* seventy thousand times a day, and that he urged his followers to use beans as an aid in counting the number of times they chanted the name of Buddha Amitābha. As a result, every person over age seven in his province chanted the name. Clearly Tao-ch'o's vision of nembutsu established a foundation for Shan-tao's Pure Land thought.

Shan-tao (631–81) was a disciple of Tao-ch'o, and he based his idea of nembutsu upon the works of both T'an-luan and Tao-ch'o, but each of these three masters had his own interpretation of nembutsu. As the concept of nembutsu evolved through these proponents, one sees the practice go from ambiguity to clarity, from subordinancy to centrality. Whereas T'an-luan only indirectly alluded to nembutsu as a kind of meditation and Tao-ch'o referred to it equally as both meditation and recitation, Shan-tao was the first to put nembutsu recitation at the center. Initially, he recognized equally the importance of both meditation and recitation, but eventually he came to advocate solely the vocal nembutsu, with saving the masses as his expressed objective.

Shan-tao was born in Shang-tung Province in 613, entered religious life at the age of nine, and studied primarily the *Lotus Sutra* and the *Vimalakīrti Sutra*. He later found Pure Land Buddhism and strictly observed the meditative practices described in the *Meditation Sutra*. Sometime between 629 and 636, after hearing the name of Tao-ch'o, Shan-tao went to the Hsüan-chung Temple in Shan-hsi Province to meet with him. Shan-tao's meeting with Tao-ch'o is described in *Further Biographies of Eminent Monks*:

> Recently, there has been a monk called Shan-tao living on the mountain. He traveled through various provinces searching for the true teaching of Buddha Śākyamuni. One day, he went to Hsi-ho and met the religious group headed by Ta-ch'o. From them on, Shan-tao only practiced the recitation of nembutsu, the essential practice of Buddha Amitābha.[13]

Around the age of thirty-two, Shan-tao returned to Ch'ang-an, the cultural, economic, political, and religious capital of the Sui and T'ang dynasties. He devoted himself to spreading the teaching with great industry, producing his five major works including his *Commentary on the Meditation Sutra*, making tens of thousands of copies of the *Smaller Sutra*, and painting three hundred Pure Land pictures. At the age of forty-nine, Shan-tao supervised the carving of the great image of Buddha Vairocana in Lung-men. And in 681, at the age of sixty-eight, he died.

Shan-tao established the vocal nembutsu by re-interpreting the eighteenth vow of Buddha Amitābha. His *Hymns in Praise of Birth in the Pure Land* reveals the reason for his shift from mental to vocal practice:

> Stay alone in a quiet place and free yourself from all wayward thoughts. Then fix your mind on the single Buddha and, instead of being mindful of his physical features, only recite his name. If this is done, you can perceive Buddha Amitābha and all other buddhas.
>
> Question: Why is the exclusive recitation of the name of Buddha Amitābha urged instead of meditation?

> Answer: Sentient beings are burdened with weighty karmic obstacles; their conscious worlds are limited; their minds are unrefined; their senses are disturbed; their spirits are frivolous. Therefore, the Great Sage [Buddha], with sympathy, urged them to recite the name of Buddha Amitābha exclusively. Because the recitation of his name is easy, they can do so continuously to attain birth in the Pure Land.[14]

This passage is seminal for understanding Shan-tao's notion of nembutsu: reciting the name of Buddha Amitābha is not only "easy" for everyone to perform but also possible to do "continuously" in order to realize birth in the Pure Land.

Shan-tao unmistakably valued the vocal nembutsu more than meditation. Presumably, this transformation in thought was inspired by his own religious experiences. The rigor of his discipline during his stay in Ch'ang-an is well documented:

> Even in the cold season, Shan-tao practiced to the extent that he perspired…For more than thirty years, he had no particular place to sleep, nor did he take robes off except when bathing…He stringently observed the precepts without breaking a single one. He neither raised his eyes to look at a woman nor entertained any desire for fame or wealth.[15]

Shan-tao's austere religious discipline astonished even his fellow monks. His contemporaries respectfully referred to him as "Meditation Master" or "Precept Master." Nonetheless, he often confessed, "I am a common mortal with worldly passions."[16] Because of his deep awareness of human nature, he recognized that he, like other ordinary people, was weak and karmically unvirtuous.

This kind of moral introspection is apparent in his interpretation of the threefold devotional heart, the three being the genuine heart, the profound heart, and the heart that seeks birth in the Pure Land through the dedication of merit. This threefold idea was originally introduced in the *Meditation Sutra*, where the term *threefold devotional heart* originally meant the three aspects of faith indispensable for attaining birth in the Pure Land. According to the *Meditation Sutra*, however, the threefold devotional heart applies only to superior beings. Shan-tao, on the other hand, regarded them as applying equally to every sentient being aspiring for birth in the Pure Land. Among the three hearts, the profound heart was particularly significant to him. Shan-tao describes the profound heart in his *Commentary on the Meditation Sutra*:

> The *profound heart* is the heart filled with profound faith. This has two aspects. First, we must firmly believe that we are unwholesome common mortals who have wandered though the delusive triple realms of saṃsāra for innumerable eons and will never have a chance to escape from these delusive realms. Second, we must firmly believe that Buddha Amitābha welcomes and embraces all sentient beings by the grace of his forty-eight vows and that we can rely on the compassionate power of his vows, without doubt or anxiety, to achieve the certain attainment of birth in the Pure Land.[17]

Accordingly, Shan-tao's vision of the profound heart consists of two parts: (1) the total recognition of how deeply the human heart is consumed by worldly passions; and (2) unquestioning faith in the power of Buddha Amitābha. That is to say, Shan-tao had been convinced through his austere discipline that common mortals, including himself, could only be saved through relying upon the compassion of Buddha Amitābha and that the vocal nembutsu was the sole means to birth in the Pure Land.

Because of Shan-tao's accomplishments and his far-reaching catechization in Ch'ang-an, Pure Land Buddhism rapidly gained popularity in China during the T'ang dynasty. Among all of the disciples who followed Shan-tao's nembutsu tradition, three monks stand out in particular: Huai-kan (seventh to eighth century), Huai-yün (639–701), and Ching-yeh (665–712).

Huai-kan was originally a Yogācāra monk, a disciple of Hsüan-tsang (600 or 602–64), the famous pilgrim who strictly observed the Buddhist precepts. Although Huai-kan met with Shan-tao for instruction in Pure Land Buddhism and even performed the meditative nembutsu without cessation for twenty-one days, his efforts were in vain; Buddha Amitābha did not appear before him. In a final futile attempt at repenting his karmic defilements, Huai-kan tried to starve himself to death. Shan-tao stopped this, encouraging him to continue calling the name of Buddha Amitābha. Huai-kan eventually reached the samādhi of nembutsu three years later and engaged in extensive propagation of Pure Land Buddhism in Ch'ang-an.

Huai-kan's primary academic contribution to Pure Land Buddhism is his *Treatise Clarifying Doubts Regarding Pure Land Buddhism*. As the title indicates, this work elucidates contemporary problems posed by other Buddhist scholars, in particular those belonging to the Sanlun, or "Three Treatise," school, which was based on the Indian Madhyamaka tradition. In this work, Huai-kan employed Yogācāra terminology as well as Hsüan-tsang's view of Consciousness-only, which served to clarify Shan-tao's Pure Land tradition, making it more comprehensible and acceptable to his peers.

Huai-yün, another distinguished disciple of Shan-tao, entered the religious order and joined Shan-tao at Shih-chi Temple in Ch'ang-an when Shan-tao was about fifty-six years old. There Huai-yün served the master for more than ten years, and when Shan-tao died in 681, Huai-yün buried his ashes at the foot of Mount Chung-nan. Huai-yün later built a temple there, where he lectured on the three sutras of Pure Land Buddhism and practiced the recitation with other monks. In 689 Huai-yün was appointed by the emperor to be the head priest of Shih-chi Temple. His teaching was undoubtedly made more effective by royal patronage, and he was granted the posthumous title "Great Master Lung-shan." Unfortunately, none of his works are extant, and so his full contribution to Pure Land Buddhism remains unknown.

Shan-tao's third leading disciple, Ching-yeh, is said to have ordained at a young age and studied the *Meditation Sutra* intensively. He died at the age of fifty-eight while sitting erect and reciting the name of Buddha Amitābha. Ching-yeh's funeral was attended by a great number of monks and lay followers, and his ashes were buried beside Shan-tao's. Unfortunately, none of his works have survived either.

In addition to Shan-tao's three leading disciples, there were other Pure Land masters of the T'ang dynasty. Tz'u-min (680–748), Fa-chao (eighth century), and Shao-k'ang (d. 805) are excellent examples.

Tz'u-min was given his name by Emperor Hsüan-tsung. He journeyed extensively in South Asia before settling in India for eighteen years. In Gandhāra, he was instructed in vocal nembutsu for achieving birth in the Pure Land, and it was there that he converted to Pure Land Buddhism. He returned to Ch'ang-an in 719 with images of buddhas as well as with voluminous Pure Land manuscripts written in Sanskrit. He continued teaching in Ch'ang-an the rest of his life and died in Lo-yang in 748.

Tz'u-min had great influence on Chinese Pure Land Buddhism despite the fact that his idea of nembutsu deviated from that of Shan-tao. His principal work, *Collection of the Teachings of Birth in the Pure Land*, severely criticizes the Zen (Chinese: Ch'an) view, but unlike Shan-tao, Tz'u-min was by no means an opponent of Zen. He thought of it as a useful part of a triad—the "unity of nembutsu, precepts, and meditation," *meditation* here being the Sanskrit *dhyāna*, which in Chinese is *ch'an*. In this sense, he was a forerunner of the synchronization of Pure Land Buddhism and Zen in China.

Japanese Pure Land followers later established the theory of the "three streams" of the Pure Land tradition: (1) the Hui-yüan stream, which stresses meditation, (2) the Shan-tao stream, which relies exclusively on recitation of nembutsu, and (3) the Tz'u-min stream, which integrates the practice of nembutsu with Zen. Japanese Pure Land devotees, however, follow Shan-tao's nembutsu tradition exclusively.

Fa-chao, another prominent Chinese Pure Land master, was widely regarded as Shan-tao's successor, though his Pure Land thought is unique. He greatly admired Hui-yüan and, like him, went to Mount Lu to meditate with the members of the White Lotus Society. Later, Fa-chao moved to Mount Nan-yo-heng to study under Ch'eng-yüan (712–802), a well-known student of Tz'u-min.

In 766, while on Mount Lu, Fa-chao pledged to practice *pratyutpannasamādhi* meditation each summer for ninety days. During this meditation, he received the instruction of the fivefold rhythmic chanting of *nien-fo* (nembutsu) from Buddha Amitābha himself. The *fivefold rhythmic chanting of nien-fo* is the five steps of the chanting practice of nembutsu, moving from low to high voice and from slow to quick tempo. In the first step, a practitioner chants *Namo A-mi-t'o-fo* slowly, in an ordinary voice; in the second, it is recited slowly in a higher voice; in the third, it is chanted neither slowly nor quickly; in the fourth, it is chanted quickly; in the fifth, only *A-mi-t'o-fo* is chanted very quickly. Fa-chao was convinced that this practice was the most effective way for ordinary practitioners to awaken faith in Buddha Amitābha.

In 770, Fa-chao went to Mount Wu-t'ai in Shan-hsi Province.[18] There too, during meditation, he received confirmation of his faith from the bodhisattvas Mañjuśrī and Samanthabhadra.

Fa-chao was substantially influenced by the *constant walking of samādhi* from the T'ien-t'ai school. *Constant walking of samādhi* consists of walking around an image of Buddha Amitābha for ninety days while constantly keeping him in mind and reciting his name. Thus he innovatively combined T'ien-t'ai meditation with the vocal nembutsu. Although he deviated from Shan-tao on this point (stressing meditation as well as reciting nembutsu), this was more a product of Fa-chao's time than a conscious deviation on his part from Shan-tao's thought. Many Buddhist practices were combined during this period, especially the integration of Zen meditation and nembutsu recitation mentioned above.

Shao-k'ang, the final Chinese Pure Land master we will treat here, had two mystical experiences that profoundly affected him and led to his conversion to Pure Land Buddhism. First, in about 785, he was studying Shan-tao's writings at White Horse Temple in Lo-yang when, miraculously, the writings began to emit dazzling lights. This naturally left a lasting impression upon him. Second, after visiting the image of Shan-tao in Ch'ang-an, he began to spontaneously receive instruction on Shan-tao's Pure Land doctrines. Moved by these experiences, he began preaching Shan-tao's nembutsu tradition in the south. Legend recounts that he had a regular congregation of three thousand people, many of them children. It is said he rewarded children with prizes if they recited Buddha Amitābha's name.

Shao-k'ang's *Selected Biographies of Devotees Who Attained Birth in the Western Pure Land* is a collection of forty-eight short biographies of Pure Land practitioners who were active from the period of the Eastern Chin dynasty (317–420) through the middle of the T'ang dynasty (618–907). In 794, Shao-k'ang built a nembutsu center on Mount Wu-lung in Che-chiang Province and also composed special melodies to accompany the chanting of nembutsu at the center in order to help his congregation with their practice. Shao-k'ang further incorporated Fa-chao's fivefold rhythmic chanting of nien-fo into his own practice regimen.

Recitation of Buddha Amitābha's name for birth in the Pure Land was established in China by Shan-tao, but after his death, there was a marked tendency to integrate various Buddhist practices. The Zen, Vinaya, and T'ien-t'ai schools, each especially active, all incorporated the vocal nembutsu into their established regimens. This combining of practices is not unique to Pure Land Buddhism in China; a tendency to fuse different practices has long been a feature of Chinese religion more generally. But while Shan-tao's own nembutsu tradition lost its individuality in China, his advocacy of exclusive recitation of the name of Buddha Amitābha was championed in Japan by Hōnen.

3. Hōnen and the Establishment of Nembutsu Recitation in Japan

Buddhism came to Japan in 552, and Pure Land Buddhism was introduced into Japan during the middle of the seventh century. At that time, Japanese Buddhism was under the control of the court, and monks were concerned primarily with the prosperity of their country. Shan-tao's nembutsu tradition had not yet gained a foothold in Japan.

Two Tendai monks, En'nin (794–864) and Genshin (942–1017), played important roles in the development of Pure Land Buddhism in Japan. In 838, En'nin traveled to China and studied Fa-chao's fivefold rhythmic chanting of nien-fo on Mount Wu-t'ai. After about ten years in China he returned to Mount Hiei, the center of Japanese Buddhist studies, bringing with him 559 Chinese works. These included Tao-cho's *Collection of Passages on the Blissful Land*, Fa-chao's *Liturgy for the Rite of the Fivefold Rhythmic Chanting of Nien-fo*, and Shan-tao's *Hymns of the Nien-fo Liturgy*.

En'nin taught his disciples on Mount Hiei the practices of the constant walking of samādhi and of the fivefold rhythmic chanting of nien-fo. En'nin built a center for this practice, and his disciples were the first to observe the practice in Japan. The fivefold rhythmic chanting of nien-fo, an easy discipline, spread rapidly among the Japanese people, particularly among the aristocracy. Elaborate and ornate temples were built in Kyōto and Nara, with jeweled interiors decorated so as to resemble the Pure Land itself. This was an age of visual representation, and as a result, Japanese Buddhist art flourished in the eleventh century.

The monk Genshin, who died at the beginning of this flourishing, entered the monastery on Mount Hiei as a child and at the age of fifteen became a lecturer on the *Lotus Sutra*. He was known as the most distinguished scholar in Buddhist logic at that time. His greatest contribution to Japanese Pure Land Buddhism was his *Collection of Essentials on Attaining Birth in the Pure Land*, a three-fascicle work in which he graphically describes birth in the Pure Land as a means for saving common people. The work first gives a fearful and detailed description of hell in order to deter readers from attachment to this defiled world. It then offers the method for detaching from this world of suffering and attaining birth in the Pure Land. These methods include both the meditative and vocal nembutsu.

The Japanese people at that time, apprehensive about the imminence of the era of the decline of the Dharma,[19] may have been particularly receptive to the Pure Land doctrine and methods. It was widely accepted, based on scriptural evidence, that this degenerate age would begin after 1052. The view of this period of decline is outlined in the *Lamp for the Period of the Decline of the Dharma* by Saichō (767–822), the founder of the Tendai school. In it Saichō emphasizes the need for repentance of karmic nonvirtue even for monks. However, although Pure Land Buddhism gained popularity in Japan after the composition of this treatise, it was not until Hōnen that the distinctive Japanese Pure Land school called Jōdo Shū was first established.

Hōnen (1133–1212) was born the son of a warrior in the Mimasaka Province of Okayama at the end of the Heian period. Tragedy struck him at the age of nine when his father, Uruma no Tokikuni, by then the constable for the province, was fatally wounded in a night attack by adversaries. His last words to his son were, "Never entertain ill-will toward your enemy. This tragedy is the result of my own residual karma... Enter the monastery to pray for my attainment of buddhahood and seek your own deliverance."[20] Hōnen listened to his father and at thirteen became a monk and went to Mount Hiei to study the Tendai doctrines under the mentorship of Genkō and Kōen.

In 1150, Hōnen moved to Kurodani (a holy site located on the western side of Mount Hiei) to live a life of seclusion. His religious training was under the guidance of Eikū, who gave Hōnen the name "Hōnen-bō Genkū." At twenty-four Hōnen left the mountain for Kyōto, the capital, and Nara in order to learn from the eminent monks of the Hossō, Sanron, and Kegon schools.[21] His efforts were in vain, however, as none of these famous masters could instruct him in the teaching for deliverance that Hōnen sought.

While in the capital, Hōnen was struck by the contrast between the terrible suffering endured by the common people as the result of civil wars and natural disasters and the magnificence of the ornate Buddhist temples. Thereafter, he returned to Kurodani, seeking in solitude the right teaching that would allow him to lead all people to deliverance, enabling them to realize eternal peace, irrespective of age, sex, class, or occupation. It is said that Hōnen read the Buddhist scriptures and commentaries in their entirety five times. At the age of forty-three, he founded Jōdo Shū after being deeply impressed by the following passage in Shan-tao's *Commentary on the Meditation Sutra*:

> To recite intently and exclusively the name of Buddha Amitābha while walking, standing, sitting, or lying down, without regard for length of time; to engage without cessation in the recitation of nembutsu for life: This is called the *rightly established practice* because it is in accordance with the essential vow of Buddha Amitābha.[22]

Hōnen asserted his unshakable faith through citing this passage, which declares that by relying on the compassionate power of Amida Buddha completely and reciting his name continually, all sentient beings in the period of the decline of the Dharma will cultivate the karmic causes necessary to assure birth in the Pure Land of Ultimate Bliss.

The following was written by Hōnen in his major work, *Collection of Passages on the Nembutsu Chosen in the Essential Vow* (*Senchaku Hongan Nembutsu-shū*,[23] hereafter abbreviated as the *Collection on Nembutsu*):

> Shan-tao's *Commentary on the Meditation Sutra* is the guidebook to the Western Pure Land. It should be regarded as the eyes and feet of nembutsu devotees... I, an ordinary monk,

> happened to read this *Commentary* one time and grasped its general idea. Thereafter, I immediately abandoned practices other than the recitation of the name of Amida Buddha and immersed myself exclusively in recitation.
>
> Since then, I have practiced the recitation of nembutsu myself and taught only the practice of nembutsu to others. To those who seek deliverance from this world of suffering, I have preached the way to attain birth in the Western Pure Land. To those who have asked me about the means to birth in the Pure Land, I have taught the special practice of reciting nembutsu. Multitudes believe in my teaching; a few remain unbelievers. It should be known that only Pure Land Buddhism will encompass the potential of all people during this period...[24]

Hōnen adopted the nembutsu tradition of Shan-tao in its entirety and declared, "I rely exclusively upon Master Shan-tao." It is reported that Hōnen devoted himself to reciting the name of Amida Buddha sixty thousand times a day in accordance with the instruction of Shan-tao. He became convinced that deliverance was possible only through the recitation of nembutsu, but that the practice was available to anyone, anywhere, anytime. After nearly thirty years, Hōnen descended from the mountain and dwelled in a peaceful retreat in Yoshimizu, Kyōto, continually engaging in the intensive recitation of nembutsu.

The political situation in Kyōto changed dramatically, however, during the period from 1175 to 1190. Wars between the Genji and Heike, both vying for power, plunged the country into disorder. Hōnen later reminisced, saying, "Not a day passed without my reading the holy teaching of Buddha Śākyamuni, except for the day when Kiso no Kanja [Minamoto no Yoshinaka] invaded the capital of Kyōto." Along with war, natural calamities threatened many lives, and people were fearful of the decline of the Dharma. As a result, numerous people, of all ages and of both sexes, began visiting Hōnen to hear the teaching of nembutsu and find peace.

The popularity of Hōnen's nembutsu teaching drew much attention from the established Buddhist schools. In 1186, at the request of Kenshin, a leading Tendai monk, Hōnen engaged in a public dialogue on Pure Land Buddhism in Ōhara, a suburb of Kyōto. Known as the Ōhara Controversy, the dialogue was held before an audience of approximately three hundred, including such leading monks of other Buddhist schools ("the holy gate") as Chikai of the Sanron school and Jōkei of Hossō school. Hōnen stated,

> During the Ōhara debate on the holy gate and the Pure Land gate, both schools were equal with regard to the essence of their teachings. I, Genkū, however, emerged victorious in terms of the practitioners' capabilities. Although the teachings of the holy gate are indeed profound, they do not suit the people of today. The Pure Land gate may seem overly simplistic, but it is the right practice for the people of this era.[25]

It is reported that the entire audience recited the name of Amida Buddha for three days and nights after the debate. This incident was a major factor in the spread of Hōnen's vocal nembutsu thought throughout the country. Regent Kujō Kanezane (1149–1207), the chief minister of the state, became one of Hōnen's most ardent supporters after this discussion.

The heart of Hōnen's nembutsu is elaborated in the *Collection on Nembutsu* mentioned above, which was compiled in 1198 when Hōnen was sixty-six years old. The work, written at the request of Kanezane, consists of sixteen chapters and reveals Hōnen's view of nembutsu, with references to the Pure Land scriptures as well as to Shan-tao's *Commentary on the Meditation Sutra*. The text opens, "*Namu Amida Butsu*, the recitation of nembutsu, is foremost among practices for birth in the Pure Land."[26] The contents of the *Collection on Nembutsu* are:

1. *The Holy Gate and the Pure Land Gate*
   Hōnen presents the doctrinal foundation of Jōdo Shū, referring to Tao-ch'o's theory of the two gates and encouraging the reader to follow the teachings of the Pure Land gate. Hōnen also establishes the three sutras of Pure Land Buddhism as the authoritative texts of Jōdo Shū and clarifies the Jōdo Shū transmission lineage.
2. *The Right Practices and the Miscellaneous Practices*
   Following Shan-tao's classification of right practices and miscellaneous practices, Hōnen instructs us to abandon miscellaneous practices and to choose from among the right practices the *rightly established practice*. The rightly established practice is the recitation of nembutsu for birth in the Pure Land.
3. *The Essential Vow for Birth in the Pure Land through Nembutsu*
   Hōnen explains the meaning of the essential vow of Amida Buddha as one of all-encompassing compassion, emphasizing that nembutsu recitation is the actualization of the essential vow.
4. *The Three Categories of Aspirants for Birth in the Pure Land*
   Although the *Larger Sutra* logically analyzes the three categories of devotees aspiring to birth in the Pure Land, Hōnen defines the underlying principle as the recitation of nembutsu for all three categories of devotees.
5. *The Merit of Nembutsu*
   The unparalleled merit of just a single utterance of nembutsu is covered in great detail.
6. *The Teaching of Nembutsu Alone Will Prevail*
   Hōnen shows that after the period of the Dharma's decline that will last ten thousand years, the teaching of nembutsu alone will endure, even one hundred years after the Three Jewels have become extinct.
7. *The Light of Amida Buddha Embraces the Nembutsu Devotee*
   Hōnen explains that the light of Amida Buddha embraces and shines exclusively upon nembutsu practitioners. It does

not shine over those who engage in other practices not in accord with the essential vow.

8. *The Threefold Devotional Heart*

   On the basis of Shan-tao's *Commentary on the Meditation Sutra*, Hōnen describes the threefold devotional heart in detail: (1) the genuine heart, (2) the profound heart, and (3) the heart that seeks birth in the Pure Land through the dedication of merit. These three aspects of faith are indispensable for birth in the Pure Land of Ultimate Bliss.

9. *The Four Modes of Exercise*

   The four modes of exercise for the nembutsu practitioner are detailed in order to encourage and develop faith and practice. The four are to exercise nembutsu in reverence, purity, continuity, and infinity.

10. *In Praise of Nembutsu*

    Hōnen states that Amida Buddha delights in the utterance of his name when he welcomes the nembutsu devotee of the low category at the time of his death; Amida Buddha does not extol the virtuous act of hearing the names of Mahāyāna texts.

11. *In Praise of the Nembutsu Devotee*

    Referring to Shan-tao's *Commentary on the Meditation Sutra*, Hōnen clarifies that Buddha Śākyamuni praised the nembutsu devotee as the most outstanding, in contrast to practitioners engaged in other wholesome acts.

12. *Buddha Śākyamuni's Entrustment of Nembutsu to Ānanda*

    In the *Meditation Sutra* Buddha Śākyamuni expounded various types of meditative practices, some involving a focused mind and some a distracted mind. After completing these instructions, however, he entrusted to Ānanda the practice of nembutsu alone. Because of this, Hōnen is convinced that the true intention for posterity of Buddha Śākyamuni was to transmit nembutsu.

13. *The Unparalleled Virtues of Nembutsu*

    Referring to the *Smaller Sutra*, Hōnen proves that vocal

nembutsu, in contrast to the miscellaneous practices, is the most excellent and virtuous cause for birth in the Pure Land.

14. *The Authentication of Nembutsu by Various Buddhas*
Hōnen states that buddhas in all six directions, as countless as the grains of sand of the Ganges, indeed authenticated solely reciting nembutsu as the right practice for birth in the Pure Land. In contrast, they did not endorse practices other than nembutsu.
15. *The Protection of the Nembutsu Devotee by Manifold Buddhas*
Hōnen clarifies that because the nembutsu devotee is always protected by all buddhas in the six directions as well as by various bodhisattvas and holy beings, the devotee can live in peace until the time of death.
16. *Buddha Śākyamuni's Entrustment of Nembutsu to Śāriputra*
Hōnen describes the entrustment of the name of Amida Buddha to Śāriputra by Buddha Śākyamuni and concludes that the ultimate concern of Amida Buddha, Buddha Śākyamuni, and all buddhas is the propogation of nembutsu recitation, the sole means for birth in the Pure Land.

The purpose of composing the *Collection on Nembutsu* was to clarify for the ignorant, weak, and karmically defiled the means of deliverance through recitation of nembutsu while at the same time confronting the established Buddhist schools of the Nara and Heian periods. This was the first time the doctrine of the recitation of nembutsu was expressed in such a systematic manner in the history of Buddhism. Hōnen knew, however, that this revolutionary teaching would cause a confrontation with the established schools. He therefore stated, "It is my earnest wish that once you have read this work, you should conceal it in a mud wall and never leave it by your window."[27]

Day by day, Hōnen's propagation of nembutsu spread throughout the country, and a great number of people came to follow his teachings, including emperors, empresses, regents, monks, nuns, court nobles, warriors, merchants, townspeople, and even burglars. Among these followers, however, some, as a result of their misunderstanding of the teaching of Hōnen, criticized the traditional schools and indulged in wine and meat. This misconduct angered the monks on Mount Hiei, who asked Archbishop Shinshō of the Tendai school to prohibit the nembutsu practice.

On November 7, 1204, upon hearing this, Hōnen presented to Shinshō the *Monition in Seven Articles* (*Shichikajō kishōmon*), which he summarized as follows:

> To all of my followers and priests who practice the recitation of nembutsu, I admonish you:
>
> 1. Do not abuse the practices of the Shingon or Tendai schools, nor despise the buddhas and bodhisattvas not from your school, without understanding the profound meanings of the texts and commentaries.
> 2. The ignorant must not engage in disputes with the learned or with followers who differ from them in understanding and practice.
> 3. Do not insist that followers with different views and practices from your own abandon their practice. Never despise or scorn them.
> 4. Do not encourage people to commit adultery, drink wine, or eat meat by saying that the teaching of nembutsu does not require them to observe the precepts. Never refer to those observing the precepts as "people of the miscellaneous practice" or insist that followers who rely upon the essential vow of Amida Buddha need not be afraid of committing misdeeds.
> 5. The ignorant, who cannot yet discern right from wrong, must not depart from the teachings of the holy texts, nor should they disregard the teachings of their masters. They should not arbitrarily dispute with and be scorned by the learned, or confuse or disturb others.
> 6. The ignorant must not willingly teach nembutsu, preach

falsity without fundamental knowledge of the true Dharma, or teach innocent monastics or lay people.

7. Do not give arbitrary instruction with views contrary to the teaching of the Buddha and pretend that these views are those of the master.[28]

A copy of this text is housed at Nison-in Temple in Kyōto. Along with the articles, Hōnen presented the signatures of more than eighty of his disciples pledging to follow them. Kanezane also sympathized, sending a letter to Shinshō explaining the true intention of Hōnen: that Hōnen only sought deliverance for the populace through the recitation of nembutsu. There was no intention to dispute with the monks of other more traditional schools. Over time, resentment of the monks on Mount Hiei subsided.

In 1207 Hōnen was tragically exiled to the island of Shikoku as a result of the secret conversion to Pure Land Buddhism by two ladies of the court after they attended a special nembutsu retreat held by Hōnen's disciples. Perhaps out of jealousy, the traditional schools had been alarming the court with claims of misconduct among Hōnen's followers. The disciples and followers were greatly overwhelmed with sorrow and grief. To his closest disciple, Hōren-bō Shinkū, Hōnen said:

> Do not resent this penalty of exile, as I am now nearly eighty years old. Even if we, master and disciple, were both living in the capital, our separation in this delusive world would come soon. And though we are at present separated by mountains and oceans, I firmly believe we will meet again in the Pure Land. Even he who abhors this world of suffering still lives here as long as there is life in his body. On the other hand, though he may desire a longer life, he may leave this world sooner than expected. What difference does it make where we live? When I resided in the capital Kyōto for many years to teach nembutsu, it was long my desire to preach the

> nembutsu to innocent people in the countryside, yet my wish was never fulfilled. Now, however, thanks to imperial benevolence, I am able to accomplish my long-held wish; this is a matter of cause and effect.[29]

When the boat carrying Hōnen reached the coast of Takasago on the way to Shikoku, an old couple came to him, palms together, and said, "We fish for a living in this bay. It has been our livelihood since childhood to take the lives of fish day and night. We heard that one who took the life of another would fall to hell and be unbearably tormented there. Is there any way to avoid such torment?" Hōnen replied, "If you only recite *Namu Amida Butsu,* you will be born in the Pure Land by means of the compassion of Amida Buddha."[30]

Later, his boat had almost reached Muro no tomari in the same province when a small boat carrying a woman of ill-fame approached him. She begged him to show her the way for her own deliverance. Speaking gently, Hōnen said, "A life such as yours is not slight in offense. If there is any other livelihood for you, then stop this conduct. If you can find no other way to make a living, however, or if you cannot sacrifice all of your interests to seek the way to buddhahood, just stay as you are and recite nembutsu exclusively. Amida Buddha established the universal vow in order to save an undesirable person such as you. Rely implicitly upon his essential vow and never disparage yourself. Once you recite the name of Amida Buddha and rely on the essential vow, birth in the Pure Land will certainly be realized."[31]

These two accounts verify Hōnen's spirit of tolerance and deep concern for the masses. Hōnen often called himself Ignorant Hōnen. This does not indicate that Hōnen was indeed ignorant. He was actually known as the "most knowledgeable monk" of his time and was thoroughly acquainted with many Buddhist texts, commentaries, and doctrines. The term *ignorant* indicates his total recognition of the human essence. He knew that the human mind was deeply consumed by worldly passions such as greed, anger, and ignorance.

It is not known exactly where Hōnen spent his days of exile in

Shikoku. On the eighth of December of the same year, however, the emperor rescinded Hōnen's exile, but still he did not grant Hōnen permission to enter the capital. Hōnen thus remained in Kachiō-ji Temple in Ōsaka for four years until he finally returned to Kyōto late in 1211, where he stayed at a small temple in Yoshimizu. By that time, Hōnen's physical condition had greatly deteriorated.

In the waning days of his life, on January 23, 1212, Hōnen wrote the *Single-Sheet Covenant* at the behest of his disciple Seikan-bō Genchi. The essence of his nembutsu doctrines is presented in the *Covenant*, which states, "The nembutsu I preach is not the meditation taught by the learned men of China and Japan; nor is it recitation of scholarly works in order to master their profound meanings. To attain birth in the Pure Land, nothing is required but an implicit faith that the recitation of *Namu Amida Butsu* causes the certain attainment of birth in the Pure Land. The teachings of the threefold devotional heart and the four modes of exercise are encompassed in the firm belief that birth in the Pure Land is assured by reciting *Namu Amida Butsu*."

Hōnen's approach demands faith in the all encompassing compassion of Amida Buddha. In this sense Hōnen takes Shan-tao's notion of nembutsu to extremes. Every religious practice is combined into the intense and exclusive recitation of nembutsu. Hōnen concludes his *Single-Sheet Covenant* with the words, "Refrain from flaunting knowledge and devote yourself to reciting nembutsu." He passed away two days later at the age of eighty.

4. Conclusion

From an academic viewpoint, the discrepancy between the scriptural depiction of nembutsu as one meditation practice among many on the one hand and Shan-tao and Hōnen's praise of a vocal nembutsu as singularly efficacious on the other could be a problem, but from a religious perspective, this shift is not so problematic. That is to say, the innovations of these monks emerged from their personal religious experiences. Both were known for their overwhelming rigorous discipline, and Hōnen clarified his reason for regarding Shan-tao as his forerunner in his *Collection on Nembutsu* when he said, "Master Shan-tao indeed realized the state of samādhi."[32] *Samādhi*, as we have noted, is the state of tranquility full of insight, and by it one is able to perceive the physical features of Amida Buddha. That both Shan-tao and Hōnen attained samādhi through the recitation of nembutsu is the crucial validation for the efficacy of nembutsu.

Buddhism talks about the Three Jewels: the Buddha, the Dharma, and the Sangha. The Buddha and the Dharma are the ideals of the tradition, and the historical reality is the Sangha, which interprets the Buddha and the Dharma and is constantly changing. In this way, the Buddha and the Dharma are shaped by history and culture. In Indian Buddhism, for example, monks, following Brahmanic traditions, were prohibited from engaging in physical labor, yet in China and Japan, monks were required to work. They plowed fields, harvested crops, and prepared their own meals. Further, in both China and Japan, temples were built near commercial centers, and although the Vinaya prohibits monks from engaging in financial transactions, temples were frequently used as marketplaces. Thus, the interpretation of the Buddha and the Dharma have been subject to great change. This does not invalidate those expressions of the Buddha and the Dharma; it just means that those ideals are modified by the Sangha in response to historical circumstances.

Such was the case with Shan-tao and Hōnen, who reworked Pure Land Buddhism by de-emphasizing the difficult bodhisattva practices and valorizing the recitation of nembutsu. Their modifications presupposed that humans by and large were incapable of realizing enlightenment through their own efforts using the traditional methods. The transformation from the meditative nembutsu to the vocal nembutsu was a major shift in Buddhism's historical development.

An Outline of *Collected Teachings of Hōnen: The Japanese Anthology*

After Hōnen's death in 1212, his disciples and followers, in order to praise Hōnen's religious and academic accomplishments and to transmit his nembutsu tradition to future generations, attempted to compile his voluminous writings and compose his biography.

Seikan-bō Genchi (1183–1238),[33] a disciple of Hōnen, edited the *Biography of Hōnen-shōnin* approximately thirty years after the death of Hōnen. Shinran (1173–1262),[34] the founder of Jōdo Shin Shū, compiled the *Guide to the Western Pure Land* forty-four years after Hōnen's death. Ryōe Dōkō (1243–1330) searched all over the capital of Kyōto and other provinces for more than twenty years compiling Hōnen's literary remains. These consisted of works in both Chinese and Japanese, and the resulting compilation, called the *Collected Teachings of Kurodani-shōnin*, had four parts:

1. The *Collected Teachings of Kurodani-shōnin: The Chinese Anthology* (ten fascicles and twenty-two chapters), completed on December 8, 1274
2. The *Collected Teachings of Kurodani-shōnin: The Japanese Anthology* (five fascicles and twenty-four chapters), completed on January 25, 1275
3. The *Supplement to the Collected Teachings of Kurodani-shōnin: The Chinese Anthology* (one fascicle and three chapters), completed on December 8, 1274
4. The *Supplement to the Collected Teachings of Kurodani-shōnin: The Japanese Anthology* (two fascicles and eight chapters), completed on January 25, 1275

Kurodani is a holy place on the west side of Mount Hiei, the center of the nembutsu practice at the time of Hōnen. Kurodani-shōnin ("eminent monk of Kurodani") refers to Hōnen, who studied the entire Buddhist scriptures at Seiryū-ji Temple in Kurodani and who established Jōdo Shū as an independent school there in the spring of 1175.

The Japanese collection and supplement in the above list, compiled by Ryōe Dōko in 1275, were published by Enchi in July of the first year of the Genkō era (1321), just over a hundred years after Hōnen's death. Accordingly, these two Japanese works, one of the most comprehensive collections of Hōnen's teachings, are referred to as the Genkō edition of the *Japanese Anthology* (*Wago Tōroku*). "Japanese" in the title means that it is written in the *hiragana* syllabary mixed with Chinese characters. An almost perfect copy of the Genkō edition of the *Japanese Anthology* is preserved at Bukkyō University in Kyōto, and it is this edition that has been used as the basis for the present translation. The *Chinese Anthology* (*Kango Tōroku*) and its supplement were not published until 1715 during the Edo period, over five hundred years after Hōnen's death. Apart from one work—the *Collection on Nembutsu* outlined above—this collection has yet to be translated into English.

Ryōe Dōkō was one of the leading disciples of the third Jōdo Shū patriarch Ryōchū (1199–1287),[35] who had received Hōnen's Pure Land Buddhism from the second patriarch, Shōkō-bō Benchō (1162–1238).[36] Born in Kamakura, Dōkō went to Mount Hiei at the age of eleven, mastering both exoteric and esoteric Buddhism as well as the doctrine of the *Lotus Sutra*. It is uncertain precisely when he converted to Jōdo Shū, but he began compiling the Genkō edition of Hōnen's collected teachings at the age of thirty-one, and he inscribed the original manuscript for the printer's engraving block when he was seventy-nine. He then received the Buddhist precepts from Ryōchū in 1279 and established Goshin-ji Temple in Kyōto, where he propagated Hōnen's teaching.

Dōkō was greatly concerned about misinterpretations of Hōnen's nembutsu thought that emerged after the death of Hōnen. In the epilogue to the Genkō edition of the *Japanese Anthology*, Dōkō states,

"The purpose of this compilation is to encourage all sentient beings to enter the *right path* toward birth in the Pure Land" (emphasis added).

Several collections of Hōnen's works exist in addition to the Genkō edition. Gizan (1647–1717), a scholarly monk of Jōdo Shū active in the middle of the Edo period, published the Gizan edition of the collected works in 1711. This included both the Chinese and Japanese collections but also many of Gizan's own interpretations.

The so-called Ekū edition of the *Chinese Anthology* is based on a copy made in 1694 by Ekū (1644–1721), a priest of the Ōtani branch of the Jōdo Shin sect. This work excludes, however, a part of the supplement. There is also the Daitoku-ji Temple edition of the supplement to the *Chinese Anthology*, which was inscribed in 1702.

We will now briefly summarize each chapter of the Genkō edition of Hōnen's collected teachings in the *Japanese Anthology*.

Part I: Collected Teachings of Hōnen: The Japanese Anthology

First Fascicle (Three Chapters)

Prologue (*Jo*)

Dokō shows his respect to Hōnen and describes the situation prevailing after the death of Hōnen, stating, "The eminent monk of Kurodani appeared in the world as an emanation of the bodhisattva Mahāsthāmaprāpta. He explicated the meaning of the essential vow of Amida Buddha for the first time in Japan and encouraged people to practice exclusively the vocal nembutsu for attaining birth in the Pure Land... Many follow the nembutsu tradition of Hōnen-shōnin today, but each interprets its meaning differently." This alludes to Dōkō's main motivation for compiling the literary heritage of Hōnen.

Dōkō then concludes the prologue, stating, "I sincerely hope that those who seek birth in the Pure Land regard this work as a 'light' shining on the path toward the Pure Land. If someone finds any additional teaching of Hōnen that I have omitted, please amend this work."

1. Commentary on the Three Sutras of Pure Land Buddhism (*Sanbukyō-shaku*)

As for the *Larger Sutra*, Hōnen states that the forty-eight vows of Amida Buddha were made specifically for the establishment of the essential eighteenth vow—the vow that all sentient beings will be born in the Pure Land through nembutsu recitation. Hence, the eighteenth vow is regarded as the most outstanding of all forty-eight vows.

In general, all vows made by bodhisattvas have two aspects: one is the vow to attain enlightenment, and the other is the vow to save mortals from suffering. The primary concern of bodhisattvas, however, is the second aspect, saving mortals from suffering. Thus Amida Buddha created the Pure Land so that he could welcome all sentient beings into his Pure Land of Ultimate Bliss for their attainment of enlightenment there.

Regarding the *Meditation Sutra*, Hōnen believes that the essence of the *Meditation Sutra* is to clarify the merit of nembutsu, as taught in the passage: "Each ray of light from Amida Buddha shines over the worlds of the ten directions. Those who recite nembutsu are embraced by that light and will never be abandoned."[37] In order to validate this view, Hōnen refers to several vows of Amida Buddha: the vow that the light of Amida Buddha is immeasurable and illuminates countless other buddhalands (twelfth vow); the vow that the life of Amida Buddha is infinite (thirteenth vow); the vow that all the innumerable buddhas praise the name of Amida Buddha (seventeenth vow); the vow that all sentient beings will be born in the Pure Land through the repetition of nembutsu (eighteenth vow); and the vow that Amida Buddha, surrounded by the host of celestial beings, welcomes nembutsu devotees into the Pure Land at their time of death (nineteenth vow).

Following this, Hōnen explains the theory of the threefold devotional heart for birth in the Pure Land, stating, "The elements of the threefold devotional heart are thought of as separate, but closer inspection reveals that the essence and core of the threefold devotional heart is the profound heart."

Concerning the *Smaller Sutra*, Hōnen explains that nembutsu, as taught in the essential vow, is not only the teaching of Amida Buddha but also that of Buddha Śākyamuni and of all buddhas in the ten directions.

2. The Covenant (*Goseigon no sho*)

This is the document generally known as the *Single-Sheet Covenant*, the essential teaching of Jōdo Shū focusing on nembutsu recitation. As noted above, it was composed just two days before Hōnen's death. At the end of this document, Dōkō has appended a note stating, "This covenant was written by Hōnen-shōnin himself and given to his disciple, Seikan-shōnin." Almost the same document appears within chapter 24 of this work, "The Sayings of Hōnen-shōnin as Stated by His Disciples."

3. An Outline of the Doctrine for Birth in the Pure Land (*Ōjō taiyōshō*)

Hōnen first explains about the four vehicles taught in the holy gate, but he then encourages people to enter the Pure Land gate since the teachings of the four vehicles are too difficult for ordinary people. He further states: "Both heart and practice should be in concert," and "The threefold devotional heart is connected to the nine grades of aspirants for birth in the Pure Land."

This text lacks the commentary on the third aspect of the threefold devotional heart—the heart that seeks birth in the Pure Land through the dedication of merit. Dōkō attaches a note to the end of this work, saying, "This text alludes to the existence of a second fascicle, but I have not found it. It may be lost in obscurity. Should anyone discover it, amending this dissertation would be desirable."

SECOND FASCICLE (FIVE CHAPTERS)

4. Essential Discourse on Birth in the Pure Land through Nembutsu (*Nembutsu Ōjo yōgishō*)
This is the essential teaching for attaining birth in the Pure Land through nembutsu in the period of the decline of the Dharma.[38] Thirteen questions and answers are recorded, including the issues of "power other than self and self-power," "a single utterance and the ten repetitions of nembutsu," "nembutsu in daily life and at death," and "nembutsu recited by the learned and the ignorant." A Chinese version of this work is in the collection of Nishi Hongwan-ji Temple in Kyōto.

5. The Significance of the Threefold Devotional Heart (*Sanjingi*)
Basing himself upon the interpretations of Shan-tao, Hōnen discusses the essentials of the threefold devotional heart, including the five advantages of the right practices and the five disadvantages of the miscellaneous practices.

6. Instruction in the Seven Articles (*Shichikajō no kishōmon*)
After a general explanation of the threefold devotional heart, Hōnen delineates seven instructions for the success of nembutsu:

1. Not taking the vows of buddhas and bodhisattvas lightly
2. Reciting nembutsu, while relying on the power other than self
3. Possessing the threefold devotional heart through nembutsu
4. Encouraging a special nembutsu retreat for a fixed period of time
5. Establishing the rightly settled state of mind for birth in the Pure Land at the time of death
6. Continuing nembutsu for life
7. Vigilantly avoiding conceit

This *Instruction in the Seven Articles* is different from the *Monition in Seven Articles,* despite the fact that their Japanese titles are identical. The same composition appears in chapter 21 of the *Illustrated Biography of Hōnen-shōnin.*

7. An Outline of Nembutsu (*Nembutsu tai'i*)
Hōnen encourages those who aspire for birth in the Pure Land to enter the nembutsu gate based on the instruction of Shan-tao. Hōnen emphasizes that exclusively practicing nembutsu has great merit because it is the practice most suitable to the ability of the common people in the period of the decline of the Dharma and nurtures the threefold devotional heart. He also states that nembutsu devotees should not be overly concerned about criticisms from people of other Buddhist schools because nembutsu was validated and observed by great masters such as Tao-ch'o[39] and Shan-tao. The work is also recorded in *Guide to the Western Pure Land.*

8. An Outline of the Essentials of Jōdo Shū (*Jōdo Shū ryakushō*)
According to Dōkō, this is Hōnen's reply composed at the behest of a powerful nun in the court of Kamakura, Hōjō Masako[40] (1157–1225), who had earlier been the consort of Shōgun Minamoto no Yoritomo (1147–97). In this reply, Hōnen first explains the holy gate and the Pure Land gate and then expounds upon the steadfast heart and the practice for attaining birth in the Pure Land.

THIRD FASCICLE (FOUR CHAPTERS)

9. A Reply to the Lady Kujō (*Kujō-denka no kita no mandokoro e mairasu gohenji*)
This is Hōnen's reply to the Lady Kujō Kaneko (1152–1201), the consort of Regent Kujō Kanezane (1149–1207), a close patron-disciple of Hōnen. She received the Buddhist precepts from Hōnen a year before her death.

Hōnen encourages Lady Kujō to seek birth in the Pure Land exclusively through nembutsu practice for the following reasons:

nembutsu is a wondrous practice for common people in this period; nembutsu is the practice taught in the essential vow of Amida Buddha; the practice of nembutsu was validated by Buddha Śākyamuni; nembutsu was validated by all the buddhas in the six directions.

The contents of this text are similar to those in "A Reply to the Lay Priest Saburō in Tsunoto," chapter 15 of the present work. The reply is also recorded in *Guide to the Western Pure Land* and in chapter 21 of the *Illustrated Biography of Hōnen-shōnin*.

10. A Reply to the Nun Holding the Second Rank in the Court of Kamakura (*Kamakura no ni'i no zen'ni e mairasu gohenji*)

This is another reply to Hōjō Masako. Hōnen elucidates the extensive virtues of nembutsu, encourages her to exclusively practice nembutsu, and then answers the questions posed by Masako about:

1. The establishment of a karmic relationship with Amida Buddha
2. Various virtuous roots
3. Virtuous acts for the life to come
4. The easiest practice for birth in the Pure Land
5. Not arguing with a nonbeliever in nembutsu

The work is also recorded in *Guide to the Western Pure Land* and in chapter 25 of the *Illustrated Biography of Hōnen-shōnin*.

11. Dialogue on the Essentials of Nembutsu (*Yōgi mondō*)

Hōnen teaches thirteen fundamental understandings for the nembutsu devotee in question-and-answer form. They are:

1. Renouncing the secular life
2. Departing from this delusive world
3. The attainment of birth in the Pure Land for common mortals
4. Aspiration for birth in the Western Pure Land
5. The recitation of nembutsu for birth in the Pure Land
6. The sole practice for birth in the Pure Land

7. Pure Land texts and commentaries
8. The threefold devotional heart
9. Nembutsu with a single heart
10. The four ways to perform nembutsu for birth in the Pure Land
11. Negative conditions
12. The elimination of karmic defilements through nembutsu
13. Reciting nembutsu

This work is also recorded in *Guide to the Western Pure Land.*

12. A Reply to Tarō Sanehide in Ōgo (*Ōgo no Tarō Sanehide e tsukawasu gohenji*)

This is a reply to Tarō Sanehide (d. 1246) in Ōgo,[41] a lay disciple of Hōnen, regarding the issue of the threefold devotional heart. Hōnen stresses that nembutsu is in accord with the essential vow for birth in the Pure Land. The work is also recorded in *Guide to the Western Pure Land* and in chapter 5 of the *Biography of Hōnen-shōnin* (nine fascicles).

FOURTH FASCICLE (NINE CHAPTERS)

13. A Reply to the Lady of Tarō Sanehide in Ōgo (*Ōgo no Tarō Sanehide ga saishitsu no moto e tsukawasu gohenji*)

According to Dōkō, this is a reply to the lady of Tarō Sanehide that Hōnen sent in 1199 when he was sixty-seven years old. In it Hōnen clarifies that no practice is superior to nembutsu for common mortals to attain birth in the Pure Land because nembutsu is the very practice prescribed in the essential vow of Amida Buddha. Hōnen also discusses the relative merit between exclusive practice of nembutsu on the one hand and the miscellaneous practices on the other and encourages the lady to devote herself to nembutsu. The work is also recorded in *Guide to the Western Pure Land* and in chapter 25 of the *Illustrated Biography of Hōnen-shōnin.*

14. A Reply to the Lay Priest in Kumagai (*Kumagai no nyūdō e tsukawasu gohenji*)

This is Hōnen's reply to Jirō Naozane (1141–1207)[42] in Kumagai. Since Naozane became a lay disciple of Hōnen in 1193, the letter was probably composed thereafter. Hōnen encourages Naozane to have unshakable faith in the attainment of birth in the Pure Land through nembutsu. The work is also recorded in *Guide to the Western Pure Land*.

15. A Reply to the Lay Priest Saburō in Tsunoto (*Tsunoto no Saburō-nyūdō e tsukawasu gohenji*)

Hōnen responds to four concerns posed by the lay priest Saburō Tamemori:[43]

1. Amida Buddha does not discriminate between the learned and the unschooled.
2. Virtuous acts do not become a hindrance to nembutsu.
3. Nembutsu does not require a particular time or place for its practice.
4. You should not debate those who do not believe in nembutsu.

These four replies are dated April 26, September 18, September 28, and October 18. Dōkō notes that this reply was written on September 18, but the year is uncertain. The work is also recorded in *Guide to the Western Pure Land*, in chapter 3 of the *Biography of Hōnen-shōnin*, and in chapter 28 of the *Illustrated Biography of Hōnen-shōnin*.

16. A Letter to an Eminent Monk in Kuroda (*Kuroda no shōnin e tsukawasu on-fumi*)

This document is as essential to understanding Hōnen's Pure Land thought as is his *Single-Sheet Covenant*. In this letter, Hōnen examines the attitudes of nembutsu devotees, focusing on the issue of faith in Pure Land Buddhism. The work is also recorded in *Guide to the Western Pure Land* and in chapter 21 of the *Illustrated Biography of Hōnen-shōnin*.

17. A Reply to Kōmyō-bō in Ecchū (*Ecchū no kuni Kōmyō-bō e tsukawasu gohenji*)

In this reply, Hōnen severely protests the idea that a single utterance of nembutsu is sufficient to attain birth in the Pure Land. He encourages Kōmyō-bō[44] to practice the repetition of nembutsu throughout his life. The work is also recorded in *Guide to the Western Pure Land* and in chapter 29 of the *Illustrated Biography of Hōnen-shōnin*.

18. A Letter to the Nun Shōnyo-bō (*Shōnyo-bō e tsukawasu on-fumi*)

Shōnyo-bō,[45] a daughter of Emperor Go-Shirakawa, died on January 25, 1201, and this letter shows that she was seriously ill and nearing her end. Hōnen encourages her to devote herself to the practice of nembutsu in order to establish the properly settled state of mind for Amida Buddha to welcome her into the Pure Land at the time of her death. The work is also recorded in *Guide to the Western Pure Land* and in chapter 19 of the *Illustrated Biography of Hōnen-shōnin*.

19. Instruction to Zenshō-bō (*Zenshō-bō ni shimesu on-kotoba*)

This is Hōnen's short yet important instruction to Zenshō-bō (1174–1258),[46] who became a disciple of Hōnen when the master was seventy. Hōnen instructs him:

1. Continuously recite nembutsu throughout your life up to the moment of death so that you are guaranteed birth in the Pure Land.
2. Recite nembutsu in your natural state even at birth.
3. Persist in reciting nembutsu throughout your life while still believing that even a single utterance of nembutsu assures birth in the Pure Land.
4. Do not doubt that the recitation assures birth in the Pure Land, for without faith, every utterance is futile.

20. Dialogue on Twelve Topics (*Jūni no mondō*)

The twelve topics in this teaching are responses to questions about:

1. The establishment of Jōdo Shū
2. The miscellaneous practices, including the practices of the *Lotus Sutra* and the Shingon tradition
3. Virtuous deeds
4. The nine classes of aspirants for birth in the Pure Land
5. Observing and violating the Buddhist precepts
6. The vocal nembutsu
7. Unbroken daily nembutsu
8. Faith and practice
9. The essential vow for attaining birth in the Pure Land through nembutsu
10. Self-power and the power other than self
11. Possessing the threefold devotional heart
12. The final utterance of nembutsu at the time of death

Dōkō notes: "In *Clarifying the Essentials and Promoting Wholesome Conduct*,[47] these questions are attributed to Zenshō-bō. Another source names Monk Ryūkan. More research is necessary." The work is also recorded in *Guide to the Western Pure Land*, in chapter 4 of the *Biography of Hōnen-shōnin*, and in chapter 35 of the *Illustrated Biography of Hōnen-shōnin*.

21. Dialogue on Twelve Issues (*Jūnikajō-mondō*)

This is another set of responses on twelve topics:

1. Birth in the Pure Land through relying on the power other than self
2. Unwholesome karma
3. The precious gem
4. The continuation of nembutsu
5. Nembutsu without cessation
6. The threefold devotional heart
7. Aspiration to birth in the Pure Land
8. The attitude of the nembutsu devotee
9. Wholesome conditions

10. Virtuous acts other than nembutsu
11. An unwholesome person
12. The single-hearted nembutsu

FIFTH FASCICLE (THREE CHAPTERS)

22. Dialogue on One Hundred Forty-Five Topics (*Ippyaku shijū gokajō mondō*)
This is a dialogue between Hōnen and some nembutsu devotees. The questions are simple, relating to their daily life; through them one can see the customs, religious life, and views of nembutsu in those days. The work is also recorded in chapter 22 of the *Illustrated Biography of Hōnen-shōnin*.

23. A Dialogue Between Hōnen-shōnin and Myōhen-sōzu (*Shōnin to Myōhen tono mondō*)
Myōhen-sōzu (1142–1224)[48] was a Sanron monk. In this short dialogue, he and Hōnen discuss detachment from this delusive world of transmigration and distracted thoughts during nembutsu. Hōnen answers that detachment is possible only through nembutsu and that even he is powerless over distractions during the recitation. This work is also recorded in the second fascicle of *Clarifying the Essentials and Promoting Wholesome Conduct*.

24. The Sayings of Hōnen-shōnin as Stated by His Disciples (*Shonin denzetsu no kotoba*)
This is a collection of the sayings of Hōnen narrated by his six leading disciples: Ryūkan, Jōgan-bō Sōgen,[49] Hōren-bō Shinkū,[50] Shōkō-bō Benchō, Zenshō-bō, and Dōhen.[51] This is based on quotations from *Clarifying the Essentials and Promoting Wholesome Conduct*, the *Solution to Problems Regarding Shōkō's Jushuin*, the *Dialogue on Twenty-Eight Topics*, the *Dialogue on the Next Life*, the *Letters of Shirakawa*, the *Collection of Stories*, the *Personal Seal Attesting to the*

Transmission of Hōnen's Teaching of Nembutsu for the Future Generations, the *In-depth Study of the Collection on Nembutsu*, the *Collection of Dialogues on Nembutsu*, and the *Collection of Essentials on Jōdo Shū*. The sayings are also recorded in chapters 6, 21, 30, 44, 45, and 48 of the *Illustrated Biography of Hōnen-shōnin*.

Part II: First Supplement to Collected Teachings of Hōnen: The Japanese Anthology

(ONE FASCICLE AND FOUR CHAPTERS)

25. The Statement Sent to Mount Hiei (*Tozan-jō*)

Sent to Enryaku-ji Temple on Mount Hiei, the headquarters of the Tendai school, this document was intended to stop the traditional Buddhist schools' persecution of Jōdo Shū. Hōnen dictated these essentials of Jōdo Shū to his disciple Seikaku (1167–1235), who wrote them down between 1204 and 1205.

Based on literary style, this work seems to consist of two parts: the first half is written in a flowery style and the latter in a traditional style. In the first part, Hōnen teaches that we should lament having transmigrated for so long in the delusive triple realms, rejoice at the good fortune of experiencing a precious encounter with the teachings of Buddha Śākyamuni in this life, and aspire to detachment from the delusive worlds. He then advocates entering the Pure Land gate and articulates that the essence of the meditative practices with focused and with distracted minds narrated in the *Meditation Sutra* lies in the recitation of nembutsu.

The second half explains that:

1. Jōdo Shū was established based on the teachings of both Buddha Śākyamuni and Amida Buddha. This presents the academic tradition of Shan-tao.
2. Nembutsu as taught in the essential vow of Amida Buddha was validated by Buddha Śākyamuni and other buddhas.
3. The only thing that conflict between Jōdo Shū and other

schools accomplishes is disregard for the intent of Buddha Śākyamuni.

4. Nembutsu devotees should devote themselves exclusively to the practice of nembutsu.

The work is also recorded in chapter 32 of the *Illustrated Biography of Hōnen-shōnin*.

26. Instruction to a Devotee (*Aruhito ni shimesu kotoba*)

This writing seems to be Hōnen's reply to a nembutsu devotee regarding several issues: the way to relieve oneself, the fulfillment of filial duties, Shan-tao's interpretation of the essential eighteenth vow, and nembutsu for repentance.

27. Replies to Saburō in Tsunoto (*Tsunoto no Saburō e tsukawasu gohenji*)

The first reply, dated October 18th, was probably composed around 1205–6: Saburō was an ardent devotee of the exclusive practice of nembutsu. One day, he was summoned to the Shōgun's court because someone reported that Saburō had criticized the teachings of other traditional schools. Saburō was then ordered before the court to explain his real intentions in performing nembutsu. He immediately sent a letter to Hōnen requesting that Hōnen write out the essentials of nembutsu, making sure it matched Saburō's explanation about nembutsu at the trial. The reply is also recorded in chapter 28 of the *Illustrated Biography of Hōnen-shōnin*.

In the second reply, dated September 28th, Hōnen expresses how happy he is to hear that more than thirty people were performing nembutsu in the province where Saburō lived. The letter is also recorded in chapter 28 of the *Illustrated Biography of Hōnen-shōnin*.

The third reply, dated April 26th, is Hōnen's response to the get-well letter sent by Saburō, who was seriously concerned about Hōnen's physical condition. Hōnen discouraged Saburō from visiting but encouraged him to continue performing nembutsu for attaining birth in the Pure Land.

28. Instruction to a Lady (*Aru nyōbō ni shimesu hōgo*)
This is Hōnen's reply to a lady who posed the question, "Is it true that one who attains birth in the Pure Land in the lower level of the middle category does not receive the welcome of Amida Buddha because there is no mention of his arrival in that category in the *Meditation Sutra*?" Hōnen answers that Amida Buddha will arrive for any nembutsu devotee in any level. The work is also recorded in chapter 24 of the *Illustrated Biography of Hōnen-shōnin*.

Part III: Second Supplement to Collected Teachings of Hōnen: The Japanese Anthology

(ONE FASCICLE AND FOUR CHAPTERS)

29. Essentials for Birth in the Pure Land through Nembutsu (*Nembutsu Ōjōgi*)
In this text, Hōnen plainly explains that birth in the Pure Land through nembutsu is certain; birth in the Pure Land becomes uncertain only if one doubts that nembutsu will bring birth in the Pure Land. Nembutsu should be performed even if mundane affairs keep one busy. He further encourages a nembutsu devotee to perform the exclusive practice of nembutsu with the threefold devotional heart.

30. Dialogue on Ten Issues at Tōdai-ji Temple (*Tōdai-ji jūmondō*)
This is a dialogue between Hōnen and Shunjō-bō Chōgen (1121–1206),[52] a prominent disciple of Hōnen, held at Tōdai-ji Temple on March 13, 1191. Hōnen replies to questions posed by Chōgen on ten topics:

1. Jōdo Shū and the complete teachings of Buddha Śākyamuni
2. Nembutsu as the essential vow
3. Nembutsu with the threefold devotional heart
4. Reciting nembutsu with a string of prayer beads
5. The Three Jewels
6. Aspiration for birth in the Pure Land

7. The merit of embracing Amida Buddha
8. The light of Amida Buddha
9. Continuous nembutsu after awakening the heart for birth in the Pure Land
10. Amida Buddha's welcoming at the time of death

31. Letters (*Goshōsoku*)

This chapter contains four letters:

1. *A Reply*

   It is unknown to whom this letter was composed. However, the style of this writing indicates that the addressee is a person of distinction. There are some similar descriptions in "A Reply to the Nun Holding the Second Rank in the Court of Kamakura" (chapter 10). In the present letter, Hōnen gives a full account of the steadfast heart for birth in the Pure Land: that is, the threefold devotional heart.

2. *A Letter to Someone*

   In this short letter, Hōnen writes that in this period of the decline of the Dharma, nembutsu is the sole practice for attaining birth in the Pure Land, even if it is just uttered once. It is not certain who this "someone" is.

3. *A Reply to the Lay Priest Kumagai*

   This is Hōnen's reply, dated May 5th, to a question posed by the lay priest Naozane. Honen explains that general Buddhist practices, such as observing the precepts, chanting a mystic phrase (Skt. *dhāraṇī*), meditating on the noumenal aspects of reality, using a Buddhist walking staff, refraining from committing adultery, and refraining from being angry are secondary to nembutsu. Hōnen then urges Naozane to devote himself to the exclusive recitation of nembutsu. At the very end of this reply, Hōnen kindly says, "Attending dutifully to one's parents is not in the practice of the essential vow. Nevertheless, your mother is eighty-nine years old now. Please encourage her to recite nembutsu within her heart so that Amida

Buddha may come to welcome her this year." The work is also recorded in chapter 27 of the *Illustrated Biography of Hōnen-shōnin.*

4. *A Reply on One Occasion*
   This is another reply to Naozane by Hōnen, dated April 3rd. Naozane seems to have experienced an auspicious augury, in which he predicted the specific date of his attainment of birth in the Pure Land. Hōnen enjoys hearing this and urges him to practice nembutsu even more.

The above four letters are also recorded in chapter 27 of the *Illustrated Biography of Hōnen-shōnin.*

32. Admonitions for the Attainment of Birth in the Pure Land (*Ōjō Jōdo yōjin*)

This is Hōnen's reply to a nembutsu devotee who asked nine questions regarding birth in the Pure Land. The nine topics are:

1. Daily nembutsu
2. Residual virtuous deeds
3. Exchanging words during the practice of nembutsu
4. One million recitations of nembutsu
5. A memorial service for the departed
6. Faith in birth in the Pure Land through nembutsu
7. Amida Buddha's welcome at the time of death
8. Continuous nembutsu for life
9. Eating meat

The work is also recorded in chapter 23 of the *Illustrated Biography of Hōnen-shōnin.*

Epilogue (*Kōjo*)

Dōkō states, "For more than twenty years, I searched for the literary remains of Hōnen-shōnin all over the capital Kyōto and the provinces. I carefully examined their sincerity and have properly selected them." He asks for help in correcting any errors in his selection and adding to the supplement any new genuine texts that come to light.

The Auspicious Dream of the Japanese Anthology (*Gotōroku zuimu no koto*)
Following the epilogue, Dōkō adds this account of a court lady in Saga, Kyōto, whose heart had great depth in aspiring to be born in the Pure Land in the life to come. One day, she encountered the *Japanese Anthology* in an auspicious dream. After reading it, she devoted herself to reciting nembutsu and eventually attained birth in the Pure Land. It also mentions that many people have possessed the steadfast heart for birth in the Pure Land through nembutsu and realized birth in the Pure Land through reading this work.

Colophon (*Okugaki*)
Dōkō states that he, filled with great admiration and excessive rejoicing, rubbed his seventy-nine-year-old eyes and composed the original engraving block of the *Japanese Anthology* in seven fascicles.

Now, we take great pleasure in offering an English translation of the Genkō edition of the *Japanese Anthology*. It is hoped that the publication of this work will serve as an important step in fostering an understanding of Hōnen's Pure Land Buddhism among our friends in the West.

A Chronology of Events During the Lifetime of Hōnen

Year	Events
1133	*April 7*: Hōnen is born as the son of a warrior in Mimasaka Province in Okayama and named Seishimaru. *July*: Monks of Enryaku-ji Temple destroy the halls of Kiyomizu-dera Temple in the capital of Kyōto.
1134	Floods, famines, and plagues spread. Kakuban becomes the head priest of the Shingi Shingon school.
1135	Monks of Tōdai-ji Temple take arms against Kōfuku-ji Temple in Nara.
1138	A great fire breaks out in Kyōto.
1139	Chikai of the Sanron school composes the *Collection of the Certain Attainment of Birth in the Pure Land* (*Ketsujō Ōjō-shū*).
1140	Kakuban is removed from Mt. Kōya to Mt. Negoro.
1141	*Spring*: Uruma no Tokikuni, Hōnen's father, is killed in a night raid by Akashi no Sadaakira, a local official. *Winter*: Hōnen is sent to the temple of his uncle, Kangaku, in order to take ordination.
1142	Monks of Onjō-ji Temple burn down the halls of Enryaku-ji Temple.
1145	*Spring*: Hōnen goes up to Mt. Hiei to learn Buddhism under the guidance of Genkō. *March*: Monks of Kōfuku-ji Temple clash with the monks of Tōdai-ji Temple.

1146 Monks of Onjō-ji Temple set fire to the hall of Enmei-in Temple.

1147 *Spring*: Hōnen begins to study the three major works of the Tendai school: the *Profound Meanings of the Lotus Sutra* (*Hokke Gengi*), the *Excellent Words of the Lotus Sutra* (*Hokke Mongu*), and the *Great Concentration and Insight* (*Maka Shikan*). *November*: Hōnen joins Kōen's fold and receives the Mahāyāna Buddhist precepts under the supervision of Kōen.

1148 With encouragement from Kōen, Hōnen begins to study the Tendai doctrines.

1150 *September*: Hōnen moves to Saitō Kurodani to join Eikū's fold and live a life of seclusion. He is given the name, Hōnen-bō Genkū.

1151 Another great fire breaks out in Kyōto.

1152 Chinkai of the Sanron school dies.

1153 Many temples are destroyed by fire in Kyōto.

1154 The halls of Hokke and Jōgyōdō of Enryaku-ji Temple are destroyed by fire.

1156 Hōnen visits Shakadō Hall in Saga on the way to Nara, a Buddhist center, where he meets eminent Buddhist scholars and learns the way to enlightenment. *July*: Hogen no ran (a military conflict arising from rivalries within imperial families) breaks out.

1157 Hōren-bō Shinkū enters Eikū's fold.

1158 Emperor Go-Shirakawa administers state affairs.

1159 *December*: Heiji no ran (a military conflict between the Minamoto and Taira clans) breaks out.

1160 Minamoto no Yoshitomo is killed and Yoritomo is exiled to Izu.

1163 Another great fire breaks out in Kyōto.

1165 Kōfuku-ji Temple is attacked by the monks of Enryaku-ji Temple.

1166 Another great fire breaks out in Kyōto.

1167 Taira no Kiyomori is appointed as the chief minister of the state.

1168 *February*: Approximately two thousand houses in Kyōto are destroyed by fire. *April*: Eisai goes to China.

1169 Emperor Go-Shirakawa enters the priesthood.

1170 The retired Emperor Go-Shirakawa and Taira no Kiyomori receive the Mahāyāna Buddhist precepts.

1171 Shinkan-bō Kansei becomes Hōnen's disciple.

1175 *Spring*: Hōnen establishes the Jōdo school based on Shan-tao's Pure Land thought. Hōnen then leaves Kurodani and goes to Higashiyama Yoshimizu in Kyōto.

1176 The retired Emperor Go-Shirakawa receives Mahāyāna Buddhist precepts at Enryaku-ji Temple.

1177 Yūren-bō Enshō dies.

1179 Hōnen preaches the nembutsu doctrine to Jōsaimon-in.

1180 Minamoto no Yoritomo attacks Taira. Taira no Shigehira burns down both Tōdai-ji Temple and Kōfuku-ji Temple, which are supported by the Minamoto clan.

1181 Hōnen is named to supervise fundraising to rebuild Tōdai-ji Temple but declines to do so. Taira no Kiyomori dies. Famine spreads all over the country.

1182 Death by famine overwhelms Kyōto.

1183 Minamoto no Yoshinaka invades Kyōto.

1184 Minamoto no Yoshitsune enters Kyōto.

1185 The Taira clan is defeated by the House of Minamoto. The image of the Great Buddha at Tōdai-ji Temple is enshrined.

1186 *Autumn*: Hōnen engages in a public discussion on the teachings of nembutsu before an audience of approximately three hundred, including leading monks of the holy gate, at Shōrin-in Temple in Ōhara, Kyōto.

1187 Eisai goes to China a second time.

1189 Kujō Kanezane, the chief minister of the state, becomes one of Hōnen's most ardent supporters and receives Mahāyāna Buddhist precepts from Hōnen in August.

1190 Hōnen preaches the teachings of the three sutras of Pure Land Buddhism at Tōdai-ji Temple.

1191 *March*: Hōnen answers ten questions posed by Chōgen regarding the attainment of birth in the Pure Land through the recitation of nembutsu. Eisai returns from China and introduces Rinzai Zen.

1192 Emperor Go-Shirakawa dies. The Kamakura period begins. Kumagai no Naozane becomes Hōnen's disciple.

1195 *September*: Seikan-bō Genchi becomes Hōnen's disciple. Hōnen replies to Tsuto no Saburō through letters.

1197 Benchō, a succesor to Hōnen, becomes Hōnen's disciple.

1198 Hōnen compiles his major work, *Collection on Nembutsu*, at the request of Kanezane. Hōnen often attains the ultimate religious state through nembutsu. Jōkaku-bō Kōsai becomes Hōnen's disciple.

1199 *February*: Hōnen conveys the *Collection on Nembutsu* to Benchō. Minamoto no Yoritomo dies.

1200 *September*: Over three days Hōnen gives Mahāyāna precepts to the wife of Kanezane.

1201 *March*: Shinran, the founder of Jōdo Shin Shū, becomes Hōnen's disciple. Hōnen conducts a dialogue on 140 topics regarding birth in the Pure Land through nembutsu.

1202 *December*: Kanezane becomes ordained under the supervision of Hōnen. Chōsai becomes Hōnen's disciple.

1204 *March*: Hōnen conveys the *Collection on Nembutsu* to Ryūkan (possibly in 1206). *October*: Monks of Enryaku-ji Temple request Archbishop Shinshō of the Tendai school to prohibit nembutsu. *November*: Hōnen presents the *Monition in Seven Articles* to Shinshō in remonstration of his followers.

1205 *April*: Hōnen conveys the *Collection on Nembutsu* to Shinran. *September*: Monks of Kōfuku-ji Temple appeal to the court to prohibit the practice of nembutsu.

1206 Hōnen's followers Anraku and Jūren are executed.

1207 *February*: The practice of nembutsu is banned by Emperor Go-Toba, and Hōnen is exiled to Tosa, Shikoku. Shinran is exiled to Echigo. Kanezane dies. *December*: The emperor rescinds Hōnen's exile although he does not grant Hōnen permission to enter the capital. Hōnen remains in Kachio-dera Temple in Ōsaka.

1208 *November*: Utsunomiya Zen'mon visits Hōnen and takes ordination under the guidance of Hōnen.

1200 Hōnen writes a reply to Kōmyō-bō in Ecchū Province to protest the idea advocated by Jōkaku-bō Kōsai that birth in the Pure Land is attained by a single utterance of nembutsu.

1211 *August*: Hōnen is permitted to enter Kyōto. *November*: Hōnen returns to the capital and stays at a small temple in Higashiyama Yoshimizu.

1212 Hōnen writes the *Single-Sheet Covenant* at the behest of his disciple, Seikan-bō Genchi. *January 25*: Hōnen attains birth in the Pure Land.

Part I

Collected Teachings of Hōnen: The Japanese Anthology

Prologue

Collected and recorded by Monk Ryōe Dōkō, who loathes this defiled world and longs for birth in the Pure Land

IN THE SAME manner as medicine prescribed by a skilled physician proves efficacious in accordance with the type of illness, the teaching of the Tathāgata Amida prevails when man's karmic condition ripens.

Throughout Japan, the time has now come for the teaching of attaining birth in the Pure Land of Ultimate Bliss[53] through the recitation of the name of Amida Buddha. All of the people in the court as well as the public living near and far from the capital of Kyōto rely on this teaching of Amida Buddha for attaining birth in the Pure Land. Without exception, the clergy and the laity, the noble and the humble, wish for the attainment of birth in the Pure Land.

The teaching of Amida Buddha for birth in the Pure Land first spread in this country with the first holy images of Buddha Śākyamuni and Amida Buddha presented by the Korean kingdom of Paekche[54] during the reign of Amekuni Oshiharaki Hironiwa no Tennō (Emperor Kinmei, r. 531/39–71).

Buddha Śākyamuni is the lord master who encourages people to achieve birth in the Pure Land, and Amida Buddha is the principal buddha who comes to welcome them into the Pure Land. These Two Honored Ones, with identical hearts of compassion, manifested to propagate the path of birth in the Pure Land.

During the reign of Oharida no Tennō (the Reigning Empress

Suiko, r. 592–628), Prince Shōtoku (574–622),[55] in accordance with the intent of the Two Honored Ones, praised the name of Amida Buddha for seven days out of gratitude for a favor from Emperor Kinmei. Just after, Prince Shōtoku wrote a letter to Tathāgata Amida of Zenkō-ji Temple[56] and received a reply from the Tathāgata Amida himself.

Prince Shōtoku wrote:

> I have devoted myself to praising the name of Tathāgata Amida for seven days. This I did from my heart, in gratitude for the extensive benevolence that was bestowed upon me. O, Principal Master Amida Buddha, I respectfully request that you help save me from suffering, lead me to the Pure Land, and protect me at all times.

Tathāgata Amida replied:

> [The merit of] praising my name once has more [merit] than simple gratitude. How much more meritorious praising my name for seven days is. I welcome sentient beings in order to save them all the time. Your attainment of birth in the Pure Land is ensured, and I will protect you without fail.

Prince Shōtoku eventually achieved birth in the Pure Land, validating its merit for all throughout the country.

During the reign of Ōi no Tennō (Emperor Jun'nin, r. 758–64), both Amida Buddha and Bodhisattva Avalokiteśvara transformed themselves into human beings in this world in order to weave a pictorial representation of the Pure Land of Ultimate Bliss, presenting it as a principal image for birth in the Pure Land.

At that very moment [when they presented the principal image in this world], the merit of the six Chinese characters, *Na mo A mi t'o fo* (Jp. *Namu Amida Butsu*, meaning, "I take refuge in Amida Buddha") virtually manifested itself, and the true intent of the Two Honored Ones finally prevailed.[57]

Earlier prominent senior masters in Japan, such as Gyōki-bosatsu[58] and Jikaku-daishi En'nin,[59] departed from this defiled world of suffering with longing for birth in the Pure Land. Eshin-sōzu Genshin[60] collected essential passages on birth in the Pure Land under the moonlight at Ryōgon-in Temple on Mount Hiei. Yōkan-risshi[61] composed the *Ten Conditions for Attaining Birth in the Pure Land* beneath the flowers of Zenrin-ji Temple in Kyōto.

Each master was engaged in propagating the teachings and practices of Pure Land Buddhism. Nevertheless, the precious teaching that leads one on the path for achieving birth in the Pure Land had not yet become universally accepted.

Finally, the eminent monk of Kurodani [Hōnen] appeared in the world as an emanation of Bodhisattva Mahāsthāmaprāpta. He clarified the true meaning of the essential vow made by Amida Buddha for the first time in Japan and encouraged people to perform the exclusive recitation of the name of Amida Buddha for the attainment of birth in the Pure Land.

As a result, the teaching of nembutsu spread throughout the country and everyone received its merit. From that time, the teaching of Jōdo Shū spread. For this reason, those who study and practice nembutsu for birth in the Pure Land refer to Hōnen-shōnin as Founding Master.

Today there are many who follow the nembutsu tradition of Hōnen-shōnin, but each interprets its meaning differently. They dispute topics: "Are Buddhist practices other than nembutsu for birth in the Pure Land in accord with the essential vow of Amida Buddha?" "Is the attainment of birth in the Pure Land really possible?" "What should be the condition of the threefold devotional heart?" There are also disputes regarding exclusive practice of nembutsu versus the miscellaneous practices, as well as regarding the single utterance of nembutsu versus multiple recitations of nembutsu.

Unfortunately, they are unable to distinguish between gold and brass or tell right from wrong. A number of people who hear these misinterpretations lose sight of the essentials of the teaching of nembutsu and are easily swayed by public opinion. They respect the new interpretations and disregard the old teachings.

The *Book of Documents*[62] states: "Among human beings, the sages of old deserve the greater esteem; among utensils, newer is better." Amazed by this passage, I decided to follow the legacy of Hōnen-shōnin and to abandon the new interpretations of nembutsu.

For this reason, I have collected letters and other works of Hōnen-shōnin and have made a copy of some other writings that were recorded in Japanese. Compared to the Chinese writings, the Japanese is easier to read and its content less difficult to understand.

I sincerely hope that those who seek birth in the Pure Land regard this work as a "light" shining on the path to the Pure Land of Amida Buddha. If someone finds any additional teaching of Hōnen-shōnin that I have omitted, please append it to this work.

On the twenty-fifth of January in the twelfth year of Bun'ei (1275), the anniversary of the death of Hōnen-shōnin, I made this declaration with heartfelt gratitude for his benevolence.

1. Commentary on the Three Sutras of Pure Land Buddhism

by Kurodani

THE TWO-FASCICLE SUTRA [hereafter, the *Larger Sutra*],[63] the *Meditation Sutra*,[64] and the *Smaller Sutra*[65] are collectively called the three sutras of Pure Land Buddhism.

The *Larger Sutra* expounds on the forty-eight vows made by Amida Buddha in the first fascicle and clarifies the fulfillment of these vows in the second fascicle. The forty-eight vows refer to the covenant Bodhisattva Dharmākara made in front of Tathāgata Lokeśvararāja.[66] Arousing the heart for enlightenment, Bodhisattva Dharmākara vowed that he would establish his own pure buddhaland and welcome all sentient beings there to save them from suffering.

Thus the forty-eight vows include: the vow that the three lower realms do not exist in the Pure Land [first vow], the vow that no one returns to the three lower realms after birth in the Pure Land [second vow], and the vow that all beings in the Pure Land are golden in color [third vow]. The vows, however, were made specifically for the establishment of the eighteenth vow: the vow that all sentient beings will be born in the Pure Land through the recitation of the name of Amida Buddha.

The eighteenth vow states, "If, when I [Bodhisattva Dharmākara] am to attain buddhahood, all sentient beings in the ten directions who have faith with genuine hearts and who wish to be born in my buddhaland are not born there within just ten moments of being mindful of me, I will not realize enlightenment."[67]

This essential vow of Amida Buddha is the most essential of all the forty-eight vows, because if no one were born in the Pure Land, the realization of the other vows, such as the vow that all beings in the Pure Land are golden in color and the vow that there is no distinction in the personal appearance of all beings in the Pure Land [fourth vow], would be impossible. Only through birth in the Pure Land would one become golden in color, would there be no distinction between beauty and ugliness, would one acquire the five transcendent faculties, and would one possess the ability to know all former existences of himself and others. Accordingly, Master Shan-tao explained, "Bodhisattva Dharmākara made the forty-eight vows. Each of the vows state that, when he attains buddhahood, if all sentient beings in the ten directions who wish to be born in his buddhaland and who recite his name at least ten times are not born there, he will not realize enlightenment."[68] Master Shan-tao further commented that each of the forty-eight vows bore this message.

As a rule, the vows any buddhas make arise from within the heart of their aspiration for enlightenment in order to save sentient beings from suffering. A Mahāyāna text states, "There are two aspects of a vow made by a bodhisattva: one aspect is the vow aspiring for enlightenment, and another aspect is the vow to save sentient beings from anguish. The true intention of the vow aspiring for enlightenment, however, is saving sentient beings from suffering and leading them to the shore of deliverance."[69] Therefore, the real intention of a bodhisattva is in the vow to save sentient beings. The reason that Tathāgata Amida established his own Pure Land is to welcome all sentient beings there in order to save them from suffering.

After having attained buddhahood, all buddhas possess the merit of the inner realization (enlightenment), its external activities, and the oath to save sentient beings by leading them to the far shore of enlightenment. The merit and oath of every buddha is equally profound and cannot be deemed more or less superior to another. However, the supremely skillful means of the vows made by bodhisattvas during practice to attain buddhahood are diverse.

Tathāgata Amida, when he was in the state of a bodhisattva [as Bodhisattva Dharmākara], vowed that he would welcome into the Pure Land all those who exclusively recited his name, and he dedicated the merit of his austere practices from an eternity of eons[70] to all sentient beings. This essential vow is what we, who reside in this world of defilement, rely upon. It is also the main path for sentient beings in the period of the decline of the Dharma to depart from this defiled world of suffering. Is there anything else in which to rejoice but his essential vow?

Amida Buddha proclaimed, "I have made vows that are unsurpassed."[71] Numerous buddhas in the past, present, and future have yet to make such a vow, not to mention all the bodhisattvas in the ten directions [i.e., everywhere]. Amida Buddha further stated, "If the vows are fulfilled, may the whole universe quake. And may various heavenly beings rain wondrous blossoms from the sky."[72] Thereupon, the six elements constituting all existence trembled, flowers rained from the sky, and he received a prophecy, stating, "You will, with certainty, realize enlightenment."[73]

Even if someone said that Bodhisattva Dharmākara did not accomplish buddhahood, this vow should not be questioned. For, in truth, Bodhisattva Dharmākara did attain buddhahood, and ten eons have elapsed since then. We must believe in this fact. This is what Master Shan-tao meant when he said, "Amida Buddha did, indeed, attain buddhahood and presently resides in the Pure Land. It should be known that his essential vow was not made in vain. If sentient beings recite his name, they will, with certainty, attain birth in the Pure Land."[74]

The *Larger Sutra* states, "If any sentient beings hear the name of Amida Buddha, rejoice in faith, and wish to be born in that buddha-land, then within just one moment of being mindful of Amida Buddha, through the dedication of their merit, they will immediately attain birth in the Pure Land and will remain in the state of nonregression; the exception are those who have committed the five grave offenses and who have abused the true Dharma."[75] This is a passage about the fulfillment of the eighteenth vow of Amida Buddha. Incidentally, the eighteenth vow states, "within just ten moments of being mindful of Amida Buddha," but in this passage citing the fulfillment of the eighteenth vow, the words are, "within just one moment."

The passage that follows in the *Larger Sutra* sets forth the three types of aspirants seeking birth in the Pure Land.[76] This passage relates to the fulfillment of the nineteenth vow, which describes Amida Buddha's appearance in front of nembutsu practitioners at their time of death.[77] Those who wish for birth in the Pure Land are divided into three categories based on their karmic deeds and how much they have awakened the heart of enlightenment (Skt. *bodhicitta*). Regarding the karmic deeds for birth in the Pure Land, all three categories share the teaching of "reciting single-heartedly and exclusively the name of the Buddha of Immeasurable Life [Amida Buddha]." This is because this teaching is part of the essential vow of Amida Buddha.[78]

Another passage in the *Larger Sutra* states, "The power of the essential vow of Amida Buddha enables those seeking birth in the Pure Land that have heard his name to attain birth in that buddhaland without exception, and once there, they will naturally proceed to the state of nonregression for attaining buddhahood."[79] The following account reveals the power of the essential vow of Amida Buddha:

> In China there was a precept master Hüan-t'ung,[80] who lived by the Hīnayāna precepts. Once when he was staying in a hermitage far away, the person in the adjoining room was reciting this passage. Hearing this, Hüan-t'ung also repeated the passage once or twice and then put it out of his mind.
>
> As time passed, Hüan-t'ung violated one of the precepts, and as a result, found himself before the judgment seat of King Yama [the lord of the realm of the dead]. King Yama said, "You were born in a place where the teachings of Bud-

> dha Śākyamuni prevail. Now teach what you have learned, if anything." Then he made Hüan-t'ung sit on a throne.
>
> Hüan-t'ung, on the throne, searched his memory to no avail. The only thought that came to mind was the passage of the *Larger Sutra* he had heard in the hermitage. He proceeded to recite the passage on the power of the essential vow of Amida Buddha.
>
> King Yama listened, his crowned head bowed low. He said, "This is the very passage that elucidates the merit of Tathāgata Amida who resides in the Pure Land of Ultimate Bliss in the West," and he prostrated himself.[81]

The power of the essential vow is inconceivably profound.

The *Larger Sutra* also states, "Buddha Śākyamuni said to Bodhisattva Maitreya, 'If someone hears the name of Amida Buddha, and having faith with great joy, is mindful of Amida Buddha even for just one moment, then that person will receive great benefit and possess unsurpassed merit.'"[82] When Buddha Śākyamuni instructed the *Larger Sutra* to Bodhisattva Maitreya, Buddha Śākyamuni said that the mindfulness of Amida Buddha for a single moment would have great benefit and unsurpassed merit. These passages clarify the essentials of the *Larger Sutra*.

In the *Meditation Sutra*, Buddha Śākyamuni expounded on the [thirteen] meditative practices with a focused mind and [the three] meditative practices with a distracted mind.[83] Also in this, he entrusted the practice of the recitation of the name of Amida Buddha to Ānanda with the statement, "Thou, hold these words carefully in your heart."[84]

In the ninth perception [among the sixteen meditative practices] of the true physical features of Amida Buddha described in the *Meditation Sutra*, there is a passage that states, "Each ray of light from Amida Buddha shines over the worlds of the ten directions. Those who recite the name of Amida Buddha are embraced by that light, and will never be abandoned."[85] Although the vow that Amida

Buddha made, which saves all sentient beings, is equal and nondiscriminatory, those with no karmic relationship to him will not merit his favor. For this reason, Amida Buddha, in his all-encompassing compassion, in order to establish a karmic relationship with all sentient beings, made a vow so that the light of Amida Buddha will be infinite and shine throughout all the ten directions of the universe. This is the twelfth vow.

So that all sentient beings would know that the recitation of his name was the primary karmic cause for birth in his Pure Land, Amida Buddha made the seventeenth vow: "If, when I am about to attain buddhahood, all the innumerable buddhas of the ten directions do not praise and call out my name, I will not realize enlightenment."[86] Amida Buddha continued with the eighteenth vow, "If, when I am about to attain buddhahood, all sentient beings are not born in my Pure Land within just ten moments of being mindful of me, I will not realize enlightenment."[87]

In accordance with these vows, Tathāgata Śākyamuni and all the buddhas of the whole universe, as countless as the grains of sand in the Ganges, taught this truth. Thus the light of Amida Buddha shines without exception over all the ten directions, and the innumerable buddhas in the universe, in unison, praise the name of Amida Buddha. Therefore, there should be no place where his name fails to be heard. As Amida Buddha vowed, "Upon my attaining buddhahood, if my name is not heard everywhere in the ten directions, I will not realize enlightenment."[88]

Thus, if the karmic relationship established by the light and the karmic cause established by the recitation of the name of Amida Buddha are in harmony, do not doubt that one will receive the benefit of being embraced by Amida Buddha, who abandons no one.

Therefore, in the beginning of *Hymns in Praise of Birth in the Pure Land*, Master Shan-tao writes, "The enlightenment of all buddhas is equal and the same, but their vows and practices have distinct causal effects. Amida Buddha, especially, having made his profound [essential] vow, has embraced all sentient beings in the ten directions in order to bring deliverance by means of his light and name."[89]

Moreover, in order to provide eternal deliverance for sentient beings through the essential vow, Amida Buddha vowed that his lifespan will be immeasurable. This is the thirteenth vow. To summarize, while the vow of immeasurable light was designed to reach all sentient beings throughout space; the vow of infinite life was designed to benefit all sentient beings throughout time. If, as mentioned above, karmic cause (his name) and relation (his light and life) are in harmony, then the buddhas and bodhisattvas will manifest in the light enveloping the sentient beings, protecting them, and surrounding them hundredfold and thousandfold. As a result, their devotion will be enhanced, and this will cause their sufferings to diminish.

Another passage states, "At the time of death, Amida Buddha himself arrives to welcome the nembutsu devotee, so that various nonvirtuous karmas that tie one to this delusive world cannot get in the way of birth in the Pure Land."[90] That is to say, as one's life comes to an end, one is assailed by hundreds of torments, and there is no peace. Externally one has undesirable karmic conditions; internally one experiences turbulent thoughts. At the time of death, the three kinds of attachment: (1) attachment to one's family, relatives, and material possessions, (2) attachment to one's own life, and (3) attachment to one's rebirth in a good situation in the future, will arise, furiously vying with each other. King Māra of the sixth heaven in the realm of desire, seizing this as an opportune moment, comes to obstruct one's birth in the Pure Land.

In order to free us of these hindrances, Amida Buddha, with hosts of bodhisattavas and celestial beings, vowed to appear to nembutsu devotees at the time of death. This is the nineteenth vow.[91] By the grace of the nineteenth vow, Amida Buddha appears at one's time of death. The nembutsu devotee, upon witnessing this welcome, experiences great joy, as if entering into a state of samādhi, and promptly mounts the lotus platform offered by Bodhisattva Avalokiteśvara and proceeds to the jeweled pond of the land of serene sustenance [the Pure Land]. Because of these benefits, it is taught that, "Those who recite nembutsu are embraced by the light of Amida Buddha and will never be abandoned."[92]

The *Meditation Sutra* declares, "One who embodies the threefold devotional heart will be born in that buddhaland without fail."[93] The threefold devotional heart, or the three aspects of faith, are: (1) the genuine heart, (2) the profound heart, and (3) the heart that seeks birth in the Pure Land through the dedication of merit. Though the threefold devotional heart is divided into three, the essence and core of the threefold devotional heart is the profound heart.

Master Shan-tao interpreted the genuine heart (Ch. *chih-ch'eng-hsin*) thus:

> The Chinese term, *chih*, refers to truth, and the term *ch'eng* refers to the quality of being sincere. The author, with this interpretation of *chih* and *ch'eng*, would like to clarify that both understanding and practice performed by all sentient beings through their physical, verbal, and mental acts must be done with a genuine heart. Do not outwardly pretend to be wise, virtuous, and diligent while inwardly harboring falsity and fickleness.[94]

Here "understanding" and "practice" mean that one has implicit faith that even a common mortal with negative karma who has wandered throughout the six delusive worlds of saṃsāra is assured of achieving birth in the Pure Land by the power of the essential vow of Amida Buddha with ten recitations, or even just a single utterance, of nembutsu. This assumes, though, that one truly understands and practices nembutsu. If one outwardly manifests the appearance of believing in the essential vow while inwardly entertaining doubt, then this is not the genuine heart.

[The second aspect of the threefold devotional heart is the profound heart.] Master Shan-tao explained,

> The profound heart is the heart of profound faith, which has two aspects. The first is to firmly believe that one is a common mortal with worldly passions who has transmigrated through the six delusive worlds of saṃsāra for countless eons up to this day, and that one does not possess the karmic conditions needed to detach oneself from the six delusive worlds. The second is to have unshakable faith that Amida Buddha will embrace all sentient beings with his forty-eight vows. If one firmly believes in these two instructions, one will, with certainty, attain birth in the Pure Land through the power of his essential vow.[95]

The passage on this first belief states, "Firmly believe that one is a common mortal with worldly passions who has transmigrated through the six delusive worlds of saṃsāra for countless eons until now, and that one does not possess the karmic condition to detach oneself from the six delusive worlds." This statement refers to those who have no intrinsic goodness and no possibility for achieving enlightenment in this life. If they recite just a single utterance, or ten repetitions, of nembutsu, even though they have wandered throughout the six delusive worlds from beginningless time until now, they will now be able to extricate themselves from the six delusive worlds and attain birth in the Pure Land of nonregression. This is what nurtures the faithful heart for birth in the Pure Land.

Generally speaking, it is impossible for the common heart to understand the inconceivable power of the essential vow of Amida Buddha. A buddha, and only a buddha, is able to comprehend this. Nonetheless, by the recitation of the name of Amida Buddha, even those who have committed the five grave offenses or the ten transgressions will be born in the Pure Land without exception. Amida Buddha's essential vow has inconceivable power. Who can doubt this?

In his *Commentary on the Meditation Sutra*, Master Shan-tao writes:

> Someone said, "You, a mortal, have, for innumerable eons until now, in all your former and present states from a commoner to a sage, perpetrated various negative karmas with your physical, verbal, and mental acts; you have committeded the ten transgressions, the five grave offenses, and the four grave offenses. You have abused the Dharma. You have no intrinsic goodness. You have violated the Buddhist precepts and have refuted right views. You have not been able to eradicate this defiled karma. This karma binds you to the delusive triple realms. How, through merely performing meritorious acts and the recitation of nembutsu for the rest of your life, can you be born into that undefiled and eternal Pure Land and realize the state of nonregression forever?"
>
> You should answer thus: "The teachings and practices of various buddhas are more numerous than specks of dust and sand. Innumerable also, are the potential and karmic conditions of sentient beings. Therefore, the teaching of a buddha is not the only one. Put in concrete terms that people can see and believe: light penetrates dark, the sky envelops all things, the earth supports and nurtures life, water makes things grow, and fire forms and destroys matter. This is called the law of mutuality. In other words, one should discern all existence in an infinite variety of ways. Further, can it not be said that there is manifold merit in the inconceivable power of the Dharma?"[96]

It is wondrous, but the water, birds, and trees in the Pure Land of Ultimate Bliss create the exquisite sound of Dharma. If one believes that this is a manifestation of the power of the vows of Amida Buddha, how could it be possible to doubt the eighteenth vow, which assures birth in the Pure Land with just ten repetitions of nembutsu? If, in general, one believes in the teachings of Buddha Śākyamuni, this, too, is the teaching of Buddha Śākyamuni.

The *Flower Garland Sutra* expounds upon the doctrine that there is no difference in substance between the mind of the Buddha and that of sentient beings. The *Perfection of Wisdom Sutra* explains that all forms of existence, in and of themselves, are not substantial [i.e., they do not exist intrinsically]. The *Lotus Sutra* teaches the concept that all phenomena are ultimate reality. The *Nirvāṇa Sutra* propounds the theory that all sentient beings innately possess buddha nature. Would anyone doubt these doctrines? These are all teachings of Buddha Śākyamuni. Would it be possible to believe one and not another?

The Japanese designation for Amitābha—*Amida*—consists of only three characters. Within this name, however, is the merit of the inner realization of Tathāgata Amida and his external activities, as well as the merit of Buddha Śākyamuni's extremely profound teachings, which are as numerous as the grains of sand in the Ganges. Who can fathom this?

Master Shan-tao, in the chapter "Essentials of the *Commentary*" of the *Commentary on the Meditation Sutra*, interpreted this name thus:[97]

> The Chinese term for Amida Buddha, *A-mi-t'o-fo*, is a transliteration of the language of India. It was interpreted into Chinese as *Enlightened One Whose Life Is Immeasurable* (*Wu-liang-shou-chiao*). *Immeasurable Life* (*Wu-liang-shou*) points to the Dharma, and *Enlightened One* (*chiao*) is a person. Both the Dharma and the person are combined into *Enlightened One Whose Life Is Immeasurable.* Accordingly, he is referred to as *A-mi-t'o-fo*. The person and the Dharma are also objects of contemplation; this includes the "dependent reward" and the "primary reward."

Therefore, all of the merits of the teachings, the meditative practices on the phenomenal aspect of reality and the noumenal principle, the unmatched power acquired through meditation and wisdom, the wisdom of inner realization, and the merit of external activities, as well as all of the virtues and undefiled enlightenment of Tathāgata Amida, Bodhisattva Avalokiteśvara, Bodhisattva Mahāsthāmaprāpta, Bodhisattva Samanthabhadra, Bodhisattva Mañjuśrī, Bodhisattva Kṣitigarbha, Nāgārjuna, and the bodhisattvas and śrāvakas of the Pure Land are encompassed in the three characters of the name of Amida. This being so, would there be any Dharma not included in the teaching for birth in the Pure Land?

The three Japanese characters in the name of Amida are interpreted by other Buddhist schools in a number of different ways. The Shingon school teaches that the letter *a* in the Sanskrit alphabet indicates the origin of all phenomena and the state of nonproduction, and that the letter *a* produces forty-two Sanskrit characters. All existence is contained in the letter *a*; therefore, the name of Amida is considered to be most meritorious.

The Tendai school teaches the theory of the three aspects of truth articulating ultimate reality—the truths of emptiness, temporariness, and the middle path; the doctrine of the three causes leading to buddhahood—the innate buddha nature, the wisdom discerning the ultimate principle, and virtuous deeds that cultivate wisdom; the teaching of the three bodies of a buddha—the Dharma body, the rewarded body, and the transformed body; and the merits possessed by a Tathāgata: these theories are all contained in the three characters of the name of Amida. Hence, the merit of the letters is considerable. As illustrated, each school has interpreted the three letters in the name of Amida from its own doctrines' perspective.

Now the essence of our Jōdo Shū is the belief that the three characters, *A-mi-da*, embody the entire Buddhist teachings, including the theory of the Shingon school that the letter *a* in the Sanskrit alphabet indicates the origin of all phenomena and the state of nonproduction; the teachings of the oneness of the three aspects of truth taught by the Tendai school; the theory that the middle path emerges from the eightfold negation taught by the Sanron school;[98] the theory of the five levels of contemplation from the principles of mind-only of the Hossō school;[99] basically, all of the Dharma in the universe. This is because no Buddhist doctrines are excluded from the teaching for birth in the Pure Land.

Nevertheless, the heart of the vows of Amida Buddha does not expect one to believe in all of the above. He will come to receive all beings who simply recite nembutsu with deep devotion.

The medicinal panacea for all ills prescribed by Jīvaka[100] of India and P'ien-ch'üeh[101] of China was a compound of various herbs and medicines. Although those who were ill knew it was made of a combination of substances, no one knew the ratio of medicine to herbs or their exact amount. The herb still cured many illnesses. Regrettably, the skill of Jīvaka and the secret formula of P'ien-ch'üeh were ineffective if the patient did not have faith in the medication, believed that he was gravely ill, and doubted whether he would ever recover through the herb. The name of Amida is the same.

Worldly passions and negative karma are grave illnesses. If one wonders, "Will reciting the name of Amida bring me birth in the Pure Land?" and there is no faith in the name, then the essential vow of Amida Buddha and the teachings of Buddha Śākyamuni are in vain, and there will be no proof to contradict this doubt. So, just revere and have faith in the name. A person will perish if he does not ingest the good medicine he obtains. One would regret it deeply if one were to climb Mount K'un-lun and return without a precious gem, or enter a sandalwood forest and return without breaking off a branch. Ponder this.

We might have met Buddha Śākyamuni and had the guidance of bodhisattvas for countless eons even up to the present time. Manifold buddhas in the past as well as tathāgatas of today might have been our fathers, mothers, and friends in our many lives of transmigration. Ask yourself: How then did they realize enlightenment? Why am I still detained in the six delusive worlds of transmigration? It is indeed shameful and a sad state of affairs.

The principal master, Tathāgata Śākyamuni, vowed to lead and emancipate sentient beings who climbed the mountain of grave offenses, ensconced themselves in the forest of aberrant views, carelessly performed their three types of acts [physical, verbal, and mental], and were wanton with the six sensory organs, thus keeping them in his land [i.e., this world].

Why did Buddha Śākyamuni vow to emancipate these types of sentient beings in particular? The answer may be in the past. Long ago, before Tathāgata Amida had attained buddhahood, he was called King Araṇemi. When he resigned from the kingship, he awakened with the desire to attain enlightenment and made the vow to embrace sentient beings and help them to escape the six delusive worlds of transmigration. At that time, Tathāgata Śākyamuni called himself Brahman Samudrareṇu. At the same time, Tathāgata Śākyamuni, who was then called Brahman Samudrareṇu, also made a vow to realize enlightenment in this world of suffering and to guide sentient beings wrought with nonvirtuous karma on the correct path to enlightenment.[102]

For countless eons until now, multifarious buddhas appeared on earth and, according to karmic condition and human potential, led each sentient being to deliverance. These occurrences are more numerous than dust and sand. Some buddhas taught Mahāyāna Buddhism, and others Hīnayāna Buddhism. They spread the true teachings at one time and the expedient teachings at another.[103] Thus creating karmic relations with a buddha, all the sentient beings benefited from these teachings.

Thereupon, Buddha Śākyamuni manifested his eight major aspects in this nonvirtuous world replete with the five defilements and lamented that licentious sentient beings with aberrant views had no opportunity for escape from this baneful realm. He then taught as follows:

> The Pure Land of Ultimate Bliss lies westward. There is the buddha named Amida, who vowed, "If, when I am to attain buddhahood, all sentient beings who wish to be born in my buddhaland, and who recite my name at least ten times are not born there, I will not realize enlightenment." He then

> attained buddhahood. You should, therefore, recite his name at once.
>
> There may be numerous ways to become free from the six delusive worlds of transmigration, but for sentient beings with negative karma and worldly passions, there is no way superior to this teaching of nembutsu to extricate themselves immediately from the six delusive worlds.[104]

Buddha Śākyamuni cordially added, "You must never entertain doubt about this teaching for attaining birth in the Pure Land through the recitation of the name of Amida Buddha. All buddhas in the six directions, as numerous as the grains of sand in the Ganges, have authenticated this teaching."[105] He further stated, "If I remain in this defiled world of suffering for too long, those licentious sentient beings with aberrant views who might criticize and betray me would eventually fall into the lower realms. The sole reason for my appearance in this defiled world is to relay this teaching of birth in the Pure Land through nembutsu to all sentient beings."[106]

Buddha Śākyamuni then entrusted his teaching of nembutsu to Ānanda, carefully saying, "Thou, transmit this teaching in the distant future."[107] Then, in the spring of his eightieth year, at midnight on the fifteenth of February, lying down with his head toward the north and face to the west, he entered parinirvāṇa under the *sāla* trees on the banks of the Hiranyavatī River. At that moment, the sun and moon lost their glow, plants and trees paled, and even the eight kinds of deities, wild beasts, and birds all looked skyward, sobbed, prostrated themselves, and wailed.

Senior disciples of Buddha Śākyamuni, including Ānanda and Maudgalyāyana, contained their tears of sorrow and held a discussion. "We have benefited from the grace of Buddha Śākyamuni for eighty years. Now, the karmic conditions leading one to enlightenment are spent; the golden-complexioned Buddha has hastily departed. Sometimes we were able to approach him, and the World-Honored One gave us a response. At other times, Buddha

Śākyamuni himself delivered discourses. To whom, now, should we pose our questions regarding the means to save sentient beings from suffering and lead them to deliverance? We must record the words of Tathāgata Śākyamuni without fail in order to convey his teachings in the future. This will be his legacy."

Thus, they gathered the leaves of a *tāla* tree, recorded all of his teachings, and later *Tripiṭaka* masters translated them, spreading them to China and then to Japan. These are the holy teachings of the life of Buddha Śākyamuni still maintained by various Buddhist schools in Japan today.

Later on, Tathāgata Amida, calling himself Shan-tao, appeared in China. He thus declared:

> Tathāgata Śākyamuni appeared in this world of the five defilements, and through various skillful means he aligned with the propensities of the people and taught sentient beings. Thus he taught differently depending on the people and the situation. For example, on one occasion, he taught that one becomes enlightened by listening to many teachings. At another time, he taught that one can attain the three insights through Hīnayāna teachings. At still another time, he taught that one can remove hindrances by accumulating meritorious virtues and wisdom, and yet another time that one can develop prudence through the practice of meditation.
>
> Enlightenment can be achieved through these teachings, but no teaching supercedes recitation of nembutsu for birth in the Western Pure Land. From the life-long nembutsu recitation to just ten repetitions, or even three or five repetitions, they will all result in welcoming the arrival of Amida Buddha.
>
> The essential vow of Amida Buddha is indeed venerable. The common people who recite nembutsu will speedily attain birth in the Pure Land.[108]

The presence of Buddha Śākyamuni attests to these statements. Master Shan-tao commented, "It is the most difficult of difficulties for one to believe in the teaching of nembutsu and make others believe it too. To transmit the great compassion of Amida Buddha to others and to spread his teaching far and wide is the true repayment of the benevolence of Amida Buddha."[109] Then, how should we repay Buddha Śākyamuni's benevolence? By attaining birth in the Pure Land through nembutsu. If we merely idle away our existence, where is our resolve to extricate ourselves from the six delusive worlds? We must immediately awaken faith in Amida Buddha and detach ourselves from the six delusive worlds of transmigration.

[The third aspect of the threefold devotional heart is the *heart that seeks birth in the Pure Land through the dedication of merit.*] The heart that seeks birth in the Pure Land through the dedication of merit should be cultivated by everyone. Who would not wish for birth in the Pure Land after hearing about the pleasure and happiness of the Pure Land of Ultimate Bliss of Amida Buddha?

In the theory of the nine grades of aspirants for birth in the Pure Land, which grade of birth are we aiming for? Master Shan-tao commented, "The Pure Land is a rewarded land, and Amida Buddha is a rewarded buddha. It is said that all common people who have not severed themselves from worldly passions are not able to achieve birth in the Pure Land. The essential vow of Amida Buddha is inconceivably profound; therefore, even ignorant people with worldly passions wandering among the six delusive worlds are able to attain birth in the Pure Land by merely a single utterance or ten repetitions of nembutsu."[110]

Nevertheless, since ancient times, many commoners have been satisfied with the low category of birth in the Pure Land and have not wished to be of the high category. They do not aspire toward the high category of birth because they fear getting through the heavy burden of their nonvirtuous karma. If birth in the Pure Land were impossible due to this karmic burden, it would be impossible for everyone. If the power of the essential vow of Amida Buddha results in birth in the Pure Land, why would it be difficult to aspire for the high category of birth?

Amida Buddha established the Pure Land to fulfill his vows. This is the very buddhaland in which all nembutsu devotees will be born. Amida Buddha vowed, "If, when I am to attain buddhahood, all sentient beings who call out my name at least ten times are not born there, I will not realize enlightenment,"[111] and then he established the Pure Land.

Here, I shall enumerate each condition of the nine grades of aspirants for birth in the Pure Land as described in the *Meditation Sutra*. People in the low category of birth are guilty of the five grave offenses or the ten transgressions. Even though they are extremely negative, they will meet a virtuous teacher for the first time at the time of their death, be encouraged by that teacher to recite nembutsu, and eventually be born in the Pure Land with ten or even just one recitation of nembutsu.

Although our karmic burden is grave, we have not yet committed the five grave offenses. Although our practice is wanting, we have recited nembutsu more than once or ten times. Before facing death, we have heard of the teaching of the essential vow of Amida Buddha and cultivated faith in birth in the Pure Land in accordance with our ability. Hence, we will never fall to the low category of birth.

Those of the middle category of birth are the Hīnayāna practitioners who have observed the regulations and practiced virtuous deeds such as filial piety, benevolence, righteousness, propriety, wisdom, and sincerity. It is difficult for us to be born in this category. We are not Hīnayāna practitioners; neither do we have the regulations to observe. Therefore, birth in the middle category is beyond our ability.

People of the high category of birth are the commoners who have practiced the teachings of Mahāyāna Buddhism and awakened in their hearts aspiration for enlightenment. Aspiration for enlightenment is understood by each Buddhist school. According to the interpretation of our Jōdo Shū, "Cultivating the heart for birth in the Pure Land is referred to as aspiration for enlightenment." The recitation of nembutsu is a Mahāyāna practice and has unsurpassed merit. Hence, we should not retreat from the desire for the high category of birth.

Further, Amida Buddha established the essential [eighteenth] vow in which birth in the Pure Land is assured with just ten repetitions of nembutsu. In the [nineteenth] vow of the appearance of Amida Buddha, he promised to appear surrounded by a host of celestial beings before nembutsu devotees at their time of death. For the middle category of birth, however, śrāvakas appear before the nembutsu devotee at their death; and for the low category of birth, the three transformed bodies of Amida Buddha and his two attendant bodhisattvas, or lotus flowers with golden petals, may appear.

The real intent of the [nineteenth] vow, the appearance of Amida Buddha surrounded by a host of his attendant bodhisattvas at the time of death, was established for those in the high category of birth. Accordingly, it is not necessary to hesitate to aim at the high category of birth in the Pure Land.

Master Shan-tao also taught, "The recitation of nembutsu more than thirty thousand times a day becomes the karmic cause for the high grade of the high category of birth."[112] It follows, then, that a large number of repetitions leads to birth in the high category. In addition, concerning the threefold devotional heart, there are also the nine different grades. Therefore, it is understood that attainment of birth in the high category depends on the depth of one's belief in birth in the Pure Land through nembutsu.

The wish to be born in the high category is not for one's own sake. Its purpose is to be able to return to this defiled world, having achieved birth in the Pure Land, to offer guidance to sentient beings without a moment's delay. How can this not be in accordance with the intent of Amida Buddha?

The *Smaller Sutra* first teaches the merits of the dependent and primary rewards of the Pure Land in order to encourage the cultivation of the desire for birth in the Pure Land in the hearts of sentient beings. The *Smaller Sutra* then clarifies the practice for birth in the Pure Land, stating, "Scant roots of virtue do not make birth in the Pure Land possible, but reciting the name of Amida Buddha continually from one to seven days makes birth in the Pure Land possible."[113]

Lest sentient beings do not believe in this teaching of birth in the Pure Land through nembutsu, the *Smaller Sutra* further states that manifold buddhas in the six directions, as countless as the grains of sand in the Ganges, extended their tongues enveloping the three thousand great-thousand worlds[114] to attest to this teaching. Master Shan-tao interpreted this to mean, "If, in spite of the attestation of the tathāgatas in the six directions, birth in the Pure Land is impossible for nembutsu devotees, then their extended tongues will never again be retracted, and their tongues will fester and fall into decay."[115]

This indicates that to doubt the teaching of birth in the Pure Land through nembutsu is not to believe in the essential vow of Amida Buddha nor in the teachings of Buddha Śākyamuni. To doubt the teachings of Buddha Śākyamuni means to doubt the assertion of all buddhas in the six directions, who are as countless as the grains of sand in Ganges. If this assertion is wrong, their tongues, extended over the three thousand great-thousand worlds, would ulcerate and disintegrate.

Conversely, if one believes in the teaching of birth in the Pure Land through nembutsu, one not only believes in the essential vow of Amida Buddha but also in the teachings of Buddha Śākyamuni. Believing in the teachings of Buddha Śākyamuni is then to believe in all buddhas in the six directions. Believing in all buddhas leads to faith in the Dharma in its entirety. Believing in the entire Dharma means to have faith in all of the bodhisattvas. Accordingly, the belief in the teaching of birth in the Pure Land through nembutsu is vast and all-encompassing. Master Shan-tao also explained:

> In order to sever the attachments to doubt and perverse views of common mortals, all buddhas extended their tongues to

envelop the three thousand great-thousand worlds and validated both the teaching of birth in the Pure Land through the recitation of nembutsu for seven days and the truth of the teachings of Buddha Śākyamuni.[116]

By extending their tongues, the tathāgatas in the six directions also validated the belief that if sentient beings recite nembutsu with all their hearts, they will be able to attain birth in the Western Land. Once birth in the Pure Land is achieved, lotus blossoms will be in bloom, one can listen to wondrous teachings, and the aspiration of the bodhisattva of the ten stages will naturally be experienced.[117]

Continually recite nembutsu; do not harbor any doubt about the teaching of birth in the Pure Land through nembutsu. The tathāgatas of the six directions have attested to this teaching. If, when one recites nembutsu, the three types of acts [physical, verbal, and mental] are in unison without distraction, the lotus blossoms of a hundred treasures will appear as the occasion requires.[118]

2. The Covenant

THE NEMBUTSU I preach is not meditation as taught by the learned men of China and Japan; neither is it recitation through scholarly endeavors to master its profound meanings. To attain birth in the Pure Land of Ultimate Bliss of Amida Buddha requires nothing but implicit faith that mere recitation of *Namu Amida Butsu* ensures attainment of birth in the Pure Land. The teachings of the threefold devotional heart and the four modes of exercise are encompassed by the firm belief that birth in the Pure Land is assured by the recitation of *Namu Amida Butsu.*

If I further expound on any thought other than this, I would be excluded from the compassionate mercy of the Two Honored Ones and be at odds with the essential vow of Amida Buddha.

A person who believes in nembutsu, although he may have learned all the teachings of Buddha Śākyamuni, should consider himself an ignorant person[119] who knows not a single letter. He should conduct himself as though he were as unschooled as the lay female Buddhist devotee who simply shaves her head and becomes a nun without proper training.

Refrain from flaunting knowledge and devote yourself to the recitation of nembutsu.

*Dōkō's note: This covenant was written by Hōnen-shōnin himself and bestowed to his disciple, Monk Seikan.[120]

3. An Outline of the Doctrine for Birth in the Pure Land

by Monk Genkū[121]

According to the teaching of our Jōdo school, the teachings of Buddha Śākyamuni are divided into two categories: namely, the *holy gate* and the *Pure Land gate.*

All Buddhist teachings of Mahāyāna Buddhism and Hīnayāna Buddhism, from the *Flower Garland Sutra* and the *Āgama Sutras* taught in the early period to the later-period *Lotus Sutra* and *Nirvāṇa Sutra*, which teach the path for the realization of enlightenment by eradicating illusions in this delusive world of anguish, are called the *holy gate.*

Regarding the holy gate, there is the holy gate of Mahāyāna Buddhism and the holy gate of Hīnayana Buddhism. Within the holy gate of Mahāyāna Buddhism there is also the Buddha Vehicle and Bodhisattva Vehicle. Within Hīnayāna Buddhism, there is the Śrāvaka Vehicle and Pratyekabuddha Vehicle. These four paths are referred to as the *four vehicles.*

The first path, the Buddha Vehicle, is the teaching on how to attain buddhahood in this very life. This instruction is clarified in the following Buddhist schools of the four vehicles: the Shingon school, the Dharma [Zen] school, the Tendai school, and the Kegon school.[122]

In the Shingon school the doctrine is described as: "the immediate realization of great enlightenment in the present, within the body received from one's parents," and it is taught that one attains the state of Tathāgata Mahāvairocana.

In the Dharma [Zen] school with the heart of Buddha Śākyamuni, the instruction is: "the transmission of the Dharma from mind to mind during the era of Buddha Śākyamuni in the past and of Buddha Maitreya in the future," meaning that the practitioner is in essence already a buddha. This instruction is referred to as the "doctrine of the realization of buddhahood in one's present state" and does not speak of "attaining" buddhahood. This teaching was encompassed in a single verse, which Buddha Śākyamuni entrusted to Venerable Kāśyapa after preaching the *Nirvāṇa Sutra* while departing for parinirvāṇa.

In the Tendai school, it is taught that one should meditate on the concept that "worldly passions are themselves enlightenment; saṃsāra itself is nirvāṇa," and that the attainment of buddhahood is accomplished through the observation of the true nature of one's mind. The eight-year-old dragon girl who speedily realized enlightenment in her present state in the pure buddha-world in the south attests to this.[123]

The Kegon school teaches that "when one first awakens the heart to enlightenment, one has realized enlightenment," and it also teaches the attainment of buddhahood in one's present state. These Buddhist schools teach the accomplishment of enlightenment in one's present body and call these teachings the Buddha Vehicle.

The second path, the Bodhisattva Vehicle, is the teaching of the "attainment of buddhahood through innumerable eons of bodhisattva practices." This is followed by two Buddhist schools: the Sanron school and the Hossō school.

The Sanron school instructs that one will attain buddhahood through abiding in the meditation of the formlessness of the Middle Path (*Madhyamaka*) that manifests through the eightfold negation, by awakening the four universal vows in the heart, and by practicing the six bodhisattva perfections for three great innumerable eons.

The Hossō school teaches that one will achieve buddhahood after the passage of three great innumerable eons if one abides in the five levels of contemplation on the principles of Mind Only (*Citta-*

mātra), awakens the four universal vows, and practices the six bodhisattva perfections. These teachings are referred to as the Bodhisattva Vehicle.

The third path, the Pratyekabuddha Vehicle, says that one realizes the impermanence of all existence by observing the scattering of flowers in the spring and the falling of leaves in the autumn, and that one realizes enlightenment by meditating on the twelve links of dependent origination. This happens in four lifetimes if attainment comes quickly, or in a hundred eons if attainment takes longer.

The fourth path, the Śrāvaka Vehicle, maintains that first, in order to remove worldly passions, one contemplates the impurity of one's body, and in order to focus on one's mind, one counts one's own breaths. Ultimately, after meditating on the four noble truths, one reaches the highest stage of a great arhat and passes through the third stage of the four stages of Hīnayāna Buddhism.[124] This happens in three lifetimes if attainment comes quickly, or in sixty eons if attainment takes longer.

These two vehicles, the Pratyekabuddha Vehicle and the Śrāvaka Vehicle, are the paths taught in both the Jojitsu school[125] and the Kusha school.[126] In the case of the Śrāvaka Vehicle, the Buddhist precepts must be strictly observed. A monk is to maintain 250 regulations, and a nun, 348 regulations. These are referred to as the five and seven categories of the Hīnayāna regulations.[127]

The Ritsu school[128] includes the regulations for a male and female Buddhist novice, the six requirements for a female novice who aspires to be a nun, and the five fundamental precepts for a male and female lay Buddhist.

Regardless of whether it is of Mahāyāna Buddhism or Hīnayāna Buddhism, we cannot endure the training in these sacred teachings of the four vehicles, as they are not appropriate teachings for our present time. If one tries to follow the path of the Śrāvaka Vehicle, it is too difficult to maintain the 250 regulations and nearly impossible to meditate on the four noble truths. If one chooses to pursue the path of the Pratyekabuddha Vehicle, realizing impermanence by contemplating the scattering of flowers in spring and the falling of leaves in autumn, or through understanding the twelve links of dependent origination, it is beyond consideration. Further, it is extremely difficult to observe the threefold pure precepts and the ten cardinal Mahāyāna precepts; not to mention accomplishing the four universal vows and the six bodhisattva perfections.

It is said that Śāriputra endured religious discipline for sixty eons, but his magnanimous heart as a bodhisattva was reversed in a moment due to the ripening of a negative karmic condition that covered his eyes. It is unnecessary to state here that in this period of the decline of the Dharma, pursuit of these achievements is almost impossible, especially for those of us with minimal capabilities.

One may contemplate various teachings: the principle of the realization of enlightenment in one's present body; the Shingon theories of the unity between a buddha and oneself and the theory that the letter *a* in the Sanskrit alphabet indicates the origin of all phenomena and the state of nonproduction; the Tendai doctrines of the threefold contemplation, the six stages to enlightenment, and the middle path that is the true nature of existence; the Kegon principle that the Dharma realm is nothing but the mind; or the theory that the mind itself is the truth as espoused by the Dharma [Zen] school with the heart of Buddha Śākyamuni. The meanings of these contemplations are truly profound, but in reality one's understanding is shallow. Therefore, it is almost impossible for a practitioner in the period of the decline of the Dharma to achieve enlightenment through the meditative practices of these principles. Accordingly, Master Tao-ch'o[129] stated, "In this period, each teaching of the holy gate is too difficult to complete."[130] He also referred to the *Moon-Matrix Section of the Great Collection Sutra*[131] and explained the truth of those various practices in full detail. It is unnecessary to expound on them here.

The Pure Land gate, on the other hand, teaches that a practitioner is to first loathe and renounce this defiled world of anguish, and then by expeditiously attaining birth in the Pure Land of Ultimate Bliss of Amida Buddha, to pursue the path leading to enlightenment there.

Therefore, aspire and practice the way to birth in the Pure Land with all deliberation right now.

Birth in the Pure Land is not determined by the good or bad of all nembutsu devotees; it is dependent only on whether one believes in the essential vow made by Amida Buddha. The essence of this tenet is that even one who has committed the five grave offenses or the ten transgressions will achieve birth in the Pure Land with just a single utterance, or ten repetitions, of nembutsu.

Master Tao-ch'o, therefore, interpreted this faith thus: "The Pure Land gate is the sole teaching for entrance into the path leading to enlightenment."[132] I understand that there are two meanings of "entrance into" the Pure Land gate. One is entrance with breadth, and another is entrance with distance. *Entrance with breadth* includes even one who has committed the five grave offenses and still has the potential to attain birth in the Pure Land. Thus it goes without saying that those with a minor offense will achieve birth in the Pure Land, and this birth will naturally be for the good; no one is without the potential for birth in the Pure Land. Hence, it is called *entrance with breadth.*

As for *entrance with distance*, Shan-tao explained, "After the period of the decline of the Dharma that will last ten thousand years, when the teachings of Buddha Śākyamuni become extinct, only this *Larger Sutra* will endure another one hundred years. When listening to the teachings of the *Larger Sutra*, if the people of that time utter nembutsu once, they will realize birth in the Pure Land without fail."[133] It goes without saying that in the present day, while it is still the period of the decline of the Dharma, let alone during the periods of the true Dharma and the semblance of the Dharma,[134] no being is excluded from birth in the Pure Land. This is what is meant by *entrance with distance.*

One who desires detachment from the delusive worlds of transmigration today should abandon the unattainable holy gate and should aspire toward entrance into the Pure Land gate, where birth in the Pure Land is easily attained.

Incidentally, the holy gate is called the "difficult path" and the Pure Land gate the "easy path." To illustrate: the difficult path is akin to traversing a treacherous road on foot; the easy path corresponds to crossing the ocean on a ship. The sightless and lame are unable to travel an arduous route, but a ship will transport them with ease to the far shore.

Today, it is as if our vision of wisdom is impaired and our legs of religious discipline are paralyzed. There is no hope for trekking across the treacherous road, the difficult path of the holy gate. Only by the ship of the essential vow of Amida Buddha are we able to cross the delusive ocean of saṃsāra to reach the shore of the Pure Land of Ultimate Bliss. Here, the "ship" means the essential vow of Amida Buddha, or the essential vow of his forty-eight vows. Of the forty-eight vows, the eighteenth vow is determined to be the essential vow, which is the practice of birth in the Pure Land for sentient beings. This summarizes the doctrines of the holy gate and the Pure Land gate.

Having left the holy gate aside, those who wish to enter the Pure Land gate should learn the three sutras of Pure Land Buddhism based upon the interpretations of Master Tao-ch'o and Master Shan-tao. I have so far differentiated between the holy gate and the Pure Land gate and clarified reasons for entering through the Pure Land gate. I will now extrapolate on the essentials of the Pure Land gate.

If one desires to attain birth in the Pure Land, both heart and practice must be in concert. The interpretation of Master Shan-tao reads: "Practice alone is not sufficient for birth in the Pure Land, nor is aspiration alone. Realization occurs only when aspiration and practice are concomitant."[135] Both heart and practice must be a single discipline, not only to achieve birth in the Pure Land but also to realize enlightenment in the holy gate. This is referred to as "observing practice by awakening the heart to enlightenment." In Jōdo Shū, Master Shan-tao called this the *steadfast heart* and *practice.*

The steadfast heart is defined in the *Meditation Sutra*: "He who aspires to birth in the Pure Land will attain this birth by awakening the threefold devotional heart. What are the three aspects of the threefold devotional heart? The first is the genuine heart, the second, the profound heart, and the third, the heart that seeks birth in the Pure Land through the dedication of merit. One who embodies the threefold devotional heart will be born in that buddhaland without fail."[136]

Master Shan-tao discussed the threefold devotional heart in the *Commentary on the Meditation Sutra* and also in the opening of the *Hymns in Praise of Birth in the Pure Land.* The first aspect is the genuine heart. His statement in the *Hymns in Praise of Birth in the Pure Land* reads: "The first is the genuine heart. In worshiping Amida Buddha as a physical act, exalting and praising Amida Buddha as a verbal act, and exclusively contemplating Amida Buddha as a mental act: whenever one performs these three categories of acts, one must do so without guile. Thus, this is called the *genuine heart.*"[137]

The *Commentary on the Meditation Sutra* describes the following: "The first aspect is the genuine heart. In the Chinese term (*chih-ch'eng-hsin*), *chih* refers to truth and *ch'eng* is the quality of being sincere. The author, with this interpretation of *chih* and *ch'eng*, is clarifying that both understanding and the practice performed by all sentient beings through their physical, verbal, and mental acts must be done with the genuine heart. Do not outwardly pretend to be wise, virtuous, and diligent while inwardly harboring falsity and ficklenesss."[138] It further states, "Whenever performing virtuous physical, verbal, and mental acts, do so in the spirit of genuineness without regard to matters of the inner mind or outer appearances, whether they are visible or hidden."[139] As to these two interpretations of the genuine heart written in the works mentioned above, I understand that the genuine heart is the sincere heart. The term *genuineness* refers to the unity of the heart and appearances. All of one's physical, verbal, and mental acts must be performed without pretense and must manifest truth.

I am afraid that people frequently conflate this *genuine* heart with the *burning* heart, and they arouse a dauntless and vigorous heart while calling both of them the *genuine heart.* This contradicts the above interpretations of Master Shan-tao. *Genuine heart* and *burning heart* are written with different Chinese letters and have different meanings. Nevertheless, such a strong heart is not entirely counter to the genuine heart. The burning heart should be founded on the genuine heart. The strong state of a heart based on the truly genuine heart is excellent, while the feeble state of a heart based on the genuine heart is inferior.

It is important to be aware of the distinctions among the nine grades of aspirants for birth in the Pure Land in connection with the genuine heart. The interpretation of the nine grades of aspirants appears in the *Commentary on the Meditation Sutra*, and in each grade Master Shan-tao said that proper understanding of the threefold devotional heart is the right karmic cause for birth in the Pure Land.[140] He also commented that the threefold devotional heart is connected with all of the nine grades of aspirants.

Monk Eshin (942–1017)[141] embraced the same thought, stating, "True to the interpretation of Shan-tao, his logic is connected to the nine grades of aspirants."[142] Because the genuine heart is one aspect of the threefold devotional heart, it is related to all nine grades of aspirants for birth in the Pure Land without question.

Furthermore, the substance of the genuine heart is the profound heart and the heart that seeks birth in the Pure Land through the dedication of merit. How would the genuine heart be if it were separated from the other two aspects of the threefold devotional heart? There is no need to look further. The sincerity of both the profound heart and the heart that seeks birth in the Pure Land through the dedication of merit is called the *genuine heart.*

Once it is understood that the threefold devotional heart is connected to the nine grades of aspirants for birth in the Pure Land, it should be known that the distinctions among the nine grades derive from the relative shallowness or depth, the strength or weakness, of the threefold devotional heart. For this reason, the *Meditation Sutra* says that one attains the high grade of the high category of birth, "Because one's effort is dauntless and bold."[143]

Master Shan-tao, in the *Commentary on the Meditation Sutra*, interpreted the high category of birth to mean: "Although the number of days may be short, exercise is rigorous." Concerning the middle grade of the high category of birth, he stated that practice is less intense; on the low grade of the high category of birth, he said that practice was not intense.[144] You should understand that there are qualities of both strength and weakness in the threefold devotional heart. Those whose threefold devotional heart is feeble will still attain birth in the Pure Land, but in the lower level and only so long as they do not doubt their attainment of birth in the Pure Land. Pathetic are those who believe that if they do not arouse a vigorous heart, this birth will be impossible for a long time due to the lack of the genuine heart. Such a belief results in decadent behavior with no respect for others. It is, therefore, desirable to arouse the vigorous heart.

The virtue of reciting nembutsu sincerely is said to be the first of the ten virtues of Master Shan-tao. The writing describes him: "Master Shan-tao earnestly practiced the vocal nembutsu without stopping until he was completely spent. He repeated nembutsu to the extent that he perspired in the freezing cold. This shows the genuine heart."[145] Everyone should try to emulate his endeavor.

If we believe that this kind of wholeheartedness only applies to the genuine heart and that others are lacking in the genuine heart, we, like feeble-minded people, might doubt the attainment of birth in the Pure Land. We may think that only those who have a dauntless and bold heart, such as Master Shan-tao, whose authenticity is supreme, could achieve birth in the Pure Land and that the rest of us could not. The ten virtues refer only to the virtues of Master Shan-tao. The rest of all sentient beings, like us, need not compare ourselves with him in order to achieve birth in the Pure Land. The true intention of Master Shan-tao's *Commentary on the Meditation Sutra* is to acknowledge the genuine heart in us common mortals. Thus, we should cultivate the genuine heart to different degrees of strength or weakness commensurate with our individual potential.

As for the genuine heart, we should practice according to the details of the description of the *Commentary on the Meditation Sutra*, which states, "Do not outwardly pretend to be wise, virtuous, and diligent while inwardly harboring falsity and fickleness."[146] This passage means to be inwardly ignorant while carrying the mien of intelligence, to be inwardly malicious while pretending to be a good person, and to be lazy in truth but to feign exertion. These are manifestations of so-called falsity and fickleness.

On the other hand, "sincerity and constancy" means to be outwardly unconcerned with good or bad—with criticism or fame—to inwardly loathe this defiled world and long for the Pure Land, to refrain from committing wrongdoings and to cultivate wholesomeness, and to hope sincerely to be in harmony with the heart of Amida Buddha. Sincerity and consistency are terms directly opposite to falsity and fickleness—sincerity opposes falsity and constancy opposes fickleness.

Regarding the relationship between "sincerity and constancy" and "falsity and fickleness," there are the four distinctive qualities of the genuine heart. The first is a person who outwardly embellishes but is empty inside; the second is one who does not put on airs but is empty inside; the third is one who is outwardly empty but inwardly sincere; the fourth is one who both displays sincerity and is inwardly sincere. Of these four types of people, the first two should be called *practitioners with falsity and fickleness*, and the latter two, *practitioners with sincerity and constancy*. Accordingly, one should not opt for mere outward wisdom or ignorance, good or bad; one should make one's selection based on inward falsity or righteousness, on delusion or enlightenment.[147]

On the whole, the genuine heart is extremely difficult for people and is elusive for one reason or another. This heart seems to expose our hearts as ignorant and fleeting. Since time immemorial until now, we have borne the worldly passions for renown and personal gain. Some people may forgo combatting these worldly passions because they are not easy to eradicate. This is inexcusable. We should reflect upon ourselves and should be admonished.

Thus, we can see the measure of our own minds, and it is sorrowful and sad to perceive the outward person unable to eradicate the urge to present a facade. Those who are deeply attached only to this world believe that it is not problematic to discuss thoughts of superficial glory and fame. Among those who have renounced this ephemeral world and embarked on the journey for the true path, there are some who inspire our pity.

Because of the depth of attachment to this world in the past, there are people who deem it a wondrous blessing if they merely rid themselves of their trifling renown and personal gain. Soon they tout this accomplishment with trite sentiments and expressions. Thoughtless people praise them without knowing their real motive. The outward people then believe that to speak of outward appearances and actions is laudable and of great importance. Even if these people move to a hovel deep in the mountains, they do not understand that the real meaning of living in such a hermitage is to spend days peacefully. They are attracted by visitors or get caught up in other people's thoughts that they happen to hear secondhand. They consciously cling to the need to care for the thicket of trees inside the rough-woven bamboo fence, the appearance of the hermitage, and the adornment of the practice hall so they appear wondrous, yet inside they are desolate and pathetic. Accordingly, reflections on their negative karma or the intent of Amida Buddha is subverted; the only thought that prevails is the wish to avoid criticism from others. Thoughts are not focused on a genuine desire for birth in the Pure Land, and soon the genuine heart erodes and they arrive at a point where they feel that birth in the Pure Land is impossible.

It is also said that there are people who have renounced this secular society and who live the life of a hermit harboring the desire for renown as a sage, and that there also exist ordinary people in this world who aspire for birth in the Pure Land but do not attend to the genuine heart. The person who expresses this kind of thought does not thoroughly understand the true meaning of the genuine heart either.

To think only of being praised by others, to desire a facade adorned to draw attention to oneself—these thoughts are not restricted to those craving dream-like prosperity and social status. Since people say that it is a wondrous and blessed thing for laymen and laywomen to seek deliverance in the next life, there are people who want to adorn their outward appearances with the guise of seeking deliverance in order to share a similar good fortune and to be thought well of by others. It is like one who tells a hermit who has already renounced the secular world about the loathsomeness of this world and the horrors of the next life while feigning superficial knowledge and hiding one's true feelings.

While it is unnecessary to worry much about what other people think, it is nonetheless unacceptable to behave recklessly, heedless of criticism, believing that it is commendable to not put on a false front. The lesser precepts[148] for a bodhisattva caution one to refrain from acts that may be criticized by others. Also, to behave recklessly, saying such an act is not forbidden by the lesser precepts, is licentious and is unwholesome.

Those who following the lesser precepts to avoid the attention of others behave righteously but are still overly conscious of others' perceptions and are not truly concerned with genuine actions. Thus they pitiably prolong that which is a hindrance to birth in the Pure Land. To follow the lesser precepts, but obsessively, may result in one's heart becoming filled with falsity and fickleness. To act with "genuineness" obsessively may result in one becoming licentious. These concepts must be well understood and embraced. I feel that my explanation may be inadequate.

In connection with this genuineness, there is genuineness in seeking enlightenment for one's own merit and genuineness for the merit of others. The *Commentary on the Meditation Sutra* fully explains what it means to be genuine in all deeds: loathing, renouncing, neglecting, and despising the dependent and primary rewards for oneself and others in the six delusive worlds of the transmigration of the delusive triple realm; worship, praise, and contemplation of the dependent and primary rewards of Amida Buddha; and the physical, verbal, and mental acts of loathing this defiled world and longing for the Pure Land. This dissertation is too lengthy to cite here. This is my condensed explanation of the state of the genuine heart.

The second aspect is the profound heart. The *Hymns in Praise of Birth in the Pure Land* thus states: "The second is the profound heart. That is, it is the heart of genuine belief that we are common mortals, with worldly passions whose virtuous roots are shallow and meager, who have transmigrated through the delusive triple realms and who have no chance to escape from the 'house on fire.' We should also have the implicit faith that one who recites the name of Amida Buddha as few as ten times, or even just once, will, with certainty, attain birth in the Pure Land as taught in the universal vow. Do not harbor doubt about this even for a moment. This belief is called the *profound heart.*"[149]

The *Commentary on the Meditation Sutra* narrates the profound heart as below:

> The second is the profound heart. That is, the heart of profound faith, which has two aspects. The first is to firmly believe that one is a common mortal with worldly passions, who has transmigrated through the six delusive worlds of saṃsāra for countless eons up to this day and thus does not possess the karmic condition needed to extricate oneself from the six delusive worlds. The second is to have the unshakable faith that Amida Buddha will embrace all sentient beings with his forty-eight vows. If one firmly believes in these two teachings, one will, with certainty, attain birth in the Pure Land through the power of the essential vow.
>
> Moreover, it should be firmly believed that in order to

> urge people to aspire for birth in the Pure Land as taught in the *Meditation Sutra*, Buddha Śākyamuni elucidated the three meritorious acts, the nine grades of aspirants for birth in the Pure Land, and the meditative practices with both a focused mind and a distracted mind, and that he validated and praised the dependent and primary rewards of Amida Buddha. One should also have an unshakable faith in the passage from the *Smaller Sutra* that states that all buddhas in the ten directions, as numerous as the grains of sand in the Ganges, testified and encouraged all sentient beings to attain birth in the Pure Land.
>
> Sincerely wish that all practitioners wholeheartedly believe in the words of Buddha Śākyamuni, that they have no regard for their own lives, and that they recite nembutsu with a decisive mind while relying entirely on Amida Buddha.
>
> Abandon the teachings that Amida Buddha abandoned, observe the practice that Amida Buddha observed, and leave the practices that Amida Buddha left. This is said to be "in accordance with the teaching of Amida Buddha" and "in compliance with the intent of Amida Buddha." Such a person is referred to as the "true disciple of Amida Buddha."
>
> The profound heart is also called *profound faith*. This is because nembutsu practitioners are to establish decisively implicit faith, to practice in accordance with the teaching of Amida Buddha, to exclude perpetually doubt and falsity, and to not fall back or be swayed by all of those who have different understandings, practices, teachings, views, or misleading opinions.[150]

When I see these two interpretations of Master Shan-tao, the writings are at the same time detailed and brief, and the language is both similar and different. Although he established these two different aspects of faith in the profound heart here, their purpose is identical.

To clarify, the first is the notion of the profound belief that one is a common mortal with worldly passions and that one has no chance to escape from this house on fire and no karmic condition to escape from the six delusive worlds of transmigration.

The second notion is the profound faith that one, without harboring a single doubt even for a moment, is destined to achieve birth in the Pure Land and that one is never to be disturbed by the words of others. These two use different language and are difficult to understand. If one really thinks about them, however, the first means that one must acknowledge one's own limitations, and the second is that one must believe in the essential vow of Amida Buddha.

Master Shan-tao pointed out the first belief in order to establish the latter one. If he only mentioned the second belief in the essential vow without having first pointed out the belief that one is a common mortal with worldly passions, then those who seek birth in the Pure Land might perform the miscellaneous practices and would not rely exclusively upon the essential vow. This is why the belief in the essential vow comes second. Without the first belief, they would harbor the worldly passions of greed and anger in their hearts, commit the karmic faults of the ten transgressions, violate the precepts, become [egoistically] self-deprecating, and doubt the essential vow, even though they properly recite nembutsu as taught in the essential vow.

Moreover, inferior people such as ourselves tend to think that it is impossible for the common person to attain birth in the Pure Land according to the essential vow by as few as ten repetitions or just a single utterance of nembutsu. We think that birth in the Pure Land is only possible if nembutsu is recited by a fine person who does not entertain illusory thoughts, commits no unwholesome acts, and awakens the profound spirit with a vigorous heart. We believe that we, people who have minimal potential, cannot realize this birth with just one or ten repetitions of nembutsu. One can't blame people for harboring such thoughts.

In this regard, Master Shan-tao foresaw that such doubts might arise in the common people of the future and established the theory of the two aspects of the profound heart. He then commented that even we common mortals, who cannot sever worldly passions and who commit nonvirtues, will attain birth in the Pure Land without fail if we believe in the essential vow and recite nembutsu ten times or just once with profound faith. Without this revelation, our birth in the Pure Land would not be assured.

Likewise, people become anxious about their ability to attain birth in the Pure Land; however, this interpretation of Master Shan-tao is truly accurate with regard to birth in the Pure Land. It seems that his interpretation was designed for those who do not understand the dual meaning of faith. Having faith in the essential vow while simultaneously saying that birth in the Pure Land is impossible with an unwholesome frame of mind will ultimately make one doubt the essential vow. This interpretation helps us understand to what extent our spirit does not live up to the essential vow and to what extent we are in harmony with it.

Those who do not understand this think that, because they have not been able to rid themselves of unwholesome thoughts and cannot sever their worldly passions, now is not an appropriate time for them to desire birth in the Pure Land. Further, if one truly needed to first detach oneself from worldly passions to attain birth in the Pure Land, then this birth would be impossible for ordinary people. If this were true, how could a common mortal with worldly passions be saved by the power of the essential vow? It would then have to be said that Amida Buddha will not arrive to welcome such a mortal to the Pure Land.

How deep is the understanding of the essential vow among these people? How is it that they could interpret the power of the essential vow in their own self-serving way and harbor doubts about the essential vow? It could be said that this represents a betrayal of Amida Buddha. In short, whether we are in harmony with the essential vow based on the disposition of good or bad in our hearts depends upon the wisdom of Amida Buddha.

Consequently, Master Shan-tao commented on the universal vow in the first fascicle of the *Commentary on the Meditation Sutra*, stating, "The attainment of birth in the Pure Land for all ordinary people, good or bad, is exclusively due to the great karmic power of the essential vow, which is regarded as the dominant karmic relationship with Amida Buddha."[151] Master Shan-tao continued,

> The real intention of Amida Buddha is so extensive and profound that it is difficult to understand his teaching. Even the bodhisattvas who have reached the stages of the threefold wisdom [the stages from eleventh to fortieth] and of the bodhisattva stages from forty-first to fiftieth cannot comprehend the teaching perfectly. How much less can we, ordinary people, who have not yet reached the stages of the first ten of the fifty-two stages of bodhisattva practice, be able to know the real intent of Amida Buddha?[152]

Master Shan-tao himself expressed doubts that he could truly comprehend the intent of Amida Buddha because he did not reach the bodhisattva stages of the first ten of the fifty-two stages. We, who are so lacking in understanding, should not even venture to guess the intent of the essential vow of Amida Buddha.

There is no need to reflect on virtue or vice, or to discuss the gravity of your negative karma. Establish an unshakable faith that if you simply mouth *Namu Amida Butsu* with the aspiration for birth in the Pure Land, you will most certainly attain birth in the Pure Land. The karma of this birth will be determined by your degree of faith. Once you understand this, birth in the Pure Land will be attained easily. The attainment of birth in the Pure Land will be uncertain only if you doubt this birth; the attainment of birth in the Pure Land will be certain if you believe in this birth. After all, the profound faith is the firm belief without a shadow of doubt that the essential vow never abandons any person, regardless of the gravity of their karma, and that anyone will, with certainty, attain birth in the Pure Land with just a single utterance of the name of Amida Buddha.

The *Meditation Sutra* describes the low grade in the low category of birth in the Pure Land as follows: "Even a wretched being who has committed the ten transgressions or the five grave offenses will achieve birth in the Pure Land with just a single utterance, or ten repetitions, of nembutsu."[153] Further, a passage referring to these negative deeds describes them as "Those who commit the ten transgressions or the five grave offenses, who have the worldly passions of greed and anger, who commit the four grave offenses, who steal the property of the Buddhist Sangha, who abuse the true Dharma, and who have no sense of shame and have never repented their previous faults."[154] Another passage states, "Say a person's life is about to end and he meets a virtuous teacher who urges him to recite exclusively the name of Amida Buddha. As a result of this recitation, transformed buddhas and bodhisattvas will appear before this person. In the interval of a single thought-moment, he attains birth within a jeweled lotus flower in the Pure Land."[155] This description defines the condition of a person at the time of his death.

The second fascicle of the *Two-Fascicle Sutra* [*Larger Sutra*] states, "Sentient beings living even after the extinction of the Three Jewels will attain birth in the Pure Land by a mere single utterance of nembutsu."[156] Master Shan-tao interpreted this to mean, "Even after the period of the decline of the Dharma, which will last ten thousand years, when the Three Jewels become extinct, only this *Larger Sutra* will endure another one hundred years. When listening to the teaching of the *Larger Sutra*, if the people of that time recite nembutsu once, they will realize birth in the Pure Land without fail."[157] It is clear through these two passages that the grace of the essential vow will continue to save the masses over an infinite length of time.

The heinous will be saved and the venal embraced by Amida Buddha; the bad will be saved and the good embraced; those who live far will be saved and those who live near embraced; those who live long after Buddha Śākyamuni's entrance into parinirvāṇa will be saved and those who lived shortly after embraced. The profundity and extensiveness of the great compassionate essential vow are beyond verbal description. Believe in it in the depth of your heart and validate the truth within yourself.

It is now the period of the decline of the Dharma, but not even one hundred years have elapsed. Our karmic unvirtues may be grave, yet we have not committed the five grave offenses. Amida Buddha will save the masses one hundred years after the period of the extinction of the Dharma; how much more benevolence will there be for us living today? Amida Buddha does not abandon the most vile of beings who have committed the five grave offenses. He most certainly would not abandon us. You, with the threefold devotional heart, should recite the name of Amida Buddha exclusively. Never doubt the essential vow, not even for a moment.

In spite of this, there may be some people who interpret this teaching in their own negative way, thinking, "If I cannot prevent wrongdoings, unwholesome acts can be as acceptable as I want. Further, if a single utterance of nembutsu suffices for the certain attainment of birth in the Pure Land, I need not repeat it many times." Such misguided people appear and say, "A bad person is excusable and the recitation of nembutsu may be minimized." This is grievous.

No teaching of Buddha Śākyamuni encourages committing wrongdoings or putting an end to virtues. Master Shan-tao, therefore, admonished, "Do not entertain the worldly passions of greed and anger."[158] He taught, "Continue the recitation of nembutsu without cessation throughout your life."[159] And he encouraged, "Recite nembutsu fifty or sixty thousand times, up to one hundred thousand times daily."[160]

These statements urge us to believe that a single utterance and ten recitations of nembutsu are sufficient to achieve birth in the Pure Land because the recitation of nembutsu has the following merits: the great compassionate essential vow embraces all sentient beings; Amida Buddha saves even those who have committed the ten transgressions or the five grave offenses; and nembutsu surpasses all other practices for birth in the Pure Land. Interpreted mistakenly, these instructions may be seen as erroneous. If strengthening faith is overemphasized, aberrant views will surface; if suppressing aberrant views is overemphasized, faith cannot be strengthened. To go into detail would be too cumbersome here; this will be discussed further in the passage on the practice.

There are two meanings of this faith [i.e., belief in the essential vow], explained in the *Commentary on the Meditation Sutra*: One is profound faith with regard to Amida Buddha, the other is profound faith with regard to sutras.

First, profound faith with regard to Amida Buddha means that one has implicit faith in the following: (1) the essential vow of Amida Buddha, (2) the teachings of Buddha Śākyamuni, and (3) the protection and exhortation of all buddhas in the ten directions, who are as numerous as the grains of sand in the Ganges. Second, profound faith with regard to sutras is a belief in (1) the *Larger Sutra*, (2) the *Meditation Sutra*, and (3) the *Smaller Sutra*.

The statement,[161] "Firmly believe in the forty-eight vows of Amida Buddha" refers to belief in both Amida Buddha and the *Larger Sutra*. "Have the implicit faith in the *Meditation Sutra* taught by Buddha Śākyamuni," is to believe in both Buddha Śākyamuni and the *Meditation Sutra*. "Firmly believe in the teachings of the *Smaller Sutra*," means to believe in both the numerous buddhas in the ten directions and the *Smaller Sutra*. The next statement, "Abandon what Amida Buddha abandoned," applies to the miscellaneous practices. "Practice what Amida Buddha practiced," is the exclusive observance of the right practices. "Leave what Amida Buddha left," is to leave aside the teachings, understandings, miscellaneous karmic conditions, and aberrent thoughts diverging from the nembutsu tradition. Master Shan-tao reprimanded, "They become hindrances not only to one's own attainment of birth in the Pure Land but to others' right practice for birth in the Pure Land." These hindrances are frightening.

The statement "In accordance with the teachings of the Buddha" means to practice the teachings of Buddha Śākyamuni. "In accordance with the vow of the Buddha" refers to following the teaching of the essential vow of Amida Buddha. "In accordance with the intent of the Buddha" means to be in consensus with the compassionate hearts of the Two Honored Ones [Buddha Śākyamuni and Amida Buddha]. The intent of these statements corresponds to the meaning of the above-cited passage: "... firm belief in the three sutras of Pure Land Buddhism." In short, it is understood that abandoning the miscellaneous practices and performing the exclusive practice of the recitation of nembutsu are in accordance with the heart of Amida Buddha.

The next passage, "Do not be defeated by those who have different understandings and practices," means that those who have different understandings and practices will attempt to criticize and defeat a nembutsu devotee, but the devotee should never abandon nembutsu or doubt birth in the Pure Land. Here, the statement "those who have different understandings" indicates the scholarly monks of the Tendai school and the Hossō school. The phrase "those who observe different practices" applies to all of the practitioners of other schools, such as the Shingon school and the Tendai school. These are the studies and practices designed for the holy gate. Since they differ from the understandings and practices of the Pure Land gate, they are called "different understandings and practices."

The rationale not to be defeated by these people is elaborated by Master Shan-tao. He points out the two key aspects of faith: "establishing an unshakable faith in birth in the Pure Land with respect to persons" and "establishing an unshakable faith in birth in the Pure Land with respect to practice."

The first explanation, "establishing an unshakable faith in birth in the Pure Land with respect to persons," is so extensively erudite that I am not able to cite the entire dissertation. However, this concept is most important and cannot be overlooked, so the essence is condensed and clarified thus:

> If some with a different understanding and practice say that common people will be unable to attain birth in the Pure Land and refer to documented evidence in the sutras and

> commentaries, give them this reply: "It is not that I do not believe in the sutras and commentaries you cite. I revere and have faith in all of them. However, I cannot accept your refutation because the sutras and commentaries you cite and the sutras and commentaries in which I believe are different tenets.
>
> "Buddha Śākyamuni preached the *Meditation Sutra*, the *Smaller Sutra*, and so on. The time, the place, the listeners and their propensities, and the benefit that the listeners gained were different for each. The teachings of Buddha Śākyamuni differ with the propensities and time of the audience.
>
> "To those of the holy gate, Buddha Śākyamuni generally expounded on the understandings and practices of the schooled, celestial beings, and bodhisattvas for attaining enlightenment. In contrast, to those of the Pure Land gate, he taught the understanding and practice of birth in the Pure Land. In other words, Buddha Śākyamuni taught that birth in the Pure Land is certain for all common people who live in the period after his death, when there will be a marked increase in the five defilements.
>
> "I, now, single-mindedly, believe in this teaching of Buddha Śākyamuni and am determined to devote myself to this nembutsu practice. Numerous people such as you may say that birth in the Pure Land is impossible, but that will only intensify my belief and faith in being born in the Pure Land."[162]

Another passage of Master Shan-tao also describes "establishing an unshakable faith in birth in the Pure Land with respect to persons" as follows:

> The devotee of nembutsu should also say to those who may criticize and refute this belief, "Listen well. I will define for

you the aspect of decisive faith in the attainment of birth in the Pure Land through nembutsu."

The devotee might then mention various names, from bodhisattvas who have not attained the stages, those from the forty-first through the fiftieth of the fifty-two stages of bodhisattva practice, arhats, and pratyekabuddhas to transformed (*nirmāṇakāya*) and rewarded (*saṃbhogakāya*) buddhas. Then the devotee may add, "Should even the transformed and rewarded buddhas existing throughout the ten directions [appear to] cast their individual lights, envelop the ten directions with their broad tongues, and in unison say that it is misguided to think that common people will achieve birth in the Pure Land through the recitation of nembutsu, even though I hear these messages, I will not believe this. I will not, even for a moment, doubt, fear, or retreat from my belief that I will be born in the Pure Land."

This is because one buddha encompasses all buddhas. The great compassion of a buddha is universal, and thus there is no difference between one buddha and another. Because the great compassion of Amida Buddha is identical to that of all other buddhas, the teachings of one buddha are identical to those of all buddhas.

In fact, tathāgata Amida vowed, "If, when I am to attain buddhahood, all sentient beings who recite my name as few as ten times are not born in the Pure Land, I will not realize enlightenment."[163] Amida Buddha did fulfill the vow and realize buddhahood. Tathāgata Śākyamuni appeared in this world of the five defilements when deluded sentient beings, erroneous views, worldly passions, wrongdoers, and the faithless dominate. He then praised the name of Amida Buddha, encouraged people to recite nembutsu, and taught that nembutsu will without fail result in the achievement of birth in the Pure Land.

> Besides, all the buddhas in the ten directions, fearing disbelief in the teaching of the sole buddha, Buddha Śākyamuni, with the same heart and at the same time extended their tongues, enveloped the three thousand great-thousand worlds, and said these sincere words: "All sentient beings should believe in the teachings preached, praised, and validated by Buddha Śākyamuni. All common people must believe that regardless of the balance of vice and virtue and regardless of the time spent reciting nembutsu—once, ten times, for one day, or for seven days up to one hundred years—if one utters the name of Amida Buddha from the depth of one's heart, birth in the Pure Land will certainly be possible. The buddhas averred that you must not doubt this." This is referred to as "establishing an unshakable faith in birth in the Pure Land with respect to persons."

Thus, since all buddhas without exception and in concerted spirit made a vow and expounded on the vow, validated the vow, and encouraged the teaching of the certain attainment of birth in the Pure Land through nembutsu for all common people, one must not be alarmed over the seeming appearance of any buddha who says that birth in the Pure Land is impossible through nembutsu. If the words of such a "buddha" are unreliable, much more so the words of bodhisattvas who have reached the bodhisattva stages from forty-first through fiftieth, those who have not yet reached any of the stages, or arhats in Hīnayāna Buddhism. Do not be alarmed even for a moment over the sayings of common people.

In general, this state of faith is not easily understood. It is a mistake to believe that faith arises with the spirit being moved, hair standing on end, and tears spilling over. These emotions are called *joy, rejoicing,* and *sorrow and elation. Faith* is one's feelings regarding doubt; the removal of doubt is called *faith.* Whatever you may see, whatever you may hear, if you believe that birth in the Pure Land is a certainty, you will never think that birth in the Pure Land is uncertain. This is the true meaning of faith. If joy and rejoicing accompany faith, then all the better.

To illustrate, say someone you trust because you have seen and known his heart over the years, someone genuine and with no falsity, makes an astounding vow, makes a sincere promise, which you then trust, remember, are bound to, and cherish deep in your heart, your heart must not waver, even if another person who is not aware of this feeling says, in an attempt to create a hindrance, "You must not believe him. You will be betrayed." Accordingly, you must firmly believe in the essential vow of Amida Buddha. Do not crumble in the face of counterarguments.

Moreover, Buddha Śākyamuni—who taught precious teachings in their entirety throughout his life—entrusted the teaching of nembutsu to Ānanda. It is then natural for us to think that the numerous buddhas of the ten directions have also attested to the teaching of nembutsu. Truly, it is acceptable if one listens to the teachings without being aware of their meaning. However, one should believe that once having listened to the teaching and having embraced faith in nembutsu, one will not be distracted by the offhand comments of others.

Next, "establishing an unshakable faith in birth in the Pure Land with respect to practice" applies to a passage that states, "There are two types of practices. One is called the *right practices* and the other, the *miscellaneous pactices.*" Regarding these two types of practices, there are lengthy dissertations and many interpretations relating to the manner of practice, advantages, and disadvantages, but I will not delve into these teachings at this time. I will reveal them in my next fascicle, which focuses on the issue of practice. The gist of the profound heart is what I have described above.

*Dōkō's note: This manuscript alludes to the existence of a second fascicle, but it may be lost in obscurity. I have not found it. Should anyone discover it, this discourse should be amended.

4. Essential Discourse on Birth in the Pure Land through Nembutsu

by Genkū

Birth in the Pure Land through the recitation of nembutsu does not discriminate against those who may have committed the ten transgressions or the five grave offenses. Ten repetitions, or even a single utterance, of nembutsu accords us the welcome of Amida Buddha at the time of our death.

According to the teachings of the Buddhist schools of the holy gate, attainment of buddhahood is based on the premise that only those who possess vast merit and profound wisdom can succeed. Therefore, these teachings were designed for those capable of accomplishing the states of a śrāvaka or a bodhisattva.

It is now, however, the period of the decline of the Dharma, where all beings are wrongdoers. Rather than attempting to practice difficult teachings, it would be more expeditious to practice the easy recitation of the name of Amida Buddha in order to depart speedily from the burning house [i.e., the delusive worlds] of saṃsāra.

Nevertheless, since Buddha Śākyamuni is the source of all sutras and commentaries on Buddhism, it should be possible to attain buddhahood through the practice of the *Lotus Sutra* or the *Nirvāṇa Sutra* of Mahāyāna Buddhism. Manifold buddhas of the past, present, and future have attained buddhahood in this way, especially through the practice of the *Lotus Sutra*; numerous tathāgatas residing in the ten directionss have also realized enlightenment through the *Lotus Sutra*. Indeed, it is commendable to recite sutras such as the *Lotus Sutra*. We ordinary people today, however, do not possess the capability to embrace the teachings of the *Lotus Sutra*, which were intended for those who were destined to become bodhisattvas or śrāvakas. These precious teachings are too difficult for us common mortals.

In contrast, the essential vow of Amida Buddha was made specifically for us who live in the period of the decline of the Dharma; therefore, the merit of birth in the Pure Land is assured. We need not lament the fact that we may be women, nor need we rue our negative karma as sentient beings with worldly passions. We have fortunately encountered the essential vow that Amida Buddha established to save and welcome us wretched, defiled mortals who are beyond the help of the buddhas of past, present, and future and of the tathāgatas in the ten directions other than Amida Buddha.

Accordingly, those who firmly believe in the definite attainment of birth in the Pure Land and repeat *Namu Amida Butsu, Namu Amida Butsu*—both the virtuous and the nonvirtuous, men and women, ten out of ten, or one hundred out of one hundred beings—will achieve birth in the Pure Land.

Question: Is birth in the Pure Land possible for all who recite nembutsu?

Answer: Nembutsu relying on the power other than self [i.e., Amida Buddha] makes birth in the Pure Land possible, but nembutsu relying on self-power will never result in birth in the Pure Land.

Q. (2): What does *power other than self* mean?

Answer: *Power other than self* means having implicit faith in the repetition of nembutsu with a firm belief in the assurance of birth in the Pure Land, without looking back on one's virtuous or vicious deeds. To illustrate, a fly may alight on the tail of a Chinese mythological, fiery horse. Should the fiery horse leap, the fly will travel one thousand miles in an instant. Even a lowly and vulgar man who joins the caravan of a universal sovereign (*cakravatin*) will be able to traverse the four continents in a day.[164] This is called the *power other than self.* Further, even a large boulder, placed on a ship, will be transported to the far shore in due time. This is possible not by the mobility of the stone but by the ability of the ship. Likewise, one will see accomplishment through the power of Amida Buddha, which is referred to as the *power other than self.*

Q. (3): What is meant by *self-power*?

Answer: If common mortals who possess worldly passions and are determined to rid themselves of these passions strive to realize enlightenment and to attain buddhahood, even if they strive day and night, they will not be able to rid themselves of the worldly passions for very long. This is because they have been entrenched in the worldly passions of greed and anger from beginningless time. Thus, it is extremely difficult for us who are filled with the three poisons to rid ourselves of the worldly passions of ignorance. It would be as formidable a task as chipping away at Mount Meru with a tiny needle or emptying the ocean with a small ladle. Even if we were fortunate enough to chip away at Mount Meru with a needle and empty the ocean with a ladle the size of a poppy seed, innumerable eons of saṃsāra would not help us to achieve buddhahood. This is because we have accumulated negative karma with worldly passions. Being preoccupied by our thoughts every moment will cause us to fall into both the three lower realms and the eight difficult conditions; and our every thought, awake and asleep, will be a bond that ties us to the six delusive worlds and the four modes of birth in the illusive worlds of transmigration. Under these circumstances, no amount of practice or study would make the attainment of buddhahood a reality. This attempt to realize buddhahood by one's efforts is referred to as *self-power.*

Q. (4): Which is superior: nembutsu recited by an eminent monk or that recited by a lay person?

Answer: Unquestionably, there is no difference at all in their merit of nembutsu.

Q. (5): I am still doubtful. The nembutsu of the eminent monk, who is celibate and obtains sustenance by honest means, must be more virtuous. In contrast, the nembutsu of those who enjoy the company of women morning and evening, the pleasure of wine, and who get sustenance by unreligious means would be less virtuous. How, then, could the merit of all nembutsu be equal?

Answer: There is no difference in the merit of nembutsu. One has such doubts because one does not know the true meaning of the essential vow of Amida Buddha.

Long ago, before Buddha Lokeśvararāja, when Amida Buddha cast his eyes on the pure buddhalands of twenty-one billion buddhas and witnessed their majestic adornments, treasures, pleasures, and the pledges of these buddhas for the benefit of all sentient beings, there were no means for us common people who are filled with illusory and aberrant thoughts to attain birth in those pure buddhalands.

Master Shan-tao explained: "All buddhalands are solemn and pure. Common mortals with aberrant thoughts, however, have difficulty attaining birth in these buddhalands."[165] The intent of this passage means that although all buddhalands are wondrous, common mortals with aberrant thoughts cannot be born in these buddhalands. Each of you should reflect on yourself.

In fact, we mouth sutras and worship the Buddha, yet our hearts harbor errant thoughts and are never, even for a moment, in concentration. This being our situation, how then can we depart from the delusive worlds of transmigration? For innumerable eons up to this moment, we have lived in the three lower realms and the eight difficult conditions, and we have scorched ourselves in the raging fire of ignorance, never arriving at a point of extrication from this condition. This is indeed lamentable. Good spirit fades from year to year, and defiled thoughts become more dominant from day to day.

The ancients once said, "Worldly passions are like shadows: one cannot separate oneself from them. Enlightenment is like the moon reflected on the water: unreachable and unobtainable."

Therefore, Amida Buddha pondered for five eons and made the profound essential vow, which does not discriminate between the good or the bad, those observing the precepts or violating the precepts, the laity or clergy, and the learned or the unschooled. Amida Buddha then attained buddhahood with his all-encompassing compassion, which saves all sentient beings equally.

Consequently, we need only to believe firmly in the attainment of birth in the Pure Land through the power of the essential vow, recite nembutsu, and in an instant, we will be welcomed by Amida Buddha at the time of death.

Furthermore, among holy men who have been celibate for life, have abstained from intoxicants, meat, and the five pungent vegetables for a long time, and who have obstinately observed both the five precepts and the ten precepts, if they recite nembutsu relying on their own powers, only one out of one thousand or one or two out of ten thousand holy men may be welcomed by Amida Buddha.

Master Shan-tao, therefore, stated, "It is impossible for even one out of one thousand holy men to be welcomed."[166] So how can it be said that birth in the Pure Land is possible through self-power?

The essential vow of Amida Buddha does not require anything special; it does not require a serene frame of mind, or purification of one's defiled body. If mortals recite nembutsu with the implicit faith that Amida Buddha will come to receive them at the time of their death, and if they, awake or asleep, recite his name, they are certain to be welcomed by Amida Buddha at the time of their death. Repudiate all reservations owing to your being a woman or a layman; have unshakable faith in the assurance of birth in the Pure Land.

Q. (6): Which is more worthy: nembutsu recited with purity of mind or nembutsu recited when one is wracked by illusive thoughts?

Answer: There is no difference in the merit of birth in the Pure Land.

Q. (7): I still find this difficult to understand. The nembutsu recited when one's mind is serene without any stray thoughts is the nembutsu with exclusive thoughts of the Pure Land of Ultimate Bliss and the essential vow of Amida Buddha. Since there exists no impurity, this is considered to be the nembutsu of purity. In contrast, the nembutsu recited with distracting thoughts is an empty exercise of merely mouthing the name of Amida Buddha and of holding a string of prayer beads in hand while lacking the harmony of the three types of acts. This is considered to be the nembutsu of impurity. How, then, could these two types of nembutsu be equal in the merit of birth in the Pure Land?

Answer: These doubts come from a lack of thorough understanding of the essential vow. Amida Buddha set out the compassionate ship called the *universal vow* on the great ocean of transmigration in order to save sentient beings with unwholesome karma. It is like a ship transporting weighty rocks along with pieces of linen to the other shore. The supremacy of the essential vow is that there is no other meaning than that all sentient beings are able to attain birth in the Pure Land through the mere recitation of the name of Amida Buddha without regard for the gravity of their negative karma.

Q. (8): Which is superior in merit: a mere single utterance of nembutsu or ten repetitions of nembutsu?

Answer: They have the same merit with regard to birth in the Pure Land.

Q. (9): This is another point I do not understand because a single utterance and ten repetitions are clearly different in number. How could they be equal?

Answer: The issue of a single utterance and ten repetitions of nembutsu applies to one's time of death. When it is one's time to depart from this delusive world, one will attain birth in the Pure Land with a single utterance of nembutsu just as well as ten. There is no difference in merit, as both one and ten will result equally in birth in the Pure Land.

The passage of the essential vow Amida Buddha

states: "If, when I am to attain buddhahood, all sentient beings in the ten directions who hold faith with genuine hearts and who wish to be born in my buddhaland are not born there within just ten moments of being mindful of me, I will not realize enlightenment."[167] The meaning of this statement is described in the essential vow of Bodhisattva Dharmākara: "If, when I am to attain buddhahood, all sentient beings in the ten directions who desire to be born in my buddhaland of Ultimate Bliss and who recite *Namu Amida Butsu* ten times, or just once, are not welcomed, I will not realize enlightenment."[168] Therefore, the number of recitations is not the issue. The merit of birth in the Pure Land is equal, as is clearly stated in the essential vow. How can there be any doubt?

Q. (10): Which is more profound: nembutsu at the time of death or nembutsu in our daily life?

Answer: They are the same. Our daily nembutsu and nembutsu at the time of death are no different at all. When we are visited by death, our daily nembutsu becomes nembutsu at death; if our life is prolonged, nembutsu at death becomes nembutsu of daily life.

Q. (11): It is said that one final utterance of nembutsu at the time of death is worth more than the deeds accumulated for one hundred years. Is this so?

Answer: This statement indicates a lack of understanding of the previous answer. It simply means that one final utterance of nembutsu at the time of death is worth more than all the virtuous deeds, which are overshadowed by one's negative karma anyway, or more than all the negative karma, though it may be overshadowed by one's virtuous deeds. Nevertheless, reciting the one final nembutsu applies to a wrongdoer, not to the nembutsu devotee. This does not concern a person who recites nembutsu in his daily life while affirming his desire for birth in the Pure Land in his daily life.

Q. (12): When does one receive the protection of the light of Amida Buddha? Does one benefit in daily life or at the time of death?

Answer: The merit of protection by Amida Buddha is received in daily life. This is because one who has genuine belief in birth in the Pure Land holds no doubt and awaits the coming of Amida Buddha; this is the nembutsu devotee who embodies the threefold devotional heart. The *Meditation Sutra* teaches that one who has the threefold devotional heart will be born, with certainty, in the Pure Land of Ultimate Bliss.[169] Amida Buddha casts eighty-four thousand rays of his light of compassion upon one who is resolute in the attainment of this goal. Amida Buddha shines this light continually on the nembutsu practitioner in daily life and up to the final moment of that person's life. For this reason, it is called the "vow by which Amida Buddha never abandons the nembutsu devotee."

Q. (13): Is there a difference between the nembutsu practiced by the learned and the nembutsu of the ignorant?

Answer: The essential vow of Amida Buddha does not differentiate between the two at all. Before Amida Buddha attained buddhahood, he had vowed: "If all sentient beings in the ten directions recite my name, I will come to welcome all of them, including one who repeats my name a mere ten times."[170] This means that he does not choose the learned and abandon the ignorant.

The *Liturgy for the Rite of the Fivefold Rhythmic*

> *Chanting of Nien-fo* states: "Amida Buddha will not discriminate between the schooled who observe the precepts and the nonvirtuous who violate the precepts. If they turn their meritorious hearts toward birth in the Pure Land and recite nembutsu many times, they will be born in the Pure Land, as if broken tiles and pebbles that are turned into gold."[171] This means that the learned, the ignorant, the observers of the precepts, and those in violation of the precepts will all achieve birth in the Pure Land by performing nembutsu. Therefore, one should set aside thoughts of wholesomeness or unwholesomeness, rely on the essential vow, and earnestly recite nembutsu.

Now, there is no better way than nembutsu to take leave of the delusive worlds of transmigration. Even those who disparage my writings will be among the nine grades and born on the petals of the lotus in the Pure Land by the recitation of nembutsu. Various aspirants for birth in the Pure Land, through favorable or adverse conditions, will all become kindred spirits in the Pure Land of Amida Buddha.

Upon examination of the human potential for birth in the Pure Land, Amida Buddha never discriminates, even against one who has committed the five grave offenses, and never abandons women or those who have no intrinsic goodness. Concerning practice, anyone who chants nembutsu just once, or ten times, can attain birth in the Pure Land. Amida Buddha does not discriminate against women, who are said to be afflicted with the five hindrances and the three types of obedience.

You should rely totally on the essential vow and devote yourself to the recitation of nembutsu. Without the power of nembutsu, birth in the Pure Land is too difficult to achieve even for good people and that much more difficult for the unwholesome.

Believe that five recitations of nembutsu destroy the five hindrances for a woman, three recitations of nembutsu eliminate the three types of obedience, and a single utterance will result in one being welcomed by Amida Buddha into the Pure Land at the time of one's death.

Recite the name of Amida Buddha while you walk, while you stand, while you sit, and while you lie down. Accept and avail yourself to all conditions regardless of time, place, and various karmic relationships, and believe in the essential vow.

Respectfully yours. *Namu Amida Butsu. Namu Amida Butsu.*

5. The Significance of the Threefold Devotional Heart

THE *MEDITATION SUTRA* describes, "If there are sentient beings who aspire to be born in the Pure Land of Ultimate Bliss, they will attain this birth by awakening the three aspects of a heart. What are these three? The first aspect is the genuine heart, the second aspect, the profound heart, and the third aspect, the heart that seeks birth in the Pure Land through the dedication of merit. One who embodies the threefold devotional heart will be born in that Pure Land without fail."[172]

In the *Hymns in Praise of Birth in the Pure Land*, Master Shan-tao, after interpreting the threefold devotional heart, states, "One who possesses the threefold devotional heart will, with certainty, attain birth in the Pure Land. If one lacks even one aspect of the threefold devotional heart, birth in the Pure Land will not be realized."[173] Therefore, we should strive to cultivate the threefold devotional heart.

First, the *genuine heart* is the sincere heart. Whether worshiping physically, verbally reciting the name of Amida Buddha, or being mindful of his physical features, all actions must be performed based on the genuine heart. As a rule, one who loathes this defiled world of suffering, longs for achieving birth in the Pure Land, and engages in various karmic practices toward this birth should do so with a truly genuine heart. In doing so, if one outwardly pretends to be wise, virtuous, and diligent while inwardly harboring falsity and indolence, birth in the Pure Land becomes impossible despite continuing the practice day and night without cessation. Conversely, if a nembutsu devotee appears to harbor falsity and indolence but he practices with a truly wise, virtuous, and diligent heart, his fleeting moment of practice will be meritorious. This person will certainly attain birth in the Pure Land. This is called the *genuine heart.*

Second, the *profound heart* symbolizes the depth of one's faith. The profound heart has two aspects: the first is the belief that one is a common mortal without any virtue who has been wandering in the six delusive worlds from beginningless time to the present and who has no karmic cause to attain birth in the Pure Land; the second is the faith that, despite being a wrongdoer, one firmly believes in the certain attainment of birth in the Pure Land through the power of the vow of Amida Buddha, which is the decisive karmic cause of birth in the Pure Land. Of these two aspects, the second is further divided into two: The first is the "establishment of an unshakable faith in birth in the Pure Land with respect to persons," and the second, the "establishment of an unshakable faith in birth in the Pure Land with respect to practice."

The first faith can be subdivided into two: the holy gate and the Pure Land gate. Though there are many gates out of the delusive worlds of transmigration, the main division is between the holy gate and the Pure Land gate. The holy gate is the path toward enlightenment that pursues the eradication of worldly passions in this world. The Pure Land gate is the desire for birth in the Pure Land wherein one loathes this delusive world of anguish and cultivates virtuous deeds. Of these two gates, we should forget the holy gate and rely upon the Pure Land gate.

If someone, citing many sutras and commentaries, avers, "A common mortal with worldly passions is not able to attain birth in the Pure Land," do not be deterred by such words; rather, your belief should become even stronger. This is because the common mortal, while obstructed by karmic hindrances, *is* able to achieve birth in the Pure Land—these are the genuine words of Buddha Śākyamuni, not the remarks of common people with delusory attachments. I, [Hōnen], believe in the words of Buddha Śākyamuni and long for birth in the Pure Land with all my heart.

Even if various buddhas and bodhisattvas appear before you saying, "Common mortals who are obstructed by karmic hindrances will not attain birth in the Pure Land," you must not believe this. This is because a bodhisattva is a disciple of Buddha Śākyamuni; a true bodhisattva would not negate his teachings. Therefore, the "bodhisattva" who would say that birth in the Pure Land is impossible, counter to the teachings of Buddha Śākyamuni, should not be regarded as an actual bodhisattva.

Moreover, all buddhas equally have infinite compassion. A true buddha would not contradict the teachings of Buddha Śākyamuni. The *Smaller Sutra* clearly states, "One day or seven, if the name of Amida Buddha is repeated, birth in the Pure Land will certainly be attained."[174] Manifold buddhas in the six directions, as numerous as the grains of sand in the Ganges, validated this teaching in the same manner as did Buddha Śākyamuni. Nevertheless, some so-called buddhas, negating Buddha Śākyamuni, are claiming that birth in the Pure Land is impossible. We now know that they are not true buddhas: They are heavenly demons in the guise of buddhas. For this reason, we should not believe in the instructions of these false buddhas or bodhisattvas.

This is even more true for the extraneous sayings [of others]. You should say, "Whether the practices you are pursuing are Mahāyāna Buddhism or Hīnayāna Buddhism, they are practices in hope of enlightenment in this delusive world. This is the spirit of the holy gate. However, although there are differences between the right practices and the miscellaneous practices, our karmic practice is the one that seeks birth in the Pure Land of Ultimate Bliss, and this is the spirit of the Pure Land gate. The holy gate is the practice that is karmically related to you; the Pure Land gate is the practice that has a karmic relation to us." From each of our perspectives in either teaching, we must refrain from criticizing others. To believe in this way is referred to as the "establishment of an unshakable faith in birth in the Pure Land with respect to persons."

Next is the "establishment of an unshakable faith for birth in the Pure Land with respect to practice." Although there are various practices for birth in the Pure Land, they can be divided into two categories: the right practices and the miscellaneous practices. The right practices are practices intimately related to Amida Buddha, and the miscellaneous practices are practices estranged from him.

These right practices include the five practices. The first is the *recitation of sutras*: that is, the recitation of the three sutras of Pure Land Buddhism. The second is *contemplation*: that is, the contemplation of Amida Buddha and the majestic adornments of his Pure Land. The third is *worship*: that is, the worship of Amida Buddha. The fourth is *recitation*: that is, the recitation of the name of Amida Buddha. The fifth is *praise and offering*: that is, the praise of Amida Buddha and the act of making offerings to him.

These five right practices can be put into two categories. One is to recite single-heartedly and exclusively the name of Amida Buddha while walking, standing, sitting, or lying down, without regard for length of time, and thus to engage in nembutsu without cessation throughout one's life. This is called the *rightly established practice* because it is in accordance with the essential vow of Amida Buddha.[175] With the exception of the rightly established practice, the other four right practices, such as worship and recitation of sutras, are named the *auxiliary practices.*

The miscellaneous practices are all the other practices—including the recitation of Mahāyāna texts, awakening the heart for enlightenment, the observation of the Buddhist precepts, and encouraging people to the path leading to deliverance—not included in the above-mentioned right practices and auxiliary practices.

The right practices and miscellaneous practices have five pairs of advantages and disadvantages. The first is the intimate/extraneous condition: one who performs the right practices has an intimate relationship with Amida Buddha, but observance of the miscellaneous practices estranges one from him. The second is the familiar/unfamiliar condition: one who observes the right practices is familiar with Amida Buddha, but observance of the miscellaneous practices distances one from Amida Buddha. The third is the constant/inconstant condition: one who observes the right practices constantly maintains one's devotion to Amida Buddha, but observance of the miscellaneous practices results in a severance of devotion from him. The fourth is the condition of the dedication/nondedication of merit. This means that the right practices themselves become the karmic cause of birth in the Pure Land, but the miscellaneous practices require special attention in order to dedicate merit to birth in the Pure Land. The fifth is the pure/impure condition. The right practices become a pure cause for birth in the Pure Land, while the miscellaneous practices are practices for birth in various pure buddhalands in the ten directions and for rebirth in the realms of human beings and celestial beings. To believe in the above is referred to as the "establishment of an unshakable faith for birth in the Pure Land with respect to practice."

Third, the heart that seeks birth in the Pure Land through the dedication of merit means to dedicate with a genuine heart all of one's meritorious physical, verbal, and mental virtues cultivated in the past and also in this present life for the singular purpose of attaining birth in the Pure Land. This is called the *heart that seeks birth in the Pure Land through the dedication of merit.* If one embodies the threefold devotional heart, birth in the Pure Land is assured indeed.

6. Instruction in the Seven Articles

ALTHOUGH THERE ARE many substantial teachings for attaining birth in the Pure Land of Ultimate Bliss, the most essential teaching for our Jōdo Shū lies in the theory of the threefold devotional heart.

Even he who endeavors day and night, without rest, as though trying to put out a fire in his hair, will not achieve birth in the Pure Land after all without possession of the threefold devotional heart. Those who aspire to birth in the Pure Land should by all means recite nembutsu with the proper understanding of the threefold devotional heart, the three aspects of faith indispensable for birth in the Pure Land—the genuine heart, the profound heart, and the heart that seeks birth in the Pure Land through the dedication of merit.

First is the genuine heart. Master Shan-tao stated, "The Chinese term *chih* refers to truth, and *ch'eng* is the quality of being sincere."[176] He interpreted the genuine heart to mean a truly sincere heart. Genuineness indicates the state of the heart absent of any falsity or fickleness. The heart that holds falsity and fickleness produces the worldly passions of greed and anger and loses the rightly settled state of mind for birth in the Pure Land. All worldly passions arise out of greed and anger, which are considered to be the mother of the undesirable passions.

Regarding the issue of greed, there are two categories: (1) greed that may be satisfied with small gratification, and (2) greed that may remain unsated even with enormous gratification. Jōdo Shū prohibits entertaining the latter greed of worldly passions: that is, greed that may remain unsatisfied even with enormous gratification. The nembutsu devotee should recite nembutsu with this in mind; this is genuine nembutsu.

Greed that may be satisfied with a small gratification is justifiable. The worldly passion of anger can be tolerated so long as one venerates one's elders and nurtures one's subordinates. The worldly passion of ignorance indicates an ignorant heart. We need to strive to become wiser. If we loathe the delusive worlds of saṃsāra, long for birth in the Pure Land, treasure our precious belief in birth in the Pure Land, and devote ourselves to a life of service, then we can be free from the worldly passion of ignorance. Minimal ignorance will not be an obstacle to birth in the Pure Land.

Cultivation of these attitudes will rid us of a heart filled with falsity and fickleness because of the worldly passions of greed and anger. The result, a truly genuine heart, will emerge without difficulty. This is referred to as the heart that seeks enlightenment in Jōdo Shū. In short, to reduce the myriad worldly passions of the delusive worlds of transmigration and to recite nembutsu exclusively are together referred to as the heart of genuineness.

Second is the profound heart. The profound heart is the heart that believes profoundly in nembutsu. It also means to recite exclusively nembutsu without embracing other practices. If other practices are performed concurrently with nembutsu, one would be a nembutsu devotee lacking in the profound heart. To understand that the three sutras of Pure Land Buddhism taught by Buddha Śākyamuni exclusively propogate the sole practice of nembutsu, to believe that the essence of the forty-eight vows of Amida Buddha is the vow of the exclusive recitation of nembutsu, and to recite single-heartedly nembutsu—these indicate having the profound heart.

Third is the heart that seeks birth in the Pure Land through the dedication of merit, which means earnestly focusing all of one's virtuous deeds from the beginningless past to the present for the sake of birth in the Pure Land, and to desire exclusively this birth. It also means continually repeating nembutsu without stopping. This is the teaching of Monk Eshin. If one pursues this heart and acquires both the genuine heart and the profound heart, one should practice nembutsu continually. If one falters in the recitation of nembutsu, one will be a nembutsu practitioner lacking in the heart that seeks birth in the Pure Land through the dedication of merit.

Jōdo Shū followers should have a thorough understanding of the substance of the threefold devotional heart and recite nembutsu. If even one aspect of the threefold devotional heart is lacking, the nembutsu practitioner will be precluded from birth in the Pure Land. On the other hand, this birth becomes a simple matter if one possesses the threefold devotional heart.

All of our deeds in the realms of saṃsāra result from ties with the three worldly passions of greed, anger, and ignorance. Understand that when the worldly passions of greed, anger, and ignorance surface, an illusion arises that causes one to fall into the lower realms. Do your best to prevent such an occurrence.

If these worldly passions arise, merely think of them as a guest of the heart, and think of nembutsu as the host of the heart. In this way, birth in the Pure Land will be possible. Contrarily, if you think of the worldly passions as the host and nembutsu as the guest, nembutsu becomes virtue mixed with worldly passions and falsity, making birth in the Pure Land impossible.

In essence, even if worldly passions surface in the moments before and after nembutsu is recited, do not allow these passions to intermingle with the recitation of the six characters, *Na mu A mi da Butsu*.

1. Just because one relies solely upon Amida Buddha and believes only in nembutsu, do not make light of the compassionate vows of various buddhas and bodhisattvas, or think ill of and slander wondrous sutras such as the *Lotus Sutra* or the *Perfection of Wisdom Sutra*.

   The karma of defaming myriad buddhas and of doubting and

slandering many holy teachings is not in harmony with the heart of Amida Buddha. Such actions would certainly exclude one from his compassionate vow even if one recites nembutsu.

2. There seem to be many who say that behaving prudently and exerting efforts to become a good person in order not to commit unwholesome karma will demean the essential vow, or that reciting nembutsu sixty thousand times a day and repeating nembutsu as many times as possible will be to doubt the compassionate power of Amida Buddha. Don't lend an ear to such misguided notions.

   In the first place, where in the holy text does Amida Buddha encourage you to commit an offense? Such people are simply those who are unable to desist from their nonvirtuous deeds, who continue to commit wrongs, who fabricate such falsehood and mislead and insult innocent men and women, and who encourage others to commit karmic misdeeds and attempt to arouse worldly passions. Regard them as a kind of demon. This is also the work of non-Buddhist heretics. They are considered enemies of the attainment of birth in the Pure Land.

   Further, it is a grave misconception to call someone who recites nembutsu many times as a "practitioner of nembutsu with self-power." Someone who recites nembutsu merely once or twice, relying on his own efforts, is referred to as a devotee of nembutsu with self-power. Conversely, if one recites nembutsu continually one thousand or ten thousand times each day and night for one hundred or one thousand days, with complete reliance on the power of the essential vow and with respect for the compassionate power of Amida Buddha, this nembutsu, with each mindful utterance, is considered to be nembutsu with the power other than self. Nembutsu performed by devotees who possess the threefold devotional heart, recite moment by moment and day and night, revere the power of the essential vow, and depend on the compassion of Amida Buddha is never deemed nembutsu with self-power.

3. It need not be mentioned here that the threefold devotional heart exists in the nembutsu recited by a practitioner who thoroughly understands the meaning of the threefold devotional heart. However, it is a grave misconception to say that the threefold devotional heart does not exist in the nembutsu recited by ignorant people who are not even aware of the term *threefold devotional heart*, or that birth in the Pure Land is impossible if the threefold devotional heart is lacking even slightly.

   The threefold devotional heart is the heart of the essential vow, which Amida Buddha made when he was Bodhisattva Dharmākara after contemplating day and night for five eons. Therefore, the threefold devotional heart should not be treated lightly.

   The threefold devotional heart was designed for even the most ignorant. Those who are not even aware of the name of the threefold devotional heart can also possess the three parts of it without knowing anything about them. Accordingly, when one hears that Amida Buddha will certainly receive us into the Pure Land through total reliance on him and the single-hearted recitation of his name—if, with deep faith in these words without questioning, one desires to be welcomed by him and recites his name—one will embody the threefold devotional heart naturally because one's heart is in accordance with the threefold devotional heart.

   In fact, there is proof that among the illiterate who knew not a single letter but who recited nembutsu wholeheartedly, those who had the rightly settled state of mind for birth in the Pure Land at their times of death enjoyed an auspicious birth in the Pure Land. Hence, one must not have a shadow of doubt, not even the size of a dewdrop or a speck of dust.

   To debate the threefold devotional heart without extensive knowledge and misunderstanding may even result in a grievous condition at the time of death. Everyone must have the proper understanding of the threefold devotional heart.

4. Occasionally, it is important to perform a special nembutsu

retreat for a fixed period of time to nurture our mind and body. To recite nembutsu sixty or seventy thousand times every day would suffice. But unfortunately our minds tend to be remiss in our efforts because our eyes and ears become accustomed to the mundane; our minds become restless due to the pressure of constant daily activities, and consequently, we become inattentive to the practice of nembutsu. In order to renew our spirit, we should regularly perform nembutsu for a fixed period of time. Master Shan-tao, in his benevolence, encouraged us to observe this practice, as did Monk Eshin in his work, the *Collection of Essentials on Attaining Birth in the Pure Land*.[177]

How is this accomplished? Prepare the nembutsu hall as immaculately as possible with offerings of flowers and incense. Before entering the hall, purify your body. Recite the nembutsu in three sessions a day (morning, midday, and sunset) or in six sessions a day (sunset, early evening, the beginning of the night, the end of the night, morning, and midday). If there is a group of devotees, each may take turns entering the hall, making certain that the nembutsu recitation continues without interruption. Perform this practice as the occasion dictates.

According to Master Shan-tao, the most auspicious times are the first to the eighth of the month, the eighth to the fifteenth, the fifteenth to the twenty-third, or the twenty-third to the end of the month. The special practice of nembutsu for a fixed period of time should be conducted for seven days, beginning on a day that is convenient for everyone. One must not harbor decadent and unwholesome thoughts or be influenced by those who make light of this.

5. At any cost, you must establish the rightly settled state of mind for birth in the Pure Land at the time of death, see Amida Buddha with your eyes, recite his name with your mouth, and in your heart, await the arrival of a host of celestial beings. It would be regrettable to fail to be born in the Pure Land and thus to suffer in the realms of transmigration for one life, two lives, three lives,

or four, just because you met with an undesirable karmic condition at the time of death and harbored illusory thoughts, even though you had cultivated the merit of daily nembutsu.

Master Shan-tao, therefore, encouraged us, saying, "May Amida Buddha grant that at the end of our lives, his disciples and followers, including us... may we realize birth in the high category of the Pure Land of Amida Buddha."[178]

Pray and wish daily that you will abide in the rightly settled state of mind for birth in the Pure Land at the time of death. Some say that those who pray for the rightly settled state of mind for birth in the Pure Land at the time of death are ones who do not rely on the essential vow of Amida Buddha. How much more scholarly than Master Shan-tao do these people think they are? This is regrettable and disturbing indeed.

6. Absolutely, birth in the Pure Land is attained through the diligent, uninterrupted recitation of nembutsu. Accordingly, Master Shan-tao encouraged us, saying, "Once devotees awaken in themselves the aspiration for birth in the Pure Land, they should devote themselves to the recitation of nembutsu for life, without abandoning it, always pursuing birth in the Pure Land."[179]

   He further stated, "... to recite single-heartedly and exclusively the name of Amida Buddha while walking, standing, sitting, or lying down, without regard for length of time, and to engage in the recitation of nembutsu without cessation throughout one's life. This is called the *rightly established practice* because it is in accordance with the essential vow of Amida Buddha."[180]

   Many additional passages encourage nembutsu, too, but I will not enumerate each here. Simply rely on the essential vow, revere Master Shan-tao, and do not doubt the teaching of nembutsu.

7. Once devotees assiduously practice nembutsu and become plausible nembutsu practitioners, they might begin to look upon others and see their hearts as inferior, as imperfect and wrong, and then think that, as a peerless practitioner of nembutsu,

they are superior to everyone else. Be vigilant not to indulge in conceit.

The world is vast and its inhabitants are numerous. There are countless people, unknown to you, deep in the mountains and forests, who are respectable and exemplary practitioners of nembutsu. You are not aware of them simply because you have not heard of them and do not know them. Hence, it is wrong to think that you are the most admirable nembutsu practitioner in existence.

This kind of heart is consumed by great conceit. If the conceited heart appears, undesirable conditions will prevent birth in the Pure Land. Such a person believes that birth in the Pure Land, because it is attained as a result of his own outstanding practice, will eliminate the effects of his karmic wrongs. The truth, however, is that only the power of the essential vow rids us of our worldly passions and negative karma and induces Amida Buddha to graciously extend his hand of compassion to welcome us into the Pure Land of Ultimate Bliss. If you think that birth in the Pure Land is possible through your own efforts, you will become consumed with conceit that you are wise. When you possess this heart of conceit, you will not be in accord with the essential vow, and you will lose the protection of Amida Buddha as well as that of other buddhas. You are ultimately haunted by malevolent spirits. I here repeat—be vigilant indeed against conceit.

Sincerely yours.

7. An Outline of Nembutsu

SENTIENT BEINGS in this defiled world who aspire for birth in the Pure Land during the period of the decline of the Dharma should have no other practice but the practice of reciting nembutsu. They should, in compliance with the guidance of Master Shan-tao, enter the gate of the single-hearted and exclusive practice of nembutsu.

However, I regret to say that there are very few who enter that gate with earnest hearts focused solely on nembutsu. This is because some are attracted to other Buddhist practices, and others do not take the merits of nembutsu seriously enough. I suppose that this must be the reason for the small number of people who profoundly believe in birth in the Pure Land, who realize this profound aspiration. Therefore, understand the following truth.

There are numerous sutras, commentaries, and sacred teachings of the Tendai school and the Hossō school, and even one of these teachings could bring buddhahood. However, to find the best way to buddhahood, one needs to carefully look at one's own potential and reflect on the conditions of the era. It was difficult to hone one's wisdom and to rid oneself of worldly passions even in the fourth five-hundred-year period after the death of Buddha Śākyamuni, not to mention how difficult it was to reach the state of samādhi with purity of heart. Accordingly, many entered the nembutsu gate. Master Tao-ch'o, Master Shan-tao, and other Pure Land masters lived during that period of time.

It is now in the fifth five-hundred-year period after the death of Buddha Śākyamuni, known as *the period of a steadfast engagement in doctrinal disputes*, in which one has extreme difficulty accomplishing Buddhist practices and teachings other than birth in the Pure Land through nembutsu for achieving enlightenment.

Nembutsu still will have merit even after the period of the decline of the Dharma. It need not be said that it is now the beginning of the period of the decline of the Dharma, which will last ten thousand years. Even a single utterance of the name of Amida Buddha will assure birth in the Pure Land. Although we may not have the potential to achieve this birth, we are better off than those who will live at the end of the period of the decline of the Dharma.

As for the attainment of buddhahood in one's present body even during the time of Buddha Śākyamuni, only the dragon girl achieved this realization.[181] Attaining buddhahood in one's present body is extremely difficult. Even though one may not attain buddhahood in one's present body, how many practitioners have realized enlightenment among the bodhisattvas and śrāvakas who practiced the doctrines of the holy gate? How many have attained buddhahood among other prominent and virtuous monks, male and female Buddhist clerics in later years, present-day scholarly monks who have studied sutras and commentaries, and those who hold the *Lotus Sutra*? We may endeavor today to practice the teachings of the holy gate, but there is no way we can match their achievements.

Amida Buddha with his omniscience perceived the sentient beings, including us, who would exist during the period of the decline of the Dharma and, in order to save them, contemplated for five eons, finally composing his forty-eight vows. Among them, the eighteenth vow states, "If, when I am to attain buddhahood, all sentient beings in the ten directions who hold faith with genuine hearts and who wish to be born in my buddhaland are not born there within just ten moments of being mindful of me, I will not realize enlightenment."[182] Amida Buddha, did, indeed, attain enlightenment.

Buddha Śākyamuni taught these teachings in the three sutras of

Pure Land Buddhism, one of which is the *Meditation Sutra*. These sutras merely articulate the nembutsu gate.

Even for those who have repeatedly committed misdeeds and who do not believe in the essential vow of Amida Buddha, it would not be in vain to explain to them in detail a mere single word of the three sutras of Pure Land Buddhism of Buddha Śākyamuni. Besides, verification by myriad buddhas of the six or ten directions is cited in the three sutras. There are no such testimonies in texts other than the three sutras. Therefore, since so much time has elapsed since the death of Buddha Śākyamuni, we should recite the name of Amida Buddha, a practice that has been validated by various buddhas and that speedily brings merits, rather than attempt the impossible practices of tranquility or the pursuit of wisdom.

Among those who seek deliverance in the life to come, there are some who will look lightly upon the Pure Land, thinking that true aspiration should be toward the pure buddhaland of Buddha Mahāvairocana and the world of the Lotus Treasury of Buddha Vairocana. Those who believe in the possibility of attaining birth in these buddhaworlds do not know their own limitations. Only the bodhisattvas who have completely eradicated ignorance are able to enter such supreme worlds.

There are also some who doubt the efficacy of entering the gate of the single-hearted and exclusive practice of nembutsu, repeating nembutsu 30,000, 50,000, 60,000, and up to 100,000 times daily and subsequently reciting various meritorious sutras that have been held and recited for years. They deceive the nembutsu devotee with this kind of doubt. It is not that these acts are not effective. It is simply that it is too difficult for mortals in the period of the decline of the Dharma to fulfill the practice of holding and reciting the sutras. Therefore, they should first attain birth in the Pure Land through nembutsu while relying on the essential vow, be blessed to encounter Tathāgata Amida, Bodhisattva Avalokiteśvara, and Bodhisattva Mahāsthāmaprāpta there, study various holy teachings, and then realize enlightenment.

There are many texts that state that sentient beings in the period of the decline of the Dharma should practice nembutsu exclusively. In one of these texts in particular, [the *Smaller Sutra*,] birth in the Pure Land through nembutsu is proven by all buddhas in the ten directions, who are as numerous as the grains of sand in the Ganges. Master Shan-tao, in the third fascicle of his *Commentary on the Meditation Sutra*, thus stated:

> Buddhist practices other than nembutsu may be called virtuous practices, but they do not compare with nembutsu at all. The merits of nembutsu are praised extensively throughout many Buddhist texts.
>
> For instance, the forty-eight vows described in the *Larger Sutra* articulate that birth in the Pure Land is assured through the earnest recitation of the name of Amida Buddha. In the *Smaller Sutra*, it is also written that those who recite the name of Amida Buddha for one or seven days will attain birth in the Pure Land. This was validated by all the buddhas in the ten directions, who are as numerous as the grains of sand of the Ganges.
>
> Further, in the passage about the meditative practices with a focused mind and with a distracted mind described in the *Meditation Sutra*, it is proven that birth in the Pure Land comes to pass through the mere recitation of the name of Amida Buddha. There are many examples of this. These points clarify the exclusive practice of the nembutsu samādhi.[183]

Master Shan-tao also stated in the passage on the exclusive practice of nembutsu and the miscellaneous practices in the *Hymns in Praise of Birth in the Pure Land*: "Rarely will one or two out of ten thousand practitioners of the miscellaneous practices attain birth in the Pure Land. On the other hand, one hundred out of one hundred practitioners of the exclusive practice of nembutsu will be assured birth in the Pure Land."[184] This means that regardless of the practice, when one enters a particular gate, one should practice that teaching earnestly and exclusively and avoid being distracted by other teachings.

To illustrate: If one serves a lord in this life and is dependent on that lord, there is a difference between one's loyalty to other lords and being solely dependent on one's own lord. However, if one has wealth, possesses a means of transportation, has servants, and is in a position to divide one's loyalty among many lords, the efforts may not be in vain. In contrast, if one is not in a position to be loyal to many lords, but still tries, one will exhaust oneself and one's efforts will be futile. If that person is instead reliant on one lord alone, even if they are a poor person, they will benefit from the lord's mercy. In other words, ignorant people in the difficult period of the decline of the Dharma can be likened to the poor above. The prominent and holy masters of old days are analogous to families of wealth. For the ignorant to follow the practice of the lettered is as if a poor person were to follow the practice of men of means.

To cite another analogy: A powerless person who depends on rocky protrusions and tree roots in an attempt to scale a boulder obstructing his path on a high mountain is the same as the one endeavoring to attain birth in the Pure Land through the miscellaneous practices. Contrarily, one who depends on a lifeline from above in order to scale the boulder is like the one aspiring for birth in the Pure Land based upon profound faith in the essential vow who single-heartedly recites nembutsu.

One who exercises the single-hearted and exclusive practice of nembutsu requires the threefold devotional heart. The first aspect is the genuine heart, the second, the profound heart, and the third, the heart that seeks birth in the Pure Land through the dedication of merit.

The genuine heart refers to worshiping only Amida Buddha and to reciting his name wholeheartedly and exclusively without worshiping other buddhas and observing other practices.

The profound heart is the implicit faith in the essential vow of Amida Buddha. One must believe that one is a common mortal with worldly passions who has transmigrated through the six delusive worlds from beginningless time until the present who has still not found a way to extricate himself from the six delusive worlds. Further, it is essential to believe that if a person continues to recite the name of Amida Buddha without any doubts, even a single utterance will eradicate any karmic negativity accumulated in transmigration for eight billion eons, and it will certainly bring the blessing of Amida Buddha's welcome at the final moment. This is due to the inconceivably profound power of the essential vow.

The heart that seeks birth in the Pure Land through the dedication of merit means to dedicate sincerely all the merits of the practices of one's own and of others toward aspiring for birth in the Pure Land. It would be difficult to achieve this birth if one lacked any element of the threefold devotional heart.

Although it would seem not to be a hindrance for birth in the Pure Land to perform practices in addition to nembutsu, on closer scrutiny, one can see that to do so belies a lingering doubt about the certain attainment of birth in the Pure Land through nembutsu.

Now then, is there any person who misunderstands the genuine heart and who insists on the impossibility of awakening genuineness for ordinary people? Such a person misunderstands the true intention of the essential vow and is lacking in faith. Even though we make an effort to cultivate the power of faith, how can we, common mortals with worldly passions, possess the power of faith in order to fulfill our wishes for birth in the Pure Land? Since we single-heartedly endeavor to nurture our desire for the certain attainment of birth in the Pure Land, this birth will be possible through the inconceivably profound power of the essential vow. Amida Buddha did not make his inconceivable essential vow for the elite or the monastics with the profound power of faith. Those with thorough understanding of these reasons who sincerely enter the exclusive practice of nembutsu are extremely venerable.

Master Tao-ch'o was the senior master for the certain attainment of birth in the Pure Land. He, the third generation, younger disciple of Master T'an-luan (476–542),[185] had profound wisdom and preached the *Nirvāṇa Sutra*. Although Master T'an-luan also had profound wisdom, he abandoned preaching the *Four Treatises*,[186] devoted himself to the practice for birth in the Pure Land, exercised the exclusive repetition of the name of Amida Buddha without interruption, and indeed attained birth in the Pure Land.

Master Tao-ch'o likewise abandoned the teachings of the *Nirvāṇa Sutra* and exercised the vocal nembutsu. Master Shan-tao also abandoned the miscellaneous practices and engaged in the exclusive practice of reciting nembutsu. It is also said that following the guidance of Master Tao-ch'o, all people above the age of seven in the three districts (Chin-yang, Tai-yuan, and Wen-sui) of Ping-chou in Shanhsi Province, where he lived, earnestly practiced the recitation of nembutsu.

Why then, would common mortals in the period of the decline of the Dharma in our country ever choose to engage in the miscellaneous practices? We should immediately, without fail, learn about the essential vow of Tathāgata Amida, the teachings of Buddha Śākyamuni, and the interpretations of Master Tao-ch'o and Master Shan-tao. Rather than doubt the attainment of birth in the Pure Land through the miscellaneous practices, we should strengthen our aspiration for birth in the Pure Land through the exclusive practice of nembutsu.

It is unnecessary to cite passages from Master Tao-ch'o and Master Shan-tao here, because they were the masters of the nembutsu gate [that we have already discussed]. But regarding the teachings of other schools, I understand that the Hossō school does not embrace the teaching of the exclusive practice of nembutsu. However, in the *Essentials for Birth in the West*, Master K'uei-chi (632–82)[187] writes, "All of the Buddhist teachings will be extinct after the period of the decline of the Dharma, which lasts ten thousand years. Despite that, the sole sutra (*Larger Sutra*) of Amida Buddha will endure and become even more virtuous in saving sentient beings."[188]

The same writing also states, "One can master neither the passages of the three aspects of emptiness and the eradication of the nine kinds of worldly passions nor the teachings of the ten bodhisattva stages and the five levels of concentration on the principles of Mind Only, even if one pursues them for a lifetime. Our final moment is approaching each day, so abandon diverse Buddhist studies and devote yourself to nembutsu."[189]

Further, in the *Record of Holy Chu-lin Temple*,[190] it is recorded:

> While Bodhisattva Samantabhadra and Bodhisattva Mañjuśrī sat facing each other in the east and west and were revealing the wondrous teachings to a multitude of sentient beings in the great hall of Chu-lin Temple on Mount Wu-t'ai, the meditation master Fa-chao[191] kneeled and asked Bodhisattva Mañjuśrī, "What sort of teaching would make it possible for common mortals of the future defiled world to depart from the delusive triple realms forever and to be born in the Pure Land?"
>
> Bodhisattva Mañjuśrī replied, "There is no practice superior to the recitation of the name of Amida Buddha for birth in the Pure Land. Even in the path for the instantaneous realization of enlightenment, there is the sole teaching of nembutsu. Therefore, the acclaimed holy teachings from the lifetime of Buddha Śākyamuni are the teachings of Amida Buddha, particularly for the common people in the defiled world of the future."[192]

It is truly unfortunate if one's faith is not strengthened by seeing such essential passages and teachings of the learned, and unfortunate, too, if one fails to enter the easy path to birth in the Pure Land after having received life in the world as a human being, a state extremely difficult to obtain. It is even more unfortunate that there are many who insult and deride the exclusive practitioners of nembutsu today.

These unfortunate circumstances were foretold by incarnate buddhas and bodhisattvas a long time ago. Accordingly, Bodhisattva Mañjuśrī stated, "Nonvirtuous beings in the future world will recite the name of Amida Buddha in the west, become detached from the delusive worlds of saṃsāra by relying on the essential vow, and be born in the Pure Land through the depth of their sincere heart."

In the *Hymns of the Nien-fo Liturgy*, Master Shan-tao thus stated:

> At the very moment when the World-Honored One [Buddha Śākyamuni] was coming to the end of his sermon, he entrusted to Śāriputra with great care the name of Amida Buddha.
>
> Over time, after the death of Buddha Śākyamuni, the five defilements proliferated, and many people began to slander the teaching of nembutsu. Monastics and lay people alike began to dislike the teaching of nembutsu and ceased listening to it. This gave rise to the poison of anger, and when they saw nembutsu practitioners, they struggled to incite intrigue and create grudges. Such people seem blind by nature and have no intrinsic goodness. Destroying the teaching designed for the instantaneous realization of enlightenment, they will sink into the three lower realms for a long time. They will never be released from the three lower realms, even though innumerable eons pass, more numerous than the number of particles released in the explosion of the earth.[193]

The *Sutra of Universal Enlightenment* states: "If a good man and woman listen to the teaching of nembutsu, are overwhelmed both with sorrow at their state of ignorance and with unspeakable elation at the promise of birth in the Pure Land, and attempt to escape from the three lower realms, then it is clear that they have already cultivated the path leading to enlightenment in a previous life. Conversely, if a person does not rejoice even after listening to the teaching, it is a sign that he has just emerged for the first time from the three lower realms."[194] Those who criticize and slander the teaching of nembutsu are merely obsessed with illogical reasons, which are not worthy of debate.

It is difficult for those who have not resolutely performed the ten virtuous acts to attain birth in the Trāyastriṃśa Heaven and the Tuṣita Heaven. On the contrary, even one who commits the five grave offenses can attain birth in the Pure Land through nembutsu; not to mention the possibility of birth in the Pure Land for one who commits the ten transgressions.

If one were to hope for the emergence of Buddha Maitreya, one would have to wait for 5,670 million years. There is no vow like the essential vow in any pure buddhaland other than the Pure Land. As for the attainment of birth in the Pure Land, the power of the essential vow is profoundly effective. Why would it be necessary to aspire for birth in any pure buddhaland other than the Pure Land of Amida Buddha?

There exists now those who have a karmic relation to the Buddhadharma and hope to attain enlightenment after three and four lives of transmigration, but the realization of this aspiration is not assured. There are also those who have karmic ties to buddhahood through listening to the instructions of the sixteen princes at the time of Buddha Mahābhijñājñānābhibhū and attaching the precious gem of the teaching of the one vehicle on the lining of the gown of genuine faith and repentance. Nevertheless, such people may forget the holy teaching and fall into the six delusive worlds of transmigration for three thousand eons immediately after coming into existence in the next life. Although they spend three and four lives to attain deliverance, the agony of transmigration for the sake of this deliverance is completely unbearable. It would be too long in coming. In the holy gate, one realizes enlightenment through the instructions of the three vehicles and the five vehicles, and these practices entail long hours spanning hundreds and thousands of eons.

We did not receive life as human beings for the first time in this lifetime. We have been wandering through previous rounds of saṃsāra, and in that time we must have encountered the teachings of tathāgatas and listened to the sermons of bodhisattvas. Sadly, these teachings did not usher us onto the path of enlightenment because of our lack of faith in such teachings.

All the buddhas in the past, present, and future, as well as various bodhisattvas in the ten directions, may be friends from our past. It is an incredible thought, but we may have even been connected to Buddha Śākyamuni five hundred dust-atom eons in the past, and Amida Buddha before his attainment of buddhahood ten eons ago, in the form of fathers, mothers, mentors, or disciples. Those who attained buddhahood believed in the words of previous buddhas, believed in the teachings of virtuous teachers, observed practices by awakening the heart to enlightenment, and eventually became buddhas a very long time ago. In contrast, we, who have not been faithful, are still detained in the delusive world of saṃsāra.

Looking at the transmigrations of the past, we will probably repeat the same transmigration. Although we may awaken aspiration for the two vehicles, it is still difficult to awaken the heart to enlightenment. For this reason, Amida Buddha, through wondrous skillful means, taught us the way to birth in the Pure Land by relying on the power of the essential vow.

Sentient beings of this defiled world may endeavor to attain buddhahood through their own efforts by engaging in austere religious practices for countless eons, but enlightenment will be impossible. Moreover, the teachings of the holy gate are appropriate only for those pure in heart and who are competent enough for austere practice. For those who are indolent and without faith, such endeavors would not only be difficult, they may become the cause of negative deeds.

On the other hand, within the nembutsu gate, the recitation of nembutsu is performed while walking, standing, sitting, or lying down, awake or asleep, without regard to the manner in which it is recited. Nembutsu is also recited without regard to one's ability. All ways of nembutsu lead, without doubt, to birth in the Pure Land.

In the *Liturgy for the Rite of the Fivefold Rhythmic Chanting of Nien-fo*, Monk Fa-chao stated:

> When Amida Buddha was a bodhisattva, he made the universal vow for saving sentient beings, saying, "I will come to welcome all those who listen to and meditate on my name. I will not discriminate between the poor and the rich, or between the ignorant and the erudite. I will not choose only the learned observers of the precepts or the wrongdoers who are in breach of the precepts. If they turn their meritorious hearts toward birth in the Pure Land and recite my name many times, I will welcome them to the Pure Land, like broken tiles and pebbles turned into gold."[195]

Even the schooled who have mastered holy sutras, commentaries, and sacred teachings are unable to recite them at the end of their lives. In contrast, one can utter nembutsu until the very moment of one's death.

On examining the vow of a buddha, it is notable that of the twelve vows of the Medicine Buddha (Tathāgata Bhaiṣajyaguru), there is no vow like the one in which Amida Buddha promised that he would not realize enlightenment until he succeeded in fulfilling his vows in their entirety. In the vows of Bodhisattva Sahasrabhuja Sahasranetra, he promised that he would not realize enlightenment until the fulfillment of all of his vows, but he has yet to realize enlightenment. In contrast, Amida Buddha also made the same vows as the above two yet did achieve enlightenment, and ten eons have elapsed since then.

If one is incapable of faith in the essential vow, one probably has no faith in the teachings of other buddhas as well. This is why one should believe in the exclusive practice of nembutsu, without thoughts of any other teachings, and recite nembutsu diligently day and night, morning and evening, while walking, standing, sitting, or lying down. It is said that many in the present day who endeavor in the exclusive practice of nembutsu attain birth in the Pure Land, and that very few among those following the miscellaneous practices attain birth in the Pure Land.

Despite all this, there may be some misguided individuals who remain critical of the teaching of nembutsu. These people become increasingly hostile and sarcastic, declaring: "All sutras, commentaries, and sacred teachings of old that have been taught by Buddha Śākyamuni are of no value and will eventually be laid by the wayside." However, such critical individuals are not related to the eminent monks who have served in the head temples of the Tendai school and the Hossō school, those who attained fame, or to those respectable people who have served the court in hopes of gaining official status. They are also unrelated to those who have great potential and wisdom.

Those who have the right understanding and view about the teaching of nembutsu should know that being critical of nembutsu wrongly emphasizes the holy gate. Further, pursuing the teaching of nembutsu while practicing the holy gate and nembutsu concurrently may indicate that the holy gate is being practiced as an auxiliary act to the practice of nembutsu. This fact will certainly doom one's practice of the holy gate.

I have stated these teachings of the nembutsu gate without ulterior motive. Those who worry about deliverance in the life to come sometimes hold mistaken notions and engage in the miscellaneous practices without regard for the time or abilities. They regrettably abandon the essential vow of Amida Buddha, even though they have been born through much difficulty in the world of human beings and have encountered the essential vow only after much difficulty. They will return to the three lower realms as their former abodes, where they will transmigrate in the delusive worlds of saṃsāra for immeasurable eons.

Here, I have recorded the teachings of nembutsu for birth in the Pure Land because I am concerned about their future conditions. Hence, the teaching of nembutsu should not be a source of animosity on the part of other Buddhist schools toward Jōdo Shū.

8. An Outline of the Essentials of Jōdo Shū

IN THE PRESENT DAY, no way is superior to attainment of birth in the Pure Land of Amida Buddha for departing from the delusive worlds of saṃsāra; no practice is superior to the recitation of nembutsu for the attainment of birth in the Pure Land.

Upon departure from this ephemeral world, there are many gates for entering the path leading to enlightenment. These can be categorized into two major gates: the holy gate and the Pure Land gate. First, the holy gate applies to the path of transcending delusions and realizing enlightenment in this world. The holy gate can also be categorized into two: the holy gate of Mahāyāna Buddhism and the holy gate of Hīnayāna Buddhism. The holy gate of Mahāyāna Buddhism is further divided into two: the Buddha Vehicle and the Bodhisattva Vehicle. [The holy gate of Hīnayāna Buddhism is also divided into two: the Śrāvaka Vehicle—the path to becoming an arhat through hearing the Dharma—and the Pratyekabuddha Vehicle, the path to attaining enlightenment through one's personal efforts.] These varied ways are referred to as the *four vehicles.*

However, the practices of the four vehicles are too difficult for us to perform today. Therefore, Master Tao-ch'o stated, "In the present day, the teaching of the holy gate is an extremely difficult way to realize enlightenment."[196] It would be meaningless to extrapolate here on the various practices of the holy gate. We should merely consider that because many years have passed since the death of Buddha Śākyamuni, it is difficult to comprehend the teachings of the holy gate in order to realize enlightenment. It is also a path unfit for us, delusive, common mortals.

Second, the Pure Land gate teaches us the path to loathe and renounce this world of anguish and to be born speedily in the Pure Land. Birth in the Pure Land is achieved by the grace of the essential vow of Amida Buddha, who does not discriminate between good and bad. This birth is determined by belief or nonbelief in the essential vow. Master Tao-ch'o therefore said, "The Pure Land gate is the sole teaching for the path leading to enlightenment."[197] Hence, those who desire departure from the delusive worlds of transmigration should abandon the difficult holy gate and aspire for birth in the Pure Land through the easy Pure Land gate.

The holy gate and the Pure Land gate are called the *difficult path* and the *easy path.* To illustrate, the difficult path is akin to traversing a treacherous road on foot; the easy path corresponds to crossing the ocean on a ship. The lame and sightless are unable to travel an arduous route, but the ship will transport them with ease to the far shore.

It is as if our vision of wisdom is impaired and our legs of religious discipline are paralyzed today. There is no hope for trekking across the treacherous road, the difficult path of the holy gate. Only by the ship, the essential vow, are we able to cross the delusive ocean of saṃsāra to reach the shore of the Pure Land of Ultimate Bliss. The "ship" we speak of is symbolic of the essential vow of Amida Buddha.

This essential vow is: In ancient times, when Amida Buddha's aspiration to enlightenment was first awakened and he renounced his throne to lead an ascetic life, he made forty-eight vows to establish his own Pure Land in order to save sentient beings. The eighteenth vow promised, "If, when I am to attain buddhahood, all sentient beings in the ten directions who wish to be born in my buddhaland who call my name at least ten times are not born there by the power of my vow, I will not realize buddhahood."[198] Amida Buddha realized his aspiration on the basis of the eighteenth vow and attained buddhahood ten eons ago.

Master Shan-tao's interpretation states, "The fact is that Amida Buddha did attain buddhahood and presently resides in the Pure Land. It should be known that his essential vow was not made in vain. If sentient beings recite his name, they will, with certainty, attain birth in the Pure Land."[199]

Considering this statement, nembutsu devotees who have faith in the essential vow and recite nembutsu should not have a shadow of a doubt in the attainment of birth in the Pure Land. Deeply understand the teaching of Master Shan-tao, believe in the essential vow above all, recite nembutsu with all your heart, and harbor no doubt in spite of attempts by detractors with different views to erode your faith in the essential vow.

On this authority, you should recognize that the practices of the holy gate are beyond your capabilities, abandon the holy gate, enter the Pure Land gate, place your esteem in the essential vow, and say the name of Amida Buddha. A person such as this is called a *practitioner of the Pure Land gate*. Thus, these are referred to as the holy gate and the Pure Land gate.

There is, however, one condition necessary for the practice of the Pure Land gate. It is that one's faith and one's practice should be in harmony. Here, faith is called the *steadfast heart*, and practice, the *practice*. The steadfast heart refers to the condition of the heart of the nembutsu devotee who aspires to birth in the Pure Land. The *Meditation Sutra* describes: "If there is one who aspires to be born in the Pure Land, this birth is attained by awakening the threefold devotional heart. What is the threefold devotional heart? The first aspect is the genuine heart, the second, the profound heart, and the third, the heart that seeks birth in the Pure Land through the dedication of merit. Those who embody the threefold devotional heart will be born in the Pure Land without fail."[200]

Master Shan-tao thus interpreted the [first aspect of the] threefold devotional heart:

> First is the genuine heart (Ch. *chih-ch'eng-hsin*). The Chinese term *chih* refers to truth, and *ch'eng* to the quality of being sincere. The author, with this interpretation of *chih* and *ch'eng*, would like to clarify that both understanding and practice performed by all sentient beings through their physical, verbal, and mental acts must be done with the genuine heart. Do not outwardly pretend to be wise, virtuous, and diligent while inwardly harboring falsity and fickleness.[201]
>
> One should perform these acts in the spirit of sincerity with a truly genuine heart without regard to matters of the inner mind or outer appearances, whether they are visible or hidden. This is what is meant by the genuine heart.[202]

This means that the genuine heart is a heart filled with sincerity. "Sincerity" is not disguising one's inner feelings with an embellished facade when one acts, speaks, or thinks. When we loathe this defiled world of suffering and long for birth in the Pure Land, our outer appearances and inner selves must be compatible. We should not pretend to have sagacity while harboring unwholesomeness; we should not pretend industriousness while indulging in laziness. Master Shan-tao said, "Do not outwardly pretend to be wise, virtuous, and diligent while inwardly harboring falsity and fickleness."

Regarding nembutsu, the genuine heart does not claim to have repeated the name of Amida Buddha sixty or seventy thousand times a day when this is not true; neither is it the genuine heart that dons a noble mien and recites nembutsu in public without doing so in private. This is not to say, however, that unsavory thoughts should be exposed.

In short, it is essential that we truly desire to be in tune with the heart of Amida Buddha, and that we have a sincere heart while making an effort to avoid matters that are unpleasant to others. Betraying our genuine feelings merely to avoid unpleasantness, however, surrenders the genuine heart. Whatever the circumstance, our genuineness should be steadfast, and outwardly there should be no pretentiousness in our actions. This is called the *genuine heart.*

The second aspect of faith is the profound heart. Master Shan-tao interpreted the profound heart as follows:

> The profound heart is the heart of profound faith, which also has two aspects. The first is to firmly believe that one is a common mortal with worldly passions whose virtuous roots are shallow and meager and who does not possess the karmic condition to detach oneself from the delusive triple realms through which one has transmigrated for countless eons up to this day.
>
> The second is to have unshakable faith that Amida Buddha will embrace sentient beings with his forty-eight vows, and to believe that one who recites his name at least ten times will, with certainty, attain birth in the Pure Land through the power of his essential vow. One must not harbor a doubt about this even for a moment. Hence, this implicit belief is called the *profound heart.*[203]
>
> One who possesses the profound heart establishes decisively an unshakable faith, practices in accordance with the teachings of Amida Buddha, permanently excludes doubt and falsity, and will not fall back or be swayed by all of those who have different understandings, practices, teachings, and views and misleading opinions.[204]

The meaning of Master Shan-tao's interpretation is that first, one must believe in one's own limitations, and second, one must trust the essential vow. He pointed out the first faith in order to establish the latter one. Another reason he mentioned these two aspects of belief in this order is that, without first pointing out a person's limitations, those who aspire for birth in the Pure Land and who practice the nembutsu taught in the essential vow will develop the worldly passions of greed and anger and live in fear of committing the ten transgressions and the violation of the precepts. They could, therefore, feel hopeless and doubt the essential vow.

In anticipation of the emergence of such doubts, Master Shan-tao pointed to the two aspects of devout hearts and said, "Although we may be common mortals with worldly passions, if we recite nembutsu as few as ten times, or just once, with profound reliance on the essential vow, birth in the Pure Land will be assured for all."[205] Had Master Shan-tao not stressed the reason for accepting that we are common mortals, we, with mundane hearts, would not be in accord with the essential vow regardless of how much nembutsu we performed. We might also think that birth in the Pure Land through a single utterance or ten recitations of nembutsu is possible only for those flawless mortals who have no worldly passions or karmic defilements—not for flawed mortals like ourselves.

When we are overcome with such self-doubt, and are questioning the possibility of birth in the Pure Land for those of us with human frailties, instruction on these two aspects of belief fills us with elation. Those who are unable to understand the interpretation of Master Shan-tao may say that birth in the Pure Land is impossible for them due to their wicked hearts. This birth may eventually really become impossible for them, but it will be because of their doubtful hearts. Accept this interpretation, and hereafter never question birth in the Pure Land through nembutsu.

There is no need to reflect on virtue and vice, or to discuss the gravity of your karmic defilements. Establish the unshakable faith that if you simply mouth *Namu Amida Butsu* along with the aspiration for birth in the Pure Land, you will most certainly attain this birth through the grace of the essential vow. Because of this implicit faith, the karma of birth in the Pure Land will be generated. The attainment of birth in the Pure Land will be uncertain if you doubt this birth; the attainment of birth in the Pure Land will be certain if you believe in this birth.

To put the matter simply, the profound heart is the implicit faith and trust, beyond a shadow of doubt, that if you deeply rely upon the essential vow, you will certainly be welcomed into the Pure Land, regardless of the kind of person you are.

Nevertheless, we are admonished not to be impulsive in our actions as a result of misinterpreting the concept of nondiscrimination. Master Shan-tao commented, "With a genuine heart, abandon the three categories of unwholesome karma, but in turn, nurture, with the same genuine heart, the three categories of wholesome karma."[206] He further stated, "Respectfully distance yourself from, and never willingly submit to, unwholesome karma."[207]

Accordingly, make every effort to be free of unwholesome karma and, in turn, to conduct yourself virtuously. Firmly believe that the essential vow does not discriminate between the virtuous and non-virtuous and that anyone who recites the name of Amida Buddha will be welcomed by him. Believe also that his name has the power to nullify karmic offenses, and that a single utterance, or ten recitations, will bring birth in the Pure Land. There should be no doubt in the heart of the nembutsu devotee.

Recitation of nembutsu should not be limited to a single utterance in spite of the teaching that a single utterance suffices to attain birth in the Pure Land. The true intention of the essential vow is that if you establish faith in Amida Buddha and recite *Namu Amida Butsu* for a hundred years, ten or twenty years, four or five years, one or two years, or seven days, one day, or even ten times, you will certainly be welcomed by him.

As a rule, the upper limit of continual recitation is from the first moment of the awareness of nembutsu until the moment of death; the middle term, from seven days to one day; and the lowest limit, from ten recitations to just a single utterance. Since nembutsu has the compassionate power of Amida Buddha's essential vow, you must believe that you will, with certainty, achieve birth in the Pure Land with just a single utterance. You do not need to fix the number of nembutsu in accord with the essential vow; just continue reciting without interruption until the end of your life.

There are some who sincerely aspire for birth in the Pure Land, depend on the essential vow, and recite nembutsu diligently; they do not suffer in their last moments. This is because Amida Buddha comes to escort these nembutsu devotees in their final moment in order to establish the rightly settled state of mind for birth in the Pure Land. If this is not understood, the devotee may think that he must repeat nembutsu at the time of death with the rightly settled state of mind, and only then will Amida Buddha arrive to welcome him for birth in the Pure Land. This person does not truly believe in the essential vow or understand the lessons in the sutras.

The *Sutra in Praise of the Pure Land* teaches, "Amida Buddha embraces the nembutsu devotee through his compassion and protects him from disturbances to his serenity."[208] Diligence in practicing nembutsu in daily life causes the arrival of Amida Buddha at the time of death. That is, in seeing the coming of Amida Buddha, the devotee then is able to arrive at a state called "abiding in the rightly settled state of mind for birth in the Pure Land."

Regrettably, many people feel futility in the daily nembutsu and merely desire the state of abiding in the rightly settled state of mind for birth in the Pure Land at the time of death. These are extremely misguided thoughts. Those who believe in the essential vow must not have any doubt about their time for departure. Daily nembutsu should be recited with ever-increasing commitment. Was it ever stated in the essential vow that Amida Buddha will accept only one who recites nembutsu on his deathbed?

The issue of birth in the Pure Land through nembutsu at the time of death is taught in the *Meditation Sutra*, which states that a person who has not aspired for birth in the Pure Land has lived a meaningless life. Still such a person may have his first encounter with a virtuous teacher at the time of his death, and with this encouragement recite nembutsu and nonetheless achieve birth in the Pure Land.[209]

Those with a fundamental belief in nembutsu do not need to discuss the matter of their death in particular. If belief in the arrival of Amida Buddha is unshakable, abiding in the rightly settled state of mind for birth in the Pure Land at the time of death follows as a matter of course. Hold this fast in your heart.

The forgoing instruction teaches us not to be defeated by those who have different views and practices[210] and means that we should not forsake nembutsu nor begin to question birth in the Pure Land, nor fall under the influence of those who study different teachings and observe practices different from our own. "Those who follow different teachings" are usually the scholarly monks of the eight traditional Buddhist schools, such as the Tendai school and the Hossō school. "Those who perform different practices" are all the practitioners of the Shingon school and of the Shikan [Tendai][211] school. They study and practice the teachings of the holy gate. The instructions and practices of the holy gate are different from those of the Pure Land gate; therefore, they are called "different views and practices" within the nembutsu tradition.

Incidentally, among the nembutsu practitioners there may be a devotee who does not depend on the essential vow, who relies on his personal efforts, and who devotes himself to the recitation of nembutsu. How can this type of person attain birth in the Pure Land?

There may be one who says that this birth, a matter of great importance, can be achieved through cultivating different kinds of merit from practices other than nembutsu, serving buddhas other than Amida Buddha, and combining these merits and service with nembutsu. He may also say that birth in the Pure Land is impossible if it is only through the reliance on the compassion of Amida Buddha. Even though someone questions birth in the Pure Land and tries to deter us with doubts by stating the above, we should not listen to him. I admonish you all that we must believe in the teaching of Amida Buddha, have no doubt in our hearts even for a moment, regardless of any deterrent, and never lose our absolute commitment to the assurance of birth in the Pure Land.

Master Shan-tao went into detail to explain the rationale for not being defeated by others. The essence of his warning is this: There may be myriad buddhas filling the ten directions, emanating their brilliant light, and extending their tongues, saying, "It is a misguided teaching that birth in the Pure Land is assured through nembutsu for common mortals with worldly passions. You should not believe in this." Even though you hear this, your implicit faith in birth in the Pure Land must not, even for a moment, be swayed.

This is because all buddhas, with the same compassionate hearts, save sentient beings. For instance, Amida Buddha planned to establish the Pure Land and vowed, "If, when I am to realize buddhahood, all sentient beings in the ten directions who wish to be born in my buddhaland who recite my name are not born there, I will not realize enlightenment."[212]

Upon hearing this, Buddha Śākyamuni appeared in this world and expounded on the essential vow of Amida Buddha to humankind. All the buddhas in the six directions, as countless as the grains of sand in the Ganges, extended their tongues, covered the three thousand great-thousand worlds and, showing their excellent marks without any pretense, stated: "There is no doubt that Buddha Śākyamuni extolled the essential vow and told all sentient beings that birth in the Pure Land is certainly achieved through the recitation of nembutsu. All sentient beings must believe in this teaching." Thus did the buddhas in the six directions authenticate the validity of birth in the Pure Land through nembutsu.

Since every buddha, in concert and without exception, encourages all common mortals to attain birth in the Pure Land through nembutsu with implicit faith in the essential vow, we should not be alarmed if some false buddhas repudiate the attainment of birth in the Pure Land. And if a buddha is unable to shake our resolve, so should we stand fast against a śrāvaka or pratyekabuddha who expresses a similarly dissident opinion. The misguided opinions of common people are to be ignored all the more. Knowing this, once we believe in birth in the Pure Land through nembutsu, we should neither falter nor harbor any doubt, regardless of what is said by whom. This is called the *profound heart.*

The third aspect of faith is the heart that seeks birth in the Pure Land through the dedication of merit. Master Shan-tao interpreted this heart as follows:

> The heart that seeks birth in the Pure Land through the dedication of merit means to rejoice completely in the worldly and transcendent physical, verbal, and mental virtues of oneself and other ordinary and holy beings, which have accumulated in both previous and present lives, as well as to desire to dedicate these virtues for the sake of birth in the Pure Land with the genuine and profound hearts. For this reason, this is called the *heart that seeks birth in the Pure Land through the dedication of merit.*
>
> Moreover, one who aspires for birth in the Pure Land through the dedication of merit must have implicit faith in this birth with a genuine heart. This steadfast heart must be as solid as an adamantine stone, without being swayed and defeated by those who have different views, studies, understandings, and practices.[213]

This interpretation means that all the merits we have accumulated in our previous lives must be dedicated toward the Pure Land in our desire for birth there. Besides our own merits, all the merits earned by other common people as well as holy beings will also be dedicated. Here, the term *common* refers to the merits accumulated by the common people, and the word *holy* to the merits of buddhas and bodhisattvas. By rejoicing in the benevolent acts of mortals as well as buddhas and bodhisattvas, we make these merits our own; we then ask that these merits be dedicated toward the attainment of birth in the Pure Land. In sum, we must not desire anything but birth in the Pure Land.

We must not pray for good fortune for ourselves and others in this life, neither should we wish to be born in pure buddhalands other than the Pure Land of Amida Buddha in the next life, nor should we hope to be reborn in the delusive realms of human beings or heavenly beings. We must not dedicate the merit toward anything other than the Pure Land. If, before gaining proper understanding, your prayers were concerned with occurrences in this defiled world and merits were dedicated in a mistaken direction, these merits should be reclaimed in order for you to concentrate on dedicating them toward birth in the Pure Land of Amida Buddha.

To say that all merits should be dedicated to the Pure Land does not, however, mean that one should accumulate benevolent acts at the exclusion of nembutsu for the purpose of dedication. It merely means that all previous merits should be dedicated toward birth in the Pure Land at the present time and in the future; one should continue to give alms to monks, make charitable gifts to others, and to dedicate all benevolent acts toward birth in the Pure Land. This conviction must be as solid as an adamantine stone. One should not dedicate one's own merit hither and thither under the instruction of a wrongful teacher. The heart that seeks birth in the Pure Land through the dedication of merit should be unbreakable like an adamantine stone. One should aspire for this birth with this unshakable heart.

These are the conditions of the threefold devotional heart. According to Master Shan-tao: "One who possesses the threefold devotional heart will, with certainty, attain birth in the Pure Land. If one aspect of the threefold devotional heart is lacking, the realization of birth in the Pure Land will become impossible."[214] Hence, those who desire birth in the Pure Land must be endowed with the threefold devotional heart. Thus described, the threefold devotional heart may seem divided and exaggerated; yet, if one truly comprehends the concept, it is easily possessed. The threefold devotional heart only means that one should be genuine, have profound faith in the essential vow, and aspire for birth in the Pure Land.

There may be differences in the depth of commitment; but among those who aspire for birth in the Pure Land, could there be one who lacks genuineness? A cursory view of the threefold devotional heart makes the concept seem difficult, but close examination reveals its simplicity. Close scrutiny makes it possible for the uninformed to be so endowed, and even on occasion, for the informed to be lacking in some aspects of the threefold devotional heart.

Birth in the Pure Land may be attained by the base and ignorant while an outstanding, exalted holy man, due to some grievous condition at his time of death, may not attain birth in the Pure Land. With full awareness that the threefold devotional heart should be possessed, we should verify their possession and exert effort toward being able to possess all the aspects of the threefold devotional heart. This attitude is called the *steadfast heart* and is the condition of a heart for birth in the Pure Land. We should understand this well.

Regarding the "practice" for birth in the Pure Land, Master Shan-tao stated, "Although there are various practices for birth in the Pure Land, they can be roughly divided into two: the first is the right practices and the second is the miscellaneous practices."[215] The right practices include many practices: (1) the right practice of reciting the three sutras of Pure Land Buddhism, (2) the right practice of contemplating Amida Buddha, (3) the right practice of worshiping Amida Buddha, (4) the right practice of reciting the name of Amida Buddha, and (5) the right practice of praising and making offerings to Amida Buddha. These are called the *five right practices.* When the practices of praising and making offerings are divided, the practices are referred to as the *six right practices.*

Master Shan-tao further divided the right practices into two categories, saying, "First is the devotional act of reciting the name of Amida Buddha every moment while walking, standing, sitting, or lying down, throughout the day and night, and of continuing the recitation without cessation throughout one's life. This is called the *rightly established practice*, which is in accordance with the essential vow of Amida Buddha."[216] Master Shan-tao considered the vocal nembutsu to be the essential karmic cause for birth in the Pure Land.

He continued, "If we rely on the right practices of worship and recitation of sutras and so forth for birth in the Pure Land, these acts are called the *auxiliary practices.*"[217] This means that the right practices other than the recitation of nembutsu, such as worshiping Amida Buddha, reciting the three sutras of Pure Land Buddhism, meditating on the adornments of the Pure Land of Ultimate Bliss, performing praise, and making offerings to Amida Buddha, exist to serve as enhancements to the recitation of nembutsu. That is, the rightly established practice is the recitation of nembutsu only.

Excluding the rightly established practice and the auxiliary practices, all other practices, such as the six perfections, reciting the *Lotus Sutra*, observing Shingon (verses containing mystic truth), and other various practices are called the *miscellaneous practices.*

Master Shan-tao, therefore, encouraged us, saying, "If your singular desire is birth in the Pure Land, implement the rightly established practice: that is, the repetition of nembutsu with utmost intensity. This is because the rightly established practice is the one in accord with the essential vow. If departure from the delusive worlds of saṃsāra were possible through self-power, this practice would not be limited only to the essential vow; but because birth in the Pure Land is impossible without the aid of the power other than self [i.e., the compassion of Amida Buddha], we must rely on the power of the essential vow of Amida Buddha and fervently recite his name."

Self power refers to striving to attain birth in the Pure Land through one's personal efforts, and the *power other than self* refers to unconditional faith in the compassionate power of Amida Buddha. Therefore, one who pursues the right practices is called an *exclusive practitioner*, and one who pursues the miscellaneous practices is called a *desultory practitioner.*

Master Shan-tao stated, "One who observes the right practices always holds the Pure Land close at heart, and there is uninterrupted mindfulness of Amida Buddha. On the other hand, one who performs the miscellaneous practices is interrupted while being mindful of Amida Buddha. Birth in the Pure Land is still possible for a desultory practitioner by dedicating his merit to Amida Buddha; such practice is referred to as *estranged miscellaneous practice*."[218] These practices are regarded as remote from the Pure Land. Master Shan-tao further narrates:

> Ten out of ten, one hundred out of one hundred, the exclusive practitioner of nembutsu will attain birth in the Pure Land. This is because (1) he achieves the rightly settled state of mind for birth without being disturbed by other miscellaneous karmic conditions, (2) nembutsu is in accord with the essential vow of Amida Buddha, and (3) nembutsu follows the teachings of Buddha Śākyamuni.
>
> In contrast, among those who perform the miscellaneous practices, only one or two out of one hundred and four or five out of one thousand attain birth in the Pure Land. The reasons for this are (1) the miscellaneous practices are not in accord with the essential vow of Amida Buddha, (2) the miscellaneous practices do not follow the teachings of Buddha Śākyamuni, (3) the thoughts of Amida Buddha become interrupted or (4) they are related to renown and personal gain, and (5) the miscellanous practices become an obstacle to one's own path to birth in the Pure Land as well as the path of others.[219]

Those who believe in Master Shan-tao and who wish to enter Jōdo Shū should intently exercise the rightly established practice, commensurate with their capability, and recite from ten or twenty thousand, up to fifty, sixty, or one hundred thousand nembutsu daily.

Despite this understanding, there are still many who perform other practices in addition to nembutsu. This is incomprehensible, because there is no reason for practitioners to supplement what is advised by Master Shan-tao. It is vital to perform the rightly established practice as Master Shan-tao suggested; including the miscellaneous practices unsanctioned by Master Shan-tao would be meaningless.

Some say that because even the bad can achieve birth in the Pure Land, it is possible to attain birth in the Pure Land through the meritorious practice of reciting the *Lotus Sutra*. This is a misguided view. The recitation of sutras becomes an excellent practice if it is performed as an auxiliary act toward attaining birth in the Pure Land. Some also assume that the recitation of sutras is an excellent practice because it becomes an auxiliary act for attaining birth in the Pure Land, and that therefore the recitation of sutras is superior and will never prevent birth in the Pure Land. If they practice reciting sutras together with nembutsu while having these thoughts, the practice will be ineffective.

Concerning wrongdoings, is the intention of Amida Buddha to promote nonvirtuous deeds? Amida Buddha taught that one should never indulge in nonvirtue; however, we are common mortals. From time to time, we commit unwholesome deeds because of our nature as common people. It is beyond our ability to prevent this. Amida Buddha, with his compassion, will not abandon such mortals like us. However, if one practices nembutsu together with other practices, just as with one who is happy to engage in nonvirtue, the compassionate power of Amida Buddha will not be effective. To believe that reciting a sutra is equivalent to committing base acts and that the acts become good deeds is preposterous.

As profound as the teachings of Amida Buddha may be, it mortifies and saddens us to encounter those with mistaken understandings about his teachings. You should not guide anyone who has an understanding different from yours and who does not listen to what you say, but it is proper to guide one who follows your guidance. There should never be an argument with anyone who espouses mistaken beliefs. Intently pray for birth in the Pure Land, fervently practice nembutsu, realize this birth with the high grade, and hurry back to earth in order to save the rest of humanity.

In *Hymns in Praise of Birth in the Pure Land*, Master Shan-tao expounds as follows:

Question: What virtues and merits are in this life if we recite the name of Amida Buddha, worship, and meditate on him?

Answer: If one utters the name of Amida Buddha just once, the grave offenses binding one to saṃsāra for eight billion eons are eradicated.

The *Sutra of the Ten Right Practices for Birth in the Pure Land*[220] states: "If there is someone who meditates upon Amida Buddha and aspires for birth in the Pure Land, Amida Buddha will immediately deploy the twenty-five bodhisattvas to protect him. Whether you are walking, sitting, standing, or lying down, whether it is day or night, Amida Buddha will sever your connection to malevolent spirits and deities in order to protect you."

The *Meditation Sutra* states: "If there is someone who recites the name of Amida Buddha and desires to be born in the Pure Land, Amida Buddha will immediately send innumerable miraculously created buddhas, Bodhisattva Avalokiteśvara, and Bodhisattva Mahāsthāmaprāpta in order to protect the nembutsu practitioner. The twenty-five attendant bodhisattvas of Amida Buddha, including Bodhisattva Avalokiteśvara and Bodhisattva Mahāsthāmaprāpta, surround the nembutsu practitioner a hundredfold and a thousandfold and are never apart from him regardless of time and place, whether he is walking, standing, sitting, or lying down, whether it is day or night."

One who meditates on Amida Buddha and wishes to be born in the Pure Land will always be protected by all the buddhas of the six directions, as countless as the grains of sand of the Ganges. For this reason, this *Meditation Sutra* is referred to as the *Sutra of Protection*.

> We should now rely upon this vow of the dominant karmic relationship, and all followers should prepare themselves for birth in the Pure Land.[221]

This means that all buddhas and bodhisattvas in the ten directions, Bodhisattva Avalokiteśvara, Bodhisattva Mahāsthāmaprāpta, and countless other bodhisattvas, as well as Amida Buddha, surround the nembutsu devotee who firmly believes in the essential vow and aspires for birth in the Pure Land. They are in his shadow day and night whether he is walking, standing, sitting, or lying down. They dispel malevolent spirits and deities that deceive him. They relieve him from any trouble inconsistent with reason and enable him to live in peace. They come to welcome him into the Pure Land when his end arrives. Accordingly, one who believes in nembutsu and desires birth in the Pure Land need not pray to other buddhas or deities or observe abstinence in order to ward off malevolent spirits.

Those who rely upon the Buddha, the Dharma, and the Sangha are always protected by the benevolence of the king of deities and his attendant deities, as numerous as the sands of the Ganges. How could any buddha or deity torment you or deter you from your goal when the blessings of innumerable benevolent buddhas and deities surround and protect you?

Reducing residual karma has its limits. An illness that one contracts in daily life cannot be overcome by prayers to various buddhas and deities. If prayer healed and prolonged life, there would be no illness or death. Still, the compassionate power of Amida Buddha lessens the illnesses based on one's residual karma. This is called *lessening the burden.*

Much more, Amida Buddha protects one from untimely accidental death. Whatever illness befalls the nembutsu devotee, that misfortune is the result of residual karma. It should be thought that although one was supposed to receive a heavy burden, the power of Amida Buddha lessened the burden. Amida Buddha eliminates our burden of karmic defilements and enables us to attain birth in the Pure Land, the great religious goal. There is no reason not to believe that Amida Buddha can prolong our short life and lessen our illness in daily life.

Consequently, Master Shan-tao said that those whose faith in birth in the Pure Land in the next life and in the essential vow was less than profound would not enjoy the embrace and protection of holy beings. While reciting nembutsu, we must arouse profound faith, loathe this defiled world of suffering, and long for the Pure Land.

Maintain and understand this teaching, steadfastly offer your devotion, and practice nembutsu. Never belittle this detailed teaching, saying that these are personal opinions and misrepresentations.

I studied exclusively the words of Master Shan-tao and extracted meaning from ancient writings and commentaries. Try to understand with sincerity and without question.

Please understand what I have taught here. No way is superior to the recitation of nembutsu for the attainment of birth in the Pure Land.

*Dōkō's note: This reply was composed at the behest of the nun holding the second rank in the court of Kamakura, Hōjō Masako,[222] and presented to her.

9. A Reply to the Lady Kujō[223]

WITH GREAT RESPECT to my lady, I am elated to learn that you are reciting nembutsu. Indeed, the recitation of nembutsu is a wondrous practice for the attainment of birth in the Pure Land of Ultimate Bliss. This is because nembutsu is the practice taught in the essential vow made by Amida Buddha. Practices other than nembutsu, such as Shingon and Shikan, are honorable practices, but they are not in accord with the essential vow of Amida Buddha.

Nembutsu is also the practice entrusted to Ānanda by Buddha Śākyamuni. Practices other than nembutsu are included in the meditative practices for a focused mind and for a distracted mind, both eminently worthy practices, but these are not the teachings entrusted to him by Buddha Śākyamuni.

In addition, nembutsu is the practice that has been attested by all the buddhas in the six directions. Practices other than nembutsu also exist, such as noble exoteric and esoteric teachings, and meditation on the phenomenal aspect of reality and on the noumenal principle, but they have not been validated by the various buddhas. For this reason, although there are numerous Buddhist practices, nembutsu is the single most valid practice for birth in the Pure Land.

Those who are ignorant of the path to birth in the Pure Land claim that nembutsu, which is an easy path to birth in the Pure Land, is designed for those who are unable to endure the practices of the Shingon and Shikan. This view is absolutely wrong.

I maintain that one should abandon practices other than nembutsu because such practices are not in accordance with the essential vow of Amida Buddha. Refrain from choosing them because they were not selected by Buddha Śākyamuni and were not validated by the manifold buddhas.

I instead encourage one to rely upon the essential vow, to accept the teaching chosen by Buddha Śākyamuni, to submit to the teaching of the buddhas, to rid oneself of ignorant thoughts, and to recite wondrous nembutsu while aspiring for birth in the Pure Land. This is what is meant by the passage, "The recitation of nembutsu is essential among karmic practices for birth in the Pure Land," found in the *Collection of Essentials on Attaining Birth in the Pure Land*[224] by Eshin-sōzu.

In the present age, one must cease other practices and recite nembutsu with all one's heart. Within the practice of nembutsu, the most worthy is the single-hearted and exclusive recitation of nembutsu. This is explained in the *Commentary on the Meditation Sutra* by Master Shan-tao, who truly realized the state of samādhi through reciting nembutsu.

Besides the *Commentary on the Meditation Sutra*, the *Two-Fascicle Sutra* (*Larger Sutra*) teaches, "Meditate single-heartedly and exclusively on the Buddha of Immeasurable Light."[225] Here "single-heartedly" is in contrast with twofold or threefold practices. That is, one should distinguish the practice of nembutsu from other practices and abandon all practices other than nembutsu.

Practicing nembutsu when it is time for your prayers is a marvelous act; therefore, the *Collection of Essentials on Attaining Birth in the Pure Land* has explained the reason for the superiority of nembutsu over other practices. Furthermore, Dengyō-daishi's[226] *Instructions of Destroying the Seven Disasters*[227] also prevails upon the reader to vocalize nembutsu.

Nembutsu is a real practice blessed and protected by the celestial beings of the delusive triple realms as well as numerous buddhas in the ten directions. In this life and the next, no practice surpasses nembutsu. At this time, please strive to become a single-hearted and exclusive practitioner of nembutsu for attaining birth in the Pure Land of Amida Buddha.

10. A Reply to the Nun Holding the Second Rank in the Court of Kamakura[228]

I HAVE HUMBLY read your letter in detail. Buddha Śākyamuni once stated, "The virtue of the recitation of nembutsu is so profound that even I cannot expound upon it all." Both Śāriputra, the most knowledgeable disciple of Buddha Śākyamuni, and Ānanda, the most erudite disciple of Buddha Śākyamuni, also admitted to their lack of complete knowledge regarding the merit of nembutsu. Nembutsu has an extensive root of virtue; therefore, one such as I could not possibly expound upon its merit.

I, Genkū, have studied the voluminous Buddhist scriptures that have found their way to our country; however, I do not think that all Pure Land texts are in existence here. Even the Pure Land scriptures from China cannot be fully elucidated in one or two years. Nonetheless, since you have asked, I will relate some thoughts to you.

The nonbelievers in nembutsu say that because the lay priest of Kumagai and Saburō of Tsunoto[229] are unschooled, I, Hōnen-bō Genkū, encourage them to recite nembutsu exclusively rather than pursue other practices. This is a totally mistaken criticism.

The practice of nembutsu does not discriminate between the learned and the unschooled. Long ago the essential vow of Amida Buddha was designed for saving all sentient beings. It does not promote nembutsu for the unschooled nor other practices for the scholarly. The essential vow was established for all beings in the ten directions; therefore, nembutsu does not discriminate between the learned and the unschooled, the virtuous and the nonvirtuous, those who observe the precepts and those who violate them, those of high and low status, or between male and female.

For those who lived at the time of Buddha Śākyamuni, those who lived after his death, and even those who will live during the extinction of the Three Jewels after the period of the decline of the Dharma that lasts ten thousand years, nembutsu has and will serve as the sole practice for deliverance in this world.

Master Shan-tao was the manifestation of Amida Buddha. In his compassion for all sentient beings, Master Shan-tao pursued the study of the entire Buddhist scriptures and encouraged the exclusive practice of nembutsu. Nembutsu, as a skillful means for saving all sentient beings, is the teaching suitable for this period of the decline of the Dharma.

Have faith in the essential vow that you extensively exercise, comply thoroughly with the heart of Master Shan-tao, and exhort the sole teaching of nembutsu. How can birth in the Pure Land through nembutsu be limited to the unschooled? How can it be impossible for the learned to attain birth in the Pure Land? If this were so, it would be contrary to the essential vow of Amida Buddha and a betrayal of the intent of Master Shan-tao. I, therefore, encourage all who come asking about the way to birth in the Pure Land to commit themselves to the exclusive practice of nembutsu regardless of their intellectual abilities.

Those who attempt to discourage the exclusive practice of nembutsu through such falsehoods did not hear the teachings of the nembutsu samādhi for attaining birth in the Pure Land in their previous existence, and in their next lives they are most certainly destined to return to the three lower realms. Therefore, they promote lies as if they were true. Such erroneous views are extensively described in the holy texts. To cite an example, Master Shan-tao stated:

> There are people who give rise to the poison of anger who, when they see a serious nembutsu practitioner, struggle to incite intrigue and create grudges. Such people seem blind by

> nature and have no intrinsic goodness. Destroying the teaching designed for the instantaneous realization of enlightenment, they will sink into the three lower realms for a long time. They will never be released from the three lower realms, even though innumerable eons pass, more innumerable than the number of particles released in the explosion of the earth.[230]

This passage refers to someone who generates the worldly passion of anger upon witnessing a practitioner of nembutsu who desires to be born in the Pure Land. This person contrives various dastardly schemes and ill advisedly causes termination of the exclusive nembutsu, thus succeeding in his malicious intent. Such a person, lacking an understanding of the teachings of Buddha Śākyamuni for birth in the Pure Land, has no inherent goodness; he is in want of the seeds of virtuous roots.

Someone who recites the name of Amida Buddha will extricate himself from the delusive worlds of transmigration, where he has stayed for so long, and will live eternally in the Pure Land. A person who criticizes and attempts to destroy the teaching of nembutsu, however, will sink interminably into the three lower realms. It will be impossible for such a person to escape from the three lower realms for innumerable eons. Hence, this type of person who promotes falsehoods should be looked upon with pity. It is probably futile to urge nembutsu upon one who is swayed by such thought, becomes neglectful in his exclusive practice of nembutsu, and harbors doubt about birth in the Pure Land through nembutsu.

In general, those who have little karmic relationship with Amida Buddha, and who have not discovered his notion of birth in the Pure Land, will not believe in the teaching of nembutsu even if they hear it, will become wrathful when they see the nembutsu devotee, and will get angry upon hearing nembutsu. They will also speak ill of nembutsu, which is not found in any sutra or commentary. This should be understood, and you must not deviate, no matter what you are told. Please do not force reciting nembutsu on those who do not believe in nembutsu.

If it is unfeasible even for Amida Buddha to sway the nonbelievers; it is well neigh impossible for a common mortal. Rather, look upon the nonbelievers as having been your fathers, mothers, brothers, sisters, and relatives in your previous existence. Summon your compassionate spirit, practice nembutsu yourself, speedily achieve the high grade of the high category of birth in the Pure Land, realize enlightenment there, return once again to the delusive worlds of saṃsāra, and hope to welcome into the Pure Land all those who slander and hold nembutsu in disbelief.

I implore you to thoroughly understand this:

1. When you encounter people who engage in cultivating virtuous merit through performing the miscellaneous practices, think of it as the process by which wealth begets wealth. Firmly believe that you will attain birth in the Pure Land through the single-hearted and exclusive practice of nembutsu; think of the other as one who is taking the long way and make an effort to establish a karmic relationship that encourages him to take the short way with you. To the extent that it does not interfere with your exclusive practice of nembutsu, it is acceptable to make an attempt at bringing in a nembutsu devotee.
2. As you behold the people erecting a temple, creating the image of a buddha, engaging in the reproduction of sutras, and making offerings to a monk, encourage them to believe that they must awaken unshakable faith in birth in the Pure Land and then to keep up their effort to cultivate these sundry virtuous roots.
3. There exist those who are unaware of the true meaning of the recitation of nembutsu, who pray to buddhas and gods for fortune in this world, recite and copy sutras, and erect temples. If you behold these people, you should encourage them as mentioned above. The cultivation of these virtuous acts is acceptable if they are performed for the sake of birth in the Pure Land in

their next lives. Please do not say that these acts are unnecessary. Do not consider these acts as a deterrent to the exclusive practice of nembutsu.

4. There are many implications in the recitation of nembutsu. However, the vocalization of the six characters, *Na mu A mi da Butsu*, encompasses the merit of all religious practices. To believe in the essential vow, to utter the name of Amida Buddha, to hold a string of prayer beads in hand, and to aspire for birth in the Pure Land at all times: These become the ultimate causal practices toward the certain attainment of birth in the Pure Land.

   The practice of nembutsu does not discriminate among those who are walking, standing, sitting, or lying down; the length of time, place, or various karmic conditions; or the purity or impurity of mouth and body. The practice of nembutsu is, therefore, called the "easy practice for birth in the Pure Land." We must remember, however, that maintaining the purity of our hearts when nembutsu is recited should be foremost.

   Putting your total faith in birth in the Pure Land results in the purification of your mind. It is my wish that you encourage others to recite nembutsu in this spirit. If you have this spirit all the time, nothing more needs to be said. You, too, should recite nembutsu exclusively, believe in certain attainment of birth in the Pure Land, and be stalwart in your belief.

5. Should you encounter a nonbeliever in the nembutsu practice, do not discuss the teaching of nembutsu. Neither engage in a debate over doctrine with people who follow teachings and practices other than nembutsu. Do not look down on or slander people who have views and leanings other than your own. Lamentably, criticism will result in making the other a grievously defiled person.

   Contrarily, should there be a person who has the same heart as us, desiring birth in the Pure Land through reciting nembutsu, think of him with no less compassion than that which our fathers, mothers, and masters have shown to us, however low his station is. If such a person is suffering in poverty, come to his aid. At all times, nurture anyone who shows the least bit of interest in the teaching of nembutsu. It should be done with the thought that these acts are a service to Tathāgata Amida.

Some people impudently speak about the teachings of Buddha Śākyamuni as though their own wisdom were comparable, despite knowing that wisdom and practice have gradually waned since the passing of Tathāgata Śākyamuni. For one who does not peruse the collected Buddhist scriptures and cannot speak of other writings on Buddhism, to assume a stance of wisdom is analogous to the little frog in the well [who is ignorant of the world].

I have collected and studied many Chinese and Japanese holy teachings; and reflecting on these teachings, it is clear that a nonbeliever in nembutsu is someone who committed grave offenses in his previous existence and stayed in hell for a long while and will soon return to hell.

Never believe in the sayings of a thousand false buddhas, even if they proclaim that nembutsu is not the karmic cause for birth in the Pure Land. Firmly believe that nembutsu is validated by all buddhas, as numerous as the grains of sand of the Ganges, not to mention by Tathāgata Śākyamuni as well. Keep your heart as solid as an adamantine stone, and do not change your devotion toward the single-hearted and exclusive practice of nembutsu.

Should anyone try to initiate a debate on nembutsu, suggest that he come to me to learn the meaning of nembutsu. I could recommend voluminous worthy documents concerning nembutsu to you, but this explanation suffices.

For people in this delusive world where life is the endurance of pain, desiring a pure buddhaland other than that of Amida Buddha would be as futile as hunting a bird flying high when one has no bow, or attempting to pluck a flower from a treetop when one has no legs on which to stand.

The exclusive practice of nembutsu becomes the prayer for the present and the future. This is taught in the sutras. Please encourage your kin to practice the recitation of nembutsu throughout their entire lives in order to realize the nine grades of birth in the Pure Land in accordance with their abilities.

Respectfully yours.

11. Dialogue on the Essentials of Nembutsu

IT SADDENS ME indeed if one does not rouse one's heart toward birth in the Pure Land in order to realize enlightenment; it saddens me, too, that our physical bodies are so prone to illness.

If one does not need to live in this secular world, it is unnecessary to spend life actively going about hither and thither. One may lack food and clothing, but if one is not consumed with regrets about one's mortal life, one need not bemoan this state. In order to free ourselves of concerns, we should rid ourselves of this world of anguish. The sadness of impermanence abounds before our eyes. Who can predict the date of the end of one's life?

Glory is fleeting. Living is also wrought with grief. What we must loathe is the condition of transmigration in the six delusive worlds; we must long for enlightenment through birth in the Pure Land.

Even though one may be reborn as a heavenly being and enjoy a pleasurable life, the end of life is accompanied by the pain of the five physical failings. Another may have been reborn as a human being and become a king who reigns over the whole world; but there is no escape from the sufferings of birth, old age, sickness, and death; from the suffering of separation from loved ones; from the suffering of meeting those one hates. Even if one is spared such sufferings, there is the possibility of returning to the three lower realms of hell, hungry spirits, and animals.

Sensible people should loathe this secular world. You have received life in the realm of a human being, a state extremely difficult to obtain, and you have been blessed with encountering the precious teachings of Buddha Śākyamuni, an extraordinary opportunity. On this occasion, yearn to be free from this delusive world of transmigration.

Q. (1): I agree with you in general. In accord with your instructions, I entered the monastery without hesitation; however, I have been unable to separate myself from the thoughts of renown and personal gain. My heart is not awakened to enlightenment; sometimes I am an object of censure. What am I to do now? Is this still better than remaining as a lay person and accumulating much unwholesome karma leading to a fall into the lower realms of transmigration?

Answer: Ancient writings narrate that some wore a monk's habit for fun or entered the priesthood under the influence of liquor—these things caused them to enter the Buddhist path.

The *Ten Conditions for Attaining Birth in the Pure Land* states that the eminent monk Shōnyo (781–867) entered the priesthood together with his parents when his father was forty-one years old and his mother, thirty-three. Their mentor was a priest, who lauded their entry into the monastery thus: "To desire to become a priest now, before you suffer from old age or become ill, is the ultimate cultivation of virtuous roots."[231]

Further, Tathāgata Śākyamuni, in transmitting the Dharma to Bodhisattva Maitreya, the future leader of the world, stated, "Even those who violate the precepts and commit serious transgressions will embrace your leadership once they shave their heads, don the monk's black robes, and wear a Buddhist surplice." Hence, even one who violates the precepts will be able to have a chance to accomplish deliverance through attending the three assemblies of Bodhisattva Maitreya and listening to his teaching.

It is also said in a sutra that "a priest who violates the precepts is still superior to the lay person who observes the precepts." For a lay person, to be born in the age when the teachings of Buddha Śākyamuni prevail, to have learned a path to extricate oneself from this delusive world, to have become a priest and to be wearing the vestments over the shoulder, yet to neglect the study of the ways of Buddha Śākyamuni, is as if one returns emptyhanded from a mountain of treasures.

Q. (2): Having entered the order, one must, by all means, aspire to depart from the delusive worlds of saṃsāra and realize enlightenment. How should I aspire, and how should I exert efforts toward these goals?

Answer: The *Collection of Passages on the Blissful Land* states, "According to sacred Mahāyāna texts, there are two categories of wondrous teachings for attaining birth in the Pure Land: the first is the holy gate, and the second, the Pure Land gate."[232]

All of the teachings that enable one to accomplish buddhahood in this defiled world of suffering are called the *holy gate*. To realize enlightenment through contemplating the true nature of all existence; to pursue purification of the six sensory organs through meditating exclusively on the *Lotus Sutra*; to aspire to the realization of buddhahood in one's very existent state through the observance of the three mystic practices; to pursue the four paths to achieve nirvāṇa; to aspire to attainment of the three transcendent faculties and the six transcendent faculties—these are called the *difficult path*.

In contrast, the teaching of the Pure Land gate

begins with the attainment of birth in the Pure Land in the first place, followed by the realization of enlightenment and buddhahood there—this is called the *easy path.*

Many paths lead away from the delusive worlds of transmigration, and you are free to enter the path of your choice.

Q. (3): If such is the case, would it be best for those as ignorant as we are to aspire for birth in the Pure Land?

Answer: The *Collection of Passages on the Blissful Land* describes as below:

> It is difficult today to realize enlightenment in this world through the holy gate. One reason for this is that the passing of the Great Sage [Buddha Śākyamuni] has now receded far into the distant past. Another is that since the teachings of the holy gate are extremely profound, only a few can realize enlightenment.
>
> Accordingly, the *Moon-Matrix Section of the Great Collection Sutra* states, "In this period of the decline of the Dharma, countless sentient beings have begun to practice and cultivate the way to enlightenment, yet not a single one of them has reached his goal."[233]
>
> We are now indeed in the period of the decline of the Dharma; that is, this is the corrupt world of the five defilements. In this age, the Pure Land gate is the sole gate for entry onto the path leading to enlightenment.
>
> For this reason, all buddhas, in their great compassion, encourage us to rely on the teaching of the Pure Land gate. Even if one has committed nonvirtuous deeds throughout one's life, one should still

recite nembutsu continually with a devoted heart. One will then spontaneously be free from all hindrances and with certainty will achieve birth in the Pure Land. Would people not consider nor entertain the desire to depart from this delusive world of anguish?[234]

Monk Yōkan[235] also wrote: "The doctrines of the Shingon and Shikan [Tendai] schools are too profound and difficult to embrace; the meaning of the teachings of the Sanron and Hossō schools are also difficult to ascertain and are prone to mislead."[236]

Therefore, those who are unable to contemplate and who are not learned in the ways of religious practice should think that all they need is to be born in the Pure Land and embrace the entire teaching of Buddha Śākyamuni in the most direct way.

Q. (4): There are many pure buddhalands in the ten directions. In which pure buddhaland should I hope to be born? Many aspire for birth in the Tuṣita Heaven of Bodhisattva Maitreya. How should I decide?

Answer: The T'ien-t'ai master Chan-jan (711–82)[237] stated, "Many sutras praise Amida Buddha. His Western Pure Land, therefore, is the ultimate buddhaland."[238]

In addition to this, there are in both the exoteric and esoteric Buddhist teachings countless instructions that exclusively encourage us to be born in the Pure Land of Amida Buddha.

Among the many pure buddhalands in the ten directions, Eshin-sōzu, in his *Collection of Essentials on Attaining Birth in the Pure Land*, also encourages birth in the Western Pure Land. As for the Tuṣita Heaven, he compares, in many ways, its inferiority to the Western

Pure Land; to enter the pure buddhaland of the Tuṣita Heaven requires difficult practices, in comparison with the easy entry into the Pure Land. I encourage you to explore this work.

The Pure Land has a karmically close relationship to our world of suffering; Amida Buddha is intimately related to us as the master of learning. Please understand that due to residual causes and the grace of the essential vow, we need only aspire for birth in the Western Pure Land.

Q. (5): I suppose then that we should desire nothing but birth in the Pure Land. What is the best practice for this?

Answer: Master Shan-tao answered this question as follows:

> The practices for birth in the Pure Land are divided into two categories: the first is the *right practices* and the second the *miscellaneous practices.*
>
> The right practices include the following five different practices: the first is the right practice of worship; the second is the right practice of praise and making offerings; the third is the right practice of reciting sutras; the fourth is the right practice of reciting the name of Amida Buddha; the fifth is the right practice of contemplation.
>
> The right practice of worship indicates the worship of Amida Buddha to the exclusion of other buddhas. The right practice of praise and making offerings means to praise and make offerings to Amida Buddha to the exclusion of other buddhas. The right practice of reciting sutras comprises the recitation of the three sutras of Pure Land Buddhism, such as the *Smaller Sutra*, to the exclusion of other sutras. The right practice of reciting the name of Amida Buddha

means merely to recite the name of Amida Buddha to the exclusion of other buddhas. The right practice of contemplation means to meditate upon both Amida Buddha and the adornments of the Pure Land to the exclusion of other objects. These five practices are considered the right practices for achieving birth in the Pure Land.

The right practices can be divided further into two categories: one is the *rightly established practice* and another is called the *auxiliary practices.* Reciting the name of Amida Buddha is the *rightly established practice*; other practices, such as the right practice of worship of the *Lotus Sutra* and the right practice of reciting sutras, are called the *auxiliary practices.* The many virtuous acts other than the rightly established practice and the auxiliary practices are called the *miscellaneous practices.*[239]

Master Shan-tao further stated: "Virtuous deeds other than the right practices and the miscellaneous practices are referred to as *virtuous acts*, but they cannot be compared to nembutsu."[240] Hence, devote yourself to the recitation of nembutsu if you desire to be born in the Pure Land.

Q. (6): Is attainment of birth in the Pure Land possible through practices other than nembutsu? The *Lotus Sutra* teaches that "one will go to the Blissful Land of Amida Buddha." In esoteric Buddhism there is also the teaching of Shingon, which assures the attainment of birth in the Pure Land. Various Buddhist texts expound on the power of merit that leads to birth in the Pure Land. Even though the attainment of buddhahood in this defiled world is too difficult, it seems to me that being born in the Pure Land is a simple matter if first one observes the strenuous practice that enables one to realize buddhahood in this world and brings wondrous merit, and then one dedicates this merit for the easy attainment of birth in the Pure Land. Moreover, in listening to the teachings, the merit of reading the *Lotus Sutra* and the merit of reciting nembutsu are said to be one and the same; if this is so, is there no harm in practicing both?

Answer: Buddha Śākyamuni taught the practices regarding the three categories of aspirants for birth in the Pure Land in the *Two-Fascicle Sutra* (*Larger Sutra*) and stated in each practice to "single-heartedly and exclusively meditate on the Buddha of Immeasurable Life (Amida Buddha)."[241]

Buddha Śākyamuni, in the *Meditation Sutra*, also elaborated various practices for achieving birth in the Pure Land, after which he said to Ānanda: "Thou, hold these words carefully in your mind. To keep these words in mind means to keep in mind the name of the Buddha of Immeasurable Life."[242] Master Shan-tao interpreted the passage of the *Meditation Sutra* thus: "The *Meditation Sutra* expounds on the merits of the meditative practices with a focused mind and with a distracted mind, but in reference to the essential vow of Amida Buddha, it is clear that the true intention of Buddha Śākyamuni is to make practitioners vocalize earnestly and exclusively the name of Amida Buddha."[243]

The *Meditation Sutra* reads, "Each ray of light from Amida Buddha shines over the worlds of the ten directions [the entire universe]. Those who recite nembutsu are embraced by that light and will never be abandoned."[244] Master Shan-tao offered his interpretation of this teaching: "It is not stated that those who perform the miscellaneous practices will also be illuminated and embraced."[245] This does not mean, however, that those who perform other practices will not attain birth in the Pure Land. He professed, "One can also attain birth in the Pure Land by dedicating the merit of practices other than nembutsu toward birth in the Pure Land; such practices are referred to as the *estranged miscellaneous practices.*"[246]

In the foreword to the *Collection of Essentials on Attaining Birth in the Pure Land* it further states, "The teachings of exoteric and esoteric schools are not taught in the same way. There are numerous meditative practices aimed at the phenomenal and noumenal aspects of reality. These practices are not difficult for those with keen wisdom and persistence. However, they are extremely difficult for one as ignorant as I [Genshin]. Accordingly, I have collected important sutras and commentaries relating to the nembutsu gate. Upon reading these writings and practicing their teachings, I found them easily understood and simple to practice."[247]

It is necessary to clearly understand these testimonials. It is not a matter of selecting a teaching but of understanding one's essential nature. Reconciled to the fact that one cannot depart from the delusive worlds of saṃsāra through one's own power, one should rely implicitly on the power other than self: namely, the essential vow of Amida Buddha.

Senior eminent masters pondered this. Master Tao-ch'o abandoned the holy gate and entered the Pure Land gate, and Master Shan-tao ceased the miscellaneous practices and attained the state of samādhi through the exclusive practice of nembutsu. The senior masters of the Pure Land tradition have transmitted this practice of nembutsu. I have cited only these two Chinese masters here.

In this country, masters such as Eshin-sōzu and Monk Yōkan solely encouraged the nembutsu gate for people belonging to their own schools and other schools. Hence, the classification of the *exclusive practice of nembutsu* and the *miscellaneous practices* was not first advocated by me. There are many writings regarding the teachings of Pure Land Buddhism; peruse them for a more thorough understanding.

Further, you have said that the practice of realizing enlightenment with one's present body cannot be equivalent to the practice of attaining birth in the Pure Land through nembutsu. This stands to reason. However, both are based on teachings with academic principles and traditions.

Master Shan-tao said in the *Commentary on the Meditation Sutra*: "The *Perfection of Wisdom Sutra* is of the school of wisdom based on the theory of the emptiness of all existence. The *Vimalakīrti Sutra* is from the school with the inconceivable state of enlightenment. Now, this *Meditation Sutra* is from the school of the meditative samādhi and of the school of the nembutsu samādhi."[248]

In the same manner, the *Lotus Sutra* is from the school that realizes enlightenment through ascertaining the profound principle of absoluteness and the equality of ultimate reality; and it is also from the school of the realization of the five stages and the purification of the six sensory organs in one's present state. The Shingon school is based on the theory of the realization of buddhahood in one's present existence. In addition to emphasizing the power of the merit and praise of the *Lotus Sutra*, the Tendai school teaches the immediate entrance into the heaven of the Tuṣita Pure Land; however, these are teachings for expediency and not from the school of birth in the Pure Land. The same is true of the Shingon school.

It is said that the merit of reciting the *Lotus Sutra* and the merit of nembutsu are one and the same and that both should be practiced together. As a matter of fact, Master Shan-tao could have recited the likes of the *Lotus Sutra* and the *Vimalakīrti Sutra* along with Pure Land texts. After entrance into the Pure Land gate, however, he practiced the vocal nembutsu exclusively and did not mix it with other practices. This was true not only of Master Shan-tao; all of the successive masters and patriarchs of Pure Land Buddhism recited nembutsu exclusively and suggested that other practices not be included.

Based on all of these reflections, I am saying that you should exclusively practice nembutsu.

Q. (7): In order to understand the Pure Land gate, to which text should one first refer and embrace?

Answer: In the areas of sutras, the *Two-Fascicle Sutra*, the *Meditation Sutra*, and the *Smaller Sutra* should be referred to. They are called the three sutras of Pure Land Buddhism.

Commentaries include: the *Commentary on the Meditation Sutra*, the *Hymns in Praise of Birth in the Pure Land in the Six Periods of a Day*, and the *Methods of Contemplation on Amida Buddha* by Master Shan-tao; the *Collection of Passages on the Blissful Land* by Master Tao-ch'o; the *Essentials for Birth in the West* by K'uei-chi of Tz'u-en Temple; the *Treatise Clarifying Doubts Regarding Pure Land Buddhism* by Monk Huai-kan;[249] the *Discourse on Ten Issues Regarding Birth in the Pure Land* by the T'ien-t'ai Master Chih-i;[250] and the *Collection of Essentials on Attaining Birth in the Pure Land* by Eshin-sōzu of our own country.

These commentaries are writings that should be reviewed often. However, even without perusing relevant writings, reciting nembutsu with awareness will assure you of birth in the Pure Land.

Q. (8): How should I prepare mentally for birth in the Pure Land?

Answer: Cultivate the threefold devotional heart. The threefold devotional heart has three aspects: the genuine heart, the profound heart, and the heart that seeks birth in the Pure Land through the dedication of merit. Master Shan-tao interpreted the threefold devotional heart as follows:

> The first, the *genuine heart* (Ch. *chih-ch'eng-hsin*), is the sincere heart. The Chinese term *chih* refers to truth, and *ch'eng* to the quality of being sincere. In the genuine heart, one should loathe and abandon the primary and dependent rewards, the results of the residual karma accumulated in past lives by oneself and others, and one must proceed with a sincere heart to practice the three types of acts.
>
> It is said that a person who presents a wise, virtuous, and diligent facade while harboring falsity and fickleness within could exert effort night and day, like one trying to brush live embers off one's head, but still not attain birth in the Pure Land. Consistent practice with sincerity, regardless of matters of the inner mind or outer appearances, is called the *genuine heart*.[251]
>
> The second, the *profound heart*, means profound faith, which has two aspects. The first aspect of faith

is to believe firmly that one is a common mortal who has perpetually transmigrated throughout the six delusive worlds of transmigration for countless eons up to this day, and that one does not possess the karmic conditions needed to detach oneself from the six delusive worlds.

The second aspect of faith is to have unshakable faith that Amida Buddha will embrace all sentient beings with his forty-eight vows, and to believe that one who recites his name at least ten times will, with certainty, attain birth in the Pure Land through the power of his vows...

You must also believe in the words of Buddha Śākyamuni. Even if hundreds, thousands, or tens of thousands of the learned masters gather together and cite sutras and commentaries, stating, "No common person will attain birth in the Pure Land through nembutsu," you still must not have a moment of hesitation or doubt.

Merely answer thus: "I believe in the sutras and commentaries to which you refer. However, the sutras and commentaries to which you refer now are teachings that have a karmic relation to you; what I believe are the teachings that are most relevant to me. The sutras and commentaries to which you refer are those that are equally compatible with bodhisattvas and heavenly beings. However, the three sutras of Pure Land Buddhism, including the *Meditation Sutra*, are teachings designed for common people, who are tainted with the five defilements and the ten transgressions and are lacking in virtue. Therefore, when Buddha Śākyamuni expounded on the *Meditation Sutra*, the capabilities of the audience, the place, and the merit of the teaching were different from those of the scriptures you cite. Your questioning birth in the Pure Land only serves to enhance my faith in my belief."

Even if countless arhats, pratyekabuddhas, and the bodhisattvas who have reached the forty-first to the fiftieth stages in the fifty-two stages of bodhisattva practice appear and fill the ten directions, and even if the transformed buddhas and rewarded buddhas cast their illumination each and all, and in unison extend their tongues in the sky and proclaim that "Birth in the Pure Land through reciting nembutsu is impossible," you must reply, "The teaching of one buddha is one and the same as that of all buddhas. If we were to alter the teaching of Tathāgata Śākyamuni, would we alter the prohibition of the ten transgressions—including the prohibition of taking any form of life—and would we then go on to commit these very offenses? If the first buddha's teachings were false, then the teachings of the later buddhas would also be false. If the teachings of all buddhas are one and the same, there is no need to alter one's belief in the Dharma." You should never retrogress in life. This is called the *profound heart.*[252]

The third, the *heart that seeks birth in the Pure Land through the dedication of merit*, means the act of dedicating all of one's virtuous roots in order to attain birth in the Pure Land of Ultimate Bliss. You must dedicate these virtues with an unshakable genuine heart and desire for birth in the Pure Land. This profound faith, as solid as an adamantine stone, must not be hindered by people of differing views, teachings, or practices.[253]

Now, I will tell one story for the nembutsu practitioner to protect him from the perils of distorted and different views: A man was traveling west. He traversed one hundred *ri* [about 244 miles], then one thousand *ri*, when two rivers suddenly came into view in the middle of the road. On the southern edge was a river of fire, and on the northern edge was a river of water. Each river was one hundred steps wide and bottomless.

In the middle, between the water and fire, was a narrow white path no more than four or five *sun* [a little more than five inches] in width. The white path was one hundred steps long from east to west. The waves of the river of water ebbed and flowed over the white path; the flames of the river of fire danced on the road, burning it. Water and fire continually played on the surface of the white path.

The traveler, already in a vast meadow, encountered no passersby. There was nothing but bands of bandits and herds of terrifying beasts surrounding him, and seeing the lone traveler, the bandits and beasts were set to kill him. Fearing death, the traveler immediately ran farther west and suddenly came upon the wide river of fire and water. The traveler mumbled to himself, "This river runs north and south with no end in sight, but I see an extremely narrow white path in the middle. It is a short distance, but how should I proceed? I am sure that I will die today. Turning back is impossible because the bandits and beasts are closing in. If I run toward the north or south, avoiding the fire and water, the beasts and poisonous insects will attack me. If I take the white path toward the west I will probably fall into one side or the other of the river."

Needless to say, the traveler trembled in fear. In a flash the traveler reasoned, "If I retreat, I will probably die, but I will also probably die if I make a detour. There is no escaping death. That being the case, I would rather take this path and go forward; at least then there is some chance I will make it across."

As he made his decision he heard a voice from the eastern shore, "Be resolute and seek this white path. You will be spared death. If you remain where you are, death is certain." There was another voice from above the western shore: "You must steadfastly pray with the right belief, seek your path, and proceed. You must not doubt, have fear, or desire to turn back."

When the traveler had gone up the white path one or two tenths of the way, the bandits said, "You should return. That path you are on is precipitous and dangerous. You will never make it across. There is no doubt that you will die. We harbor no evil in our hearts."

The traveler heard this voice, but paying it no attention, he steadfastly prayed he would make his way across. Then the western shore appeared, and all the longstanding perils that had haunted him dissipated. Virtuous friends in the west welcomed the traveler with great joy. This is the fable.

Within the fable of the White Path between Two Rivers, the eastern shore is the "house on fire": that is, this delusive world of endurance. The bandits and beasts that encroach upon him through deception are the six sensory organs, the six types of consciousness, the six varieties of dust, the five aggregates of sentient beings, and the four great elements. The deserted meadow refers to one's association with undesirable friends and one's inability to encounter virtuous teachers. The two rivers of water and fire point to our emotions: water stands for greed, fire stands for the flame of anger. The four or five *sun* wide white path in the middle of the two rivers alludes to the untainted, pure mind aspiring birth in the Pure Land that exists amid the worldly passions of greed and anger. Greed and anger are powerful; therefore, they are personified as water and fire.

Since our desire for birth in the Pure Land is slim, it is referred to as the narrow white path. The waves washing ashore symbolize lust that continually arises and taints our wholesome spirit. The fire that constantly licks at the road points to the fact that anger and hate continually burn away the accumulation of Dharma riches.

The meaning of the traveler going steadfastly toward the west is the allocation of merit from all of his acts and practices to his progress toward the Western Pure Land. After hearing a voice from the east encouraging the traveler to go west, his proceeding to the west means that the teachings of Buddha Śākyamuni live on, even though those of us who came after his death are unable to learn from him directly; the teachings lead us toward aspiration for birth in the Pure Land. This is what is meant by his voice.

Further, the bands of bandits attempting to lure the traveler back after he proceeded one or two tenths of the way allude to the disorder created by the teachings of various people with different understandings; those who espouse different practices and who have erroneous views that mutually deceive and confuse each other cause themselves to commit unwholesome acts and revert to a wayward life. The voice from above the western shore personifies the spirit of the essential vow of Amida Buddha.

Having reached the western shore, joyfully encountering virtuous friends symbolizes that many bodhisattvas in the Pure Land sincerely rejoice in the attainment of birth in the Pure Land by a nembutsu practitioner.

Sentient beings who have sunk into the delusive worlds of transmigration for countless eons are unable to extricate themselves. Fortunately, Buddha Śākyamuni encourages them to proceed toward the west. Amida Buddha, with his compassion, invites them to the Pure Land. Owing to the grace of Buddha Śākyamuni and Amida Buddha, they do not disregard the twin rivers of fire and water nor forget their hearts of compassion even for a moment. Through the power of the essential vow of Amida Buddha, they are able to be born in the Pure Land after death, encounter Amida Buddha, and become immersed in joyfulness.

The nembutsu practitioner always understands and thinks of the meaning of this parable of the White Path between Two Rivers whenever he performs the three types of acts while walking, standing, sitting, or lying down, day or night, without regard for time. Therefore, this is called the *heart that seeks birth in the Pure Land through the dedication of merit.*

Moreover, it is also called a dedication of merit when, after one is born in the Pure Land, one develops great compassion there and then returns to the delusive worlds of saṃsāra in order to teach and save the populace.

If one possesses the threefold devotional heart, no aspiration is beyond reach. Once aspiration for birth in the Pure Land and the practice of nembutsu are established, there is absolutely no reason for failure to attain birth in the Pure Land, even though someone may say that birth in the Pure Land is unattainable.[254]

The above passage is an interpretation of Master Shan-tao.

Q. (9): The *Smaller Sutra* uses the phrase, "a single heart and without distraction."[255] Does this mean that one must not have any other thoughts while reciting the name of Amida Buddha? If one may utter nembutsu just once, it would be easy to practice without having any other thoughts; no one would fail if just a single utterance of nembutsu assured birth in the Pure Land. If it is necessary to repeat nembutsu without distraction until the end of life, however, it would be impossible for common people to attain birth in the Pure Land. How should I reconcile these thoughts?

Answer: Master Shan-tao interpreted this to mean: "Once one possesses the threefold devotional heart, belief in birth in the Pure Land will be as solid as an adamantine stone. To continue to repeat nembutsu until death is called a *single heart*."[256] The essential vow of Amida Buddha states, "If, when I am to attain buddhahood, all sentient beings in the ten directions who hold faith with genuine hearts and who wish to be born in my buddhaland are not born there within just ten moments of being mindful of me, I will not realize enlightenment."[257]

In this statement, "genuine hearts" refers to the genuine heart of the threefold devotional heart explained in the *Meditation Sutra*. "Hold faith" points to the profound heart. "Who wish to be born in my buddhaland" applies to the heart that seeks birth in the Pure Land through the dedication of merit. Together they refer to a *single heart* if a practitioner continually aspires for birth [in the Pure Land] for the rest of his life, without distraction.

It is said that those who have possessed this implicit heart will certainly achieve birth in the Pure Land within two days or even one day of recitation of nembutsu, or even ten repetitions, or even just a single utterance. It can never be said that the hearts of common people are too distractible. This is why nembutsu is referred to as the *easy path.*

The *Two-Fascicle Sutra* (*Larger Sutra*) instructs: "If one extricates oneself from one's ties to the five defiled worlds, the path to the lower realms naturally closes after a moment, and one progresses unhindered on one's path to the Pure Land. In spite of the existence of this easy path, there are few people who traverse it."[258]

Truly, there is no other greater path than this. If it is said that birth in the Pure Land is realized after many eons of merit accumulation, one whose life is short and who is not able to live a life of endurance wonders what will happen to him. However, the essential vow states, "just ten moments of being mindful,"[259] and the passage on the fulfillment of the essential vow states, "If one is mindful of Amida Buddha even for one moment and dedicates the merit of nembutsu to birth in the Pure Land with a sincere heart, one will be born in the Pure Land after one's death."[260]

It is generally said that those who indulge in unvirtuous deeds will not be born in the Pure Land. However, the *Meditation Sutra* teaches, "Birth in the Pure Land is possible even for one guilty of the five grave offenses."[261] It is also said that as time passes and the hearts of people become ignorant, their faith will become less devout, and it will be difficult to be born in the Pure Land. The *Larger Sutra*, however, states, "In a future age, after the period of the decline of the Dharma, when my teachings are extinct, I (Buddha Śākyamuni), full of compassion and mercy, will remain alone with this *Larger Sutra* for another one hundred years. All sentient beings of that time who encounter the *Larger Sutra* will realize enlightenment according to their wishes."[262]

At that time the masses will not even hear the name of the Three Jewels. All existing sacred sutras will be secreted in the palace of the dragon king; not another sutra, except this *Larger Sutra*, will remain in this world. Only those who are wretched and without faith will exist and most likely will fall into lower realms. However, Amida Buddha, with his essential vow, and Buddha Śākyamuni, with his great compassion, will preserve the *Larger Sutra* for another one hundred years. Fortunately, we are now still in the eve of the period of the decline of the Dharma. We are no less endowed than the masses that come after the ten-thousand-year period of the decline of the Dharma. For this reason, it is said that birth in the Pure Land is easily attainable.

Nevertheless, there are very few who will be able to encounter the *Larger Sutra*, and although one might hear its teaching as a matter of course, it is difficult to believe. Accordingly, it is said that there is "no one who is truly connected." This may well be true.

The *Smaller Sutra* states, "If a good man and a good woman, who, upon hearing the merit of the name of Amida Buddha, hold steadfast to his name in their minds, with utmost concentration and without distraction, and wholeheartedly recite his name for one day, two days, or seven days, Amida Buddha, accompanied by his assembly of holy beings, will appear before them when their lives are almost at an end. With their minds free from distraction, they will be born in the Pure Land of Amida Buddha."[263]

When Buddha Śākyamuni spoke of this, various buddhas feared that some may find it difficult to believe the teachings of just one buddha. Therefore, the tathāgatas in the six directions, being of one heart at the same moment, extended their broad and long tongues to cover the three thousand great-thousand worlds and vowed, "If this teaching is false, the broad and long tongues we have extended will tear and fall into decay, never again to return to our mouths." This is clearly recorded in the *Smaller Sutra*[264] as well as in its commentary by Master Shan-tao.[265]

Any event of significance is always accompanied by validation. The *Lotus Sutra* was confirmed by Buddha Prabhūtaratna; the *Perfection of Wisdom Sutra* was validated by the four buddhas residing in the four quarters. However, the repetition of nembutsu for one through seven days for birth in the Pure Land was validated by a multitude of buddhas. Buddha Śākyamuni was well aware of this fact.

Q. (10): You have instructed us on the issue of *faith* for the attainment of birth in the Pure Land. What should we learn about *practice* for birth in the Pure Land?

Answer: Practice should be based on the instruction of the four modes of exercise for birth in the Pure Land. The first is *to exercise nembutsu in infinity*, the second is *to exercise nembutsu in reverence*, the third is *to exercise nembutsu in continuity*, and the fourth is *to exercise nembutsu in purity*.

First is *to exercise nembutsu in infinity*. The *Essentials for Birth in the West*, composed by Master K'uei-chi, interpreted this to mean, "One who has the first awakening of aspiration for enlightenment and continues the practice of nembutsu, never regressing until enlightenment is attained."[266] Master Shan-tao also interpreted, "One should continue to practice the vocal nembutsu without resting until one draws his last breath."[267]

Second is *to exercise nembutsu in reverence.* This means that one should always be mindful of and revere Amida Buddha, the Dharma, and the Sangha of the Pure Land. This is taught in the *Collection of Essentials on Attaining Birth in the Pure Land.*[268] The *Essentials for Birth in the West* also describes it:

> There are five kinds of exercising nembutsu in reverence: (1) the adoration of karmically related sages, (2) the adoration of karmically related sacred teachings, (3) the adoration of karmically related virtuous teachers, (4) the adoration of comrades traversing the same path, and (5) the adoration of the Three Jewels.
>
> First, the adoration of karmically related sages means that whether walking, standing, sitting, or lying down, do not turn your back to the west. It is said that neither should you weep or expectorate facing the west or relieve oneself in that direction.
>
> Second, the adoration of karmically related images of a buddha and sacred teachings means to create and paint the image of Amida Buddha. If it is impossible to make many images of Amida Buddha, just fabricate his image and the images of his two attendant bodhisattvas. The adoration of sacred teachings means to carefully store sutras such as the *Smaller Sutra* in a five-hued bag and to read it and

encourage others to read it. Enshrine these images and sutras in your home, offer incense and flowers, and worship them while repenting your karmic defilements during the six periods of the day.[269]

Third, the adoration of karmically related virtuous teachers means that when hearing of a teacher of Pure Land Buddhism, do not hesitate to travel a thousand *yojana*[270] to serve, respect, and make offerings to that teacher. Even if the teacher belongs to a traditional school other than Jōdo Shū, arouse in your heart a respect for him. Should you belittle and look down on such a person, you will have committed a grave offense.

Endeavor to become a virtuous teacher for the masses and encourage them to be born in the Western Pure Land. This is because living in this house on fire will cause you to sink to a depth from which there is no escape. In this world on fire, the practice of Buddhism is extremely difficult; therefore, encourage others to rely on the Western Pure Land.

Once birth in the Pure Land is achieved, you will naturally promote studying the threefold discipline, and all wholesome deeds will become part of your being because there is no basis for committing unwholesome deeds in the Pure Land of Amida Buddha.

Fourth, the adoration of comrades traversing the same path refers to the practitioners who observe the same practice you do. They may have deterrents too grave for them to practice, but the support of a good friend will certainly help them to persevere. The result of the suitable karma of comrades is to help and save one another. Accordingly, deeply trust and honor each other.

> Fifth, the adoration of the Three Jewels means that you should revere the paintings and wooden images of a buddha, the teachings of a bodhisattva, pratyekabuddha, śrāvaka, and holy adept, including even those who violate the precepts. Never be conceited. A tree may be slanted because it is bent and fallen over; likewise if there are hindrances to your facing the west, you need only to think that you are facing the west.[271]

Third is *to exercise nembutsu in continuity*, which is explained in the *Essentials for Birth in the West* as:

> Continue to recite nembutsu and nurture the heart that seeks birth in the Pure Land. At all times, direct your thoughts to birth in the Pure Land. For instance, there may be a person who loses his wealth to a trickster, descends into vulgarity, and lives a life of hardship. One day his thoughts suddenly turn toward his parents and he wishes to race home. Nonetheless, he has no escape plan from his present state and continues to live in a land far from home. He thinks of his parents day and night and can hardly bear the pain of longing for his home. In time he formulates a plan and is able to return to his homeland, care for his parents, and enjoy a carefree and happy life.
>
> This analogy holds true for nembutsu practitioners. Their good hearts have been distracted and injured by worldly passions, leading to a loss of the precious jewels of merit and wisdom. For many eons they have descended into the transmigration of the six delusive worlds and suffered physically and spiritually. Now, they have a favorable encounter that shows them there exists a compassionate father in

> Amida Buddha. They should pray in thanks for his benevolence and continue to desire birth in the Pure Land until the end of their lives.
>
> For this reason, keep birth in the Pure Land in your heart and never include practices other than nembutsu.[272]

Fourth is *to exercise nembutsu in purity*, which is stated in the *Essentials for Birth in the West*: "Exclusively aspire for birth in the Pure Land, worship Amida Buddha, and do not include practices other than nembutsu. What is essential is the daily recitation of nembutsu."[273] Master Shan-tao thus stated:

> Exclusively recite the name of Amida Buddha, worship him, and praise Amida Buddha as well as all the celestial beings of the Pure Land, excluding any other practice.
>
> One hundred out of one hundred exclusive nembutsu practitioners will be born in the Pure Land. Rarely, one or two out of one hundred practitioners of the miscellaneous practices will be born there. Those who follow the miscellaneous karmic conditions not only hinder their own birth in the Pure Land but also become a hindrance for birth in the Pure Land for others who follow the right practices.
>
> I saw everywhere that differences existed between monks and lay people in their understandings and practices: some observed the exclusive practice of nembutsu and others the miscellaneous practices. Earnest practice of nembutsu results in ten out of ten births in the Pure Land; the miscellaneous practices result in not one birth out of one thousand.[274]

Monk Huai-kan, a disciple of Master Shan-tao, said, "If one desires to perform the practice for birth in the Western Pure Land, he must not omit the four modes of exercise, he must exclude the three categories of undesirable acts, disavow all vows and practices established by buddhas other than Amida Buddha, and only aspire for birth in the Pure Land practice with the Western Pure Land in mind."[275]

Q. (11): It is said that all virtuous roots may be severed by King Māra. How can we deal with this when it happens?

Answer: The realm of demons deceives the masses because all practices and actions performed there rely upon self-power. On the contary, the nembutsu devotee perceives himself as an afflicted common mortal who has transmigrated through the six delusive worlds of saṃsāra. He, therefore, relies not on himself but merely on the power of the essential vow of Amida Buddha in his aspiration for birth in the Pure Land, so a karmic relationship with a negative condition is of no consequence.

One who practices meditation and contemplates wisdom still meets with the unfavorable conditions that occur when observing the nine objects of contemplation. On the other hand, there is no unfavorable condition in the teaching of Amida Buddha, because he has attained the state of purity. Since there exists no unfavorable karmic condition that deceives Amida Buddha, there is nothing to deter the nembutsu practitioner. This is because the power other than self [the essential vow] is relied upon. It is analogous to the ease with which a rock even one thousand feet long may cross the ocean on a ship.

Both Amida Buddha and Bodhisattva Avalokiteśvara remain before the nembutsu practitioner at all times.

In addition, the twenty-five attendant bodhisattvas of Amida Buddha surround the practitioner a hundredfold and a thousandfold in order to protect him. There is no chance for an unfavorable condition.

Q. (12): How much negative karma will be eradicated by calling the name of Amida Buddha?

Answer: It is taught that "Through a single utterance of nembutsu, the negative karma binding one to the six delusive worlds of transmigration for eight billion eons is eliminated."[276] It is also said that "If one merely hears the name of Amida Buddha and the names of his two attendant bodhisattvas, the negative karma binding one to saṃsāra for immeasurable eons is nullified."[277]

Q. (13): Does the word *nembutsu* mean to contemplate the physical features of Amida Buddha?

Answer: Contemplation on the physical features and luminescence of Amida Buddha is regarded as the meditation samādhi. To meditate on the physical features of a buddha in his rewarded body, or to contemplate the common identity between a buddha's nature and one's own potential for the attainment of buddhahood would be impossible in this world. This is because we lack wisdom and are wanting of spirit.

Master Shan-tao stated, "Merely recite the name of Amida Buddha without meditating on his physical features. Sentient beings have grave hindrances; it is difficult for them to meditate. For this reason, the Great Sage [Buddha Śākyamuni], in his compassion, encouraged us to merely repeat the name of Amida Buddha. This is because we are lacking in our desire to practice, and our hearts vacillate and are distracted in ten directions."[278]

Master Shan-tao further commented on this passage of the essential vow of Amida Buddha: "'If, when I am to attain buddhahood, all sentient beings in the ten directions who call out my name at least ten times with reliance on the power of my essential vow are not born there, I will not realize enlightenment.' Amida Buddha did, indeed, attain buddhahood and presently resides in the Pure Land. It should be known that his essential vow was not made in vain. If sentient beings recite his name, they will, with certainty, attain birth in the Pure Land."[279]

Strive to attain birth expeditiously in the Pure Land of Ultimate Bliss, and once there with Amida Buddha and Bodhisattva Avalokiteśvara as mentors, try to learn and internalize the subtle principle of all holy teachings: the school of the realization of enlightenment through ascertainment of the profound principle of absoluteness and the equality of the ultimate reality taught in the *Lotus Sutra*, the concept of the ultimate principle of emptiness presented in the *Perfection of Wisdom Sutra*, and the theory of realization of buddhahood in your present body in the Shingon school.

12. A Reply to Tarō Sanehide in Ōgo

I APOLOGIZE for the absence of a detailed reply to your previous letter. You may have thought it suspicious. Your question is not easy to address in writing. It is also regrettable that you did not question me in detail during your long stay in the capital of Kyōto.

I merely instructed that birth in the Pure Land is attainable through the recitation of nembutsu. Although I believe it implicitly and profoundly, I am not in a position to expound on the teaching of nembutsu to others. I also hesitate to address your doubts regarding the depths of the tenet in a letter. However, I would regret not responding at all, so I will explain some thoughts as they occur to me here.

Concerning the teaching about a nembutsu devotee who will achieve birth in the Pure Land through possessing the threefold devotional heart: hearing only the name of the threefold devotional heart, it must seem a grandiose thought, giving rise to the question, "What kind of heart is this?"

Actually, according to the explanation of Master Shan-tao, this is easy to understand. The threefold devotional heart may be possessed by even the unschooled with little desire for learning, as well as by women for whom it is said that enlightenment is questionable. Any nembutsu devotee who sincerely aspires for birth in the Pure Land will naturally possess the threefold devotional heart.

This is taught in the *Meditation Sutra*: "One who aspires to be born in the Pure Land of Ultimate Bliss will attain this birth by awakening the three aspects of a devoted heart. What are the three? The first aspect is the genuine heart, the second, the profound heart, and the third, the heart that seeks birth in the Pure Land through the dedication of merit. One who embodies this threefold devotional heart will be born in the Pure Land without fail."[280]

According to Master Shan-tao's thought, then, the first—a genuine heart—points to a truly sincere heart. Here, *genuineness* means a purity heart that does not desire to put on a facade. The *Commentary on the Meditation Sutra* interprets this, "Do not outwardly pretend to be wise, virtuous, and diligent while inwardly harboring falsity and fickleness."[281]

This statement means that to pretend to be sagacious when actually ignorant, to pretend to have virtue while harboring malevolence, or to appear industrious when truly indolent will not create the genuine heart; this kind of attitude does not refer to a genuine heart. When one is undisguised in appearance and in heart without desire to embellish one's true self—this is called the *genuine heart.*

The second—the profound heart—is the heart of profound faith. What we have to believe first is that we are ordinary people who possess numerous worldly passions and have committed various karmic misdeeds with no virtuous roots. We must then revere the great compassion of the essential vow of Amida Buddha and repeat his compassionate name for one hundred years, forty or fifty years, ten or twenty years, or just one or two years, from the time we begin to desire birth in the Pure Land to the moment of our passing. This should be done without idleness or indolence. We must also have implicit faith, without harboring doubts even for a moment, that one who recites the name of Amida Buddha for seven days or one day, ten recitations or just a single utterance—the number of repetitions are beside the point—will achieve birth in the Pure Land; this is called the *profound heart.*

Many people desire birth in the Pure Land and recite the name of Amida Buddha as taught in the essential vow; however, they are fearful of the rising of illusory thoughts, become self-deprecating about the inadequate number of virtuous acts they have performed, and are uncertain about their attainment of birth in the Pure Land. These feelings confirm that they already hold doubts about the essential vow.

Master Shan-tao, foreseeing the arousal of those doubts in the nembutsu practitioners of later times, and in order to remove all doubts and to encourage them to have an unshakable faith in the attainment of birth in the Pure Land, explained in great detail that ordinary people with worldly passions, who commit offenses, who have no virtuous roots, and are unable to pursue the acquisition of wisdom, will certainly achieve birth in the Pure Land with ten recitations, or merely a single utterance, of nembutsu. Master Shan-tao commented as follows:

> Even if the sky were filled with a proliferation of buddhas casting their individual lights and extending their broad tongues and in unison saying that it is misguided for the common man who has committed offenses to believe that he can attain birth in the Pure Land through the mere recitation of nembutsu, you must not believe it and must not be alarmed or doubtful for even a fleeting moment.
>
> This is because Amida Buddha, prior to enlightenment, vowed, "If, when I am to attain buddhahood, all sentient beings in the ten directions who recite my name from the upper limit of one hundred years down to ten times or even once, are not born in my buddhaland, I will not realize enlightenment." His vow was not made in vain. He did, indeed, attain buddhahood a long time ago. Know that one who recites his name will, with certainty, attain birth in the Pure Land.
>
> Further, Buddha Śākyamuni appeared in this world of anguish, preached the essential vow of Amida Buddha for

> all sentient beings, and encouraged them to achieve birth in the Pure Land through nembutsu.
>
> All the buddhas in the six directions, as countless as grains of sand in the Ganges, extended their broad and long tongues and stated, "Buddha Śākyamuni's instruction of birth in the Pure Land through nembutsu is certain. All sentient beings should firmly believe this and never entertain any doubt regarding birth in the Pure Land through nembutsu."
>
> Without exception, manifold buddhas attested to this instruction with a unanimous heart. Amida Buddha had already made the essential vow, and Buddha Śākyamuni clarified the efficacy of the vow and encouraged us to perform nembutsu. All buddhas in the six quarters, as countless as the sands of the Ganges, also proved the authenticity of the instruction of Buddha Śākyamuni.
>
> Although there may be a buddha who, counter to other buddhas, espouses the thought that ordinary people are unable to attain birth in the Pure Land through nembutsu, you must not be alarmed or doubtful of attaining this birth through nembutsu, even if other buddhas appear and say the same thing. There is likewise no reason for bodhisattvas to say such a thing, much less arhats or pratyekabuddhas.[282]

Master Shan-tao thus commented in great detail on the theory of birth in the Pure Land through nembutsu. If this is correct, why do ordinary people today promulgate erroneous explanations obstructing nembutsu? No one, no matter how esteemed, is more learned in the path to birth in the Pure Land than Master Shan-tao. He was no mere mortal: he was in truth the manifestation of Amida Buddha. He, in order to promulgate the essential vow, to make it known to all sentient beings, in order to help them attain birth in the Pure Land, took a temporary human form in Master Shan-tao. Hence, his instruction is the teaching of Amida Buddha himself.

Furthermore, Master Shan-tao, as the manifestation of Amida Buddha, really achieved the nembutsu samādhi, through which there appeared the majestic adornments of the Pure Land before his very eyes, and he was welcomed by Amida Buddha, who passed on his nembutsu teachings directly to Master Shan-tao. His teachings are the words uttered by Amida Buddha. On pondering the quintessence of Amida Buddha, or in order to delve into the emanation of the quintessence, we must revere and believe in the teachings of Master Shan-tao.

We, therefore, need not reflect on the amount of our worldly passions, nor think about the depth of our obstructing karmic misdeeds; we must simply mouth *Namu Amida Butsu* and believe that, in accordance with our voices, we will be born in the Pure Land without fail. This resolve is referred to as the *profound heart.* If we possess the profound heart, birth in the Pure Land is guaranteed. In summary, implicit faith in birth in the Pure Land through nembutsu is called the *profound heart.*

The third, the heart that seeks birth in the Pure Land through the dedication of merit, is not a particular or special heart. It points to the fervent aspiration for birth in the Pure Land that dedicates one's accumulated practices toward [birth in] the Pure Land of Ultimate Bliss.

Master Shan-tao said, "Cultivating the threefold devotional heart brings birth in the Pure Land with certainty. Lacking one aspect of the threefold devotional heart will make this birth impossible."[283]

Someone may possess a truly genuine heart with no pretension, but if he has any doubt about the essential vow, his nembutsu is devoid of the profound heart. Another may have no doubts, but if that person has pretensions and lacks sincerity, he does not have the genuine heart. Someone may possess both the genuine heart and the profound heart, and be free of both pretensions or doubts, but if he does not aspire for birth in the Pure Land, the heart that seeks birth in the Pure Land through the dedication of merit would be missing.

Examined individually, each aspect of the threefold devotional heart seems separate and distinct, but in essence one must arouse a sincere heart, have implicit faith in the essential vow, and desire birth in the Pure Land. Together, these three aspects of a heart make up the threefold devotional heart. Indeed, how is the great achievement of birth in the Pure Land possible if one cannot nurture this simple concept of the threefold devotional heart?

To achieve this is actually a very simple matter. It is essential that the concept of the threefold devotional heart be understood in this manner, but this does not mean that it is beyond your grasp. One who does not know the name of the threefold devotional heart is still able to possess this heart. Conversely, one who has a thorough understanding of the threefold devotional heart may not necessarily embody it without difficulty. Therefore, it has long been said that among those who did not understand the threefold devotional heart, some people actually attained birth in the Pure Land through their earnest recitation of nembutsu. These people did not know the name of the threefold devotional heart, but it would be safe to say that they did indeed possess the threefold devotional heart.

If even a longtime practitioner of nembutsu does not have a serene end, it may be, as I mentioned before, that this person was only putting on a facade; he was only concerned about being seen as a devout nembutsu devotee by others, but his belief in the essential vow was not profound, and he did not genuinely aspire for birth in the Pure Land. This being the case, please understand that this person did not possess the threefold devotional heart and was not able to die peacefully or achieve birth in the Pure Land. Do not think, though, that the attainment of birth in the Pure Land is extremely difficult. A person who does not believe implicitly in birth in the Pure Land is lacking the profound heart; therefore, he needs to renew his determination and remain unwavering in his belief in birth in the Pure Land.

In general, those who sincerely wish for birth in the Pure Land and have implicit faith in the essential vow, and who continue to recite nembutsu, will meet their end in the best of circumstances. That is, the purpose of Amida Buddha welcoming the nembutsu devotee is to establish the rightly settled state of mind for birth in the Pure Land in his final moments. Those who do not understand this simply think that Amida Buddha will come to welcome them when nembutsu is recited with right mindedness at the time of death. They neither believe in the essential vow nor understand the meaning of the teaching of a sutra.

Regarding the rightly settled state of mind for birth in the Pure Land in one's final moments, the *Sutra in Praise of the Pure Land* states, "Amida Buddha saves us with his compassion, fostering tranquility in our hearts."[284] Through the merit of nembutsu frequently recited in daily life, Amida Buddha is certain to come to take us to his Pure Land at our time of death. The nembutsu devotee will establish the rightly settled state of mind for birth in the Pure Land after seeing Amida Buddha's coming to welcome him. Consequently, it is indeed a misguided person who perceives the daily practice of nembutsu as meaningless and who does so merely for acquiring the rightly settled state of mind for birth in the Pure Land and the welcoming of Amida Buddha at the time of death. Those who truly believe in the essential vow never harbor doubts about their final moments. We must renew our dedication to the nembutsu that we are reciting today.

Where and when, in the essential vow, does it mention that Amida Buddha will come to receive only those who recite nembutsu at their time of death? The issue of birth in the Pure Land through nembutsu at the time of death refers to the case of a nonbeliever who did not desire birth in the Pure Land or recite nembutsu in daily life. Though he is ignorant, the nonbeliever will still achieve this birth if he meets in his final moments a virtuous teacher who encourages him to recite nembutsu and he utters nembutsu for the first time. This is explained in the *Meditation Sutra*.[285]

Those who practice nembutsu daily need not make special plans for their time of death. One should have firm belief that since Amida

Buddha's welcoming is certain, the establishment of the rightly settled state of mind for birth in the Pure Land is assured. Because of this, believe in the compassion of Amida Buddha in the depth of your heart and know that you will attain birth in the Pure Land through nembutsu.

Some people say, "Even transgressors attain birth in the Pure Land through nembutsu. If so, is there any problem if I engage in other practices, such as reciting the *Lotus Sutra*, concurrently with reciting nembutsu?" This seems to be a question for many who live in the vicinity of the capital, Kyōto; it must be more so where you live. I do not venture to pass judgment on the teachings of other Buddhist schools. Many might discontinue them if I were to say that this idea is misleading.

Regarding the instruction of Jōdo Shū, Master Shan-tao stated,

> The practices for birth in the Pure Land are divided into two categories: one is the right practices, and the other, the miscellaneous practices. The right practices include many practices. The first is the right practice of reciting sutras. This comprises the recitation of the three sutras of Pure Land Buddhism: that is, the *Larger Sutra*, the *Meditation Sutra*, and the *Smaller Sutra*. The second is the right practice of contemplation, which refers to the meditation on Amida Buddha and the majestic adornments of the Pure Land. The third is the right practice of worship, which embraces the worship of Amida Buddha. The fourth is the right practice of reciting the name of Amida Buddha, which indicates the vocalization of *Namu Amida Butsu*. The fifth is the right practice of praising and making offerings, which includes exalting and making offerings to Amida Buddha. These are called the *five right practices.* When the practices of praising and making offerings are separated, the practices are referred to as the *six right practices.*[286]

Master Shan-tao further divided the right practices into two categories, stating,

> The first is to recite single-heartedly and exclusively the name of Amida Buddha every moment, whether walking, standing, sitting, or lying down, day and night, without interruption. This practice in which one recites nembutsu without cessation is called the *rightly established practice* because it is in accordance with the essential vow of Amida Buddha.[287]

Master Shan-tao regarded vocal nembutsu as the rightly established practice for birth in the Pure Land. He further said, "If one relies on the right practice of worship and of reciting sutras for birth in the Pure Land, these acts are called the *auxiliary practices.*"[288] Devotional practices other than nembutsu, such as worship, recitation, praising, and making offerings, are called *auxiliary practices* that serve to enhance the practice of nembutsu.

The various practices beyond the rightly established practice and the auxiliary practices are called *miscellaneous practices.* The six bodhisattva perfections and virtuous practices other than nembutsu like almsgiving, observing the precepts, forbearance, and endeavor, including reciting the *Lotus Sutra* and practicing Shingon, are referred to as the *miscellaneous practices*. One who exerts effort in the right practices is called an *exclusive practitioner* for birth in the Pure Land, and one who pursues the miscellaneous practices, a *desultory practitioner*.

Master Shan-tao also narrated, "Reflecting upon the merits and disadvantages of these two practices—the right practices and the miscellaneous practices—one who observes the right practices always holds the Pure Land close to his heart, and there is no interruption in being mindful of Amida Buddha. On the other hand, one who performs the miscellaneous practices has been interrupted from being mindful of Amida Buddha. Birth in the Pure Land is still possible for the desultory practitioner of nembutsu by dedicating his merit to birth in the Pure Land. Such practices are referred to as *estranged miscellaneous practices.*"[289] They are regarded as the practices remote from the Pure Land.

Master Shan-tao further mentioned:

> Ten out of ten and one hundred out of one hundred of the exclusive practitioners of nembutsu will realize birth in the Pure Land. Why is this so? It is because the exclusive practitioners possess the rightly settled state of mind for birth in the Pure Land without being disturbed by other miscellaneous karmic conditions. It is also because nembutsu is in accordance with both the essential vow of Amida Buddha and the teachings of Buddha Śākyamuni.
>
> In contrast, among those who perform the miscellaneous practices, only one or two out of one hundred, or only four or five out of one thousand practitioners, will be born in the Pure Land. Why is this so? It is because the followers of the miscellaneous practices are distracted by miscellaneous karmic conditions and lose the rightly settled state of mind for birth in the Pure Land; they are not in accord with the essential vow of Amida Buddha and are at odds with the teachings of Buddha Śākyamuni. In addition, their devotion to Amida Buddha is not continuous and their concentration on the Pure Land is interrupted; their karmic practices for birth in the Pure Land—the attainment of this birth for other people—is hindered.[290]

Therefore, if you have profound faith in Master Shan-tao, enter Jōdo Shū and apply the right practices fervently.

Those who would go counter to the teachings of Master Shan-tao and desire to observe Buddhist practices other than nembutsu or in addition to nembutsu may follow the practices they have learned. I am not in a position to pass judgment, but to put aside the practice encouraged by Master Shan-tao and observe practices he did not encourage will be of no avail. To be too lazy to observe the right practices encouraged by Master Shan-tao and yet wish to pursue the miscellaneous practices in addition is pointless.

Although even the defiled can achieve birth in the Pure Land through nembutsu, it is ignoble to say that observing meritorious practices such as the reciting of the *Lotus Sutra* will not interfere. Supporting the attainment of birth in the Pure Land is indeed wonderful. What purpose could it serve to say that the miscellaneous practices are wonderful and then observe Buddhist practices other than nembutsu in addition to the right practices?

Is the intention of Amida Buddha, then, to promote misdeeds? He taught that one should never indulge in wrongdoing. Nevertheless, we are common mortals, and from time to time, we commit karmic errors because of our nature as common mortals. It is beyond our ability to prevent this. It cannot be helped if a common mortal should, as the degenerate do, desire to read the *Lotus Sutra* and perform other practices together with nembutsu. If one feels that to recite the *Lotus Sutra* is even minimally comparable to committing negative karma but that it cannot be helped, but then goes on to insist that there is still merit in reading the *Lotus Sutra*, this would be improper indeed. It is lamentable that even the profound teachings of Buddha Śākyamuni sound like useless talk when enjoined by a person with wicked thoughts. To put it this way may offend believers in the miscellaneous practices, so I ask you to keep this to yourself and not share these thoughts with myriad people.

Do not lend an ear to those with different understandings; just concentrate on the encouragement from Master Shan-tao and think about reciting nembutsu as many times as possible in order to make certain the attainment of birth in the Pure Land. The miscellaneous practices may not be a hindrance to birth in the Pure Land, but neither do they assure it. Therefore, you must observe the right practices so that birth in the Pure Land will be assured. Is it not a waste to substitute the miscellaneous practices, which do not assure birth in the Pure Land, when you should be observing the right practices? Give this serious thought.

This is not to say that those who observe the miscellaneous practices in addition to nembutsu are forever unable to attain birth in the Pure Land. No matter what, it is deeply immoral to criticize and disparage those followers of the miscellaneous practices. Practice restraint and keep from being contemptuous of those who perform the miscellaneous practices. Whether positively or negatively, it is better to be nonjudgmental of others.

Further, encourage those who believe in this Pure Land gate and are pursuing this nembutsu path. Never get into a debate with others who may teach different beliefs. Even the virtuous monks are diligent in restraining from such presumption. It would indeed be a great wrong for you, people of status, to become embroiled in such a debate. Personally aspire earnestly for birth in the Pure Land, strive to recite nembutsu, attain the high grade of birth in the Pure Land, and immediately return to this defiled world of anguish in order to save the populace.

It was presumptuous of me to have gone into such great detail in this discourse. Please keep these thoughts to yourself.

Sincerely yours,
Genkū
March 14th

13. A Reply to the Lady of Tarō Sanehide in Ōgo

I HAVE THOROUGHLY read your letter. I am overwhelmed by your fervent desire to learn about nembutsu, which prompted you to send your courier this great distance.

Regarding your question on nembutsu: there is no practice superior to the recitation of nembutsu in order to attain birth in the Pure Land of Ultimate Bliss. This is because nembutsu is the practice taught in the essential vow of Amida Buddha.

Before he attained enlightenment, Amida Buddha was called Bodhisattva Dharmākara, and in order to establish his own pure buddhaland and to realize deliverance for sentient beings in the land, he made the forty-eight great vows before Tathāgata Lokeśvararāja. Among those made was a particular vow that promised the achievement of birth in the Pure Land for all sentient beings. This is called the "essential vow of birth in the Pure Land through nembutsu."

The essential vow is described thus in the first fascicle of the *Larger Sutra*: "If, when I am to attain buddhahood, all sentient beings in the ten directions who hold faith with genuine hearts and who wish to be born in my buddhaland are not born there within just ten moments of being mindful of me, I will not realize enlightenment."[291]

Master Shan-tao interpreted the above to mean: "'If, when I [Amida Buddha] attain buddhahood, all sentient beings in the ten directions who call out my name at least ten times are not born in the Pure Land, I will not realize enlightenment.' Amida Buddha did, indeed, realize buddhahood and presently resides in his Pure Land. Know that his essential vow was not made in vain. If sentient beings recite his name, they will, with certainty, attain birth in the Pure Land."[292]

Nembutsu does not mean the mindfulness of the Dharma body of Amida Buddha, nor does it mean the contemplation of his physical attributes. To recite exclusively the name of Amida Buddha with unwavering dedication—this is called *nembutsu.* Master Shan-tao, therefore, referred to nembutsu as "to call out my name."

No practice other than nembutsu is taught in the essential vow of Amida Buddha. Even though other practices are excellent, they are not superior to nembutsu. In general, if you desire to be born in a pure buddhaland, then follow the vow of that buddha. It is apparent that one who wishes specifically to be born in the Pure Land of Amida Buddha should abide by his essential vow. Do not compare the nembutsu taught in the essential vow with Buddhist practices other than nembutsu to see which is superior. It is for these reasons that there is no better practice than nembutsu for the attainment of birth in the Pure Land.

As for teachings other than birth in the Pure Land, some are also excellent teachings. In fact, the teachings of Buddha Śākyamuni include many sundry teachings for sentient beings to depart from the delusive worlds of saṃsāra. For people living today, however, taking leave of the delusive triple realms of transmigration is accomplished by merely attaining birth in the Pure Land. This is the very teaching that reveals the heart of the holy teaching of Buddha Śākyamuni.

There are also many practices for attaining birth in the Pure Land, but for us, this birth is only possible through reciting nembutsu. This is because nembutsu is taught in the essential vow; birth in the Pure Land will easily be attained if we rely on the power of the essential vow. In short, if we do not achieve birth in the Pure Land, it will be impossible for us to depart from the delusive worlds of transmigration; and birth in the Pure Land is impossible without nembutsu. You should believe this exclusively; single-mindedly aspire for birth in the Pure Land, earnestly recite nembutsu, and resolve to depart from the delusive worlds on this occasion.

Amida Buddha stated at the end of each vow: "If all sentient beings are not born in the Pure Land, I will not realize enlightenment." In reality, ten eons have already passed since he attained buddhahood. Please know that every one of his forty-eight vows has been fulfilled and that they were not made in vain: the essential vow for birth in the Pure Land through nembutsu is not the only vow he has fulfilled. Therefore, as long as sentient beings recite nembutsu, all will attain birth in the Pure Land without fail. If no one has attained this birth through nembutsu, who would believe that Amida Buddha realized buddhahood?

Even in the period of the extinction of the Three Jewels, birth in the Pure Land is still possible with just a single utterance of nembutsu. Even one who is guilty of the five grave offenses will attain birth in the Pure Land with ten repetitions of nembutsu. It goes without saying that since we are born in this world during the time of the Three Jewels and have not yet committed the five grave offenses, there is no doubt that we are able to attain birth in the Pure Land by calling out the name of Amida Buddha. For us to have encountered the essential vow results from extraordinary karmic conditions. Rejoice over this good fortune.

To be blessed to encounter the teaching of the essential vow but not to believe in it would be the same as never having had the encounter. Please have profound faith in the essential vow now and never entertain doubt about birth in the Pure Land. Have implicit belief in your heart, recite nembutsu wholeheartedly, and depart from the delusive worlds of transmigration to be born in the Pure Land on this occasion.

Furthermore, the *Meditation Sutra* describes, "Each ray of light from Amida Buddha shines over the worlds of the ten directions; those who practice nembutsu, embraced by that light, will never be abandoned."[293] This means that the light of Amida Buddha shines exclusively over the devotees of nembutsu; it does not shine over those who engage in any other practice. Nevertheless, the light also shines upon and embraces the latter if they aspire for birth in the Pure Land.

Why does the light of Amida Buddha shine exclusively upon the devotees of nembutsu? Master Shan-tao explained, "The color of the body of Amida Buddha is similar to that of a golden mountain. The rays of light emanating from his physical features shine over the ten directions; however, the light illuminates and embraces only the devotees of nembutsu. Know that this is where the influence of the essential vow is most evident."[294]

Since nembutsu is the practice taught in the essential vow, the light emitted by Amida Buddha shines upon those who practice nembutsu of the essential vow; therefore, his light makes a distinction and does not shine upon practitioners other than the nembutsu devotee. Those who desire birth in the Pure Land now must practice nembutsu of the essential vow and wish to be illuminated by his all-encompassing light. Thus, nembutsu is the most important practice for birth in the Pure Land. We must recite it often.

As described in the *Meditation Sutra*, Tathāgata Śākyamuni expounded on the meditative practices with a focused mind and those with a distracted mind. After these instructions, he entrusted the sole practice of reciting nembutsu to Ānanda, without the teaching on the three meritorious acts with a distracted mind or of the thirteen types of contemplation with a focused mind that are taught in the *Meditation Sutra*. The *Meditation Sutra* narrates, "Buddha Śākyamuni said to Ānanda, 'Thou, hold these words carefully in your heart. To hold these words means to keep in mind the name of the Buddha of Immeasurable Life [Amida Buddha].'"[295]

Master Shan-tao commented on this passage thus: "The purpose of the sentence after Buddha Śākyamuni said to Ānanda, 'Hold these words carefully in your heart,' is to clarify that Buddha Śākyamuni meant to entrust the name of Amida Buddha to Ānanda for its transmission into posterity. Buddha Śākyamuni preached the merits of the meditative practices with both a focused mind and with a distracted mind. In the final analysis, however, he exhorted sentient beings to recite nembutsu intently and exclusively, on the basis of the essential vow of Amida Buddha."[296]

Because these meditative practices with both a focused mind and a distracted mind are not founded on the essential vow, Tathāgata Śākyamuni did not teach these meditative practices when he entrusted the practice for birth in the Pure Land to Ānanda. He chose and transmitted only the vocal nembutsu, which is in accordance with the essential vow, as the right practice of the essential vow. It is incumbent upon those who now seek birth in the Pure Land according to the teachings of Buddha Śākyamuni to concentrate on the practice of nembutsu that was entrusted by him to Ānanda in compliance with this intent. Thus, you should recite nembutsu to be in accord with the teaching commended by Buddha Śākyamuni.

Further, all the buddhas in the six directions, as countless as the grains of sand in the Ganges, extended their tongues throughout the three thousand great-thousand worlds and proclaimed, "It is true that the exclusive recitation of the name of Amida Buddha will indeed bring about one's attainment of birth in the Pure Land."[297] This proclamation is testimony that these buddhas of the six directions authenticated the tenet that nembutsu is in accordance with the essential vow. Practices other than nembutsu are not consistent with the essential vow; hence the buddhas did not endorse them.

Therefore, devote yourself to nembutsu and receive the benevolence of the buddhas of the six directions. The essential vow, the teachings endorsed by Buddha Śākyamuni, and the protection of the buddhas of the six directions would not then be in vain. For this reason, it can be said that the practice of nembutsu is superior to other practices.

Master Shan-tao is the manifested body of Amida Buddha. There are many patriarchs of Pure Land Buddhism, yet I rely totally on Master Shan-tao alone.

Although there are many practices for birth in the Pure Land, they can be roughly divided into two. The first practice is the exclusive practice—the recitation of nembutsu; the second is the miscellaneous practices—all Buddhist practices other than nembutsu. The latter practices are defined as the meditative practices with a focused mind and those with a distracted mind as detailed above.

Master Shan-tao stated in *Hymns in Praise of Birth in the Pure Land*:

> If people recite nembutsu continuously throughout their entire lives in the manner mentioned previously, ten out of ten and one hundred out of one hundred people will realize birth in the Pure Land. Why is this so? It is because the exclusive practitioners of nembutsu possess the rightly settled state of mind for birth in the Pure Land without being disturbed by other miscellaneous karmic conditions. It is also because nembutsu is in accordance with the essential vow of Amida Buddha, is consistent with the teachings of Pure Land texts, and is in agreement with the words of Buddha Śakyamuni.
>
> If there are people who abandon the exclusive practice of nembutsu and desire to perform the miscellaneous practices, only one or two out of one hundred practitioners, or only three or five out of one thousand practitioners, will realize birth in the Pure Land. Why is this so? It is because the followers of the miscellaneous practices are distracted by miscellaneous karmic conditions and lose the rightly settled state of mind for birth in the Pure Land. Also the miscellaneous practices are not in accord with the essential vow of Amida Buddha, they are inconsistent with the teachings of Pure Land texts, and they do not agree with the words of Buddha Śākyamuni. In addition, devotion to Amida Buddha would not be continuous; concentration on the Pure Land would be interrupted.[298]

This statement clarifies the qualities of merit and demerit in comparing the exclusive practice and the miscellaneous practices. Here, *merit* means the attainment of birth in the Pure Land. That is, the statement "ten out of ten and one hundred out of one hundred people will realize birth in the Pure Land" reflects the merit of the exclusive practice. On the other hand, *demerit* means losing the merit of birth in the Pure Land. Only rarely will practitioners of the miscellaneous practices—"one or two out of one hundred"—achieve birth in the Pure Land; the rest cannot realize this birth. Only rarely—"three or five out of one thousand"—will practitioners of the miscellaneous practices be born in the Pure Land; the rest cannot be born there.

The reason it is possible only for all nembutsu devotees of the exclusive practice to be born in the Pure Land is that nembutsu is in accordance with the essential vow of Amida Buddha, and it is also consistent with the teachings of Tathāgata Śākyamuni. The reason so few who follow the miscellaneous practices attain birth in the Pure Land is that the miscellaneous practices are not in accordance with the essential vow; nor are they consistent with the teachings of Buddha Śākyamuni. The nembutsu devotees who aspire for birth in the Pure Land are indeed following practices in accordance with the compassionate hearts of two venerable buddhas [Buddha Śākyamuni and Amida Buddha]. The followers of the miscellaneous practices who aspire for birth in the Pure Land are not in accordance with the hearts of these two buddhas.

This is not the only statement of Master Shan-tao relative to the merit and demerit regarding the exclusive practice of nembutsu and the miscellaneous practices. He repeatedly elaborated on this issue in the *Commentary on the Meditation Sutra*. However, I will not pontificate on this topic any further because it would be too long-winded for me to dwell on it here.

In sum, those who vilify nembutsu will fall into the realm of hell and endure suffering for five eons; but those who believe in Amida Buddha will be born in the Pure Land and enjoy a good life for an eternity of eons. Please renew your commitment to your belief, dispel your doubting spirit, and recite nembutsu. It is impossible to provide more details in a letter. Please ask your courier for further explanation.

Sincerely yours,
Genkū
January 28th

*Dōkō's note: This reply was sent in the first year of Shōji (1199) using Renjō-bō Sonkaku[299] as the courier of the Lady of Tarō Sanehide in Ōgo.

14. A Reply to the Lay Priest in Kumagai

I HAVE CAREFULLY read your letter. I am extremely grateful to learn that you are earnest in pondering the profundity of birth in the Pure Land of Ultimate Bliss. Truly believe that you will certainly attain birth in the Pure Land through the recitation of nembutsu on this occasion.

You already received life in the realm of a human being, a state extremely difficult to realize, and have fortunately encountered the precious teaching of birth in the Pure Land through nembutsu. You also possess a heart that loathes this delusive world of suffering, and you have awakened aspiration for birth in the Pure Land.

The essential vow of Amida Buddha is so profound that birth in the Pure Land is within the palms of your hands. Please be diligent in your practice of nembutsu and firmly believe that you will certainly achieve birth in the Pure Land. I have nothing further to say now.

Sincerely yours,
Genkū
September 16th

15. A Reply to the Lay Priest Saburō in Tsunoto

I HAVE READ your letter carefully. Here is a brief answer to the questions you have asked.

First, it is being said that since both the lay priest Naozane in Kumagai and the lay priest Saburō in Tsunoto are unschooled, they encourage people to observe the sole practice of the recitation of nembutsu. It is also said that the learned need not limit themselves to nembutsu alone. This is a grave misunderstanding.

The practice of nembutsu was taught without regard to whether the practitioner is learned or unschooled. Long ago Amida Buddha designed his essential vow for the deliverance of all sentient beings in the ten directions; he did not make the essential vow advocating nembutsu for the ignorant and make the profound practices other than nembutsu for the intellectuals.

Here "all sentient beings in the ten directions" encompasses the learned and the unschooled, the guilty and the innocent, the virtuous and the unvirtuous, those who observe the precepts and those who do not, the wise and the ignorant, the male and female. It also includes people from the era of Buddha Śākyamuni, the mortals now present after his death, and even those who will appear after the period of the decline of the Dharma, which will last ten thousand years, when the Three Jewels vanish from this earth.

Further, Master Shan-tao appeared on this earth as the transformed body of Amida Buddha to encourage the exclusive practice of nembutsu to all sentient beings. Master Shan-tao did not intend his nembutsu teaching to be for the ignorant alone. If so, then how could one who relies upon the essential vow and attempts to spread the extensive teaching of Master Shan-tao to various people limit the teaching to merely the ignorant and exclude the educated?

If nembutsu were limited, it would betray the essential vow of Amida Buddha and would not be in keeping with the intention of Master Shan-tao. For this reason, I teach the practice of nembutsu to all who come here to ask about the path to birth in the Pure Land, regardless of their intellectual capacity.

Those who tell falsehoods to halt the practice of nembutsu are the people who in their previous existence had not listened to the teaching of the nembutsu samādhi taught in the Pure Land gate. They are also the people who, spreading lies, will return to the three lower realms in their next life. This is taught in the holy sutra as follows:

> There are people who give rise to the poison of anger who, when they see a serious nembutsu practitioner, struggle to incite intrigue and create grudges. Such people seem blind by nature and have no intrinsic goodness. Destroying the teaching designed for the instantaneous realization of enlightenment, they will sink into the three lower realms for a long time. They will never be released from the three lower realms, even though innumerable eons pass, more innumerable than the number of particles released in the explosion of the earth.[300]

This passage means: There are some people who become enraged upon seeing the nembutsu practitioner who aspires to birth in the Pure Land. They also become overwhelmed with malicious thoughts, formulate a plan, utilize misguided schemes in order to undermine the practice of nembutsu, and fight to outdo each other in their impious deeds to cause a suspension of the practice of nembutsu. These people are referred to as "people with no intrinsic goodness"

(Skt. *icchantica*), who since birth lack the ability to understand the teachings of Buddha Śākyamuni and the seed for the attainment of buddhahood.

If they vilify and destroy this nembutsu teaching of instantaneous enlightenment [that is, to detach immediately from the perpetual transmigration of the delusive realms and to live eternally in the Pure Land through the recitation of the name of Amida Buddha], they will fall into the three lower realms for an extremely long time and will not extricate themselves from the three lower realms due to the gravity of their karmic transgressions. The sutras state that these people will not escape the three lower realms for innumerable eons. In one view, such people who would scheme to spread untruths should be rather pitied. To preach to a person like this who doubts nembutsu and becomes distrustful of the teaching would nonetheless be in vain.

As a rule, one whose karmic relationship with Amida Buddha is shallow and who has not thought as far as birth in the Pure Land will not believe what he hears about the teaching of nembutsu, will fume on witnessing its practice, and in anger will try to impede the practice of nembutsu. Bear this in your mind, and despite what people say, maintain a stalwart heart.

The power of Amida Buddha is ineffective on those who do not believe in birth in the Pure Land through nembutsu at all; the word of a common mortal is even more ineffective. If you are compassionate toward nonbelievers and desire to help them attain birth in the Pure Land, you yourself must first attain birth in the Pure Land immediately. After achieving enlightenment there, return to this delusive world of transmigration and lead those who criticize and do not believe in the teaching of nembutsu to achieve birth in the Pure Land, thus saving all sentient beings. Remember this well.

Second, we need not even discuss the matter of encouraging the establishment of a karmic relationship with nembutsu for all members within an entire family. This is simply the right thing to do. To obstruct nembutsu is not allowed under the observance of the exclusive practice of nembutsu. Erecting a temple, creating the image of a buddha, writing a sutra, and giving alms to the priest are virtuous deeds that foster the karmic relationship with nembutsu. These do not become a hindrance to nembutsu or a hindrance to the exclusive practice of nembutsu.

Third, in order to recite nembutsu, it is preferable that you always be mindful of Amida Buddha and remember to vocalize his name. The practice of nembutsu is to be carried out while walking, standing, sitting, or lying down, without regard to time, place, or various karmic relationships. Even though your body and mouth may be contaminated, it is admirable indeed to keep your heart pure and to remember to recite nembutsu. To continually recite nembutsu in this manner is blessed and felicitous. Remembering to recite nembutsu in all places and at all times will become the karmic cause of birth in the Pure Land. Try to instruct those whose hearts lack this devotion.

When you are unable to practice nembutsu, think that you will strive to recite it more. When you are able to recite nembutsu, what reason could there be for failing to do so? This should never be. Wherever you may be, at any time, wholeheartedly vocalize nembutsu.

Fourth, avoid debating with those who do not believe in nembutsu. Do not force the teaching of nembutsu on those who observe practices other than nembutsu or pursue studies different from yours. As I previously said, do not be disdainful of people with different views and training, but respect them.

In contrast, if there are people who have the same heart as you and aspire for birth in the Pure Land with nembutsu, consider them to be fellow devotees of nembutsu and desire birth together in the Pure Land of Amida Buddha, even though they may live in different circumstances from you.

On occasion, it cannot be helped that some people have no karmic relationship with Amida Buddha and the Pure Land or have no arousal of devotion or desire for birth in the Pure Land. For those who follow their hearts and behave in various ways, encourage them to find a favorable condition after death to not fall into the three lower realms, according to their heart's desire.

Nevertheless, you should encourage those who have a glimmer of faith in nembutsu to follow the teaching of Amida Buddha and to desire birth in the Pure Land. No matter what is said, birth in the Pure Land and detachment from the delusive realm of transmigration is certainly realizable by anyone in this world through nembutsu. Ponder these ideas with the hearts of the people in mind.

Never, under any circumstance, create conflict with others. Think of critics and nonbelievers of nembutsu as those who have lived in hell for long periods and are going to return there; without fear, pacify and soothe them while encouraging nembutsu.

You may by chance have a fleeting moment of doubt, but whatever anyone says, do not falter in your nembutsu spirit. One thousand buddhas may appear on earth and tell you that birth in the Pure Land is impossible through nembutsu. Believing that nembutsu is the teaching of Buddha Śākyamuni and Amida Buddha, attested to by buddhas as countless as the grains of sand of the Ganges, renew your unshakable faith, be adamant, and aspire to find yourself in the presence of Amida Buddha.

Understand that I have only touched upon these matters, and continue reciting nembutsu for the benefit of yourself and others.

*Dōkō's note: Shinkan[301] wrote this reply for Master Hōnen on September 18th.

16. A Letter to an Eminent Monk in Kuroda[302]

WITH RESPECT to the potential of sentient beings for attaining birth in the Pure Land of Ultimate Bliss in the period of the decline of the Dharma, I mention the following views.

Do not doubt birth in the Pure Land even if your religious practice is minimal; birth in the Pure Land is assured with just a single utterance, or ten recitations, of nembutsu. Have no doubt that even a wrongdoer can attain birth in the Pure Land; Amida Buddha will never turn away anyone, even one who is filled with grave evil.

Do not entertain any doubt about birth in the Pure Land through nembutsu, even though much time has elapsed since the age of Buddha Śākyamuni. Sentient beings who will live in the age after the extinction of the Dharma can also achieve birth in the Pure Land; our contemporaries are even more definitely assured of this birth. Although one may perceive oneself as reprehensible, never doubt the attainment of birth in the Pure Land. Truly, Master Shan-tao said of himself, "I am a common mortal with worldly passions."[303]

There are numerous pure buddhalands in the ten directions, but we desire to be born specifically in the Western Pure Land of Amida Buddha because even one who commits the ten transgressions or the five grave offenses can be born there. Among all buddhas, we rely exclusively upon Amida Buddha because he will personally welcome into the Pure Land the nembutsu devotees who recite his name a mere three to five times.[304] We choose the practice of nembutsu over all other practices because nembutsu is in accordance with the essential vow of Amida Buddha.

Now, if we desire birth in the Pure Land through nembutsu by relying upon the essential vow, then birth in the Pure Land is definitely assured. Reliance on the blessing of the essential vow is a presupposition of our depth of faith.

It is extremely difficult to be born as a human being, to encounter the essential vow, to awaken the aspiration for birth in the Pure Land, to detach ourselves from the delusive worlds of transmigration, and to be born in the Pure Land; this is our ultimate good fortune.

Believing that even a person who has committed the ten transgressions or the five grave offenses will be born in the Pure Land, strive not to commit even the most minor of offenses. As even a wrongdoer can attain birth in the Pure Land, there is no doubt the virtuous can. Further, believing that just a single utterance of nembutsu, or ten repetitions, is never futile, you must exercise nembutsu continuously for life. If a single utterance assures birth in the Pure Land, think how much more powerful many repetitions are.

Amida Buddha fulfilled his vows, wherein he promised that he would not realize enlightenment until he succeeded in fulfilling the vows in their entirety, and he presently resides in the Pure Land. Therefore he will, without fail, come to welcome us into the Pure Land when our time on this earth comes to end.

Buddha Śākyamuni will look upon us with joy as we, devotees of nembutsu, abide by his teachings and depart from the delusive worlds of transmigration. All the buddhas in the six directions will also rejoice in the birth of mortals in the Pure Land of nonregression through our faith in the practice of nembutsu, which is endorsed by the buddhas. With great joy, express sincere appreciation for your encounter with the essential vow of Amida Buddha, and be so moved that you look skyward and prostrate yourself with joy. Walking, standing, sitting, or lying down, always recite nembutsu and be thankful for the benevolence bestowed by Amida Buddha. Rely upon the words of Amida Buddha, who vowed, "The attainment of birth in the Pure Land is assured with just ten recitations of nembutsu";[305] and further believe the declaration of Master Shan-tao, who stated, "Birth in the Pure Land will most certainly come to pass."[306]

17. A Reply to Kōmyō-bō in Ecchū

I HEARD that the idea that birth in the Pure Land is assured by a mere single utterance of nembutsu and it is unnecessary to continue the recitations after reciting nembutsu once has become widespread in the capital of Kyōto. This is clearly an unpardonable outrage; you need not have even asked.

The second fascicle of the *Two-Fascicle Sutra* (*Larger Sutra*) teaches, "Even a single utterance of nembutsu causes joy to well up in one's devout heart."[307] And Master Shan-tao instructed in *Hymns in Praise of Birth in the Pure Land*, "Believe, without doubting even for a moment, that the upper limit—lifelong nembutsu—and the lowest limit—ten repetitions or a single utterance of nembutsu—enable you to achieve birth in the Pure Land."[308] Those who misinterpret these statements have proposed the great heretical view that birth in the Pure Land is assured by just a single utterance of nembutsu. In truth, the words "even" and "the lowest limit" imply that one should continue to recite nembutsu for life.

Recently, however, many ignorant people have become exclusively attached to the ten repetitions, or even a single utterance of nembutsu, and have thereby abandoned the lifelong practice of nembutsu. This is most certainly shameful.

You must believe that nembutsu possesses supreme merit and that Amida Buddha, with his great compassion of the essential vow, will come to embrace one who recites nembutsu even ten times or just once. Thus believing this, practice nembutsu for your entire lifetime without negligence. Although there are many writings that attest to this teaching, citing these sources is unnecessary. The advocacy of the attainment of birth in the Pure Land through a single utterance of nembutsu is not worth mentioning.

Regarding this perverse view, someone replied upon encountering criticism, "I, too, advocate extreme devotion to a single utterance of nembutsu, and although a single utterance guarantees birth in the Pure Land, I do not advocate forsaking nembutsu thereafter." These words seem logical, but his heart is attached to an aberrant view. This implies the belief that if one utters nembutsu once with steadfast faith, one is free to commit the ten transgressions or the five grave offenses after the single utterance of nembutsu, much less other venial offenses.

How can someone who espouses such a belief be in compliance with the intent of Amida Buddha, even if he recites multiple nembutsu? In which sutra and commentary is such a teaching found? Such a belief is indicative of total indolence; it is a lack of aspiration for birth in the Pure Land and is an attempt of unjust and depraved people to cause iniquity. Further, if one does not continually recite nembutsu after a single utterance, one's karmic negativity would be a hindrance toward accomplishing birth in the Pure Land and would ultimately cast one down into the three lower realms.

Nevertheless, one who has committed a lifetime of wicked deeds may still attain birth in the Pure Land through reciting nembutsu ten times at the time of death. This is due to the compassionate power of nembutsu in repentance. This person should not be confused with one who has the mistaken notion that vice is nullified by a single utterance of nembutsu. The former is one in repentance; the latter is one with a perverse view. There is no need for further explanation.

Upon hearing of this erroneous view, even one who strives to practice nembutsu may succumb to the temptation of laziness. A person who strives to abide by the precepts may become one without compunction.

In summary, one who believes in the erroneous view that birth in the Pure Land is assured by merely a single utterance of nembutsu is a pseudo-practitioner of Buddhism and actually a Buddhist heretic. It is like a snake in one's bosom.

Investigating further, could it be that some people have lost their right understanding due to the undesirable influence of the king of heavenly demons attempting to hinder the masses who wish to attain birth in the Pure Land? This is a frightfully suspicious thought, and it is extremely difficult for me to elaborate upon it.

Sincerely yours.

18. A Letter to Nun Shōnyo-bō

I WAS DISMAYED on learning of your present condition. Against my intention, I've not been in touch, though I've wondered about your faith in nembutsu for the attainment of birth in the Pure Land. Since nothing required immediate attention, I had no particular reason to write, and so even though you were on my mind, I let the days go by. When news arrived of the seriousness of your situation, however, I wanted to see you once again. You must be feeling helpless regarding nembutsu for birth in the Pure Land for the time of your death; I am deeply embarrassed and regretful that you have, instead, inquired about my well-being. I had just decided to stay in my abode to observe the special nembutsu retreat for this time. Considering the circumstances, perhaps I should postpone the practice so that I may visit you?

On further consideration, seeing you again in this world is not important. Visiting you now may even increase my attachment to your lifeless form. No one remains here forever. The only difference is that some will leave here before me and some will leave after. Pondering this thought, it is impossible to predict the length of our lives, and although we may live a long time, the past is in the end like a phantom dream.

Therefore, remember that together we will enter the same buddhaland of Amida Buddha. Upon the lotus flower we will dispel memories of sadness in this defiled world of suffering, we will reminisce about our past karmic connection, and we will vow to save and lead people to enlightenment in the future. I shared the importance of this with you when we first met.

Believe deeply in the essential vow of Amida Buddha; do no doubt even for a moment that you will attain birth in the Pure Land; and believe that with ten repetitions of *Namu Amida Butsu* you will definitely achieve birth in the Pure Land through the power of the essential vow, however much negative karma you may have. Please focus on reciting nembutsu.

Birth in the Pure Land will never depend upon our goodness or lack thereof. It is possible solely through the power of the essential vow. No matter how brilliant and admirable we may be, it is extremely difficult during this age of the decline of the Dharma to be born immediately into the Pure Land through one's own efforts. Because the power of the essential vow is the crucial factor, there is no reason that even one who is nonvirtuous, simple, and incompetent cannot attain birth in the Pure Land. The essential condition is whether we believe in the essential vow of Amida Buddha.

The *Meditation Sutra* teaches this: One who, from birth on, has never uttered a single nembutsu, has no virtuous roots, and indulges in taking the life of living creatures and in stealing day in and day out—even such an immoral person as this, who lives years without a shred of repentance, will have the negative karma accumulated through five billion eons in the delusive worlds of transmigration dissipate should he accept the nembutsu teaching of a virtuous teacher at the time of death and utter *Namu Amida Butsu* even once. The transformed features of the three revered ones [Amida Buddha and his two attendant bodhisattvas] will then come to welcome him with praise, saying, "Your utterance of my name has absolved your karmic misdeeds. Therefore, I come to welcome you." The unrighteous mortal then attains birth in the Pure Land without delay.[309]

It is also taught that someone who commits the five grave offenses—including killing one's father, killing one's mother, defiling the blood of the Buddha with malicious thoughts, and destroying the harmony of the Sangha—should be destined to the hell of interminable pain and great suffering for infinite eons if he lacks repentance for even a moment. However, if such a person recites *Namu Amida Butsu* ten times under the guidance of a virtuous teacher at his time of death, each utterance will nullify his negative karma accumulated in the delusive worlds of transmigration for eight billion eons and assure him of birth in the Pure Land.[310] Thus, even a depraved mortal, with ten repetitions, or even a single utterance, of nembutsu, will achieve birth in the Pure Land. Know that this attainment of birth in the Pure Land is possible only by the power of the essential vow. Through these statements, we see that the essential vow was not made in vain.

This is truly the teaching of Buddha Śākyamuni. There is not one word of falsehood in the words uttered by Buddha Śākyamuni. Simply revere and believe them. Also know that if you were to doubt his teaching, it would be harmful and you would be karmically unfortunate. Please have implicit faith in his teaching.

It is indeed lamentable and regrettable that there are those who say birth in the Pure Land is impossible. Please, do not ever be swayed by such words, even if the speakers are wise and honorable. They may be people who are learned and respected in their individual paths of endeavor, but the instructions of those with different understandings and practices will be troublesome for those who are aspiring for birth in the Pure Land. These proponents of other practices are referred to as "undesirable teachers who will serve to distance the aspirants from their karmic relationship with Amida Buddha." You must not lend an ear to such misguided people but continue to rely steadfastly on the essential vow for birth in the Pure Land. Master Shan-tao thus stated:

> Even if the sky were filled with a proliferation of buddhas casting their individual lights and extending their broad tongues and in unison saying that it is misguided for the common mortal who has committed offenses to think he or

she can attain birth in the Pure Land through a mere single utterance of nembutsu, you must not believe it and must not be doubtful for even a fleeting moment.

This is because Amida Buddha, prior to attaining buddhahood when he first awoke the heart of enlightenment, vowed, "If, when I am to attain buddhahood, those who recite my name ten times or just once are not born in my buddhaland, I will not realize enlightenment." His vow was not made in vain; he did realize buddhahood a long time ago.

Further, Buddha Śākyamuni appeared in this delusive world of anguish, preached the essential vow of Amida Buddha for all sentient beings, and encouraged them to achieve birth in the Pure Land through nembutsu. All the buddhas in the six directions, as countless as the grains of sand in the Ganges, stated, "Buddha Śākyamuni's instruction of birth in the Pure Land through nembutsu is certain. No sentient beings should entertain any doubt regarding this birth through nembutsu even for a moment."

Without exception, many buddhas attested to this instruction with a unanimous heart. Amida Buddha had already made the essential vow, Buddha Śākyamuni clarified the efficacy of the essential vow, and all buddhas in the six quarters also proved the authenticity of the instruction of Buddha Śākyamuni.

Although there may be a buddha who, counter to other buddhas, espouses the theory that ordinary people are unable to attain birth in the Pure Land through nembutsu, you must not be alarmed or doubtful of attaining this birth through nembutsu, even if other buddhas appear and say the same thing. There is likewise no reason for bodhisattvas to say such a thing, much less arhats or pratyekabuddhas.[311]

Master Shan-tao thus commented in great detail on the theory of birth in the Pure Land through nembutsu. For this reason, you need not be disturbed by false comments made by ordinary people around you today; you must not doubt the certainty of birth in the Pure Land through nembutsu.

Even those said to be great scholarly monks do not surpass Master Shan-tao in his knowledge of the path toward birth in the Pure Land. Master Shan-tao was not an ordinary person; he was the manifestation of Amida Buddha. He appeared on earth in the form of Master Shan-tao in order to preach the essential vow and save all sentient beings. It follows, then, that the teaching of Master Shan-tao is the teaching of Amida Buddha himself. This is gracious indeed. You must never doubt this.

Since your faith was first awakened, I have known how much you have believed in the essential vow of Amida Buddha. Then why do you doubt birth in the Pure Land now? The *Meditation Sutra* contains teachings for those sentient beings who are as yet unaware of the way toward birth in the Pure Land. However, you have heard much about the teaching of nembutsu, and moreover, you have accumulated the merit of nembutsu. Your birth in the Pure Land is guaranteed, even if you do not have an encounter with a virtuous teacher at the end of your life.

It is regrettable to have someone around you of a different faith. Encourage all people, any person at your side—even female Buddhist practitioners without proper training who have merely shaved their heads—to recite nembutsu at all times. Hear their voices and remain stalwart of heart. Abandon thoughts of the virtuous teacher who is an ordinary person and rely instead on the virtuous teacher who is Amida Buddha. I ask this of you.

The arrival of Amida Buddha at the time of death is to establish the rightly settled state of mind for birth in the Pure Land. Unfortunately, some people think that if they establish the rightly settled state of mind first and then recite nembutsu, Amida Buddha will come for them. Actually this indicates a lack of belief in either the essential vow or in the teachings of the sutras. The *Sutra in Praise of the Pure Land* states, "Amida Buddha brings compassion to the nembutsu devotee and offers him tranquility of the heart."[312] Due to his merit accumulated from reciting nembutsu throughout his daily life, the nembutsu devotee abides in the rightly settled state of mind for birth in the Pure Land at the time of Amida Buddha's arrival.

It is a grave mistake to rely little on Amida Buddha, to believe in the undesirable ordinary teacher, to think that previous nembutsu recitation was in vain, and yet to pray for the rightly settled state of mind at the time of death. Bear this well in your mind.

Whenever reciting nembutsu, hold your palms together with your eyes always closed and with tranquility in your heart. Recite nembutsu with the belief that Amida Buddha, in accordance with the essential vow, will definitely appear before you at the time of death, and that he will impart his compassion to you and make you abide in the rightly settled state of mind. This is the ultimate stance for birth in the Pure Land. Your heart must not falter.

I have decided to perform a special nembutsu retreat in seclusion, but I do not do it for myself alone. Having learned of your illness, I will, during my nembutsu practice, say each nembutsu with special care and dedicate its merit toward your birth in the Pure Land. It is my heartfelt desire to help you attain birth in the Pure Land according to your wishes. If my resolution is genuine, how can Amida Buddha not extend help to you? Please know that you may rely on him.

The words I have expressed to you, which are now in your mind, are probably not limited to this world alone. The words also seem to be related to our previous existences, to which I indefinably feel an intimate karmic connection. Therefore, it is not certain that you will precede me in death, as you have informed me, or that I must embark on my journey with unexpected suddenness. What is certain is that ultimately we will meet again in the Pure Land of Amida Buddha.

In this world of phantom dreams, the wish to see each other once more may be impossible to fulfill. Abandon this thought, renew your profound desire for birth in the Pure Land, recite the nembutsu, and think of waiting for my arrival in the Pure Land. I repeat, never doubt birth in the Pure Land.

Even the wicked who have committed the five grave offenses or the ten transgressions have attained birth in the Pure Land with ten, or even just a single, nembutsu. What karmic negativity have you committed? Even if you do have foul karma, how grave could it be? Compared with the evils described in the *Larger Sutra*, your karma would be of no consequence. You are one whose heart awakened to enlightenment, who made a karmic relationship with the teaching of Buddha Śākyamuni by renouncing secular life; over the years you have been able to accumulate roots of virtue.

In addition, you have profound faith in the certainty of birth in the Pure Land, you have entered into the exclusive practice of nembutsu, and you have spent long years relying on the essential vow wholeheartedly. You must not doubt birth in the Pure Land for even a fleeting moment. Master Shan-tao taught that one hundred out of one hundred, and ten out of ten, exclusive nembutsu practitioners will attain birth in the Pure Land;[313] there is no reason why you would be excluded from these numbers. Trust Master Shan-tao and rely on the essential vow of Amida Buddha. Do not falter within your heart.

I meant only to explain my reason for being unable to come to you, and instead my letter has become extremely long. At a time such as this, when you are gravely ill, I realize this is insensitive. But you may yet ail for a long while. No one can know. If I do not say all this to you now, would there be another opportune time? I wish to relate this to you while you are able to absorb my message with a serene heart and help you nurture your desire to make even a single utterance of nembutsu more fervent. Therefore, I have not been able to condense my letter. I regret I could not adjust the length of my letter to your disposition.

If you have indeed become very frail, this letter is too long. Please ask someone to digest the gist of it and read it for you. The news of your illness melted my heart with sorrow and reminded me of you once again.

Respectfully yours.

19. Instruction to Zenshō-bō

The essential vow of Amida Buddha means that a single birth in the Pure Land can be attained through the merit of a single utterance of nembutsu. The merit of ten recitations, then, increases the possibility of birth in the Pure Land tenfold. If one becomes a single-hearted and exclusive practitioner of nembutsu, then continual recitation throughout one's life, up to the moment of death, guarantees birth in the Pure Land of Ultimate Bliss.

Regarding the potential for a nembutsu devotee, I would say that one should recite nembutsu in whatever is the natural state one was born into. Since one is born into this world through the power of one's residual karma, rectification is impossible. To illustrate, one born as a woman cannot become a man in this life even if she fervently desires to be a man. The wise should recite nembutsu as wise people do; the unlearned should recite nembutsu in their natural state; the compassionate should recite nembutsu with compassion; and one with aberrant views may recite nembutsu as a person with aberrant views. Each should recite nembutsu in his own manner. This is because Amida Buddha awakened his all-encompassing essential vow for all sentient beings in the ten directions.

Although it is said that birth in the Pure Land is assured by a single utterance or ten repetitions of nembutsu, irreverent recitation of nembutsu results in faith becoming a hindrance to practice. Conversely, continual recitation of nembutsu without cessation throughout one's life while doubting that a single utterance or ten repetitions of nembutsu assures birth in the Pure Land results in practice becoming a hindrance to faith. Hence, one must both be convinced that a single utterance of nembutsu guarantees birth in the Pure Land and continue nembutsu throughout one's entire life.

Further, if one entertains doubt that a single utterance assures birth in the Pure Land, every recitation of nembutsu, thus lacking in faith, becomes a futile exercise. The essential vow teaches that each utterance of nembutsu assures a single birth in the Pure Land; therefore, each nembutsu validates the causal karma for birth in the Pure Land.

20. Dialogue on Twelve Topics

Q. (1): If a practitioner of another Buddhist school asks, "Are you free to establish a distinct school, the Jōdo school, on top of the eight or nine traditional schools of Japanese Buddhism?" how should I address this question?

Answer: The establishment of the name of a school is not addressed in the teachings of Buddha Śākyamuni. The naming of a school is the result of deliberation based on the teachings of the sutras and commentaries to which a master aspires, resulting in mastery of its import. All Buddhist schools were named through this process. The name Jōdo Shū was determined by senior monks who mastered the significance of the attainment of birth in the Pure Land of Ultimate Bliss on the basis of the authentic Pure Land scriptures. Misconceptions are expressed by those who are not aware of this process.

Q. (2): How should I address the comment, "People say that it is not right to include the practices of the *Lotus Sutra* and Shingon in the miscellaneous practices."

Answer: Senior Master Eshin (947–1017)[314] compiled the essentials of the entire teachings of Buddha Śākyamuni and composed the *Collection of Essentials on Attaining Birth in the Pure Land*, which has ten chapters. In chapter 9, "Various Practices for Birth in the Pure Land," he discusses many Mahāyāna texts, including the *Lotus Sutra* and Shingon texts.[315] Here, "various practices" and the "miscellaneous practices" are two different labels with the same meaning. Certainly, it can be said that these critics are not superior to Senior Master Eshin.

Q. (3): Would encouraging a karmic relationship with a practitioner who is cultivating virtuous deeds based upon buddhas and sutras other than Amida Buddha and the three sutras of Pure Land Buddhism be considered a miscellaneous practice?

Answer: If you establish unshakable faith that places your heart in the essential vow in order to attain birth in the Pure Land with certainty, fostering virtuous deeds beyond vocal nembutsu would not be the miscellaneous practices. Rather, these deeds become your own auxiliary practices. Master Shan-tao commented, "Virtuous deeds other than nembutsu should be rejoiced in and praised."[316] You should understand this.

Q. (4): Was the distinguishing of aspirants who are born in the Pure Land into nine levels systematized by Amida Buddha?

Answer: The teaching of the nine grades of aspirants is found neither in Amida Buddha's essential vow nor in any other of his forty-eight vows. It was a skillful means used by Buddha Śākyamuni to guide the masses. If it were taught that the good and the errant were to be born in the same place, those with unwholesome karma would tend toward complacency; therefore, Buddha Śākyamuni ranked birth in the Pure Land into nine levels. Within the nine grades, a good person proceeds to higher categories, and an errant one will fall into the lower, according to Buddha Śākyamuni. At any rate, you should attain birth in the Pure Land speedily and validate the truth of this explanation for yourself.

Q. (5): Between an observer of the precepts who is not a conscientious reciter of daily nembutsu and one who violates the precepts but diligently recites daily nembutsu, who will progress to a higher level of birth in the Pure Land and who will fall to a lower level?

Answer: [Hōnen pressed down upon the straw mat on which he sat.] The placement of this mat here allows us to ask whether it is torn or not. Were there no mat, there would be no debate. Dengyō-daishi Saichō (767–822)[317] stated, in *Lamp for the Period of the Decline of the Dharma*, "In the period of the decline of the Dharma, there is no observance or nonobservance of the Buddhist precepts. There are merely monks in name only."[318] Why then should there even be a debate on observance and nonobservance of the precepts? Since the essential vow was promised for every common person, please hasten to recite the name of Amida Buddha.

Q. (6): Some practitioners of nembutsu vocalize the name of Amida Buddha on a daily basis, while others recite it in their hearts while counting its numbers. Which is preferable?

Answer: Recitation of nembutsu is the name of Amida Buddha, and meditative nembutsu is also the name of Amida Buddha; therefore, both will become karmic practices for birth in the Pure Land. However, you should vocalize nembutsu simply because the essential vow is the vow of recitation. For this reason, the *Meditation Sutra* states, "With an uninterrupted voice, a person says *Namu Amida Butsu* manifesting ten moments of thought."[319] Master Shan-tao also commented in the *Hymns in Praise of Birth in the Pure Land*, stating, "One who calls out my [Amida Buddha's] name at least ten times..."[320] If the voice can be heard, it would be considered nembutsu in an audible voice. Nevertheless, it is not desirable to recite so loudly as to make yourself a nuisance. Please understand that in general, nembutsu should be recited vocally.

Q. (7): What number of daily nembutsu can be considered the recitation of nembutsu in succession?

Answer: According to the interpretation of Master Shan-tao, it is more than ten thousand times a day.[321] However, to recite ten thousand nembutsu in a hurry and not to continue your recitation subsequently would be wrong. Day and night, ten thousand should be repeated. In general, to remember to recite nembutsu three times during a meal is a desirable session. However, each individual is different by nature; we cannot set up a certain number for a session. If your aspiration for birth in the Pure Land is profound, you will maintain continuous nembutsu as a matter of course.

Q. (8): A section on the profound heart in *Hymns in Praise of Birth in the Pure Land* states, "Attaining birth in the Pure Land will definitely come to pass through ten repetitions or just a single utterance of the name of Amida Buddha. Never doubt this, not even for a moment."[322] The passage on the profound heart in the *Commentary on the Meditation Sutra* also explains, "Reciting nembutsu without cessation throughout one's life is called the *rightly established practice*."[323] Which teaching should I consider more suited to me?

Answer: The interpretation of "ten recitations or just a single utterance" is the method of faith in nembutsu, and the interpretation of "reciting nembutsu without cessation throughout one's life" is the method of practice of nembutsu. These teachings, therefore, encourage you both to believe that birth in the Pure Land is possible with just a single utterance of nembutsu and also to practice recitation of nembutsu for life. Regard Master Shan-tao's comments as basic to this teaching: "Once you awaken within yourself the desire for birth in the Pure Land, you should continue for life, holding on to the aspiration for birth in the Pure Land."[324]

Q. (9): Is the teaching "a single utterance of nembutsu for birth in the Pure Land"[325] as expounded in the essential vow applicable to one's daily life as well as to a person in his final moments?

Answer: The issue of "a single utterance" refers to the person who is so close to the end of his life that he is unable to utter nembutsu more than once. If it were applicable to one's daily life, there would be no reason to teach the "upper limit of life-long nembutsu practice."[326] From this interpretation, we can understand that "a single utterance" is not the essence of the essential vow. Therefore, Master Shan-tao preached, "The practice in which one recites nembutsu continually for life is called the *rightly established practice*, which is in accord with the essential vow of Amida Buddha."[327] This interpretation of Master Shan-tao seems to mean that to recite nembutsu as many times as possible would be in accordance with the essential vow. However, the matter of timing is important in our individual encounters with the essential vow. Therefore, we must understand the essential vow in which Amida Buddha embraces all nembutsu practitioners, from the upper limit of life-long nembutsu practice to its lowest limit, the single utterance. This is, as Master Shan-tao explained, the "essential vow for birth in the Pure Land through nembutsu."

Q. (10): How am I to understand the issues of self-power and the power other than self?

Answer: I, Genkū, am not of such lofty station to be allowed entry into the imperial palace, but I had the honor of going there twice on the invitation of the emperor. It was neither my ability nor my achievements that brought me this honor; it was due to the power of the emperor. Much less, there is no doubt that Amida Buddha, by the power of the essential vow, will arrive to take us at our time of death.

One who wonders how Amida Buddha will save a man who is karmically negative and ignorant and does not know the meaning of the essential vow at all. Since the essential vow was designed to easily embrace such errant beings, one must not have a fraction of doubt when reciting the name of Amida Buddha. In the essential vow, the phrase "all sentient beings in the ten directions" encompasses the learned and the unschooled, the guilty and the innocent, the good and the bad, those who observe the precepts and those who violate them, male and female, and all sentient beings who will live a hundred years after the extinction of the Three Jewels.

If the nembutsu devotees after the extinction of the Three Jewels were to be compared with the monks of today, the monks would be more buddha-like. After the extinction of the Three Jewels, the lifespan of men will be a mere ten years. They will not even hear the name of the threefold discipline of precepts, meditation, and wisdom. There will be no one to speak of these nembutsu teachings; therefore, even if they know that they will be blessed with the coming of Amida Buddha, they will merely wonder over the method with which to extricate themselves to enter the path leading to enlightenment. For them, imminent birth in the Pure Land will be without the aspiration for birth in the Pure Land and without the ability to recite nembutsu. This is why both "the essential vow that expounds on the attainment of birth in the Pure Land through total reliance on the power of Amida Buddha" and "the unsurpassed compassionate vow" are taught.

Q. (11): How should I understand possessing the threefold devotional heart, one aspect of which is the genuine heart?

Answer: There is no particular method for cultivating the threefold devotional heart. The essential vow of Amida Buddha states, "If all sentient beings recite my name, I will, with certainty, come to welcome them into my Pure Land."[328] Therefore, the threefold devotional heart will be yours as a matter of course if you believe firmly that Amida Buddha will come to take you, if you hold him in your heart and sincerely call his name, and if you persevere until the very last utterance as if you have already attained birth in the Pure Land. Lay people do not need to contemplate so elaborately. They need only to believe in birth in the Pure Land through nembutsu and repeat it continuously; then the threefold devotional heart will naturally be theirs. This is why even ordinary people attain splendid birth in the Pure Land of Ultimate Bliss through nembutsu.

Q. (12): It is said that one's final nembutsu is more meritorious than the daily nembutsu performed for a hundred years. Does this mean that there is a lack of intensity in nembutsu in daily life?

Answer: If nembutsu is repeated with the threefold devotional heart, the merit of nembutsu is the same. The *Meditation Sutra* reads: "Those who embody the threefold devotional heart will be born in that buddhaland without fail."[329] The words "without fail" indicate that the daily recitation of nembutsu is the same as the final recitation.

*Dōkō's note: In *Clarifying the Essentials and Promoting Wholesome Conduct*, these questions are attributed to Zenshō-bō.[330] Another source names Monk Ryūkan.[331] More research is necessary.

21. Dialogue on Twelve Issues

Q. (1): I am familiar with the teaching that attainment of birth in the Pure Land of Ultimate Bliss is possible through the recitation of nembutsu, but I have not grasped its meaning. Please explain to me in detail how I, a woman deemed to bear the five hindrances, will not be abandoned by Amida Buddha.

Answer: Although there is more than one practice for extricating oneself from the delusive worlds of transmigration, you should first desire birth in the Pure Land of Ultimate Bliss and recite the name of Amida Buddha. This teaching is extensively expounded in the collected teachings of Buddha Śākyamuni. This is because Amida Buddha formulated the essential vow, saying, "If one who recites my name is unable to be born in my Pure Land, I will not realize enlightenment."[332] Amida Buddha did realize enlightenment. For this reason, those who recite his name will surely attain birth in the Pure Land.

Amida Buddha, together with his host of celestial beings, will certainly come to receive you at the time of death. Therefore, your unwholesome karma will not hinder your birth in the Pure Land, and no detrimental condition may detain you. Without distinction between male and female, noble and humble, or good and bad, all who devotedly recite the name of Amida Buddha will, without fail, realize birth in the Pure Land.

It is like an ocean liner transporting a heavy load of boulders a long distance across the sea without sinking. Though the burden of our negative karma is like the heavy boulders, if we should board the vessel of the essential vow, we will surely cross the delusive ocean of transmigration to reach the shore of birth in the Pure Land. Never fear your negative karma relative to the transcendent power of the essential vow. This is called the "realization of birth in the Pure Land through the power other than self."

If you desire to escape from the delusive worlds of transmigration through your own power, you can try abstaining from worldly passions and negative karma completely, attaining birth in the Pure Land, and realizing enlightenment. This, however, is like walking a treacherous path.

Q. (2): The light of wisdom can save one who has negative karma by removing the darkness of worldly passions, yet an ignorant one such as I who has accumulated so much undesirable karma cannot eliminate them. How can I get rid of my negative karma?

Answer: Only implicit faith, without any doubt in the words of Amida Buddha, will lead you, by his power, to achieve birth in the Pure Land. As the previous metaphor illustrated, once aboard the ocean liner, both the blind and sighted move forward together. One may possess the eye of wisdom, but without reciting nembutsu, it will not be in accord with the power of the essential vow. Even an utterly dim-witted ignoramus can rely on the power of the essential vow through the vocal nembutsu.

Amida Buddha always casts his light upon those who practice nembutsu and will not abandon them. The nembutsu devotee will not encounter any undesirable conditions and, at the time of death, will abide in the rightly settled state of mind and surely attain birth in the Pure Land. So do not assume that wisdom or the lack of it determines your capacity for birth in the Pure Land. It is determined solely by the depth of your faith.

Q. (3): For an individual who has renounced the world, it is a simple matter to devote himself to nembutsu for birth in the Pure Land. I, however, work day and night for worldly fame, and on my mind yesterday and today are thoughts of personal gain. Can one such as me recite nembutsu and be in accord with the heart of Amida Buddha?

Answer: It is like the precious gem that purifies muddy water with its special power. The human mind, like muddy water, is always in pursuit of renown and personal gain. If we cast the precious gem into the murky waters of our minds, the waters naturally become purified, and we will achieve birth in the Pure Land. This means that birth in the Pure Land is attained by the power of nembutsu. It is not taught that you should have tranquility of mind, remove all deterrents, and then recite nembutsu. Rather, you should recite nembutsu incessantly and rid yourself of your negative karma in that way. History has proven that countless lay people have attained birth in the Pure Land. If you do not have tranquility of mind, engage yourself in reciting nembutsu exclusively, praying with all your heart for the power of Amida Buddha.

Q. (4): Some encourage me to repeat nembutsu many times; others tell me that a few times will suffice. Whose opinion should I follow?

Answer: These opinions may come from either an enlightened one or a learned one. Not knowing the source of their hearts, it is difficult to make a judgment. Nonetheless, it is regrettable when lay people create only undesirable karmic conditions, do not practice nembutsu, spend days in vain, and pass their nights idly. The nature of the common mortal deteriorates easily in response to unwholesome karmic conditions; therefore, he should strive to practice nembutsu. That is why it is said everywhere, "Recite nembutsu continually and as many times possible. Do not forget nembutsu throughout your life."[333]

Q. (5): Remembering to repeat nembutsu continually seems to be difficult. Although I hold a string of prayer beads in my hand, my thoughts wander. Under these circumstances, would my nembutsu not be the true practice for birth in the Pure Land? If it is not, would my attainment of this birth become uncertain?

Answer: The teaching of the continual recitation of nembutsu without cessation[334] means to do your best given your capacity. Reflect upon yourself and evaluate yourself mentally and physically as to what extent you can devote yourself to nembutsu. To think undesirable thoughts during nembutsu is a matter of habit for all common mortals. However, the wandering of your mind does not become a hindrance for birth in the Pure Land if you recite nembutsu with the aspiration for birth in the Pure Land. For example, there may be misunderstandings at times between parent and child, but as long as they do not think of disowning each other, these misunderstandings do not sever the relationship. One who wishes to attain birth in the Pure Land through nembutsu may, during recitation, stray toward the worldly passions of greed and anger. But if one maintains faith in the promise of Amida Buddha for birth in the Pure Land through nembutsu, one will certainly achieve birth in the Pure Land.

Q. (6): If the attainment of birth in the Pure Land is so easy, everyone who practices nembutsu should achieve this birth. There are many who aspire for birth in the Pure Land and recite nembutsu. Why do so few attain birth in the Pure Land?

Answer: Since we cannot look into another's mind, it is impossible to determine impiety or righteousness in the mind of others. The *Meditation Sutra* states, however, "Those who possess the threefold devotional heart will realize birth in the Pure Land of Ultimate Bliss without fail."[335] One cannot realize birth in the Pure Land through nembutsu without these three aspects of the heart. The threefold devotional heart consists of the genuine heart, the profound heart, and the heart that seeks birth in the Pure Land through the dedication of merit.

The first aspect is the genuine heart. Master Shan-tao interpreted the genuine heart as the "sincere heart,"[336] indicating the unity of the heart and appearances. Nothing gets accomplished without a sincere heart. Most people, with their ordinary hearts, pretend to dislike this defiled world of suffering though they actually do not mind it; they pretend to aspire for birth in the Pure Land though they truly do not desire it. Master Shan-tao was afraid of discordance between "within" and "without" and taught us to possess the genuine heart within and without, to loathe this defiled world of suffering, and truly desire birth in the Pure Land.

The second aspect is the profound heart. It refers to the heart full of faith in the essential vow of Amida Buddha. If after hearing the reasons that although we are karmically defiled with worldly passions, we will certainly attain birth in the Pure Land through the power of the essential vow, we deeply believe this without a shadow of doubt, not even one the size of a dewdrop or a speck of dust—this is the *profound heart.* We should be steadfast, even if many people despise and hinder the teaching of nembutsu. This is also called the *profound faith.*

The third aspect is the heart that seeks birth in the Pure Land through the dedication of merit. This is the heart that dedicates the merit accumulated through our practice toward birth in the Pure Land. Do not think it is the power of our practice or our superior hearts that brings birth in the Pure Land. Believe instead that even the undeserving can attain birth in the Pure Land through the supremacy of the power of the essential vow. Your belief that Amida Buddha will definitely come to welcome you at your time of death should be as solid as an adamantine stone that nothing can destroy. For those who can maintain this implicit faith until the time of death, ten out of ten or one hundred out of one hundred will attain birth in the Pure Land.

Accordingly, without possessing the threefold devotional heart, one will not attain birth in the Pure Land after death, and one's karmic relationship to birth in the Pure Land will become distant. No one knows except oneself whether or not the threefold devotional heart has arisen within.

Q. (7): I wish to attain birth in the Pure Land, but my aspiration is not steadfast. Neither do I consider nembutsu to be an unfavorable practice, but I spend my daily life reciting nembutsu only idly. Therefore, it cannot be said that I indeed possess the threefold devotional heart. Should I despair in my desire for birth in the Pure Land on this occasion?

Answer: You deplore your lack of vigorous spirit in desiring birth in the Pure Land and your lack of vigilance in practicing nembutsu, but this does not mean that you have no aspiration for birth in the Pure Land. One who has no aspiration toward birth in the Pure Land never regrets his lack of vigilance or laments his lack of intensity. One deplores one's slow feet when in a hurry but not when not in a hurry. It is said that desire brings aspiration for birth in the Pure Land spontaneously, so your heart will gradually move in the right direction and bring you to birth in the Pure Land with certainty.

Even someone who commits the ten transgressions or the five grave offenses in his daily life may, at his time of death, encounter a virtuous teacher and achieve birth in the Pure Land. For someone who is desirous of birth in the Pure Land who recites nembutsu, Amida Buddha will have compassion, the bodhisattvas will protect this individual and remove obstacles, and he will encounter a virtuous teacher and realize birth in the Pure Land, even if he feels he is not devout of spirit.

Q. (8): What thoughts should always be in the mind of a nembutsu practitioner?

Answer: Ponder periodically the transience of the world and recognize the brevity of your time in mortal life. Also reflect on the essential vow and implore Amida Buddha to welcome you into the Pure Land.

On occasion, rejoice at having received life in the realm of a human being and bemoan the approaching end to a meaningless life. To have been granted life as a human being within the six delusive worlds of transmigration is as unlikely as thread from the Brahma heaven entering the eye of a needle in the depths of the ocean.

From time to time, reflect on your providential encounter with the teachings of Buddha Śākyamuni, and ponder when, if you do not practice now, you will, through observing his teachings, extricate yourself from the delusive worlds. Once you have been plunged into the lower realms, you will be unable to hear the name of the Three Jewels for countless eons. How, once there, will you be able to steadfastly believe in the essential vow?

Further, rejoice in the residual virtue you have cultivated in previous existences. The numbers in the wise and varied classes of people are many, but rare is the person who has faith in the teachings of Buddha Śākyamuni and who aspires to birth in the Pure Land. It is extremely difficult to become a believer. Most people bear ill will toward others and are critical of the teachings of Buddha Śākyamuni; this causes our descent onto the treacherous path.

Belief in the teachings of Buddha Śākyamuni, reverence for them, and the desire for birth in the Pure Land while relying on Amida Buddha are induced by virtue we cultivated in previous lives. It is not merely the result of our virtuous acts in this life. This validates the fact that the time for birth in the Pure Land has come and you should rejoice with elation. These are the thoughts upon which one should reflect.

Q. (9): An ignorant one such as me has not looked at a sacred text, and I am singularly plagued with many negative conditions. By what means can I protect my mind and cultivate faith?

Answer: There is more than one way. You may witness suffering and imagine the suffering of yourself in the three lower realms. You may witness death and know the truth of impermanence. You may recite nembutsu continually and encourage your heart. You may meet with virtuous friends frequently and feel shame in your heart. The human mind tends to grow in negative thoughts upon meeting unwholesome conditions. Stay away from such conditions and strive for contact with wholesome conditions. There is not only one practice; each should be followed as the occasion dictates.

Q. (10): How can I understand the idea that virtuous deeds other than nembutsu are not the practices for birth in the Pure Land and should therefore not be pursued?

Answer: This idea can be linked to the many attendants of a master walking with him along the road. Among the practices for birth in the Pure Land, nembutsu is the master while other deeds are the attendants. However, it is not necessary to belittle the retinue of virtuous deeds.

Q. (11): Some will choose to amass immoral deeds, knowing that the essential vow does not discriminate against a depraved person. How do you explain this?

Answer: Amida Buddha will not abandon an errant mortal. However, one who chooses unwholesome deeds does not qualify to become a disciple of Buddha Śākyamuni. Among all the teachings of Buddha Śākyamuni, there are none that do not discourage wrongful deeds. Buddha Śākyamuni encourages those who find it impossible to refrain from undesirable deeds to expiate their wrongs through the recitation of nembutsu.

To blame one's crimes and errors on Amida Buddha because one finds the burden unbearable is terribly wrong. If one finds it impossible to refrain from unwholesome deeds, one should implore, "Please, Amida Buddha, with your compassion, dissipate my failings and receive me into the Pure Land." No school of Buddhism teaches the commitment of wrongful acts.

To illustrate, though parents love all their children, some children may be good and some may be delinquent. Although the parents love them all equally, they scold with glaring eyes and discipline the unruly one with a cane.

If one hears that because the compassion of Amida Buddha is infinite, wicked deeds are acceptable, this may lead one to fall out of Amida Buddha's grace. Upon learning that the essential vow promises to save even the depraved, a wrongdoer should be evermore awed by his brilliance and insight, and thus reflect upon and have remorse for his conduct. Just because parents love their children, will they be joyous if one child commits unvirtuous deeds? The parents will grieve, but not abandon; they will feel pity, yet abhor the child's action. Amida Buddha feels the same way.

Q. (12): All common mortals have undesirable thoughts. The reason these thoughts are not overt is that, feeling no shame before Amida Buddha, people simply avoid the eyes of others. To avoid this, should one instead behave as one's thoughts dictate?

Answer: Some may put on a facade to gain the trust of others, which can lead to great problems. In order to avoid committing an unwholesome deed, one may restrain oneself from exhibiting one's true feelings and thereby conceal the unwholesome thoughts. This actually indicates a sense of shame before Amida Buddha.

Whatever the case, you just need to diminish unwholesome thoughts and accumulate the merit of nembutsu. If nembutsu is not habitual, it may be difficult to have the rightly settled state of mind for birth in the Pure Land at the time of death. Always keep in mind the time of your departure from earth and repeat nembutsu ten times whenever you are lying down. In other words, remember nembutsu whether you are awake or asleep.

As a rule, the reasoning is no different in the secular world than in the spiritual realm. Thoughtful people love their parents and honor their master; they also refrain from nonvirtuous deeds and desire to perform virtuous deeds.

Upon hearing that the essential vow saves even offensive mortals, think how much more a virtuous person is embraced. Having heard that a single utterance or ten repetitions of nembutsu will result in being welcomed by Amida Buddha, strive toward one hundred or one thousand recitations with utmost devotion.

Do not doubt the welcoming of Amida Buddha by saying that birth in the Pure Land is impossible because your ability is insufficient. The wish to live to seventy or eighty years is but a phantom dream. We cannot predict our time of death; no law of nature says the old must die before the young. Neither should we anticipate our life after death. Only aspire for birth in the Pure Land. There is more than one reason for the teaching of the single-hearted recitation of nembutsu.

"Whenever you see this, remember to recite *Namu Amida Butsu.*" [Hōnen's Poem]

22. Dialogue on One Hundred Forty-Five Topics

Q. (1): In the renovation of an aged temple and Buddhist monument, is it necessary to have a veneration ceremony consisting of making offerings?

Answer: Such a service is not always necessary, but neither is it a bad idea. The act is meritorious, but its omission is not karmically negative or wrongful.

Q. (2): Is the inaugural ceremony of opening the spiritual eyes of a buddha image the same as a veneration ceremony?

Answer: The ceremonies are actually different, though people often conflate them. First, "opening the spiritual eyes" means that the sculptor of the image inserts eyes into the representation of a buddha upon completion of his work. This is called the *physical* opening of the eyes. Following this, the priest chants Shingon to open the eyes. Then the holy lines of Tathāgata Mahāvairocana are chanted to confer on the image all the virtues of the tathāgata. This ceremony is called the *spiritual* opening of the eyes. Second, "a veneration ceremony consisting of making offerings to the image of a buddha" refers to the offering of flowers, incense, foods, a votive light, and other precious things.

Q. (3): For attaining birth in the Pure Land, is it necessary to observe meditation on the ultimate reality?[337]

Answer: This is said to be an idea espoused by Eshin-sōzu (942–1017), but it is an undesirable practice. Typically, such a meditative practice not easily observed by common mortals, and so I do not think that this practice is required for common mortals to attain birth in the Pure Land. Accordingly, it is a practice with no merit for us.

Q. (4): In relation to the above, it is taught that one must realize the universal state of the emptiness of all existence. Would this be the "meditation on emptiness"? If so, it seems to be taught that in order to practice the contemplation, one must be detached from all delusory attachments to this worldly life. I was sent here so that you would teach me the fundamentals of this meditative practice.

Answer: All of it is meditation on the noumenal aspects of real ity and quite impossible for us to practice. Even monks cannot gain this meditation despite long years of study. Those who lack erudition, especially women, would find it an impossible task. It is unnecessary to ask about this practice.

Q. (5): Others have suggested that I should recite the names of the past seven buddhas who appeared in succession in this world. If I do as they say, would I be absolved of all my negative karma? I ask this question because everything you say is reliable.

Answer: You need not do as you have described because your negative karma will be absolved through the recitation of nembutsu.

Q. (6): Is it true that neglecting even an insignificant master will detract from all that has been learned and make it impossible to receive the divine protection of a buddha or other deities?

Answer: You must never be neglectful of a master. Nothing surpasses the depth of benevolence bestowed by your master.

Q. (7): If I recite nembutsu with all my heart, will nembutsu alone help me to achieve birth in the Pure Land, even though I have a distracted heart and am lacking in any sort of practice?

Answer: It is the nature of common mortals to experience distractions, which are impossible for them to control. But if you earnestly recite nembutsu, Amida Buddha will cleanse your negative karma and make you achieve birth in the Pure Land. Even grave offenses more serious than illusory thoughts will be eradicated by nembutsu.

Q. (8): Is *dhāraṇī* [mystic phrases] as described in the sutras what we should receive from the priest in the ceremony in which purified water is sprinkled over the head of a devotee?

Answer: The *dhāraṇī* described in the *Lotus Sutra* is justifiable in the ceremony, but the mystic phrase performed by the priest in that ceremony is different from the one of the *Lotus Sutra*. I do not remember clearly the words of the phrase you have mentioned.

Q. (9): What does it mean to "meditate upon the mother of Buddha Śākyamuni" as taught in the *Sutra of Bodhisattva Samantabhadra*?

Answer: I do not remember such a concept.

Q. (10): People say that a newborn baby is impure for the first hundred days and that it is not right to take the baby to a Buddhist temple or a Shintō shrine.

Answer: The impurity of a newborn baby for the first hundred days does not matter. Impurity is not limited to the baby, who is physically soiled. Others are unclean as well.

Q. (11): It is taught that if one observes the one million recitations of nembutsu one hundred times, one will be assured of the attainment of birth in the Pure Land. What happens if one does not live long enough to do so many repetitions?

Answer: This, too, is a mistaken notion. Reciting one million nembutsu one hundred times will assure birth in the Pure Land; so will ten repetitions; so will even a single utterance of nembutsu.

Q. (12): It is said that the *Smaller Sutra* should be recited one hundred thousand times. What are your thoughts?

Answer: This means that one may go as far as possible. It also means that one should recite the *Smaller Sutra* as many times as one can.

Q. (13): Is it okay to just perform as many daily nembutsu as one can without setting a predetermined goal?

Answer: It is better to have a daily goal, for without a goal one tends to get lazy.

Q. (14): Is it allowable to recite nembutsu at all times with leeks, onions, garlic, and meat on one's breath?

Answer: Nothing affects nembutsu.

Q. (15): Before having a religious meal for purification[338] during the six days of observance of the precepts for lay people,[339] should one attempt to observe religious abstinence, perform ablutions for purification of the body, and put on freshly laundered clothing?

Answer: It is absolutely unnecessary to do so.

Q. (16): I am taking medication once a week. What should I do if a medication day falls on one of the six days of observance of the precepts?

Answer: It cannot be helped. It is not wrong to take medication.

Q. (17): Should I practice the six days of observance of the precepts throughout my life or just for a number of years?

Answer: The decision is yours. There is no hard and fast rule.

Q. (18): What is an appropriate number of repetitions for daily nembutsu?

Answer: The initial goal is ten thousand recitations, which increases to twenty, thirty, fifty, sixty, and one hundred thousand. You may set your goal to repeat it as many times as your heart desires.

Q. (19): How many times should one recite the *Smaller Sutra* in a day?

Answer: Master Shan-tao stated that reciting the *Smaller Sutra* one hundred thousand times during one's lifetime guarantees birth in the Pure Land. At fifteen times a day, you will be able to recite the *Smaller Sutra* one hundred thousand times in twenty years. Thirty times a day will take you ten years.

Q. (20): It is taught that a strand of five-colored thread is placed in the left hand of the image of Amida Buddha when someone is about to die. With which hand should I hold the [other end of the] thread?[340]

Answer: Holding in either hand is fine.

Q. (21): It is said that burning unwanted writings of the name of Amida Buddha or of the holy teachings in order not to handle them disrespectfully would be karmically problematic. What do you think of burning them while chanting Buddhist passages?

Answer: There may be some passages to chant that are appropriate for this purpose. The sacred teachings must be revered; therefore, if you wish to burn such precious writings, do it in a place that is clean and pure.

Q. (22): In the ceremony for receiving the Buddhist precepts, we ask a certain priest to become our *master* or our *eminent master*.[341] However, I do not fully understand the roles of these two masters. What do they mean?

Answer: The *master* is the one who instructs us in the teachings of Buddha Śākyamuni within the ceremony of receiving the Buddhist precepts. The *eminent master* is the one who specifically bestows the precepts; he is referred to as a *karmācārya*.

Q. (23): Is there merit in the observance of a religious meal for purification? Should we observe this practice without fail?

Answer: There is merit in this practice, especially during the six days of observance of the precepts. However, it is not necessary to observe the practice when one is seriously ill. At any rate, he who recites nembutsu frequently will remove himself from the delusive worlds of saṃsāra to attain birth in the Pure Land. This is due to the power of nembutsu.

Q. (24): When life comes to an end, should one hold the five-colored thread in the same hand position as Amida Buddha [i.e., in the meditation mudrā]? Or should one simply hold the thread in both hands?

Answer: It is absolutely unnecessary to emulate the hand gesture of meditation. Just join your palms together in homage, holding the thread between your palms.

Q. (25): It is always difficult to look up at the image of Amida Buddha, even if one is up close to the image. Is it permissible to hold the five-colored thread from a distance?

Answer: You may be close or at a distance, at your convenience. Distance does not matter.

Q. (26): Is attainment of birth in the Pure Land still possible through only hearing nembutsu recited by others, without looking up at the image of Amida Buddha or holding the five-colored thread at the time of death?

Answer: You will attain birth in the Pure Land whether or not you hold the thread, whether or not you worship the image of Amida Buddha, as long as you are reciting nembutsu. However, to achieve birth in the Pure Land by listening to others' recitation of nembutsu is reserved only for the extremely devout practitioner.

Q. (27): I fervently wish to depart from the delusive worlds of transmigration and not be reborn in the delusive three realms again. Is it true that after my attainment of birth in the Pure Land of Ultimate Bliss, I may return to this world of suffering if my karmic ties to the Pure Land come to an end?

Even if I became a ruler or a heavenly being after returning from the Pure Land, I would not want to, because I would still be in the delusive three realms.

My only hope is to detach myself from these realms. What kind of practices will prevent my return to the realms again?

Answer: These are all mistaken ideas. Once one is born in the Pure Land, one will never come back to this world of suffering. All who are in the Pure Land realize buddhahood. There are some bodhisattvas who will come back to this world for the purpose of offering guidance to others, but they are not wandering through the delusive worlds of saṃsāra.

In order to depart from the delusive triple realms and to be born in the Pure Land, no practice surpasses the recitation of nembutsu. You should devote yourself to nembutsu.

Q. (28): When a preceptor asked a woman during a service, "Will you observe the precepts or not?" she did not answer "I will" because she was worried about breaking them in the future. Is this justifiable? It is said that one should make a promise to observe the precepts for some specific span of time when a preceptor asks. Is this true?

Answer: This presents no problem. Even should she break her promise later, at the time of receiving the precepts it is proper to say "I will observe them" with a desire to commit.

Q. (29): Should one gild the image of Amida Buddha and make offerings to the image?

Answer: This is not necessary.

Q. (30): How would it be to make others recite daily nembutsu while neglecting the daily practice oneself?

Answer: It is not necessary to ask others to do so.

Q. (31): People say that to change a sutra from scroll form into a book bound with string is karmically detrimental. Is this true?

Answer: Such an act is not karmically detrimental.

Q. (32): Is it wrong to remove and give away a scripture that is presented to the image of Amida Buddha on the altar?

Answer: It is virtuous to spread Buddhism.

Q. (33): Is it wrong to remove and recite a single volume from a set of the scriptures?

Answer: It is not a wrong act.

Q. (34): Must the image of a buddha be enshrined with offerings made to it?

Answer: Not at all.

Q. (35): Should one worship other people just as Bodhisattva Sadāparibhūta[342] does?

Answer: The true meaning of this concept is difficult to understand for people today.

Q. (36): People say that it is not necessary to perform a religious abstinence for a child who has died before reaching seven years old. What does this mean?

Answer: There is no such thing as "religious abstinence" in Buddhism. This is an idea that is commonly perpetrated.

Q. (37): To apply glue to the image of a buddha is to defile it. What should I do?

Answer: True, the glue is unclean, but there is no suitable substitute for the job.

Q. (38): Is it wrong for a nun to take medication?
Answer: Medicine necessary to cure an illness is acceptable, but she should not take medication when she is well.

Q. (39): People say that it is karmically wrong to precede one's parents in death. What does this mean?
Answer: In this ephemeral world, mortals are powerless to choose whether or not children precede their parents in death.

Q. (40): Is it meritorious to accumulate virtuous deeds during one's lifetime?
Answer: It is commendable.

Q. (41): If one has received protection from another's prayers, should one make offerings?
Answer: That would be unnecessary.

Q. (42): Is giving to one who deceives others a negative act?
Answer: This would be karmically wrong.

Q. (43): Is it necessary to make offerings to a sutra when reciting it?
Answer: Just reciting suffices.

Q. (44): Should one make offerings to the scriptures after reciting one thousand sets of them?
Answer: That would be unnecessary.

Q. (45): While praying for repentance, should one use banners and adornments to embellish the altar?
Answer: They are unnecessary. The important thing is that one concentrates on repentance from the depth of one's heart.

Q. (46): How should one make offerings of flowers and incense to the image of Amida Buddha?

Answer: According to ritual, prayers should be offered at dawn. Flowers may be offered in a vase or strewn before the altar. Incense should be burned without fail. However, if it is impossible to follow the ritual, so be it.

Q. (47): Should one receive instructions on reciting a sutra from a monk?

Answer: If you are able to recite it, you need not receive instructions from a monk.

Q. (48): Must one occasionally listen to a sermon and visit a temple or a shrine for worship?

Answer: It is not necessary to do so, and indeed it may even bring negative results at times. Just quietly recite nembutsu.

Q. (49): How would it be to put your afterlife in the hands of a god?

Answer: Nothing surpasses placing your future in the hands of Amida Buddha.

Q. (50): Is it karmically wrong to become a Buddhist itinerant preacher?[343] Some say that wanting to become such a man's wife is also wrongful. Is this true?

Answer: In essence, to become an itinerant preacher is virtuous, but in the period of the decline of the Dharma, becoming such a preacher is karmically unwholesome. One who becomes his wife in this period shares in his negative karma.

Q. (51): Is it wrong to collect aromatics such as musk and clover?

Answer: Collecting such essences is undesirable.

Q. (52): How about one's wife receiving instructions in sutra chanting from a man?

Answer: This presents no problem.

Q. (53): Is it true that one should not meet the eyes of someone who has renounced monkhood and returned to secular life?

Answer: There is no such teaching. This is incorrect.

Q. (54): If one gives up monasticism and returns to secular life but not by personal choice, how karmically negative is this?

Answer: The negative karma is negligible.

Q. (55): When worshiping at a shrine or a temple, in order to purify oneself, is it better to perform religious abstinence for one day or three days?

Answer: Belief is the basis for your action. There is no dictated number of days for abstention, but three days is naturally better than one day.

Q. (56): Is it karmically problematic to compose poetry?

Answer: It depends. It may be karmically problematic or it may be meritorious.

Q. (57): Is consumption of Japanese rice wine wrong?

Answer: Rightfully, we should not drink wine, but it seems to be a custom of present-day life. It cannot be helped.

Q. (58): Is it also wrong to partake of fish, poultry, and meat?

Answer: My answer is the same as the previous one.

Q. (59): Is it commendable for a woman taking ordination to observe religious abstinence for one hundred days after she becomes a renunciant?

Answer: It is, indeed.

Q. (60): If an image of a buddha is created, must one make an offering of a scripture to the image?

Answer: It is not necessary, but a scripture may be offered.

Q. (61): Someone said that virtuous, merit-generating acts must be accumulated to one's utmost limits. Is this true?

Answer: There is no need to discuss the limit. It is best to endeavor to do as much as you possibly can.

Q. (62): Should one prepare both an image of a buddha and a scripture at the same time?

Answer: It is not necessary to do so. You may prepare each separately.

Q. (63): Must one chant the verses of a Buddhist walking staff?[344]

Answer: It's not necessary. If you have time to chant the verses, recite nembutsu even once. When a female Buddhist practitioner goes on a pilgrimage, she usually chants the verses to disperse insects around her.

Q. (64): What of visiting a shrine or a temple for worship on one's birthday?

Answer: It is all right to do so. It can also be done on the same date in the sexagenary cycle.[345]

Q. (65): Will a single utterance or ten repetitions of nembutsu eliminate the negative karma of a person who has committed the five grave offenses or the ten transgressions?

Answer: There is no doubt that such a person would be exonerated.

Q. (66): Even if one does not encounter a virtuous teacher at the time of death, will the attainment of birth in the Pure Land be possible through the daily practice of nembutsu?

Answer: Whether or not you meet a virtuous teacher, whether or not you are in control of circumstances at the end of your life, daily nembutsu makes birth in the Pure Land possible.

Q. (67): People say that to slander the true Dharma is a karmic wrong graver than the five grave offenses. Is this true?

Answer: Common people do not typically do so.

Q. (68): Should the head of the deceased be shaved?

Answer: This is not done as a rule.

Q. (69): I cannot rid myself of illusory thoughts. What should I do?

Answer: Recite nembutsu with the utmost care.

Q. (70): How would it be to loan the things I have prepared for my final moments to someone else before I use them?

Answer: You may do so without a problem.

Q. (71): Who is most appropriate for the entwining of the five-colored thread?

Answer: It would be fine to have little children do the entwining.

Q. (72): It is said that in one's final moments, people nearby should not use a wooden toothbrush with a node and that they should wear a sash without a seam, a blue sash, or a sash without a design in order to avoid any impurity.

Answer: These items may be used.

Q. (73): What might happen if a cotton swab that had been used for administering medicine to a dying person is left without washing?

Answer: This presents no problem.

Q. (74): How about if one who aspires birth in the Pure Land is dressed respectfully but finds himself in a remote place?

Answer: It is permissible. You should do so especially when you observe the eight precepts for lay people.

Q. (75): Is it all right to recite a sutra during menstruation?

Answer: There should be no problem with this.

Q. (76): How is it to think ill of Amida Buddha when one's prayers are not answered?

Answer: You must never think ill of Amida Buddha. His graces are earned through one's karmic connection and through the presence of one's faith. In this world and the next, nothing surpasses total reliance on Amida Buddha.

Q. (77): Should one perform religious abstinence for seven days in order to dissipate the undesirable effects of eating garlic and meat? Why is dried venison said to be more tainted than raw?

Answer: Garlic is fine after the odor is gone. It is not true that dried meat is more tainted.

Q. (78): Is it permissible for a woman to recite a sutra as an offering to a buddha during her menstrual period?

Answer: You may make an offering toward a Buddha during menstruation, and there is no religious abstinence for purification in Buddhism. [If you are still concerned,] you may consult a seer skilled in astrology and divination.

Q. (79): Is it true that one should abstain from visiting a temple or a shrine during the first hundred days after delivering a child?

Answer: My answer is the same as the previous one. There is no such abstinence in Buddhism.

Q. (80): Should one abstain from eating fish when one is in the process of reciting a chapter of the *Lotus Sutra*?

Answer: Eating fish is justifiable.

Q. (81): Is it possible to learn a sutra without a string of prayer beads and the red-colored ceremonial sash for religious abstinence?

Answer: There is no problem with this.

Q. (82): Is it true that soybeans and red beans are not eaten during the observation of a religious meal?

Answer: Refraining from them is unnecessary.

Q. (83): Is it acceptable to recite nembutsu, awake or lying down, without cleansing one's mouth?

Answer: This is fine.

Q. (84): Is it wrong to receive alms from a devotee?

Answer: If a priest partakes of food offered after chanting a sutra, it is acceptable. If he receives alms without prayer, his negative karma would be grave.

Q. (85): What about the saying that one will turn into a snake if one eats food that had been offered to a god?

Answer: A Shintō ritualist and priest may partake because they have devoted themselves to serving the deities. If consumption is minimal by a lay person, it would not be a grave negative karma.

Q. (86): Is it karmically wrong to eat food meant for a Buddhist priest?

Answer: It may or may not be. However, to consume food meant for a buddha, or to eat food that someone offered to a buddha for the purpose of establishing a karmic relationship with him, would be karmically wrong.

Q. (87): Is it karmically wrong for one to stay in the proximity of the Great Buddha Hall of Tōdai-ji Temple and Shitennō-ji Temple,[346] eat a priest's food, and pray for one's future life?

Answer: This is all right if one recites nembutsu.

Q. (88): On the morning of a religious meal, is it permissible to gather a great amount of food?

Answer: It is permissible.

Q. (89): How about weaving clothing in the early morning before a religious meal? Is this justifiable?

Answer: You may do so.

Q. (90): After observing the Buddhist precepts, for how many days should I perform religious abstinence for purification?

Answer: Whatever number of days is personally satisfactory is fine.

Q. (91): Is it meritorious to listen to a sermon?
Answer: It is meritorious.

Q. (92): What about a nembutsu devotee visiting a Shintō shrine for worship?
Answer: It is permissible.

Q. (93): One should dedicate the merit of sutra chanting toward birth in the Pure Land at a temple. However, some say that, beyond sutra chanting, it is also justifiable to dedicate the merit of nembutsu recitation toward birth in the Pure Land. Is this acceptable?
Answer: It is fine.

Q. (94): Is it considered taking life, and therefore a negative act, if I eat fish without praying for it?
Answer: This would not be considered the taking of life.

Q. (95): Should one cleanse the prayer beads one holds while taking a dose of medicine?
Answer: You may or may not do so, as you wish.

Q. (96): It is said that worship of both the Thousand-Armed Bodhisattva and the Buddha of Healing requires religious abstinence for purification. Is this true?
Answer: It is not.

Q. (97): Is it permissible to eat leeks and garlic during the six days of observance of the precepts for lay people?
Answer: It would be better not to do so.

Q. (98): Should one keep oneself pure when one consumes a religious meal?

Answer: According to the rules of practice, one does not necessarily need to perform ablutions or to observe religious abstinence before taking a meal. And a plain carton will suffice as a container of the meal. Concerning verses read during a religious meal, women need not chant verses and may merely recite nembutsu. If you miss a religious meal for whatever reason, recite nembutsu at another time.

Q. (99): Should a ceremony be performed on the third-year anniversary of a death?

Answer: It is not imperative to do so.

Q. (100): At the time of a religious meal, must one include vegetables with a small amount of the rice offering? Should this rice be tossed upon the roof, placed in an unglazed earthenware container, or received on my own ordinary plate?

Answer: You may do whatever you wish.

Q. (101): Is it karmically wrong for women to harbor envious feelings?

Answer: To have received life as a woman [or man] is the result of eons of karmic causes. I am indeed anxious about women's circumstances.

Q. (102): I have not taken ordination. Is the attainment of birth in the Pure Land still possible?

Answer: Many lay people have achieved birth in the Pure Land.

Q. (103): What of cutting the five-colored thread into little pieces and distributing the pieces to many people?

Answer: The thread should not be cut for distribution.

Q. (104): What should I do if various angry thoughts arise during the recitation of nembutsu?

Answer: Distracting thoughts are truly wrongful. Try to recite nembutsu earnestly.

Q. (105): What of men and women who die without shaving their heads?

Answer: The essential thing for birth in the Pure Land is not hair but whether nembutsu was recited.

Q. (106): It is said that for a nun to have a relationship with a man and to bear his child is tantamount to the five grave offenses. Is this true?

Answer: It is not as serious as the five grave offenses, but it is indeed a grave karmically wrong deed.

Q. (107): Is it karmically wrong for a nun to allow her hair to grow?

Answer: This will be a karmic cause for her to fall into the three lower realms.

Q. (108): Is it karmically wrong to sell a Buddhist scripture or an image of a buddha?

Answer: It is karmically wrong indeed.

Q. (109): Is it also a negative karma to sell people?

Answer: It certainly is.

Q. (110): People say that on days when religious abstinence is observed, one must not trim one's nails or have one's head shaved by a female. What is the reason for these beliefs?

Answer: Such beliefs are erroneous.

Q. (111): Is it wrong for me and others to write paeans to the deities?

Answer: If not done in excess, why would this be wrong?

Q. (112): It is said that religious abstinence from Japanese wine should be observed for a duration of seven days. Is this true?

Answer: This is true. However, exceptions are allowed in the case of illness.

Q. (113): After partaking of fish or poultry, should one perform ablutions to cleanse oneself before reciting a sutra?

Answer: It is proper to perform ablutions before reciting a sutra. If one does not cleanse the body, one's merit and karmic negativity will blend into each other. However, it would be more meritorious to recite than not recite a sutra, even without a cleansing.

Q. (114): When a man and his wife read a sutra together, should they first cleanse their bodies?

Answer: The answer is the same as above. Originally, a cleansing bath is to be taken before the reading of a sutra, yet a bath does not need to precede the practice of nembutsu. However, do read a sutra after a cleansing bath, even if you already read a sutra daily.

Q. (115): People say that offerings of a Japanese radish and citron are a hindrance to worship. Is this true?

Answer: There is no such effect.

Q. (116): What should be done with the hair that is shaved off the head of a female Buddhist practitioner when she enters religious life?

Answer: It may be blended into paper to be used for printing a sutra, or it can be placed in the bowels of the statue of a buddha.

Q. (117): What of a nun wearing the navy blue ceremonial robe, which is permitted to be worn only by a high-ranking clergyman?
Answer: That would be wrong.

Q. (118): Is it true that both men and women should wash their hair, or at least the tops of their heads, prior to visiting a temple or a shrine to worship?
Answer: There is no such requirement.

Q. (119): Should one ever harbor grudges toward Amida Buddha?
Answer: Under no circumstance should you be resentful of Amida Buddha. The grave wrongs of a devout person will be neutralized, but for the nonbeliever, even venial offenses will never be eradicated. One should be ashamed of one's lack of faith.

Q. (120): On which day during the eight specific dates regarded as unlucky in the sixty-day sexagenary cycle should one refrain from going to a temple to worship?
Answer: There is no such thing as this. Amida Buddha never fails to hear you, regardless of time and circumstances.

Q. (121): People say that during moxibustion treatments one should refrain from visiting a temple or a shrine to worship, and that clothing worn during treatments should be discarded. Is this true?
Answer: This, too, is a spurious view. However, one should concentrate on the treatment and not leave the home. There is no religious abstinence in the act of burning moxa.

Q. (122): People say that dying within three years after partaking of such foods as garlic and meat prevents that person from attaining birth in the Pure Land. Is this true?

Answer: This, too, is a fallacy. It is said that one who has partaken of any of the five pungent vegetables may not approach a dying person's final moments, but there is no reason to exercise religious abstinence for three years after having these foods.

Q. (123): It is said that those who die of a pestilence and women who die in childbirth are karmically reprehensible. Is this true?

Answer: Such people will also attain birth in the Pure Land through nembutsu.

Q. (124): People say that filial piety is for parents and that children should not accept the piety of parents. Is this true?

Answer: This is an erroneous understanding.

Q. (125): What is the duration of religious abstinence after childbirth? Also, what is the duration of abstinence after someone's death?

Answer: In Buddhism there is no such abstinence. Popularly, it is said that one is impure for seven or thirty days after childbirth. It is also said that religious abstinence after someone's death takes fifty days. However, one may do as one's heart dictates.

Q. (126): Is it necessary to prepare both sacred writings and the image of Amida Buddha in order to pray for one's life after death?

Answer: Yes, this is taught. You must be prepared.

Q. (127): Is it acceptable to force oneself to recite nembutsu after forgetting one's daily nembutsu, or to force oneself to recite nembutsu beforehand?

Answer: Forced recitation after forgetting one's daily nembutsu is permissible, but to do nembutsu beforehand indicates laxity in one's commitment.

Q. (128): Which one gains more merit in taking monastic ordination: one who is still young or one who is old?

Answer: An older monk is meritorious. A young monk is even more admirable.

Q. (129): Should one chant the verse "One who practices the ten bodhisattva perfections can attain birth in the Pure Land" while placing flowers on the altar? Please teach me.

Answer: There is no merit in doing so. Just recite nembutsu.

Q. (130): Is it wrong for a person to visit a shrine or a temple while performing religious abstinence for purification reasons?

Answer: There is no problem with this.

Q. (131): Is it wrong to take a different route home from the one I took on the way to visit a shrine or a temple? How about if one has fish or poultry after a visit?

Answer: Any route is fine except when visiting the Kumano shrines.[347]

Q. (132): People say there are guidelines for chanting a purification verse during a religious meal. Please let me know about this.

Answer: Merely repeat nembutsu during the religious meal. Women [in particular] need not recite the verse.

Q. (133): Is it karmically wrong for a woman to feel envy?
Answer: Just focus on reciting nembutsu from the depths of your heart.

Q. (134): It is said that to use paper made of ashes from the paulownia tree for the Buddhist and Shintō family altar is inappropriate. Is this true?
Answer: There is no truth to this.

Q. (135): Should one visit a temple or a shrine for worship on the third day or in the early morning of the fourth day after practicing religious confinement to one's home?
Answer: The early morning of the third day would be fine.

Q. (136): When practicing religious confinement to one's home for three days, should one actually confine oneself for four days? If it is for seven days, should one confine oneself for eight days before ending the confinement?
Answer: You may follow the practice of others in this ritual.

Q. (137): It is said that prayer beads made of cherry or chestnut wood are tainted. Is this true?
Answer: There is no such truth.

Q. (138): People say that the negative karma committed by a Buddhist monk is especially grave. Is this true?
Answer: This is not necessarily so.

Q. (139): What can one do if, during one's lifetime in this world, one prays without proof of its merit?
Answer: Not seeing proof of one's prayers in this world does not mean that Amida Buddha is being untruthful. The lack of proof is because one's heart is not in tune with his

intentions. Once one's heart truly reflects his teachings, one should see proof of his prayers.

If one worships Bodhisattva Avalokiteśvara with all one's heart, the answer to one's prayers will be manifested. If one does not, one's prayer will not be answered.

One whose karmic relationship with Amida Buddha in a previous existence was deeply rooted can change even undesirable karmic circumstances that were preordained. Those without a solid karmic relationship with him in times past, as well as in the present, will lament the lack of proof in response to even minor tribulations. You should never reproach Amida Buddha.

To truly serve Amida Buddha in this life and the next, one must endeavor to serve with a genuine heart. In this way one's prayers will be answered in this world, and in the next world, one will be born in the Pure Land. If one's endeavors still do not result in proof, one should be ashamed of the state of one's own heart.

Q. (140): **Dōkō's note: The following question was asked directly of Hōnen-shōnin on December 14th of the first year of Kennin (1201).* Is it true that Amida Buddha will, when he comes to receive a person in his final moments, return without taking the individual if that person is defiled?

Answer: If Amida Buddha arrives to welcome one who is defiled to the Pure Land, why would he return alone? He is not concerned with one's purity or impurity of heart. However, purity reflects impurity and impurity reflects purity in the eyes of the beholder. The mere recitation of nembutsu is sufficient. If one is pure of heart but without nembutsu, one reaps no merit. Forget all else and just repeat nembutsu. This fact has been demonstrated many times.

Q. (141): **Dōkō's note: The following questions were posed in a letter to Hōnen-shōnin.* Is the act of giving clothes and food to a family member while having thoughts of birth in the Pure Land consistent with the notion of making offerings to Amida Buddha, even if the family members may or may not be intimate?

Answer: With no thought for the depth of relationships, to give things to others in aspiration for birth in the Pure Land has great merit. I made this very clear to the bearer of this letter.

Q. (142): Is there merit in giving alms to a priest who has violated the precepts or to an ignorant priest?

Answer: In this period of the decline of the Dharma, one should have respect for priests in the same way we pay homage to Amida Buddha, even if they have violated the precepts or are ignorant. I have also clarified this thought for the bearer of the letter mentioned above; please ask him for further explanation. **Dōkō's note: The above words bear the signature of Hōnen-shōnin. The signature was found in the back of the Smaller Sutra.*

Q. (143): **Dōkō's note: The following questions were asked of Hōnen-shōnin in person.* During the daily recitation of nembutsu, which is more desirable—to recite 60,000 or 100,000 nembutsu as you thumb the prayer beads, or to recite 20,000 or 30,000 nembutsu while carefully moving the beads one at a time?

Answer: For an ordinary person, to recite 20,000 or 30,000 nembutsu according to prescribed ritual is a difficult task. However, the more nembutsu one repeats, the better, because the ritual promotes consistent recitation of the name of Amida Buddha. The number of recitations is not essential. Copious nembutsu encourages incessant practice. If one does not keep track of numbers, one may become lax; therefore, counting the prayer beads encourages the recitation of a large number of nembutsu.

Q. (144): Is the Shingon school's ceremony of making offerings to Amida Buddha a proper rite?

Answer: Although there is only one Amida Buddha, his teachings have different interpretations. The Shingon school teaches that Amida Buddha resides in one's own heart; they do not admit his existence outside of one's heart. Jōdo Shū, however, teaches that Bodhisattva Dharmākara realized buddhahood and became Amida Buddha and now resides in the west. These two viewpoints reflect great differences between the two schools.

Q. (145): Which is more commendable—to recite nembutsu while ceasing negative acts and cultivating virtuous deeds, or to recite nembutsu while relying totally upon the essential vow?

Answer: It is a universal admonition among all buddhas to cease negative acts and to perform virtuous deeds. We who are living in the present day, however, do not have the capacity to adhere to this teaching. Therefore, all that we can do is merely to believe in the essential vow and to recite the name of Amida Buddha. Without regard for whether one is learned or unschooled, or whether one observes the precepts, he will appear and take one to the Pure Land of Ultimate Bliss. Please bear this in mind.

23. A Dialogue Between Hōnen-shōnin and Myōhen-sōzu

Myōhen: How may wretched and defiled common mortals such as we are, who live in the undesirable period of the decline of the Dharma, detach from the delusive worlds of saṃsāra?

Hōnen: I believe that to detach from the delusive world of transmigration we must merely aspire for birth in the Pure Land of Ultimate Bliss of Amida Buddha through reciting *Namu Amida Butsu.*

Myōhen: I have understood this teaching in its entirety. In order to establish my steadfast faith in aspiring for birth in the Pure Land, I would like to ask you another question. Although I recite nembutsu, my heart is still distracted. What does one do?

Hōnen: Even I, Genkū, am powerless over distractions.

Myōhen: What, then, can I do?

Hōnen: I believe that birth in the Pure Land is possible by relying upon the power of the essential vow, reciting the name of Amida Buddha in spite of distractions. In brief, the primary cause for birth in the Pure Land is nothing but reciting nembutsu fervently.

Myōhen: You are right. Precisely so. This is what I came here to find out.

*Dōkō's note: Myōhen-sōzu did not utter a word either before or after this conversation, and at the end, he took his leave.

After Myōhen-sōzu's departure, Hōnen-shōnin addressed the priests in his presence as follows: "The hearts of all beings born into the realm of desire are wracked by distracting thoughts. This state is because all beings born human have eyes and noses. Therefore, it is impossible to extinguish distractions in the mind completely and then attain birth in the Pure Land. Nonetheless, birth in the Pure Land is possible through nembutsu, despite one's distracted thinking, and this is the wonder of the essential vow. I completely understand Myōhen-sōzu's doubts regarding how to cope with a distracted mind in spite of his recitation of nembutsu."

24. The Sayings of Hōnen-shōnin as Stated by His Disciples

1. Ryūkan-rishi (1148–1227)[348] stated as follows:

Hōnen-shōnin said, "I, Genkū, also used to read the *Smaller Sutra* three times a day in addition to my daily practice of nembutsu. I recited the *Smaller Sutra* in the T'ang version first, in the Wu version second, and then in the Japanese version third. However, I realized that the quintessence of the *Smaller Sutra* is the mere recitation of nembutsu; therefore, I do not read it at all anymore and exclusively recite nembutsu."

I, Ryūkan, who had read the *Smaller Sutra* forty-eight times every single day, immediately comprehended this and presently recite nembutsu thirty thousand times a day, leaving the *Smaller Sutra* aside.

*Dōkō's note: This is based on quotations from *Clarifying the Essentials and Promoting Wholesome Conduct*.[349]

2. Jōgan-shōnin (1168–1251)[350] thus stated:

Someone said to Hōnen-shōnin, "The perception of the physical features of Amida Buddha is taught in the *Meditation Sutra*. Should even the nembutsu practitioner observe this meditative practice?"

Hōnen-shōnin replied, "I, Genkū, also performed such a futile practice at the beginning, but I do not practice it now. I recite nembutsu with implicit belief in attaining birth in the Pure Land."

*Dōkō's note: This is based on quotations from the *Solution to Problems Regarding Shōkō's Jushuin*.[351]

Hōnen-shōnin also said, "The threefold devotional heart will be cultivated as a matter of course if one without pretension continuously practices the karmic act [nembutsu] for attaining birth in the Pure Land. To illustrate, one cannot see the reflection of a full moon in a reedy pond from far away. However, if one draws close to the pond, one can see the reflection of the moon among the reeds. The moon of the threefold devotional heart reflects with certainty on the pond even though the reeds of illusory thought grow thick." The late Hōnen-shōnin frequently used this parable.

*Dōkō's note: This is based on quotations from the *Dialogue on Twenty-Eight Topics*.[352]

On another occasion Hōnen-shōnin remarked, "I hope I will attain birth in the Pure Land this time!"

Hearing this, I, Jōgan, asked, "Well, if even Hōnen-shōnin uses such words of uncertainty about birth in the Pure Land, what will become of the rest of us?"

Hōnen-shōnin smiled and said, "One's wish for attaining birth in the Pure Land never comes to an end until one is truly born on the lotus platform in the Pure Land."

*Dōkō's note: This is based on quotations from the *Dialogue on the Next Life*.[353]

3. Shinkū-shōnin (1146–1228)[354] stated as below:

Hōnen-shōnin once said, "There have been many Pure Land masters, and each master encouraged people to awaken the heart of enlightenment (Skt. *bodhicitta*). Without exception they regarded meditation as the primary practice. Only Master Shan-tao considered meditation as an auxiliary practice to vocal nembutsu and did not encourage people to awaken the heart of enlightenment.

"People in our own day cannot easily attain birth in the Pure Land without relying upon the teachings of Master Shan-tao. Masters such as T'an-lun, Tao-ch'o, and Huai-kan transmitted the Pure Land tradition, each with his own interpretation regarding the issue of birth in the Pure Land.

"This should be thoroughly comprehended. Without understanding this, the distinction between the easy path and the difficult path toward birth in the Pure Land cannot be discerned."

I once said to Hōnen-shōnin, "If possessing wisdom is essential for birth in the Pure Land, I will sincerely receive instructions and devote myself to the pursuit of the Buddhist disciplines. However, if the mere recitation of nembutsu is sufficient for birth in the Pure Land, I will keep precisely what it means in my heart. Now, I would like to listen to your instruction like the golden words of Tathāgata Amida."

Hōnen-shōnin replied, "According to the interpretation of Master Shan-tao, it is obvious that the karmic activity that leads to birth in the Pure Land is the speaking of the name of Amida Buddha. It is also apparent that Amida Buddha does not discriminate between the learned and the unschooled for birth in the Pure Land. Therefore, the mere recitation of nembutsu is sufficient for this birth. Recite nembutsu exclusively rather than aspiring for birth in the Pure Land through the pursuit of the Buddhist disciplines.

"When you see Amida Buddha, Bodhisattva Avalokiteśvara, and Bodhisattva Mahāsthāmaprāpta in the Pure Land, the entire canon of the Dharma will have been thoroughly mastered. The majestic adornments of the Pure Land are expounding on the profound Dharma day and night, dawn and dusk. If you lack the understanding of the rationale for achieving birth in the Pure Land through nembutsu, you should learn it, but once you know it, do not fill your precious time with pursuing man's trifling wisdom when you could be reciting nembutsu."

On one occasion, I said to Hōnen-shōnin, "Many people encourage the observation of the precept of taking a religious meal for purification [abstention from food in the afternoon]. What do you think of it?"

Hōnen-shōnin answered, "It is right for a nun to observe the precept of a religious meal. However, people's capacity to understand the Dharma has been lowered, and provisions are scarce in the day in which we live. If they take only one religious meal a day under the existing conditions, their attention will be absorbed by food and they will be unable to focus on nembutsu. Accordingly the *Sutra of the Aspiration for Enlightenment* states, 'Though taking a meal itself does not hinder the heart that aspires enlightenment, excessive desire for a meal is a true hindrance.'[355] Do not slight your practice of nembutsu, but act according to your own conditions."

On another occasion, I said to Hōnen-shōnin, "I have firm conviction in the view of the karmic practice for birth in the Pure Land. How should I live my life in order to attain birth in the Pure Land?"

Hōnen-shōnin said, "The conduct of the clergy is based on the precepts and regulations prescribed by Mahāyāna Buddhism and Hīnayāna Buddhism, but the clergy in the period of the decline of the Dharma hardly observe these precepts. No one will be able to observe them, even though I, Genkū, admonish you to observe them. In short, live your life in a way that allows you to recite nembutsu continuously. Nembutsu is the right karmic cause for birth in the Pure Land. For this reason, you should follow the teaching of nembutsu and devote yourself to reciting nembutsu."

Someone asked Hōnen-shōnin, "Which is more commendable—reciting nembutsu while ceasing negative acts and cultivating virtuous deeds at all times, or reciting nembutsu with incessant thoughts of the essential vow of Amida Buddha?"

Hōnen-shōnin replied, "All buddhas universally advocate ceasing negative acts and performing virtuous deeds, but those of us living in the present day are unable to adhere to this teaching. Hence, all we can do is trust in the essential vow in order to detach ourselves from the delusive worlds of saṃsāra."[356]

Someone asked Hōnen-shōnin, "What do you think about the visualization of the physical attributes of Amida Buddha at the time of reciting nembutsu?"

Hōnen-shōnin replied, "I do not do this. [As Master Shan-tao said,] 'If, when I [Amida Buddha] am to attain buddhahood, all sentient beings in the ten directions who call out my name at least ten times are not born there, I will not realize enlightenment. Amida Buddha did, indeed, attain buddhahood and presently resides in the Pure Land. It should be known that the essential vow was not made in vain. If sentient beings recite his name, they will, with certainty, attain birth in the Pure Land.'[357] I have firm belief in what Master Shan-tao taught. Even if we who only have minimal potential try to contemplate the physical features of Amida Buddha, we cannot visualize him like the description in the sutras. Total reliance upon the essential vow and the vocalization of his name are not provisional practices; they are the most important practices for achieving birth in the Pure Land."

Someone said to Hōnen-shōnin, "When Master Shan-tao commented on the essential vow described in the *Larger Sutra*,[358] he deleted a part concerning the genuine heart—'all sentient beings who hold faith with genuine hearts and who wish to be born in my land'[359]—from the passage of the essential vow. Is there any reason for the deletion?"

Hōnen-shōnin answered, "It is because the threefold devotional heart will be obtained naturally if sentient beings call out the name of Amida Buddha. Master Shan-tao intentionally deleted the passage in order to clarify this reason."[360]

Someone asked Hōnen-shōnin, "Which is right—to set the number of daily nembutsu to sixty thousand or one hundred thousand but to repeat them carelessly; or to set the number to twenty or thirty thousand and recite them with one's whole heart?"

Hōnen-shōnin replied, "It is truly lamentable that the nature of common people is what it is. Even though they set the number of nembutsu to twenty or thirty thousand as a specific daily goal, they cannot accomplish the goal exactly as they plan. It is, however, desirable to repeat as many nembutsu as possible on a daily basis. In a word, a daily goal encourages people to continue to recite nembutsu. Setting the number of daily nembutsu is not essential except for such continuation. Without a daily goal for the number of nembutsu, one is prone to laziness. Hence, a numerical goal serves as an incentive for continuous practice."

Someone said to Hōnen-shōnin, "Your every utterance of nembutsu is in accord with the heart of Amida Buddha. Because you are a learned priest, you deeply understand the merits of the name of Amida Buddha and have distinctly mastered the profound meaning of the essential vow."

Hōnen-shōnin stated, "You do not yet believe in the essential vow. The name of Tathāgata Amida taught in the essential vow was designed for all people, including the woodcutter, grass trimmer, farmer, and water carrier—regardless of class or knowledge. If they firmly believe that even an illiterate who knows neither nembutsu doctrine nor other Buddhist teachings will definitely achieve birth in the Pure Land through the recitation of nembutsu and then they sincerely desire birth in the Pure Land and recite nembutsu unceasingly, then they are considered to be the ultimate nembutsu devotees.

"If one can detach oneself from the delusive worlds of saṃsāra by pursuing wisdom, why have I, Genkū, abandoned the teachings of the holy gate to follow the Pure Land gate? It should be known that the practice of the holy gate seeks to extricate one from the delusive worlds of saṃsāra through the pursuit of wisdom, and that the Pure Land gate teaches one to return to the state of ignorance in order to be born into the Pure Land of Ultimate Bliss."

*Dōkō's note: These aforementioned dialogues are the words of Shinkū-shōnin cited from *Clarifying the Essentials and Promoting Wholesome Conduct.*

Shinkū-shōnin further narrated as below:

The following are the instructions of the senior master Hōnen-shōnin, who customarily said in the morning and evening: "The recitation of nembutsu does not require any formality. Simply, one will attain birth in the Pure Land through the firm belief that the recitation of nembutsu with the genuine heart alone will lead him to birth in the Pure Land. Those who mention formality in nembutsu do not know its reason, have no desire for birth in the Pure Land, and just talk about futile things without foundation. It is they who should recite the name of Amida Buddha ten times or even once."

After Hōnen-shōnin's attainment of birth in the Pure Land, Jūshin-bō (1158–1233),[361] a scholarly monk of Mii-dera Temple,[362] asked Hōnen-shōnin a question in his dream about the way of nembutsu.

Hōnen-shōnin then replied, "There is no formal ritual for reciting the name of Amida Buddha. Recitation alone is crucial."

Jūshin-bō conducted a service for the monthly commemoration of the death of Hōnen-shōnin at Ōtani and preached this in front of a large number of attendants.

*Dōkō's note: These dialogues are based on quotations from the *Letters of Shirakawa*.[363]

4. Benna-shōnin[364] stated thus:

The late Hōnen-shōnin said, "I am a common mortal who wears no official hat. I simply state that I, Hōnen-bō, who may have committed the ten transgressions, desire birth in the Pure Land through the recitation of nembutsu and that I, the ignorant Hōnen-bō, recite nembutsu while desiring the attainment of birth in the Pure Land. Therefore, there is no distinction at all between the nembutsu chanted by Awanosuke,[365] an illiterate seer skilled in astrology and divination, and Genkū's nembutsu."

*Dōkō's note: This is based on quotations from the *Collection of Stories*.[366]

I once said to Hōnen-shōnin, "I think that your utterance of nembutsu must be superior to our nembutsu because you are a learned priest. Is this a misunderstanding?"

Hōnen-shōnin looked displeased and said, "You should not say this. If my nembutsu has a special aspect, my daily sixty thousand nembutsu will become futile, and I will fall into the three lower realms of hell beings, starving spirits, and animals. Indeed, there is no special distinction to my daily nembutsu."

Hōnen-shōnin made this assertion explicitly. Accordingly, I, Benna, strengthened my unshakable faith in nembutsu.

*Dōkō's note: This is based on quotations from the *Collection of Stories*.

Hōnen-shōnin often said, "One who plans to jump over a moat ten feet wide must make every effort to jump fifteen feet. In the same manner, one who aspires to birth in the Pure Land must establish the decisive faith in the certain attainment of birth in the Pure Land. Birth in the Pure Land will become impossible if one loosens this belief."

*Dōkō's note: This is based on quotations from the *Collection of Stories*.

Hōnen-shōnin also stated, "Regarding birth in the Pure Land through nembutsu, this nembutsu is not meditation as taught by the learned men of China and Japan; neither is it recitation through scholarly endeavors in order to master its profound meanings. To attain birth in the Pure Land of Ultimate Bliss, nothing is required but the implicit faith that the mere recitation of *Namu Amida Butsu* causes the certain attainment of birth in the Pure Land.

"The teachings of the threefold devotional heart and the four modes of exercise are encompassed in the firm belief that birth in the Pure Land is assured by the recitation of *Namu Amida Butsu.* You must believe that the recitation of *Namu Amida Butsu* causes with certainty the attainment of birth in the Pure Land.

"A person who believes in nembutsu, though he may have learned the entire teachings of Buddha Śākyamuni, should consider himself an ignorant person with minimal potential who knows not a single letter. He should conduct himself as though he were as unschooled as the female lay Buddhist practitioner who, merely shaving her head, becomes a nun without proper foundation.

"Refrain from flaunting knowledge and devote yourself to recite *Namu Amida Butsu* for the attainment of birth in the Pure Land."

*Dōkō's note: This is based on quotations from the *Collection of Stories*.

Hōnen-shōnin said, "In Genkū's eyes, the threefold devotional heart, the five aspects of meditation, and the four modes of exercise are all seen as *Namu Amida Butsu*."

*Dōkō's note: This is based on quotations from the *Personal Seal Attesting to the Transmission of Hōnen's Teaching of Nembutsu for the Future Generations*.[367]

Hōnen-shōnin also stated, "People in the world awaken their hearts to enlightenment in response to their own karmic causal conditions, such as the loss of one's parents and siblings and separation from family and friends. I, Genkū, however, spontaneously awakened my aspiration for enlightenment with no special reason; therefore, my master bestowed on me the name Hōnen.[368]

"Since I had profound aspiration for detachment from the delusive worlds of transmigration, I believed in the diverse teachings of Buddha Śākyamuni and observed various practices. The Buddhist doctrine has many facets, but its basis ultimately lies in the threefold discipline of the precepts, meditation, and wisdom. The threefold discipline is embodied in Hīnayāna Buddhism, Mahāyāna Buddhism, and in the tenets of exoteric and esoteric teachings. Upon introspection, I realized that I had not observed a single precept, nor had I succeeded in the practice of samādhi. With regard to wisdom, I did not possess the right wisdom to eliminate worldly passions and to realize the truth. A precept master once said, 'One will not enter the state of samādhi unless one becomes pure of body and mind through the observation of the precepts.' Further, the mind of the common mortal is easily distracted by the conditions around it. It is like the monkey that flits from branch to branch, confused, vacillating, and unable to concentrate.

"In what way does undefiled wisdom arise? Without the sword of undefiled wisdom, how will we extricate ourselves from the fetters of karma and worldly passions? Unable to sever ourselves from these fetters, how will we deliver ourselves from the bondage of transmigration in the delusive worlds in order to attain deliverance? This is indeed lamentable and disheartening.

"It is I who does not have the potential to perform the threefold discipline of the precepts, meditation, and wisdom. I asked various wise and learned men if there were a teaching and practice more attuned to me than the threefold discipline. However, no one was able to teach or guide me.

"In despair I entered the repository of the Buddhist scriptures, and in my grief I gazed upon the holy texts, taking a fascicle into my hands. It was the *Commentary on the Meditation Sutra*, authored by Master Shan-tao. In this fascicle I found the following passage: '...to recite single-heartedly and exclusively the name of Amida Buddha while walking, standing, sitting, or lying down, without regard for length of time, and to engage in the recitation of nembutsu without cessation throughout one's life. This is called the *rightly established practice* because it is in accordance with the essential vow of Amida Buddha.'[369] Upon reading this passage, I was convinced that ignorant people like ourselves should earnestly revere this passage, rely exclusively upon this teaching, and continually recite the name of Amida Buddha without cessation in order to meet the causal karma for certain attainment of birth in the Pure Land. Not only was I led to believe in this teaching bequeathed by Master Shan-tao, but I was also led to follow earnestly the essential vow of Amida Buddha. And that passage, 'because it is in accordance with the essential vow,' was etched deeply into my heart.

"Thereafter, I read the *Collection of Essentials on Attaining Birth in the Pure Land* authored by the senior master Eshin, which states, 'The recitation of nembutsu is essential among practices for attaining birth in the Pure Land.'[370] Further, his *Wondrous Biography* states, 'The recitation of nembutsu is foremost among practices for birth in the Pure Land.'[371]

"Kakuchō-sōzu (960–1034)[372] once said to Eshin-sōzu, 'Does your utterance of nembutsu consist of recitation or meditation on the noumenal principle?'

"Eshin-sōzu replied, 'A man's heart is always distracted by the various conditions around him. For this reason I merely recite nembutsu. Reciting nembutsu, as a karmic practice, is the most efficient method for attaining birth in the Pure Land. I will recite nembutsu throughout my entire life, and the number of my nembutsu repetitions will reach two hundred million.'

"In accordance with the teachings of Master Shan-tao of the great T'ang dynasty and with the encouragement of Senior Master Eshin, I, Genkū, have practiced my sixty thousand nembutsu daily for many years. When I felt my final moment was near, I added ten thousand more, and I became a nembutsu practitioner who recites nembutsu seventy thousand times a day."

*Dōkō's note: This is based on quotations from the *In-Depth Study of the Collection on Nembutsu*.[373]

5. Zenshō-bō (1174–1258) narrated as follows:

Honen-shōnin said, "It should be known that one who is pleased to think of being welcomed by Amida Buddha at the moment of death through the recitation of nembutsu in this life and who becomes happy enough to dance for joy will spontaneously embody the threefold devotional heart. In contrast, someone who recites nembutsu but grieves about his life to come will not possess the threefold devotional heart. Even if an individual recites nembutsu when the heart of joy has not yet arisen within, he should devote himself to nembutsu in order to gradually possess the threefold devotional heart. Those who continue to recite nembutsu should consider that they already possess the threefold devotional heart."

*Dōkō's note: This is based on quotations from the *Collection of Dialogues on Nembutsu*.[374]

Hōnen-shōnin remarked, "You should ask your own heart whether your attainment of birth in the Pure Land is possible. That is, believe that your birth in the Pure Land will be certain if you engage in the nembutsu practice incessantly. Conversely, bear in mind that your birth in the Pure Land immediately after death will become difficult if you practice nembutsu carelessly. You should think of your attainment of birth in the Pure Land in this manner, encourage your heart toward birth in the Pure Land, and discern whether you possess the threefold devotional heart."

*Dōkō's note: This is based on quotations from the *Collection of Dialogues on Nembutsu*.

Hōnen-shōnin also said, "Even if nine of ten nembutsu devotees have mental distractions at the moment of their death and fail to achieve birth in the Pure Land, you should have implicit faith that you will, with certainty, attain birth in the Pure Land."

*Dōkō's note: This is based on quotations from the *Collection of Dialogues on Nembutsu*.

Hōnen-shōnin stated, "It is a grave misconception to think, fearful of negative karma accumulated in the past, that one's birth in the Pure Land is uncertain. This does not mean that one can neglect nembutsu and behave falsely. One should be aware of the meaning of the essential vow, which is so extensive and inconceivably profound that every mortal, without exception, can attain birth in the Pure Land. Therefore, those who explain that birth in the Pure Land through nembutsu is too profound and difficult to practice do not know the true intention of the essential vow.

"According to their misinterpretations, birth in the Pure Land is achieved only by high-ranking clergy, and thus there is no possibility for me, Genkū, a mere monk called Hōnen-bō, to attain birth in the Pure Land. Hence, wisdom pursued for many years may not lead to birth in the Pure Land. Nevertheless, I was able to master the essential vow through long study, so it cannot be said simply that we do not need scholarly endeavors at all."

*Dōkō's note: This is based on quotations from the *Collection of Dialogues on Nembutsu*.

Hōnen-shōnin also narrated, "The nembutsu taught in the essential vow is sufficient and does not require additional support. One who needs some additional support will be born in a remote corner of the Pure Land of Ultimate Bliss. Here, additional support refers to pursuing wisdom, observing the precepts, awakening the heart of enlightenment, and developing a compassionate heart.

"The good person should recite nembutsu just as he is, as should the bad person. We regard faithful people, who repeat nembutsu with a mind as pure as the day they were born, as those who do not require additional support in nembutsu. If the bad rectify their misdeeds, become good, and recite nembutsu, they will truly be in harmony with the heart of Amida Buddha. On the contrary, those who are unable to attune themselves to the heart of Amida Buddha and who are unable to be resolute in their faith in birth in the Pure Land will most certainly not attain birth in the Pure Land."

*Dōkō's note: This is based on quotations from the *Collection of Dialogues on Nembutsu*.

Hōnen-shōnin once said, "There exists the principle of naturalness. Flames rise skyward, water flows downward. Some fruits are sour, some are sweet. These truths are governed by the principle of naturalness. The essential vow of Amida Buddha promises that his name is the means to save the most evil mortals. It is, therefore, obvious that if one exclusively recites nembutsu, Amida Buddha will certainly come to welcome this individual into the Pure Land in accordance with the principle of naturalness."

*Dōkō's note: This is based on quotations from the *Collection of Dialogues on Nembutsu.*

Hōnen-shōnin also stated, "To live this life means to create the conditions in which one is able to recite nembutsu in a natural way. Anything that impedes the practice of nembutsu should be abhorred and abandoned.

"If one cannot practice nembutsu as a monk, one should take a wife and recite nembutsu. On the contrary, if one cannot practice nembutsu with a wife, one should recite nembutsu as a monk. If staying in one place makes nembutsu impossible, go on a pilgrimage and practice nembutsu. Conversely, if nembutsu is difficult on a pilgrimage, stay in one place and recite nembutsu. If poverty hampers nembutsu, seek support and recite nembutsu. If the practice of nembutsu is impossible in spite of support, depend on one's own resources to repeat nembutsu. If the practice of nembutsu in seclusion is impossible, practice it with other nembutsu devotees. Conversely, if practice with other devotees is impossible, recite in seclusion. Food, clothing, and housing are considered to be supporting elements for nembutsu. In summary, if all acts and conditions mentioned above truly promote the attainment of birth with a tranquil heart in the Pure Land through nembutsu, they are regarded as the supporting elements for nembutsu.

"If you—who is destined to return to the three lower realms of hell beings, starving spirits, and animals in your future life—think tenderly of yourself, then you nurture yourself. It goes without saying that if you recite nembutsu to attain birth in the Pure Land, you should nurture and take care of yourself that much more. If you do not regard your lifestyle as a supporting element and you cling to your lifestyle out of mere stubbornness, this will be the cause of your fall into the three lower realms. Hence, to achieve birth in the Pure Land of Ultimate Bliss and to design your lifestyle in order to meet that goal—these indeed become the supporting conditions for birth in the Pure Land. Everything should be understood in this manner."

*Dōkō's note: This is based on quotations from the *Collection of Dialogues on Nembutsu*.

6. Dōhen,[375] a male Buddhist novice, thus stated:

The late Hōnen-shōnin once said, "The recitation of nembutsu is foremost for the attainment of birth in the Pure Land. Scholarly endeavors are not necessary for attaining birth in the Pure Land, but one may pursue them to the extent that one has established the implicit faith in birth in the Pure Land through nembutsu."

*Dōkō's note: This is based on quotations from the *Collection of Essentials on Jōdo Shū*.[376]

Poems of Hōnen-shōnin[377]

Grim seems each occupation that would free the heart from blame
compared with invocation of Amida Buddha's sacred name.

Pine of a thousand years, I dwell beneath thy shade,
till by Amida Buddha my welcome home is made.

The heart of man is like the water of a pot:
you know not whether it will be corrupt or not.

Foremost in the Pure Land of Ultimate Bliss, when I attain my birth,
will be the precious memory of fellow practitioners I left on earth.

The Pure Land's wondrous vision is bliss that we may claim
if we but worthily recite Amida Buddha's sacred name.

Above the thatch of my mountain home the white clouds morning
and evening hover.

Ah! When will the hour of that day come when birth in the Pure
Land purple shall me cover?

The years of this mortal life vanish hither and thither like morning
dewdrops,
yet we all keep wishing to be born in the Pure Land on the same
lotus props.

Ten times Amida Buddha's name shall pass my lips ere my final
repose.
My last long slumber shall begin sometime, and when, who knows?

There is no place where the moonlight fails to grace,
but it only abides in and purifies the hearts of those who gaze
upon its face.

Part II

First Supplement to Collected Teachings of Hōnen: The Japanese Anthology

25. The Statement Sent to Mount Hiei

by Genkū

I HAVE LONG wandered in the delusive three realms of transmigration. In which realm was I abiding, preventing me from encountering the emergence of Buddha Śākyamuni? In which of the four modes of birth in the delusive worlds of transmigration was I abiding, preventing me from listening to the sermons of Tathāgata Śākyamuni? I was not present when Buddha Śākyamuni preached the *Flower Garland Sutra*; not present at the assembly where he delivered his discourse on the *Perfection of Wisdom Sutra*; not present to hear his sermon on Vulture Peak;[378] and not present at the Crane Forest on the occasion of Buddha Śākyamuni's entrance into parinirvāṇa. Could I have been born in a house of Śrāvastī where lived the three hundred million people who were unaware of even the name of Buddha Śākyamuni? Or could I have been at the bottom of one of the eight hot hells?[379] I am overcome with regret; this is indeed grievous.

Now, then, I have wandered for innumerable eons and have finally received life in the world as a human being, a state extremely difficult to realize. After myriad eons, I have fortunately encountered the precious teachings of Buddha Śākyamuni. Though it is lamentable I did not have the opportunity to meet Buddha Śākyamuni during his lifetime, I am profoundly grateful to exist as a man during an era when his teachings proliferate. It is as if a blind turtle were to find the hole in a piece of driftwood afloat on the ocean.

The spread of Buddhism in this country began with its introduction on the first day of the tenth month in the winter of the thirteenth year of the monkey and water (552 C.E.) during the reign of Emperor Kinmei. Before this, in this country, neither the teachings of Tathāgata Śākyamuni nor listening to the way of enlightenment existed. By whatever residual karmic causes, by whatever virtuous deeds we have accumulated in a previous existence, we have been born in a world where the teachings of Buddha Śākyamuni prevail, and we are able to listen to the way to enlightenment out of the delusive worlds of saṃsāra.

We have now had the good fortune to experience a precious encounter with the teachings of Buddha Śākyamuni. To continue to live in idleness without embracing his teachings would be lamentable indeed. Some waste away long spring days just staring at splendid flowers in the Golden Glen. Some while away long autumn nights gazing at the beautiful harvest moon visible from the Southern Mansion.[380] The years fly by for others who spend time in pursuit of food on cloud-covered mountains; still others float on the ocean looking for bounties of the deep. Some live through crushing ice in the severe winter, while others toil for gainful living by the sweat of their brows. Some are encumbered by the ties of affection for wives, children, and relatives and find it too difficult to cut the attachment, while others are unable to rid themselves of the fire of anger for those who have wronged them.

Thus goes the life of people, dawn to dusk, day and night, whether they are walking, standing, sitting, or lying down. They exist for themselves, and their desires accumulate undesirable karma, which will with certainty lead them to the three lower realms and the eight difficult conditions in their future lives.

Therefore, a sutra describes, "Eight hundred and forty million delusive thoughts arise every single day in the heart of man, and each of these thoughts is the karma that will condemn him to the three lower realms."[381] Thus did night fall yesterday; and so, purposeless, the morning dawns today. How many more empty days and nights await us?

The petals of the beautiful flower that blooms in the morning are lightly scattered by the breeze of nightfall; dewdrops of the evening disappear in the light of the morning sun. Unaware of the impermanence of life, man always seeks to prosper; unaware of the frailty of life, man hopes for longevity.

However, once the wind of impermanence blows, life disappears permanently as if it were a dewdrop; man's mortal body is left in the wilderness and his spirit is sent to some distant mountaintop. Eventually, moss gathers over the dead body while the spirit continues to wander alone in the sky. The wives, children, and relatives who remain in the home do not accompany him, and his storehouse filled with the seven kinds of precious jewels and ten thousand treasures are of no avail. He takes with him only bitter tears of regret.

In time, this man appears before the judgment seat of King Yama, the lord of the realm of the dead, who evaluates the degree of guilt and the karma of the departed and determines their future. The king asks, "Having been born in a world where the teachings of Buddha Śākyamuni prevailed, why did you come back without having practiced them?" How can we respond? I implore you, here and now, to embark upon your search for the way to deliverance from the delusive worlds; never return to the three lower realms.

In the various teachings of Buddha Śākyamuni, there are exoteric and esoteric teachings, Mahāyāna Buddhism and Hīnayāna Buddhism, the expedient and true teachings, and many commentaries. Buddhism was divided into eight schools in Japan, the teachings of which are quite diverse. One school teaches the emptiness of all existence, another clarifies the essence of the ultimate reality of all phenomena, another establishes the theory of the five distinctive natures of sentient beings based on their capabilities, yet another discusses the fact that all sentient beings innately possess buddha nature.

Every school argues the superiority of its doctrines, asserting that its doctrines are profound and right. Undoubtedly, these are all true teachings expounded in sutras and commentaries; these are the golden words of the Tathāgata Śākyamuni. Buddha Śākyamuni delivered his teachings in accordance with the potential and circumstances of the people. Therefore, it would be impossible to determine which is shallow or which is profound. That is his teaching, and this is also his teaching. One must not be obsessed by the teaching of one or another.

Consequently, practicing according to the interpretation of any school will result in total extrication from the delusive worlds of saṃsāra; practicing according to the teaching of each school will equally enable you to realize enlightenment. To be critical of other schools and to argue about advantages and disadvantages without practicing their teachings is like the sightless debating shades of color or the hearing-impaired debating voice quality. Hence, one should practice the teaching of the school in which one believes; the teaching of every school paves the way to detachment of the delusive worlds of saṃsāra.

In recent times, however, students of one school are envious of another school; students tout one sutra over another. For this reason, the unschooled becomes doubtful, uncertain which teaching he should believe; those with minimal aptitude become confused. One gets embroiled in disputes with other schools when one embraces the teachings of a particular school, hoping to accumulate merit. On the other hand, if one attempts to study a broad spectrum of the teachings of various schools, one's lifetime will be too short.

It is said that there is an elixir of life in the three divine mountains in China called Mount P'eng-lai, Mount Fan-chang, and Mount Ying-chou. One may wish to take this elixir and extend one's life in order to learn the teachings of all the schools in turn. But not knowing where these mountains are, there is no way to pinpoint their location. Emperor Shih Huang-di (259–210 B.C.) of the Ch'in Dynasty and Emperor Wu (156–87 B.C.) of the Han Dynasty sent couriers to look for this elixir. However, young boys and girls spent long years aboard ships, getting old while seeking the elixir. It is said that Pen-tsu, a fictitious Chinese hermit, lived for seven hundred years, but this is an ancient legend, and there is no record that this was accomplished.

The Dharma Master T'an-luan of China was one who had a thorough understanding of the Buddhadharma. He believed that one's life may end tomorrow; therefore, he learned the teaching of the longevity of Taoism in order to further study Buddhism. At that time, an Indian Tripiṭaka master named Bodhiruci was living in China. T'an-luan visited Bodhiruci and asked, "Is there any teaching in Buddhism regarding longevity and immortality superior to that of the teaching of Taoism?" Bodhiruci spat on the ground and answered, "Ridiculous! Where on earth is there a text with instructions for longevity? No matter how long a life man enjoys, it is only a part of transmigration in the delusive triple realms."

Bodhiruci then entrusted to T'an-luan the *Meditation Sutra* there, saying, "This is the great teaching of immortality. If you practice following the instructions of this *Meditation Sutra*, you will be able to attain deliverance through detachment from the delusive worlds of saṃsāra." T'an-luan, upon receiving the *Meditation Sutra*, set fire to his Taoist texts. T'an-luan then practiced based on the *Meditation Sutra* and composed the commentary on the practice of Pure Land Buddhism.

Thereafter, the teachings of Pure Land Buddhism were transmitted in China from T'an-luan to Tao-ch'o to Shan-tao, Huai-kan, and Shao-k'ang (d. 805). Consequently, if we consider these facts of the tradition of Pure Land Buddhism, we must practice according to the instructions of the *Meditation Sutra* in order to perpetuate the eternal life in the future world.

The meditation master Tao-ch'o, in his *Collection of Passages on the Blissful Land*, established the theory of the holy gate and Pure Land gate in accordance with these Pure Land traditions. The holy gate teaches one to attain enlightenment in this defiled world by eradicating one's worldly passions. On the other hand, the Pure Land gate teaches one to achieve birth in the Pure Land of Amida Buddha, where one will then eradicate worldly passions and attain enlightenment.

From the standpoint of Jōdo Shū, the karmic cause for birth in the Pure Land described in the *Meditation Sutra* is not a single practice. A variety of practices exist, such as the practices of the three meritorious acts, the nine grades of aspirants for birth in the Pure Land, and the thirteen objects of meditation with a focused mind. Each has a different and inevitable karmic result.

The thirteen objects of meditation with a focused mind involve meditation on (1) the setting sun, (2) the pure water of the Pure Land, (3) the ground of the Pure Land, (4) the jeweled trees of the Pure Land, (5) the jeweled lakes of the Pure Land, (6) the jeweled pavilions of the Pure Land, (7) the flower throne of the Pure Land, (8) the figure of Amida Buddha, (9) the true physical features of Amida Buddha, (10) the physical features of Bodhisattva Avalokiteśvara, (11) the physical features of Bodhisattva Mahāsthāmaprāpta, (12) the state of one's own birth in the Pure Land, and (13) the figures of Amida Buddha, the bodhisattvas, and all beings in the Pure Land.

The nine grades of aspirants for birth in the Pure Land with a distracted mind means (1) making an effort toward filial piety, faithfully serving teachers and elders, having a compassionate heart without taking any form of life, and undertaking the ten virtuous acts; (2) upholding the Three Jewels, observing various precepts, and maintaining proper deportment; (3) awakening the heart of enlightenment, having profound faith in the karmic causality, reciting the Mahāyāna scriptures, and encouraging those who practice the way to enlightenment. The nine grades points to the nine divisions of the practice of the three meritorious acts for birth in the Pure Land. This is described in detail in the *Meditation Sutra*.

As a rule, no practice for attaining birth in the Pure Land is omitted in the meditative practices with a focused mind or with a distracted mind. Accordingly, perform any practice you have a close connection to, amass the merits of endeavor, follow the teaching that appeals to you, and you will attain birth in the Pure Land. Do not have any doubts.

From the standpoint of Jōdo Shū, there are indeed the thirteen types of the meditative practices with a focused mind and there are the nine grades of karmic causes with a distracted mind. However, if one attempts the meditative practice with a focused mind, the stallion of illusions begins to rage in one's heart and goes on a stampede within the six objects corresponding to the six sensory organs. And if one attempts to devote oneself to the meditative practices with a distracted mind, illusory thoughts may lead one to commit the ten transgressions, much like a monkey flitting from tree to tree. It is impossible to calm the stallion and to stop the monkey.

The explanation of the three grades in the low category of birth in the Pure Land cited in the *Meditation Sutra* states, "Even those who have committed the ten transgressions or five grave offenses will attain birth in the Pure Land if, at the time of death, they encounter a virtuous teacher and recite the name of Amida Buddha once, or ten times."[382] We must admit that this practice of reciting nembutsu is the most appropriate teaching for us.

Hsiung-chün[383] of China was a villain who renounced his monastic ordination and returned to secular life seven times. When his life ended, a demon guardian of hell took him to the court of King Yama and described him as "Hsiung-chün, the top villain in the world of human beings, who returned to secular life seven times." Hsiung-chün then, with a loud voice, shouted, "I read the *Meditation Sutra* while I had life, and I am certain that there I learned that a person who has committed the five grave offenses may attain birth in the Pure Land of Ultimate Bliss by reciting the name of Amida Buddha ten times. Although I returned to secular life seven times, I have not committed the five grave offenses; although my virtuous roots are few, I have recited nembutsu more than ten times. If I am condemned to hell, it would mean that various buddhas in the past, present, and future have transgressed the commitment against falsehood." The king was impressed by this logic, tipped his jeweled crown, and bowed in reverence. Then as he had avowed, Amida Buddha placed

Hsiung-chün on the golden lotus platform and received him into the Pure Land.

Birth in the Pure Land is possible because we are not people who returned to secular life seven times and we have recited nembutsu throughout our lives. The senior master Genshin of Ryōgon-in Temple wrote: "Nembutsu does not discriminate between male and female, or noble and humble practitioners. Neither does it question the practice of recitation while walking, standing, sitting, or lying down; nor does it question time, place, and various karmic relationships. Reciting nembutsu is an easy practice. Nembutsu becomes the sole agent in my aspiration for birth in the Pure Land until the time of my death."[384] This is the genuine teaching indeed.

Master Shan-tao also commented on the *Meditation Sutra* as follows:

> Due to the request of Queen Vaidehī,[385] the Great Lord [Buddha Śākyamuni] of this world of anguish extensively expounded on the significant teaching for birth in the Pure Land. The Great Master [Amida Buddha] of the Pure Land of Ultimate Bliss also established the universal vow.
>
> This significant teaching for birth in the Pure Land applies to the instruction of the meditative practices with a focused mind and with a distracted mind described in the *Meditation Sutra*. The focused mind means to eliminate restlessness in order to concentrate deeply on the realm of Buddha Śākyamuni; the distracted mind refers to eliminating unwholesome acts and cultivating virtuous deeds. One should aspire for birth in the Pure Land while dedicating merit derived from these two types of meditative practices.
>
> The meaning of the universal vow is similarly explained in the *Larger Sutra*. The attainment of birth in the Pure Land by all common people, both the good and bad, is realized by the great power of the essential vow of Amida Buddha. The total reliance on this power of the essential vow is

> considered the dominant karmic relationship for the nembutsu devotee.
>
> Further, the real intention of Buddha Śākyamuni was so extensive and profound that it is extremely difficult to understand his teachings. Even the bodhisattvas who have reached the stages of the threefold wisdom[386] and the stages from the forty-first to the fiftieth of the fifty-two stages of bodhisattva practice cannot comprehend his teachings perfectly. How much can we, common mortals with distracted thoughts who have not reached even the first ten of the fifty-two stages of bodhisattva practice, know the true intention of Buddha Śākyamuni?
>
> Respectfully and with deep consideration, I believe that Buddha Śākyamuni encourages us to extricate ourselves from this world of anguish and that Amida Buddha will come to welcome us into the Pure Land. Hither Buddha Śākyamuni sends us and thither Amida Buddha calls us. How can we remain here, refusing to be born in the Pure Land?[387]

Master Shan-tao thus mentioned the three ways of teaching: that is, the meditative practices with a focused mind, the meditative practices with a distracted mind, and the universal vow of Amida Buddha.

The universal vow is described in the *Larger Sutra*: "'If, when I [Amida Buddha] am to attain buddhahood, all sentient beings in the ten directions who hold faith with genuine hearts and who wish to be born in my buddhaland are not born there within just ten moments of being mindful of me, I will not realize enlightenment.' Excluded only are those who have committed the five grave offenses and those who have abused the true Dharma."[388] Master Shan-tao interpreted this to mean, "'If, when I am to attain buddhahood, all sentient beings in the ten directions who call out my name at least ten times are not born there, I will not realize enlightenment.' Amida Buddha did, indeed, attain buddhahood and presently resides in the

Pure Land. It should be known that his essential vow was not made in vain. If sentient beings recite his name, they will, with certainty, attain birth in the Pure Land."[389]

Moreover, in the *Meditation Sutra*, after Buddha Śākyamuni has expounded on the two types of meditation with focused and with distracted minds, it states "Buddha Śākyamuni addressed Ānanda, 'Thou, Ānanda, hold these words carefully in your heart. To keep these words means to keep in mind the name of the Buddha of Immeasurable Life [Amida Buddha].'"[390] This statement reveals the true intention of the universal vow of Amida Buddha.

Master Shan-tao also points to the passage of the perception of the true physical features of Amida Buddha described in the *Meditation Sutra*: "The color of the body of Amida Buddha is similar to that of a golden mountain. The rays of light emanating from his special physical features shine over the ten directions. However, the light illuminates and embraces only the nembutsu practitioners. It should be known that this is where the influence of the essential vow is most evident."[391] This interpretation also reveals the meaning of the universal vow.

The *Smaller Sutra* states: "One cannot be born in the Pure Land through dependence on the merit of a few virtuous roots. If a good man and good woman, who, upon hearing the merit of the name of Amida Buddha, hold steadfast to his name in their minds with utmost concentration and without distraction and earnestly recite his name for one day, two days, or seven days, they will attain birth in the Pure Land when their lives are nearing the end and their minds are free from distractions."[392]

The passage following the above paragraph in the *Smaller Sutra* states, "Manifold buddhas in the six directions, as countless as the grains of sand in the Ganges, extended their broad and long tongues throughout the three thousand great-thousand worlds and proclaimed that nembutsu would indeed cause one's birth in the Pure Land. You should believe in the teachings of the *Smaller Sutra*."[393] This passage also explains the meaning of the universal vow.

Further, the *Sutra of the Samādhi of All Buddhas' Presence* states, "Bodhisattva Bhadrapāla asked Amida Buddha, 'What kind of practice will allow me to attain birth in the Pure Land?' Amida Buddha replied, 'Those who wish to be born in my land can do so by reciting my name ceaselessly.'"[394] These are the words of Amida Buddha himself regarding the essence of the universal vow.

The *Record of Holy Chu-lin Temple on Mount Wu-t'ai* of China describes as follows:

> The meditation master Fa-chao was met by two boys upon arrival at Holy Chu-lin Temple on Mount Ch'ing-lin. One boy was named Shan-ts'a, and the other was named Nan-t'o. Ushered into the temple by the two boys, Fa-chao entered the lecture hall and found Bodhisattva Samantabhadra surrounded by countless attendants. Bodhisattva Mañjuśrī was also seated, surrounded by ten thousand bodhisattvas.
>
> Fa-chao paid homage to Bodhisattva Mañjuśrī and asked, "Which practice should common mortals pursue in the period of the decline of the Dharma?"
>
> Bodhisattva Mañjuśrī replied, "You should now practice the recitation of nembutsu. This, indeed, is the appropriate time."
>
> Fa-chao continued, "Which buddha's name should I recite?"
>
> Bodhisattva Mañjuśrī replied, "In the western world beyond this world resides Amida Buddha. The vow of Amida Buddha is profound indeed. You should recite his name."[395]

The great sage Bodhisattva Mañjuśrī averred thus before Fa-chao's eyes. From the standpoint of an extensive view, it is said that the nembutsu practice is taught in various Buddhist schools. However, there is not enough time to expound on this teaching here.

Nonetheless, there are scholarly monks in various schools today who criticize the spread of the teaching of nembutsu, saying that the

Buddhadharma will be destroyed as a result. Accordingly, many people are said to have ceased their practice of reciting nembutsu. This is very difficult to understand. The teachings of Buddha Śākyamuni will not perish for ten thousand years. Even if there are attempts to destroy it, there are many heavenly beings and virtuous deities who protect the Buddhadharma; destroying it is beyond human power.

This is similar to the historical fact that Minister of State Mononobe no Moriya[396] attempted to destroy the Buddhadharma when Buddhism was introduced into Japan, and yet it has endured until the present day. It is impossible to destroy the Buddhadharma through the power of ignorant priests and lay people; through the recitation of nembutsu, the Hossō school and Sanron school will not perish, and neither will the Tendai school or Kegon school. Do followers of other schools expect their schools to flourish if nembutsu recitation comes to an end? The result would only be a meaningless cessation of nembutsu, and it is impossible to study the essential teachings of all the schools anyway. This would be a grievous loss for the Buddhadharma.

Scholars of the profound teachings of various schools, who are in the southern capital [Nara] and northern capital [Kyōto], and the priests of the head temples who study the great teachings of the Diamond Realm and the Womb Realm of esoteric Buddhism[397] should not alter their own beliefs, regardless of whether one or ten million nembutsu devotees proliferate in this world. Conversely, nembutsu should not be abandoned due to the belief that it would cause the decline of the Buddhadharma. To believe thus is analogous to facing lions while trying to escape from tigers and wolves. Nembutsu is also the teaching of Buddha Śākyamuni.

To vilify nembutsu or Buddhist practices other than nembutsu is a serious transgression. To be harmed by tigers and wolves or to be harmed by lions will ultimately result in death. Therefore, this nembutsu teaching must not be vilified; teachings other than nembutsu must not be privileged. Both are teachings of Buddha Śākyamuni.

Believers in the teachings of all schools should not be too obsessed with their beliefs.

The *Sutra Resolving Doubts Regarding the Period of the Imitative Dharma* states that if the practitioners of the threefold discipline of the precepts, meditation, and wisdom defame each other, they will fall into hell faster than an arrow flies.[398] The *Great Commentary on the Perfection of Wisdom* also teaches that even a practitioner who observes the Buddhist precepts will not escape agony in hell if, out of deep attachment to his own school, he criticizes people who are followers of other schools.[399] Master Shan-tao thus stated:

> At the very moment when the World-Honored One was coming to the end of his sermon, he entrusted with great care the name of Amida Buddha to Ānanda. With the passage of time, after the death of Buddha Śākyamuni, the five defilements proliferated, and many people began to slander the teaching of nembutsu. Monastics and lay people alike began to dislike the teaching of nembutsu and ceased listening to it. This gave rise to the poison of anger, and when they saw nembutsu practitioners, they struggled to incite intrigue and create grudges. Such people seem blind by nature and have no intrinsic goodness. Destroying the teaching designed for the instantaneous realization of enlightenment, they will sink into the three lower realms for a long time. They will never be released from the three lower realms, even though innumerable eons pass, more numerous than the number of particles released in the explosion of the earth.[400]

Practitioners of nembutsu must not vilify practices other than nembutsu. This would be counter to the compassionate vow of Amida Buddha. By the same token, followers of practices other than nembutsu should also refrain from vilifying nembutsu. Such an act would be counter to the vows of various buddhas.

Nevertheless, from the temple halls of the Shingon and Tendai schools today, criticism of nembutsu can be heard beyond their doors. At the same time, devotees of the single-hearted and exclusive recitation of nembutsu sit on the floor and are equally critical of practices other than nembutsu. These people are steeped in bias, justify their self-serving belief, determining that they are right and others are wrong, interpreting the teachings of other schools in their own way. This does not mean that these interpretations are appropriate. They are in contradiction with the true intention of Amida Buddha.

Some who criticize nembutsu say: "There are nembutsu devotees now who interpret nembutsu conveniently, claiming that one who is afraid of committing negative karma has no faith in the essential vow. Reciting nembutsu many times indicates doubt that a single nembutsu will suffice for birth in the Pure Land. As far as karmic practice for birth in the Pure Land is concerned, a single utterance, or ten repetitions of nembutsu will suffice; therefore, one should not repeat nembutsu. As for negative karma, even a person who commits the four grave offenses and five grave offenses will also attain birth in the Pure Land, and therefore one should not be afraid to commit wrongdoings." These are entirely groundless ideas. They are not found in the teachings of Buddha Śākyamuni; nor are they found in the interpretations of Master Shan-tao. Those who interpret nembutsu in this way are contrary to the spirit of all buddhas and are not in accord with the essential vow of Amida Buddha.

The *Meditation Sutra* clarifies that attaining birth in the Pure Land is possible through a single utterance, or ten repetitions of nembutsu by one who has committed the five grave offenses or the ten transgressions. This does not mean, however, that one should commit the five grave offenses and then recite nembutsu ten times, or commit the ten transgressions and utter nembutsu once. Rather, recite nembutsu ten times while observing the ten cardinal Mahāyāna precepts.[401] Be mindful also of the lesser forty-eight Mahāyāna precepts[402] while heavily relying upon the forty-eight vows of Amida Buddha. I, Hōnen, earnestly desire this.

In general, to whatever Buddhist practice you devote yourself, you must keep in mind that observance of the precepts is a protection like swimming with a life preserver. Your demeanor must be beyond reproach, as deliberate as if you were walking with a vessel brimming with oil, without a drop of spillage. Otherwise, the goal of your practice cannot be attained, and your wish cannot be realized.

In reality, however, we have perpetrated the four grave offenses or are guilty of committing the ten transgressions. Every one of us is karmically defiled in that we have committed these grave offenses and wrongful acts. No one is without reproach. Various buddhas of the past, present, and future have admonished, "Do not indulge in unwholesome acts, but cultivate wholesome deeds." Those who are virtuous will be reborn in a favorable world; those who are nonvirtuous will fall into a defiled world. If one who hears this law of causation continues to engage in unwholesome deeds, it is futile to admonish him.

This is not the first time it has been said that we should strive to avoid unwholesome karma within our capabilities and practice nembutsu in aspiration of birth in the Pure Land as often as we possibly can. If Amida Buddha does not abandon even a nonvirtuous person, how could he have antipathy toward the good person? To say that one who fears committing a negative karma doubts the essential vow is absolutely false in Jōdo Shū.

The words "One will attain birth in the Pure Land with just a single utterance, or ten repetitions, of nembutsu" is the golden saying of Buddha Śākyamuni. This is clearly taught in the *Meditation Sutra*.[403] Master Shan-tao interpreted this to mean: "One should also have unshakable faith that one who recites the name of Amida Buddha as few as ten times, or even just once, will, with certainty, attain birth in the Pure Land. This implicit belief is called the *profound heart*."[404]

Master Shan-tao continues, "... to recite single-heartedly and exclusively the name of Amida Buddha while walking, standing, sitting, or lying down, without regard for length of time, and to engage in the recitation of nembutsu without cessation throughout one's life. This is called the *rightly established practice* because it is in accordance with the essential vow of Amida Buddha."[405] This means that Master Shan-tao encouraged us from the standpoint of faith to believe birth in the Pure Land is attainable with just a single utterance of nembutsu. From the standpoint of practice, however, the recitation of nembutsu should continue in earnest for life.

How can it be said that one does not believe in the *power* of the essential vow when that person believes in the truth of the essential vow, accumulates the merits of nembutsu, and maintains a pure and sincere heart for many years? Relying upon the power of the essential vow is the sole means to enable common mortals with minimal potential to attain birth in the Pure Land. If one does not embrace belief in his compassionate power, the path to birth in the Pure Land is closed.

Generally speaking, manifold buddhas in the ten directions attained buddhahood in this delusive world of suffering in order to lead sentient beings to the way of deliverance, while Amida Buddha realized buddhahood in the Pure Land and made the essential vow in order to save sentient beings from suffering in the delusive world.

Buddha Śākyamuni achieved enlightenment in this world and, after a short stay, entered parinirvāṇa. He tailored the Dharma to suit the capacities of mortals for their convenience. The buddhas who attained buddhahood in their pure buddhalands are regarded as rewarded buddhas, and their pure buddhalands are considered the buddhalands where outstanding bodhisattvas reside.[406]

Fundamentally, common mortals who have not severed themselves from worldly passions are unable to be born in a pure buddhaland straightaway. However, unlike the other buddhas, Amida Buddha, residing in his Pure Land, is practicing even now to lead them to the path to birth in the Pure Land. His intent is to lead common mortals—who commit undesirable deeds, have no virtues, and are wandering among the delusive worlds of saṃsāra endlessly—to birth in the Pure Land. He has pity and extends his compassion, desiring to save from suffering those who violate the precepts, are ignorant, and have no chance of detaching themselves from the delusive worlds of transmigration.

It may be said that only those holy beings who have attained the threefold wisdom and the ten bodhisattva stages after endeavoring for a long period, and the high-ranking bodhisattvas who have mastered the six bodhisattva perfections and other virtuous practices are able to be born in the Pure Land; this is not the true intention of the great compassion of Amida Buddha.

Amida Buddha, embracing the theory that endeavor begets merit, and with immeasurable compassion in his heart, delineated the way of deliverance for all sentient beings for the endless period of five eons. Amida Buddha employed various skillful means to seek the way of deliverance and thus avowed:

> I [Amida Buddha], having fulfilled my essential vow and having resided in the Pure Land, should lead common mortals with minimal potential to attain birth in the Pure Land. It is impossible for them to achieve this goal by their own karmic power. For these people I will spend countless eons observing innumerable austere practices, completing tens of thousands of admirable practices and virtuous deeds, and attaining the practice that brings enlightenment to both myself and other beings. Through these efforts, I will attain buddhahood, having acquired all virtuous and undefiled merits.
>
> I will see that my name embodies these merits, and I will induce sentient beings to utter my name. If sentient beings believe in the essential vow and recite my name, they will realize birth in the Pure Land in accordance with the essential vow. This is because I vowed that my attainment of buddhahood would be impossible should the essential vow—that birth in the Pure Land is possible for the mortal through nembutsu—not be fulfilled. If the essential vow

> is not accomplished, I will not realize enlightenment for countless eons.[407]

At the same time, Amida Buddha foresaw that since the masses in the defiled world of the future would be vain and lazy, they would find it difficult to awaken faith in the essential vow. Doubt will arise regarding birth in the Pure Land through nembutsu, even if one or two buddhas attest to it. Therefore, having wished that all buddhas in the ten directions extol the essential vow, Amida Buddha stated in the seventeenth vow: "If, when I am to attain buddhahood, all the countless buddhas of the ten directions do not praise and call out my name, I will not realize enlightenment."[408]

Following this, in the essential vow, Amida Buddha stated, "If, when I am to attain buddhahood, all sentient beings who recite my name at least ten times are not born in my Pure Land, I will not realize enlightenment."[409] This implies that the seventeenth vow was created so that the intent of the eighteenth vow would be extolled by all of the countless buddhas.

After the fulfillment of the essential vow, all buddhas in the six directions, as countless as the grains of sand in the Ganges, extended their broad and long tongues that enveloped the three thousand great-thousand worlds and in unison attested to the teaching of birth in the Pure Land through nembutsu.[410] Master Shan-tao interpreted this to mean: "If, in spite of the attestation of the buddhas in the six directions, birth in the Pure Land is impossible for nembutsu devotees, the extended tongues of these buddhas will never again be retracted; they will fester and fall into decay."[411]

The nonbeliever of birth in the Pure Land through nembutsu will, in essence, be just like one who decomposes the tongues of all the buddhas in the ten directions. This should be known. To cause the decay of the tongues of one or two buddhas is a frightening occurrence; would we think nothing of causing the decomposition of the tongues of all the buddhas in the ten directions? Master Shan-tao said that such nonbelievers would be unable to extricate themselves from the three lower realms for a period longer than the number of particles resulting from the explosion of the earth.[412]

The forty-eight vows of Amida Buddha include the first vow that the three lower realms do not exist in the Pure Land, the second vow that there is no return to the three lower realms after birth in the Pure Land, and the eighteenth vow that all sentient beings will be born in the Pure Land through nembutsu. Amida Buddha fulfilled the forty-eight vows entirely; no vow was made in vain. This is because Amida Buddha promised that he would not realize enlightenment until he succeeded in fulfilling each vow, and he did attain buddhahood. Accordingly, if one believes in the first vow that the three lower realms do not exist in the Pure Land, how could one say that there are the three lower realms in the Pure Land? No one would have such thoughts. If one believes in the second vow that there is no return to the three lower realms after birth in the Pure Land, no one would say that after life ends in the Pure Land, one will descend into the three lower realms. If one believes in the third vow that all beings in the Pure Land are golden in color, no one would say that some beings are gold and others are white. If one believes in the fourth vow that there is no distinction in the personal appearance of all beings in the Pure Land, no one would say that there are beautiful ones as well as homely ones in the Pure Land.

So it follows that no one doubts the fulfillment of the vows, from the sixth vow that all beings in the Pure Land possess divine eyes that see countless buddhalands, the seventh vow that all beings in the Pure Land possess divine ears that hear the teachings of countless buddhas, the twelfth vow that the light of Amida Buddha is immeasurable, the thirteenth vow that the life of Amida Buddha is infinite, to the forty-eighth vow that all the bodhisattvas of other buddhalands, on hearing the name of Amida Buddha, acquire the three kinds of wisdom.

In spite of this, there remain some who simply do not believe in the eighteenth vow, the attainment of birth in the Pure Land through nembutsu. However, if one has no faith in this vow, it is impossible to believe in the rest of the forty-seven vows. Conversely, if one believes in the forty-seven vows, it is impossible to disbelieve only the eighteenth vow. Further, if it is said that Bodhisattva Dharmākara has not attained buddhahood, it would be an evil mockery of the teachings of Buddha Śākyamuni. If we accept his attainment of buddhahood, would there be reason to doubt the eighteenth vow? The truth is that Buddha Śākyamuni proclaimed that Amida Buddha, who made these forty-eight vows, realized enlightenment ten eons ago.

All the buddhas and tathāgatas in the six directionss, as countless as the grains of sand in the Ganges, extended their tongues to envelop the three thousand great-thousand worlds and attested to the truth of the attainment of birth in the Pure Land through nembutsu. Who would doubt this? Master Shan-tao interpreted this spirit of belief in the essential vow thus: "Even if one or many transformed buddhas or rewarded buddhas were to pervade the ten directions, emitting light and enveloping the ten directions with their tongues, and teach that the attainment of birth in the Pure Land through nembutsu is a falsehood, the nembutsu practitioner must not have a shadow of a doubt and fall back."[413]

However, nembutsu practitioners today are easily swayed by those with different teachings and different views and become doubtful. They become even more doubtful when they are told by the rewarded buddhas and transformed buddhas that birth in the Pure Land through nembutsu is a hoax. What is there to practice if they abandon this practice of nembutsu? Those with little wisdom, who open a sutra, do not have the vision to study the teachings, and if they possess no wealth, they are incapable of offering alms even if they desire to.

Long ago, in Vārāṇasī, India, there lived a prince. He was known as Prince Great Giver,[414] and had great sympathy for the poor. He opened his storage rooms, and gave all his treasures to the needy. Eventually his riches were gone, but the poor continued to abound. The prince heard that at the bottom of the ocean was a magical gem with the power to fulfill any wish and desire of its possessor. He vowed to go to the sea in order to find the magical gem so as to share the riches with the poor. Thus, he appeared before the palace of the dragon king (Skt. *nāgarāja*).

The dragon king was surprised and perplexed. Seeing that this was an unusual human being, he greeted the prince personally, asked him to have a seat on the floor of gems and asked, "What do you seek, having come all this distance to my kingdom?" The prince replied, "There are so many poor people in my world, and they are all suffering. I have come to ask for the gem that you hold in your topknot." The dragon king replied, "In that case, stay here for seven days and receive my offerings. I will then award you the gem." The prince stayed there for seven days and was given the magical gem. The dragon king saw the prince off, and the prince returned quickly to the shores of his land.

Many dragon deities regretted the king's decision after a while and lamented to the king, saying, "That gem is really a treasure belonging to the ocean and should be retrieved." One dragon deity decided to bring it back. He disguised himself as a human being and appeared before the prince, saying, "You are known to have acquired a most unusual and precious gem. May I see it?" When the prince showed it to him, the dragon deity snatched it away and returned to the ocean.

The sorrowful prince vowed, "If the gem is not returned, I will empty the ocean." The dragon deities laughed, "You are a most foolish man. It may be possible to make the sun fall out of the sky. It may also be possible to dam a rushing river. But it would be impossible to empty the ocean." The prince replied, "I known that the benevolent bond of love [between parent and child] is difficult to sever, but I wish to do so. I also wish to exhaust the inexhaustible world of life and death. No matter how much water there may be in the sea, it is finite. Still, if I am not able to empty the sea in this life, I vow I will commit many lifetimes to making the ocean dry."

Having made the vow, the prince took a seashell and began to scoop out water from the ocean. The sincerity of the prince's vow touched the hearts of the heavenly beings. They all gathered round, filled the sleeves of their celestial robes with water, and emptied it beyond the Cakravāḍa Mountains. When the prince took one or two shells full of water, he emptied one fifth of the sea. The dragon king panicked, thinking that he would lose his abode. He then begged the prince's forgiveness and gave back the gem. The prince returned to the capital with the magical gem and showered the people with riches; there was no one in the human world who did not receive the blessings of the prince.

To hold steadfast in the face of extreme adversity is called *forbearance*. In the past, the benevolent Prince Great Giver crossed ten thousand leagues of ocean and succeeded in obtaining the magical gem from the dragon king. At present, we have traversed the path that lies between the river of water [i.e., greed] and the river of fire [i.e., anger] and have attained the magical gem called the *essential vow of Amida Buddha*.

Prince Great Giver lost his magical gem when the dragon deities had misgivings about the relinquished gem and wished it back in their possession. We devotees of nembutsu have also lost our faith in the essential vow due to criticism from those who hold teachings and views different from our own. Prince Great Giver emptied the waters of the ocean with a seashell in order to retrieve the magical gem. Impressed by the prince, both the six heavenly beings in the realm of desire and the four meditative celestial beings in the realm of form helped the prince succeed in emptying the ocean. Thus, if devotees of nembutsu, like Prince Great Giver with his seashell, try with implicit faith to dispose of doubt and criticism from those who hold teachings and views different from their own, all of the buddhas in the six directions will extend their protective hands to enable the practitioners to achieve their goal.

With great effort the prince succeeded in emptying the ocean. The tiled roof of the palace of the dragon king appeared, and the prince retrieved the magical gem. When the nembutsu devotee emptied the ocean of censure, the roof of the abode of one who criticizes nembutsu appeared, and the gem called the *essential vow* was retrieved. The prince regained possession of his gem and saved the poor in this world; the nembutsu devotee must retrieve the essential vow and attain birth in the Pure Land in order to save all of the masses.

It is my wish that all the practitioners of nembutsu keep fast the gem called the *essential vow of Amida Buddha* and hold it deep within through faith. If you have lost it, you must speedily remove the waters of doubt and criticism with a hand from a devout heart. You must not return to this delusive world with an empty heart.

Why did Amida Buddha establish the compassionate vow to make birth in the Pure Land possible through just ten repetitions of nembutsu, embracing all sentient beings in the ten directions? Why can we attain birth in the Pure Land in the forms of the three categories after reciting the six syllables, *Na mu A mi da Butsu*? For whom did Amida Buddha endeavor for countless eons? It was only so the merit would be bestowed upon sentient beings in the future. For what reason did Amida Buddha establish the unsurpassed compassionate vow? It was to bestow upon us his compassionate wish of birth in the Pure Land for those of us who live in the period of the decline of the Dharma.

How could Amida Buddha have realized enlightenment if we are not able to attain birth in the Pure Land through nembutsu? We are able to attain birth in the Pure Land because Amida Buddha attained buddhahood. The enlightenment of Amida Buddha enables us to attain birth in the Pure Land.

Hence, we should understand the very words of his vow, "If sentient beings are not born in the Pure Land," in this context. The other words of his vow, "I will not realize enlightenment," verify our attainment of birth in the Pure Land, surpassing all definition.

26. Instruction to a Devotee

1. Refrain from facing west or turning your back to the east when relieving yourself; face either north or south to do so. Also turn your head toward the west as much as possible while sitting and lying down at home. When you inevitably have to turn your back to the west, say to yourself, "Inexcusably, my backside is now facing the west where Amida Buddha resides." Someone who is not looking toward the west but sets his heart on the west is more commendable than one who faces the west without any attentions to the Pure Land of Amida Buddha.

2. A person with filial piety who wishes to respect and be dutiful to his parents should rely on the compassion of Amida Buddha first. He then should think: To have been given life as a human being and to be able to recite nembutsu in aspiration for attaining birth in the Pure Land is due entirely to the nurturing of my parents. Therefore, if you ask Amida Buddha, in reward for your merit cultivated through the practice of nembutsu, to welcome your parents into the Pure Land and to eliminate their unwholesome karma there, Amida Buddha will, with certainty, welcome your parents into the Pure Land.

   To illustrate, there was a nun called Miao-yün in China who lost her parents in her early years. She recited nembutsu for thirty years while praying for their attainment of birth in the

Pure Land. Her parents then got rid of their hellish agony and finally realized birth in the Pure Land of Ultimate Bliss.

3. Master Shan-tao interpreted the essential vow in his *Hymns in Praise of Birth in the Pure Land*, "'If, when I [Amida Buddha] am to attain buddhahood, all sentient beings in the ten directions who call out my name at least ten times are not born in the Pure Land, I will not realize enlightenment.' Amida Buddha did, indeed, attain buddhahood and presently resides in the Pure Land. It should be known that the essential vow was not made in vain. If sentient beings recite his name, they will, with certainty, attain birth in the Pure Land."[415]

Recite, call to mind, and look upon this passage at all times. Amida Buddha realized the essential vow fully and established the Pure Land with majestic ornaments. He is now day and night carefully searching for those devotees who recite his name and listening for any voice calling his name. Amida Buddha knows even the person who merely utters his name once as well as those who contemplate him for just a moment. The light of Amida Buddha embraces and never abandons nembutsu devotees like us, and his arrival to welcome us during our final moments is unfailing.

The aforementioned passage is the eyes [essence], liver [vital point], and core spirit of the forty-eight vows of Amida Buddha. Master Shan-tao then skillfully arranged the real intention of the essential [eighteenth] vow into forty-eight Chinese letters.

Thoroughly purify your body and hands, hold a string of prayer beads, wear a religious robe, and recite nembutsu. With your ordinary, defiled body, do not enter a religious hall in which the image of Amida Buddha is enshrined. Even a lord is respected and awed in this world; how much more so is the unparalleled Honored One [Amida Buddha] revered by various great bodhisattvas? How then could common mortals like us act disrespectfully toward Amida Buddha? All the heavenly beings in the delusive three realms respect him with their heads bowed; without question we should revere and worship Amida Buddha.

It is a grave misconception to say that fearing one's negative karma slights the essential vow, and that behaving prudently and cultivating virtuous deeds is tantamount to relying on one's self-power. Never lend your ears to these falsehoods, which are not worthy of thought even the size of a dewdrop or a speck of dust. Those who say this willfully misinterpret the nembutsu doctrine; this was not taught in the three sutras of Pure Land Buddhism or other Pure Land texts composed by masters in China and Japan. These people will definitely fall into the three lower realms. There is no such interpretation in the entire lifetime of teachings of Buddha Śākyamuni.

Those who have committed the five grave offenses or the ten transgressions may still be welcomed by Amida Buddha at their time of death through just a single utterance, or ten repetitions, of nembutsu. This is because they repent in grief their wrong deeds, ask for their deliverance, and recite nembutsu. Then Amida Buddha will certainly eliminate their negative karma and arrive to welcome them through the power of the essential vow.

I have noted here the meaning of the essential vow and am sending it to you. Please believe in what I have taught and devote yourself to practicing nembutsu. I hope that you will become by all means a respectable nembutsu devotee.

Sincerely yours.

27. Replies to Saburō in Tsunoto

1. A Reply to Saburō Dated October 18th

I HAVE THOROUGHLY read your letter. You need not explain the teaching of nembutsu in detail when the Shōgun's [Minamoto no Sanetomo (1192–1219)] court summons you to ask about nembutsu. In fact, you have not yet been fully instructed in the doctrine of nembutsu. Therefore, when they ask you questions regarding the exclusive practice and the miscellaneous practices, you are encouraged to answer in the following manner:

> I do not know all the details of the teaching of nembutsu. When the Shōgun [Minamoto no Yoritomo (1147–99)] went up to the capital, Kyōto, I attended to him. During my stay in the capital, I heard about the holy monk [Hōnen], visited him, and asked, "What shall I do now to prepare for deliverance in the life to come? Is there any teaching for lay people like me to attain this goal?"
>
> The holy monk answered, "There are many teachings designed to detach oneself from the delusive worlds of saṃsāra. However, for ordinary people in this period of the decline of the Dharma to part from saṃsāra, there is no alternative except attainment of birth in the Pure Land of Ultimate Bliss. This is the sole path that Amida Buddha

himself encourages people to follow in order to detach from the delusive worlds of saṃsāra.

"Likewise, various practices have been designed to attain birth in the Pure Land, but none is superior to recitation of nembutsu. Practices other than nembutsu are too difficult for common mortals to perform. This is because nembutsu is the practice taught in the essential vow, which Amida Buddha himself vowed in order to realize enlightenment for all sentient beings. Nembutsu is beyond comparison with other practices for achieving birth in the Pure Land. Hence, devote yourself to reciting nembutsu if you desire birth in the Pure Land."

The holy monk continued, saying, "Common mortals with minimal potential, who are ignorant of the teachings of Buddha Śākyamuni and who have no wisdom, are unable to attain birth in the Pure Land through practices other than nembutsu. Even though I studied the teachings of Buddha Śākyamuni from my early age, I have no idea how to accomplish birth in the Pure Land through practices other than nembutsu. I merely recite nembutsu now and desire birth in the Pure Land while relying on the essential vow of Amida Buddha. How can common mortals with minimal potential achieve birth in the Pure Land through practices other than nembutsu?"

Upon hearing these words, I firmly believed in the teaching of Hōnen-shōnin and presently devote myself to reciting nembutsu.

The holy monk also said, "The recitation of nembutsu is taught in the essential vow—this is not merely my own teaching. There was a prominent monk in China called Master Shan-tao, who advocated nembutsu for birth in the Pure Land. He divided practices for birth in the Pure Land into two categories, the exclusive practice and the miscellaneous practices, and encouraged common people to perform the former one. The exclusive practice refers specifically to the recitation of nembutsu, and the miscellaneous practices to practices other than nembutsu.

"It is said that one hundred out of one hundred people who observe the exclusive practice will attain birth in the Pure Land, but only one or two out of one thousand people who perform the miscellaneous practices will attain birth in the Pure Land.[416]

"There also was a man named Hsin-chung[417] in China, who wrote down the merits and demerits of these two types of practices in his *Treatise of the Exclusive and Right Practices*[418] and propagated the vocal nembutsu to various people in China. This writing is most likely in Jōshō-bō's[419] hands now. It may be convenient for you to bring it to the court at the time of summons."

The holy monk added, "The exclusive practice also includes the five right practices, which are further divided into two categories, the rightly established practice and the auxiliary practices. The former applies to the recitation of nembutsu, the fourth among the five right practices, and the latter includes the rest of the four practices.

"Now, if one aspires to birth in the Pure Land with the definitely settled mind, one should select the exclusive practice between the exclusive practice and the miscellaneous practices and earnestly recite nembutsu in accordance with the principle of the exclusive practice. In the same manner, one should further select the rightly established practice between the rightly established practice and the auxiliary practices and engage in the recitation of nembutsu with singleness of heart.

"Please tell the court that you [Saburō] do not know the detailed and the profound meaning of nembutsu. You believe that nembutsu is so commendable that you simply recite nembutsu."

> The holy monk further stated, "Master Shan-tao was not an ordinary monk; he was a manifestation of Amida Buddha. Accordingly, you [Saburō] should firmly believe that his teaching of nembutsu is absolutely right and perform nembutsu.
>
> "There are also many writings being attributed to Master Shan-tao. However, as you are illiterate and have only heard the import of the writings, recite nembutsu while wishing for deliverance and birth in the Pure Land in the life to come. Those who are close to you most likely saw you, felt envy, and reported this type of thing without any authority from the court."

If you indiscreetly speak about the teaching of nembutsu in detail at the time of the summons, I am afraid that you might commit an error, and your situation will become worse. In the letter, you requested my detailed instructions regarding nembutsu, but no one can predict what their questions will be at that time in the court. My full account of written instructions may cause things to become worse. I appreciate your deep consideration regarding this matter and have thus answered questions in accordance with your situation.

Those who aspire for birth in the Pure Land are not swayed by the command, "Do not practice nembutsu!" Contrarily, those who have no desire for birth in the Pure Land do not listen to the words, "Recite nembutsu diligently!" In any case, you, apart from others, should be firmly resolved to achieve birth in the Pure Land on this occasion.

I really feel sorry for the courier who brought your letter here from far away. It is inappropriate and useless for you to explain nembutsu in more detail than what I have mentioned here at the time of the summons. Trouble will not arise if you answer questions as the occasion demands. Were I to give a full account of the teaching of nembutsu using both Chinese characters and Japanese syllables, my reply would be unexpectedly long, and it would be difficult to compose a timely response, which also may cause you trouble, as I have said.

The thoughtful will understand if you say, "I do not know particulars about nembutsu. I will just answer as much as I have heard." Conversely, those who have no heart for the attainment of birth in the Pure Land will never be satisfied, even if you explain nembutsu as thoroughly as you can.

The Shōgun is said to be a very reasonable person and says nothing false; therefore, I do not suppose that he will say, "Nembutsu is erroneous. Do not recite nembutsu," upon hearing your answer. You do not have to worry about what they will say or think of your explanation of nembutsu. It is indeed difficult to write everything about the teaching of nembutsu in a letter.

Sincerely yours,
October 18th

2. A Reply to Saburō Dated September 28th

I am very delighted to receive and read your letter, as I have been concerned for you. It is truly impressive to hear that more than thirty people are now observing the exclusive practice of nembutsu in your province, even though there are not many exclusive nembutsu devotees in our country. Even in the vicinity of the capital, Kyōto, where people are accustomed to hearing the recitation of nembutsu and can easily learn nembutsu, we hardly see exclusive nembutsu practitioners. It is said that a place called Ping-chou was the center of the exclusive practice of nembutsu in China at the time of Master Tao-ch'o. The fact that more than thirty nembutsu devotees exist in a Japanese province is really impressive. This success is due completely to the good offices of your great efforts, as well as the lay priest Kumagai. It also indicates that the time may have come for many aspirants to attain birth in the Pure Land.

If karmic relations are not ripe, no matter how much one encourages the recitation of nembutsu, the result will be in vain. Besides, nembutsu has never spread through the remarks of someone who does not fully understand nembutsu. I assume that the karmic conditions with nembutsu are ripe now; that is why such a large number of nembutsu devotees have gathered around you. It is impressive, indeed.

However, it is a grave misconception to say that nembutsu is encouraged merely for the unschooled in accordance with their potential and karmic conditions. The essential vow of Amida Buddha does not discriminate between the learned and the unschooled, those who observe the precepts and those who transgress them, people in the age of Buddha Śākyamuni and people after his entrance into parinirvāṇa, and lay people and monastics. The essential vow was designed on the basis of all-encompassing compassion that saves all sentient beings equally; it never discriminates. The *Meditation Sutra* therefore states, "The mind of Amida Buddha is the mind of great compassion."[420]

Master Shan-tao, in commenting on this passage, said, "Amida Buddha embraces all sentient beings equally with his all-encompassing compassion."[421] Here, the phrase "all sentient beings" denotes "without exception." Buddha Śākyamuni also encouraged all bad, good, and ignorant people to equally accomplish birth in the Pure Land through nembutsu.

For this reason, the vow for birth in the Pure Land through nembutsu is Tathāgata Amida's quintessential vow. All other practices are inconsistent with the most critical teaching of Amida Buddha. Although Tathāgata Śākyamuni taught various practices in accordance with the karmic conditions of all sorts of practitioners, the purpose of his presence in this world was to preach the essential vow of Amida Buddha.

Besides nembutsu, Buddha Śākyamuni taught various modes of practices attuned to the potential and karmic conditions of sentient beings. This form of eclectic teaching is called the "instruction in accordance with one's potential." These practices, however, did not convey the true heart of Buddha Śākyamuni. Nembutsu, then, is not only the practice taught in the essential vow for the emancipation of all beings but is also the true intent of Buddha Śākyamuni's presence in this world.

Nembutsu is indeed different from any other practice. It is a misinterpretation to say that nembutsu was designed specifically for the ignorant.

Someday, I will write you important passages on nembutsu. The letter I previously sent to the lay priest Kumagai needs correction; therefore, I will rewrite it and send it again. It is impossible for me to express myself completely in a letter. In any case, I will write you again at a propitious time.

Sincerely yours,
September 28th

3. A Reply to Saburō Dated April 26th

Please accept my sincere appreciation for your immediate inquiry upon hearing of my illness. Your kindness is beyond description. On this occasion, my illness was so serious that I had to take great care of myself. Still, it is not so severe that one must fear I will only be in this world for another day or two.

I developed a slight cold around the end of the last year. Despite that, I participated in the fifty-day special nembutsu retreat in January, and that truly aggravated my physical condition. Although I felt very dehydrated around February 10th, I forced myself to keep practicing until February 20th, the fiftieth day of the nembutsu retreat. Overexerting myself like this made the condition worse; my parched throat craved water continuously, and even today every joint in my body aches.

It has taken me a long time to recover from this illness, but the condition is not so serious now. My doctor told me to take care of myself; therefore, I have started moxibustion treatments again, and

I use hot compresses as well as take some Chinese medicines internally. I feel that I am getting better these days, little by little.

Your offer to immediately come to the capital to visit me is truly appreciated, but it is not necessary for you to travel such a great distance. It has been our long-held wish to attain birth in the Pure Land together, wherever we may live.

It is impossible for me to express everything in this letter. I will write to you again.

Sincerely yours,
April 26th

*Dōkō's note: Hōnen-shōnin was treated as described above not to preserve his life but so that he could recite nembutsu with a peaceful mind. Please refer to the passage in the end of *Admonitions for the Attainment of Birth in the Pure Land*.[422]

28. Instruction to a Lady[423]

THE ESSENCE for the nembutsu devotee is nothing but the repetition of nembutsu. The practitioner should recite nembutsu exclusively while contemplating the fear of falling into the lower realms in the life to come, aspiring to birth in the Pure Land, and having faith that, through the recitation of nembutsu, Amida Buddha will come to welcome him into the Pure Land at his time of death.

In the same manner, the threefold devotional heart is nothing more than just the heart aspiring to birth in the Pure Land. The wish to achieve birth in the Pure Land, truthfully and without pretension, is called the *genuine heart.* The purity of this heart, which carries no doubt that nembutsu leads Amida Buddha to welcome one at the time of death, is called the *profound heart.* One's desire for birth in the Pure Land and the dedication of one's accumulated merits of practice and virtuous deeds for attaining birth in the Pure Land are called the *heart that seeks birth in the Pure Land through the dedication of merit.* Therefore, if one wishes for birth in the Pure Land with purity of heart, one will spontaneously embody the threefold devotional heart.

Incidentally, regarding your question, "Is it possible that one who achieves birth in the Pure Land in the low grade of the middle category will not receive the welcome of Amida Buddha at the time of death, simply because there is no account of the arrival in the passage on the low grade in the middle category in the *Meditation Sutra*?"[424]

The fact is that Amida Buddha's welcome actually applies to all of the nine grades of aspirants. His welcome is merely abridged in the passage of the low grade in the middle category.

According to the interpretation of Master Shan-tao, the threefold devotional heart is embodied in each aspirant throughout the nine grades. Although each grade is described in various ways, both the threefold devotional heart and Amida Buddha's arrival certainly apply to each grade. The nembutsu devotees who desire birth in the Pure Land must have all aspects of the threefold devotional heart; therefore, the *Meditation Sutra* mentions the threefold devotional heart in the passage of the high grade in the high category of aspirants. Nonetheless, we should understand that each grade comprehends the teaching of the threefold devotional heart.

It is impossible for us to cross the ocean of the delusive worlds of saṃsāra because our raft and boat of the precepts have been destroyed. The light of wisdom becomes clouded and does not illuminate the darkness of the delusive worlds, and there is no way to detach ourselves from the delusive worlds.

Amida Buddha, with his compassion, designed the teaching of the power other than self. The nineteenth vow states that Amida Buddha will welcome the nembutsu devotee to the Pure Land at the time of death in order to embrace those of us who have been excluded from entering the holy gate.[425]

The passage of the low grade of the middle category as described in the *Meditation Sutra* did not mention Amida Buddha's welcome. This is due to the fact that it is a self-evident truth. Hence, you need not entertain any doubts regarding Amida Buddha's welcome of the nembutsu devotee at the time of death.

Sincerely yours,
Genkū

Part III

Second Supplement to Collected Teachings of Hōnen: The Japanese Anthology

29. Essentials for Birth in the Pure Land through Nembutsu

AMIDA BUDDHA VOWED: "If, when I am to attain buddhahood, all sentient beings who recite my name are not born in the Pure Land, I will not realize enlightenment."[426] He did, indeed, realize enlightenment. Birth in the Pure Land through nembutsu, therefore, signifies certain attainment of birth in the Pure Land by those who recite his name.

If one deeply believes in this vow of Amida Buddha and does not entertain any doubts about birth in the Pure Land through nembutsu, ten out of ten and one hundred out of one hundred people will achieve birth in the Pure Land through just a single utterance of nembutsu.[427] Conversely, one who doubts birth in the Pure Land through nembutsu will not attain this birth, even if this individual recites nembutsu.

People entertain various doubts about birth in the Pure Land: some feel that even though they recite nembutsu, birth in the Pure Land is impossible due to their own accumulated nonvirtuous karma; others think that birth in the Pure Land is impossible through nembutsu because they are too busy with everyday life; and some suppose that birth in the Pure Land through nembutsu is impossible because their hearts of nembutsu are not strong enough to attain this birth. Those who entertain these doubts about birth in the Pure Land do not know the efficacy of nembutsu.

In reality, a mortal's karmic burden is so grave that nembutsu is encouraged in order to eradicate it. Do not harbor doubts about birth in the Pure Land by saying that such birth is unattainable through nembutsu because your karmic burden is too heavy. Nembutsu is just like medicine: one who gets seriously ill must take medicine. If one has a serious condition but does not take medicine, the disease will never be cured.

The *Meditation Sutra* teaches, "With the instruction of a virtuous teacher, those who have committed the ten transgressions or the five grave offenses will accomplish birth in the Pure Land through just a single utterance, or ten repetitions of nembutsu."[428] In addition, Master Shan-tao said, "A single utterance of nembutsu eliminates the negative karma accumulated in many eons."[429] Hence, one with grave karmic negativity should not doubt his attainment of birth in the Pure Land through nembutsu.

It is also said that if one is lacking in virtuous roots, one should repeat nembutsu and receive unsurpassed merit. Some may believe that since they have cultivated great virtuous roots other than nembutsu, they can attain birth in the Pure Land without nembutsu. Master Shan-tao, however, exhorted us to rely on the essential vow of Amida Buddha and to repeat his name, saying that our virtuous roots are shallow and meager.[430]

The *Larger Sutra* reads, "A single utterance of the name of Amida Buddha brings us enormous virtue, an unsurpassed merit."[431] How much more merit can one receive through the continual recitation of nembutsu for life? It follows that we must not doubt the certainty of birth in the Pure Land through nembutsu, even if we did not cultivate virtuous roots.

The nature of the common mortals in the period of the decline of the Dharma is that their vigorous hearts for nembutsu do not appear, even if they practice nembutsu. This does not mean they have no reliance upon Amida Buddha. It is as if one is grateful to his lord yet hesitates somewhat to serve his lord at the court. This hesitation does not signify a lack of his gratitude to the lord.

If one lacks diligence in performing nembutsu, how can one strive in practices other than nembutsu? Further, if one practices halfheartedly and one's life passes by idly, what sort of conditions will one meet at the end of one's life?

Having the intention to practice nembutsu proves that one has aspiration for birth in the Pure Land even if one lacks diligence in nembutsu. A proverb says: "If one comes to be so minded, the heart will awaken to enlightenment as a matter of course." A vigorous heart for nembutsu sometimes appears as one accumulates merit and strives after virtue. If one lacks diligence in nembutsu from the beginning and idles one's time away, one's life will end in vain followed by regret.

Master Shan-tao taught that the essential vow of Amida Buddha does not discriminate against those with distracted and vacillating hearts.[432] Hence, one should not doubt the attainment of birth in the Pure Land, even though one lacks diligence in nembutsu.

Moreover, that mundane affairs keep us so busy means we should recite nembutsu even more. The reason is that nembutsu is designed for all people, without distinction as to whether one is male or female, high or low, walking, standing, sitting, or lying down, and without regard for length of time, place, or various karmic relationships. Nembutsu can be practiced easily. Only nembutsu can be uttered even in one's final moment. Contrarily, practices other than nembutsu are difficult to perform in this hectic world. The practice of nembutsu does not discriminate between a lay person and a monk, or between the learned and the unschooled. Everyone who recites nembutsu will receive the merit of birth in the Pure Land equally. The attainment of birth in the Pure Land must be realized without being hindered by various worldly affairs.

In short, the attainment of this birth depends on whether one has aspiration or not. We cannot abandon mundane affairs, but if the affairs become a true hindrance for nembutsu, we lose our resolve and diligence in nembutsu.

We have received life in the realm of a human being, a state extremely difficult to obtain, and with the precious teachings of Buddha Śākyamuni, we have fortunately encountered an extraordinary opportunity. Life, however, is transient: no law of nature dictates that the old must die before the young. No one can predict his own illness or death. At all times, we must make the best of our opportunities and devote ourselves to reciting nembutsu.

The instruction that nembutsu is recited with the threefold devotional heart is included in my aforementioned sayings. The threefold devotional heart is as follows: the first aspect is the genuine heart, the second, the profound heart, and the third, the heart that seeks birth in the Pure Land through the dedication of merit.

The genuine heart is the sincere heart. Aspiration for birth in the Pure Land and the recitation of nembutsu must come from the bottom of one's heart. This is called the *genuine heart.* Conversely, the expression that should be foreign to one's heart is referred to as the "unfruitful heart of falsity and fickleness." Birth in the Pure Land will be achieved through conviction if one is resolved not to return to the state of the delusive three realms of transmigration, one desires birth in the Pure Land, and one recites nembutsu. Consequently, some who achieve birth in the Pure Land seem on the outside to hold no aspiration for this birth, while others who appear to desire birth in the Pure Land do not attain this birth. The genuine heart will abide naturally in one who firmly perceives the reality of the impermanence of all phenomena, abhors existence in the delusive world, and recites nembutsu.

The profound heart is the heart of belief. That is, one believes that one is a common mortal who has wandered through the delusive worlds of saṃsāra, and that Amida Buddha without fail will embrace sentient beings through the power of the essential vow. Amida Buddha vowed, "If, when I am to attain buddhahood, all sentient beings who recite my name are not born in the Pure Land, I will not realize enlightenment."[433] Since Amida Buddha *did* attain buddhahood, then if one believes in the certain attainment of birth in the Pure Land through nembutsu, one will naturally possess the profound heart.

The heart that seeks birth in the Pure Land through the dedication of merit refers to aspiration for birth in the Pure Land of Ultimate Bliss by dedicating the merit of all of one's virtues cultivated in the past and in the present life.[434] There is no meaning other than this.

The name *threefold devotional heart* seems to indicate three separate hearts, but they are encompassed entirely within the "single-hearted and exclusive practice of nembutsu"[435] taught in the *Larger Sutra*—that is, it is the exclusive reliance on Amida Buddha and the exclusive recitation of nembutsu without the mingling of other practices.

Amida Buddha will transform one's unsettled karma for attaining birth in the Pure Land into the definitely settled karma for birth in the Pure Land and welcome one to the Pure Land if one exclusively relies on him with a singleness of heart. This is more meritorious for attaining birth in the Pure Land than thoughtlessly invoking buddhas or gods, without seeing that the length of one's life and the depth of one's penalty for previous acts are due to one's residual karma.

To pray for a good fortune in this ephemeral world and forgetting crucial deliverance in the next life are not the true meaning for nembutsu devotees. Amida Buddha designed nembutsu as the "rightly established practice" for birth in the Pure Land in the life to come; therefore, one should not ignore nembutsu and observe other practices. For this reason, I encourage you to recite nembutsu.

Nevertheless, knowing that birth in the Pure Land is possible through nembutsu and yet indulging in nonvirtuous acts, neglecting compassionate deeds, and not devoting oneself to nembutsu violates the teachings of Buddha Śākyamuni. It is like parents, who compassionately nurture all of their children, whether they are good or bad, yet rejoice in good children and grieve for the bad children. Amida Buddha extends his mercy equally to all beings and saves both the good and bad, but he finds joy in the good and feels sorrow for the bad. Elation over the good is analogous to the good seed sown in fertile soil resulting in a good crop. Still, even the good should recite nembutsu. They are then, in the true sense, the follower of the teachings of Buddha Śākyamuni.

In summary, recite nembutsu at all times while desiring birth in the Pure Land and await the arrival of Amida Buddha. Aspire to the attainment of birth in the Pure Land without fearing illness or death.

Namu Amida Butsu. Namu Amida Butsu.

30. Dialogue on Ten Issues at Tōdai-ji Temple

Posed by Shunjō-bō Chōgen

Q. (1): Are the entirety of the holy teachings of Buddha Śākyamuni found in the teaching of Jōdo Shū, or is Jōdo Shū based only upon the teachings of the three sutras of Pure Land Buddhism?

Answer: All of the teachings of the eight or nine traditional schools in Japanese Buddhism are, as a part of the lifetime teachings of Buddha Śākyamuni, embodied in our Jōdo Shū, and they are further divided into two categories: the holy gate and the Pure Land gate.

Within the holy gate are Mahāyāna Buddhism and Hīnayāna Buddhism as well as the "expedient teachings" for those not yet ready to understand the true teachings, and the "true teachings" that directly reveal the intent of Buddha Śākyamuni.

Within the Pure Land gate are pure buddhalands in the ten directions and the Pure Land in the west. The teaching of birth in the Western Pure Land contains the miscellaneous practices and the right practices, and within the right practices are the auxiliary practices and the rightly established practice.

The practice of the holy gate is interpreted to be difficult, and the practice of the Pure Land gate is said to be easy.

Only those who are ignorant in the meaning and substance of establishing the Jōdo school would say that Jōdo Shū is based upon only the teachings of the three sutras of Pure Land Buddhism.

Q. (2): Are the right practices and miscellaneous practices taught in the essential vow of Amida Buddha?

Answer: The essential vow teaches the recitation of nembutsu. Amida Buddha, in order to embrace those abandoned by the buddhas and bodhisattvas in the ten directions of the past, present, and future, contemplated for five eons, investigating the nature of those suffering in the six delusive worlds of transmigration and thereby established his path to deliverance. This path entails the recitation of the name of Amida Buddha as taught in the essential vow.

Those who insist that the miscellaneous practices are rooted in the essential vow would doubt the five wisdoms. If such a person were born in the Pure Land, he would find himself isolated in a secluded corner and not benefit from the blessings of seeing Amida Buddha or listening to his teachings.

Those who espouse birth in the Pure Land through the miscellaneous practices are misguided individuals who lack the heart leading to enlightenment. They do not consider the intent of Buddha Śākyamuni and make statements just to receive praise from the armed monks on Mount Hiei.

Q. (3): Is birth in the Pure Land always certain for the nembutsu practitioner who possesses the threefold devotional heart?

Answer: Birth in the Pure Land is possible without exception. There are two types of the threefold devotional heart;

the threefold devotional heart that encompasses wisdom and the threefold devotional heart that encompasses practice.

The threefold devotional heart that encompasses wisdom means thus: It is hard for those who have studied in Buddhist schools other than the Jōdo school to believe in the teaching of attaining birth in the Pure Land through nembutsu. Therefore, in order to understand the nembutsu teaching, they need to refer to Pure Land texts, interpret their meaning, and gradually develop faith in nembutsu.

Regarding the threefold devotional heart that encompasses practice, it is the genuine heart if one totally relies on Amida Buddha; it is the profound heart if one has no doubt about attaining birth in the Pure Land; and it is the heart that seeks birth in the Pure Land through the dedication of merit if one sincerely desires birth in the Pure Land. Therefore, the threefold devotional heart with practice points to devotion in the recitation of nembutsu, unshakable faith, and aspiration for birth in the Pure Land.

Both the five aspects of meditation and the four modes of exercise will be naturally embodied with the nembutsu practitioners.[436]

Q. (4): Is it all right if one does not always finger a string of prayer beads in the recitation of nembutsu?

Answer: A string of prayer beads must be held in one's hand at all times. In song and dance, there must be a beat to guide you in rhythm and timing. In the repetition of nembutsu, the prayer beads are considered to be the score that guides your tongue and hands. If one does not rid oneself of ignorance, illusory thoughts will arise.

This is like the relationship between a host and guests. When one holds the prayer beads, one's intention should not be to count the number of illusory thoughts but to count the number of nembutsu. Nembutsu is the host and illusory thoughts are the guests. It is Amida Buddha's benevolence that allows illusory thoughts to rise while reciting nembutsu.

It would be terribly misguided to talk privately while holding the prayer beads.

Q. (5): If I worship this Great Buddha of Tōdai-ji Temple before me, will this Great Buddha, through his compassionate power, dispatch me to the Pure Land?

Answer: Such a thought is unthinkable. There are three interpretations regarding the Three Jewels.

First, the incorporation of the Three Jewels into one. This is the interpretation that the Three Jewels are based on the principle of *dharmakāya* [the form of the ultimate reality of a buddha] because all phenomena have their genesis in *dharmakāya*.

Second, the individual existence of the Three Jewels. According to this theory, the various buddhas in the ten directions are considered to be the Jewel of the Buddha; their wisdom and teachings are the Jewel of the Dharma; and the disciples of the three vehicles—bodhisattvas, pratyekabuddhas, and śrāvakas—are the Jewel of the Sangha.

Third, the preservation of the Three Jewels. This is the interpretation that the painted and wooden images of a buddha are regarded as the preservation of the Jewel of the Buddha; the recorded sutras, as the preservation of the Jewel of the Dharma; and the painted and carved images of the bodhisattvas, pratyekabuddhas, and śrāvakas, as the preservation of the Jewel of the Sangha.

If the Great Buddha were to welcome you into the Pure Land, the order of the three interpretations of the Three Jewels would be disrupted. The reason for this is that the teachings of the preservation of the Three Jewels and the individual existence of the Three Jewels must be separate.

It would be especially unimaginable that the principal image of the Great Buddha remains in this delusive world of anguish while the practitioner proceeds to the Western Pure Land. Nevertheless, to be captivated by Amida Buddha in the Pure Land, to construct an image of Amida Buddha, and to be truly devoted to Amida Buddha will bring you merit.

Q. (6): Who is more superior—the wise one who lives an ordinary life or the unschooled who seems to have aspiration for birth in the Pure Land?

Answer: One who may have some wisdom but who lacks aspiration for birth in the Pure Land is infinitely less superior to one who may lack wisdom but possesses aspiration for birth in the Pure Land. Recitation of nembutsu by such an unschooled person is in concert with the essential vow of Amida Buddha. This person will attain birth in the Pure Land. One who possesses some wisdom but lacks aspiration for birth in the Pure Land is one who preaches the Dharma with a tainted intent, or who teaches deception and untruths, and will certainly descend into hell.

Nevertheless, one who lacks wisdom but who possesses aspiration for birth in the Pure Land will believe falsehoods to be truths, will fear that which need not be feared, and not fear that which should be feared. On the other hand, the wise one who possesses aspiration for birth in the Pure Land has the wisdom to pursue his goal and will attain birth in the most expeditious way.

It is wrong to compare the sighted with those lacking sight. If aspirations for birth in the Pure Land were equal, one with just a little wisdom is a billion times more superior to one with no wisdom. One without wisdom who pursues birth in the Pure Land is striving through hardships to attain his goal.

Q. (7): Can a practitioner of nembutsu receive the merit of Amida Buddha embracing and welcoming him into the Pure Land?

Answer: It will come to pass with certainty.

Q. (8): It is said that once the light of Amida Buddha embraces mortals, they become nonregressive forever. Is this true?

Answer: This is a grave mistaken belief. The light of Amida Buddha shines because one recites nembutsu. If the recitation of nembutsu ceases, upon what would Amida Buddha shine his light? If what you say is right, there will be no one who recites nembutsu even once after completing the necessary recitation. Further, if your saying is true, many will realize birth in the Pure Land, but doesn't reality prove that there are few who obtain birth in the Pure Land and many who do not? There should be no doubts in this.

Q. (9): It is taught in the section on the essential vow in the *Larger Sutra* that "ten recitations will result in birth in the Pure Land";[437] and in the section on the fulfillment of the essential vow that "a single utterance will also result in birth in the Pure Land."[438] Are these nembutsu meant to be performed during one's lifetime or only at the time of death?

Answer: It is as I stated last year. The holy gate teaches that if a person concentrates on a single practice in his daily life, his negative karma will be nullified immediately, and he will realize buddhahood even if the practice is discontinued. This is simply a skillful means devised by Buddha Śākyamuni to establish a karmic relationship to his teaching. However, this does not mean that the observance of the practice only once naturally leads to the attainment of buddhahood.

Incidentally, the schools that have the extremely profound teachings, such as the Kegon school, Zen school, Shingon school, and Shikan [Tendai] school, employ such skillful means.

Sentient beings are by nature indolent. In Jōdo Shū, uttering a single nembutsu with a doubting heart, believing that this guarantees birth in the Pure Land, and ceasing the recitation of nembutsu after a few more repetitions is truly regrettable.

"Ten recitations" applies to the period in contrast with the upper limits of the lifelong practice of nembutsu. The lifelong practice continues to shorten for one who has encountered the teaching of nembutsu late in life. This is why one hundred repetitions is abbreviated into ten; ten recitations are abbreviated into a single utterance.

If the robe that I, Genkū, am wearing is burned, the karmic relationship to the linen may also be burned away. As long as the robe exists, the relationship to the linen will continue to be. Likewise, our bodies that have accumulated karmic defilements from a past with no beginning to the present have also remained unchanged. If, when we cease the practice of nembutsu, our bodies as well as our hearts remain unchanged, what would be proof of the eradication of the karmic defilements to make the attainment of buddhahood possible?

One who eliminates one's nonvirtuous karma is able to detach oneself from the delusive worlds of transmigration, and one so enlightened will be golden in color. Amida Buddha vowed that all beings in the Pure Land are golden in color.[439] However, which nembutsu practitioner can become golden in color before the end of his or her life?

Refrain from knowledge; believe in the instruction of Shan-tao that one should never cease the practice of nembutsu after one awakens the aspiration for birth in the Pure Land;[440] and await the welcome of Amida Buddha at the end of life.

Q. (10): Is the form of Amida Buddha that arrives to welcome the nembutsu devotee into the Pure Land at the time of death regarded as a rewarded buddha?

Answer: One who attains birth in the Pure Land through nembutsu is welcomed by a rewarded buddha. On the other hand, one who attains birth in the Pure Land through the miscellaneous practices is greeted by a transformed buddha. Even if one practices nembutsu, if one involves oneself with practices other than nembutsu or harbors just a shadow of a doubt about birth in the Pure Land through nembutsu, one will be greeted by a transformed buddha instead of the rewarded buddha.

*Dōkō's note: This dialogue is the record of Genkū-shōnin's replies to questions by Chōgen of Tōdai-ji Temple held on the thirteenth of March in the second year of Kenkyū (1191).

31. Letters

1. A Reply

I HAVE CAREFULLY read the letter you sent to me. If my comments add to your understanding of nembutsu even a little and enhance your aspiration for birth in the Pure Land, I will repeat them many times with all respect.

I sincerely wish that everyone, without dwelling on lowly or petty things, may depend on the essential vow of Amida Buddha and proceed toward the path of the certain attainment of birth in the Pure Land. What people are concerned about, however, varies from person to person. Some seek mere pleasure and prosperity in this dreamlike ephemeral world without thinking of deliverance in the life to come. Others fear descending into the three lower realms of hell, starving spirits, and animals in the next life and practice hard, but they follow diverse practices, never focusing on one particular practice. There are also those who start to practice a teaching but still firmly regard the practice they first observed as best without reconsidering their deep attachment to the first practice and in spite of having heard of other precious teachings. Others commendably awaken belief today but simply abandon it the next day as if nothing happened, even though people expect them to devote themselves solely to this teaching.

The ephemeral world is like this. I personally lament that very few people actually enter the sole path of the Pure Land gate and strive for the exclusive practice of nembutsu. Even those who know the principle "Rely upon the Dharma; do not depend upon a man"[441] are rare.

Regarding the teaching of nembutsu that I encourage, I feel real sorrow to think that people belittle the rationale of nembutsu because of my own incompetence. Therefore, I believe that making a vow is the only means to comfort my heart. The vow states, "I [Hōnen] shall be born in the Pure Land without a moment's delay, realize enlightenment there, and speedily return to this defiled world of suffering. With the transcendent power I will possess in the Pure Land, I will welcome everyone into the Pure Land, including those who have a karmic relationship with nembutsu and those who do not, as well as those who praise nembutsu and those who criticize it."

After reading your letter, I feel that my heart communicates well with you. This pleases me indeed. I certainly see the improvement of your aspiration for birth in the Pure Land in your letter. Therefore, I would like to encourage you to devote yourself to the practice of nembutsu in the same manner that you have engaged before, and to continue nembutsu with the decisive faith in a bright future and the certain attainment of birth in the Pure Land. I am in no position to state this; but you, through deliberation, have probably realized that your present aspiration for birth in the Pure Land is a matter of grave concern. Many are attracted by worldly renown and personal gain. There is no special need to mention it here, but we frequently hear and see the vanity of everyday mundane matters. Please compose your mind and carefully consider what I have said above.

In my previous letter, I mentioned the two types of teaching, the holy gate and the Pure Land gate, and I explained reasons for entering the sole path of the latter one. I will now discuss the practice of the Pure Land gate.

Should one wish to be born in the Pure Land of Amida Buddha, one's faith and practice should be in concert. Here, faith is called the *steadfast heart*, and practice, *the practice*.

Regarding the steadfast heart for birth in the Pure Land, the

Meditation Sutra describes: "If there is a person who aspires to be born in the Pure Land, he will attain birth in the Pure Land by the awakening of the three aspects of faith. What are these three? The first aspect is the genuine heart, the second, the profound heart, and the third, the heart that seeks birth in the Pure Land through the dedication of merit. One who embodies the threefold devotional heart will be born in the Pure Land without fail."[442]

Master Shan-tao thus commented on the threefold devotional heart: "The first aspect is the genuine heart (Ch. *chih-ch'eng-hsin*). The Chinese term *chih* refers to truth, and *ch'eng* to the quality of being genuine. The author, with this interpretation of *chih* and *ch'eng*, would like to clarify that both understanding and practice performed by all sentient beings through their physical, verbal, and mental acts must be done with a sincere heart. Do not outwardly pretend to be wise, virtuous, and diligent while inwardly harboring falsity and fickleness. One should perform these acts in the spirit of genuineness without regard for matters of the inner mind or outer appearances, whether they are visible or hidden, with a truly sincere heart. This is what is meant by the *genuine heart*."[443]

These interpretations mean that the genuine heart is a heart full of sincerity. "Sincerity" refers to the state in which one acts, speaks, and thinks with a guileless heart. In short, it is the heart that does not disguise inner feelings of futility with an elaborate facade. Those who loathe this defiled world of transience while longing for a true path to enlightenment should keep this genuine heart in their minds at all times.

Everyone, including me, has become accustomed to heavy attachment to this dreamlike world of evanescence. There are those who think of themselves as gracious and respectable by discarding their renown and personal gain just a bit, and after a while they become greatly proud of this act. When they project this demeanor of finding worldly fame and wealth insignificant, other ignorant people, not knowing their real intention, actually respect them. Upon hearing about their favorable reputation, these people feel even more elated and dwell in a thatched hut in some lonely spot away from the neighborhood of the capital. Without cultivating tranquility of the heart, they merely pay attention to the adornment of the principal image of a buddha and the arrangement of the practice hall, to the miserable-looking thicket of trees inside in the rough-woven bamboo fence around the hut, and to the eyes and opinions of other people regarding the looks of the garden. They only care about the appearance of the hut and try not to bring public reproach upon their huts. In this manner, one who does not aspire for birth in the Pure Land through relying on the essential vow of Amida Buddha soon loses the genuine heart and comes to a state by which one cannot achieve birth in the Pure Land.

This does not mean, however, that one should not care about the public eye at all, nor should one be oblivious to others' blame. One should sincerely reflect upon each criticism. But it is regrettable indeed if one is obsessed by criticism, which becomes a hindrance for the awakening of one's aspiration for birth in the Pure Land. I venture this here so that you may realize the essentials for birth in the Pure Land.

Related to the genuine heart are four distinct aspects. The first is a person who looks outwardly respectable but is despicable inside; the second is one who is despicable both outwardly and inwardly; the third is one who is outwardly despicable but inwardly respectable; the fourth is one who is respectable both outwardly and inwardly. Of these four types of people, the first two lack the genuine heart and are undesirable; they are called the *practitioners with falsity and fickleness.* Conversely, the latter two possess the genuine heart; they are called the *practitioners with genuineness and authenticity.*

In short, it is wholesome if one has the heart of genuineness inwardly, regardless of whether one displays sincerity or falsity. One should nurture a sincere loathing for this world and long for the Pure Land without worrying how other people think. This is referred to as the *genuine heart.*

Second is the profound heart. Master Shan-tao interpreted it as follows:

> The profound heart has two different aspects. The first is to believe firmly that one is a common mortal with worldly passions whose virtuous roots are shallow and meager and who has transmigrated through the delusive triple realms for countless eons up to this day, and that one does not possess the karmic conditions to detach from the delusive triple realms. The second is to have unshakable faith that Amida Buddha will embrace sentient beings with his forty-eight vows, and to believe that one who recites his name as few as ten times, or even just once, will, with certainty, attain birth in the Pure Land through the compassionate power of the essential vow. One must not harbor doubt about this for even a moment. This belief is referred to as the *profound heart*.[444]
>
> One who possesses the profound heart decisively establishes implicit faith in birth in the Pure Land through nembutsu, practices in accordance with the teachings of Buddha Śākyamuni, eliminates doubt perpetually, and does not fall back or become disturbed by all of those who have different understandings, practices, teachings, and views or misleading opinions.[445]

The meaning of Master Shan-tao's interpretation is that first, one must recognize one's own limitations, and second, one must trust the essential vow of Amida Buddha. He pointed out the first kind of faith in order to establish the latter one. The reason he mentioned two aspects of belief in this order is that without pointing out the first kind of faith, he believed that those who aspire for birth in the Pure Land and practice nembutsu of the essential vow would continue to increase their worldly passions of greed and anger and would live in fear of committing the ten transgressions or in fear of violating the precepts. They would, therefore, become self-obstructing and doubtful of the essential vow.

They may also think that birth in the Pure Land through ten repetitions or just a single utterance of nembutsu, as taught in the essential vow, is possible only for those flawless mortals who have no illusory thoughts or negative karma—not for those karmically defiled mortals like themselves. They will then entertain doubt that the attainment of birth in the Pure Land through just ten nembutsu repetitions or merely one is possible for those like them.

In anticipation of such doubts among the masses in the future, Master Shan-tao pointed out the two aspects of the devout heart and said, "Although we may be karmically defiled mortals with worldly passions, if we recite nembutsu with profound reliance on the essential vow even once, birth in the Pure Land will be assured for us all."[446] This comment truly inspired my heart, and I am grateful for it. Without this comment, the attainment of birth in the Pure Land would become uncertain. Those who do not understand this comment might say that birth in the Pure Land is impossible due to their unwholesome hearts. This kind of doubt surely makes the heart become unworkable for birth in the Pure Land.

Consequently, there is no need to reflect on virtue and vice, or to discuss the gravity of your karmic wrongs. You must firmly believe that the vocalization of *Namu Amida Butsu* along with unfaltering aspiration for birth in the Pure Land will most certainly assure you of birth in the Pure Land. Unshakable faith in birth in the Pure Land establishes the karma for birth in the Pure Land. There should be no doubt if you think in this manner. Attainment of birth in the Pure Land will be uncertain if one doubts this birth; attainment of birth in the Pure Land will be certain if one believes in this birth.

In essence, the profound heart is implicit faith without a shadow of doubt that if you vocalize *Namu Amida Butsu*, as taught in the essential vow, Amida Buddha will certainly welcome you into the Pure Land, regardless of what kind of person you are.

Further, the teaching "Do not be defeated by those who have

different understandings and practices"[447] means that one should not forsake nembutsu nor begin to question birth in the Pure Land because of influence by those who study different teachings and observe practices different from your own. "Those who study different teachings" refers to scholarly monks of the eight traditional Buddhist schools, such as the Tendai school and the Hossō school. "Those who observe practices different from your own" refers to all of the practitioners of the Shingon school and the Shikan [Tendai] school. They study and practice the holy gate. The teachings and practices of the holy gate are different from those of the Pure Land gate; therefore, they are called "different understandings and practices" within the nembutsu tradition.

Master Shan-tao went into detail explaining the rationale for not being defeated by those with different views. It is impossible for me to quote his entire explanation here because too many teachings exist. However, the essential point is this: even if a buddha appears, emanating his brilliant light, extending his tongue, and saying, "The teaching that birth in the Pure Land is assured through nembutsu for common mortals with worldly passions is misguided. Do not believe in it!" your implicit faith in birth in the Pure Land through nembutsu must not be swayed, even for a moment.

This is because all buddhas save sentient beings with the same compassionate hearts. For instance, Tathāgata Amida vowed, "If, when I am to attain buddhahood, all sentient beings in the ten directions who wish to be born in my buddhaland through the power of my essential vow and who recite my name as few as ten times or just once are not born there, I will not realize enlightenment."[448] Amida Buddha fulfilled the essential vow and indeed achieved buddhahood.

Upon hearing this, Buddha Śākyamuni appeared in this world and expounded on the essential vow of Amida Buddha to sentient beings. All the buddhas in the six directions, as countless as the grains of sand of the Ganges, also appeared and extended their tongues, covered the three thousand great-thousand worlds, showed their excellent marks with no pretense, and praised the essential vow.

They encouraged all sentient beings, stating, "There is no doubt that Amida Buddha extolled the essential vow and told all sentient beings that birth in the Pure Land is certainly achieved through nembutsu. All sentient beings must believe in this teaching." The buddhas in the six directions thus authenticated it.

Thus, all the buddhas, without exception and with a single heart, vowed that all sentient beings would achieve birth in the Pure Land through nembutsu, then expounded this and encouraged sentient beings. Therefore, we should not be swayed by the words of any buddha who disclaims the attainment of birth in the Pure Land through nembutsu.

If even a buddha cannot shake our resolve, certainly we should stand fast when a śrāvaka or pratyekabuddha expresses a similar dissident opinion, to say nothing of the mistaken guidance of common people. Once we hear and believe in birth in the Pure Land through nembutsu, we should never entertain any doubt, regardless of what is said by whom. This is what is meant by the *profound heart.*

Third is the heart that seeks birth in the Pure Land through the dedication of merit. Master Shan-tao interpreted it as follows:

> The heart that seeks birth in the Pure Land through the dedication of merit means to rejoice fully in the worldly and transcendent physical, verbal, and mental virtuous roots, accumulated in past and present lives both by oneself and by other ordinary and holy beings, as well as to desire to dedicate these virtuous roots for the sake of birth in the Pure Land with the genuine heart and the profound heart.
>
> Further, one who aspires birth in the Pure Land through the dedication of merit must have implicit faith in the attainment of birth in the Pure Land with genuineness in his heart. This steadfast heart must be as solid as an adamantine stone, without being disturbed or defeated by those who have different views, studies, understandings, or practices.[449]

This interpretation means that first, all the merit accumulated through the physical, verbal, and mental activity in all previous and present lives must be dedicated toward the Pure Land in the desire for birth in the Pure Land. Second, by rejoicing not only in one's own merit but also in all the merit of others, including in that of buddhas and bodhisattvas, make these your own then ask that the merit be dedicated toward the attainment of birth in the Pure Land.

One should not pray for good fortune for oneself or others in this life. Regarding the life to come, one should not aspire for birth in a pure buddhaland other than the Pure Land of Amida Buddha, nor should one hope to be born in the Tuṣita Heaven of Buddha Maitreya, nor desire to be reborn in the delusive worlds of human beings or heavenly beings. One should not dedicate merit toward anything other than the Pure Land of Amida Buddha; it should be exclusively toward birth in the Pure Land. If, before gaining proper understanding of this, one's prayers were concerned with occurrences in this defiled world and merit was dedicated in a mistaken direction, these merits should be reclaimed in order for one to concentrate on dedicating them specifically toward birth in the Pure Land of Amida Buddha.

To say that all merit should be dedicated to birth in the Pure Land does not mean that a nembutsu devotee should accumulate benevolent acts to the exclusion of nembutsu for the purpose of dedication. It simply means that all previous and future merits accumulated through virtuous acts other than nembutsu should be dedicated toward birth in the Pure Land.

The passage, "This heart must be as solid as an adamantine stone, without being defeated by those who who have different understandings and practices" means that as previously mentioned, one should not dedicate merit hither and thither through the instruction of an inappropriate person. An adamantine stone is unbreakable; therefore, it is being said that this heart must be like adamantine stone—one that cannot be broken by anyone. Hence, this is called the *heart that seeks birth in the Pure Land through the dedication of merit.*

Thus, I have roughly explained the conditions of the threefold devotional heart. Master Shan-tao said, "One who possesses the threefold devotional heart will, with certainty, achieve birth in the Pure Land. If one aspect of the threefold devotional heart is lacking, the realization will become impossible."[450] Therefore, one who desires birth in the Pure Land should have the threefold devotional heart.

Thus described, the threefold devotional heart seems discrete and complex; yet, if one truly comprehends the concept, one will easily obtain the threefold devotional heart. After all, the threefold devotional heart simply means that one should be genuine, deeply rely upon the essential vow of Amida Buddha, and aspire for the attainment of birth in the Pure Land. There may be differences in the depth of faith in the threefold devotional heart for each person, but you should think that it is possible to obtain the heart. A detached view of the threefold devotional heart makes the concept seem difficult, but close examination reveals its simplicity. This should be kept in mind.

One who does not know even the name of the threefold devotional heart can still possess this heart and attain birth in the Pure Land as a matter of course; conversely, even the informed may on occasion lack some aspects of the threefold devotional heart.

There is also the teaching of the four distinctive qualities with regard to the threefold devotional heart. One may feel reassured in knowing these because of full awareness of being endowed with the threefold devotional heart. It is desirable that one makes an effort to recite nembutsu in order to possess this heart, especially if one is not sure of possessing it yet. I have thus mentioned the conditions of the threefold devotional heart as they have occurred to me.

There is nothing more to tell you other than this. I would like to finish my message now. If you have any questions regarding my instruction, I will answer someday when we meet again. This is the condition of a heart ready for birth in the Pure Land. This attitude is called the *steadfast heart.*

*Dōkō's note: There seems to be another letter concerning entering the Pure Land gate. Unfortunately, I have not seen it.

2. A Letter to Someone

Birth in the Pure Land through nembutsu will be attained with certainty even if someone finds a flaw in the teaching of nembutsu and criticizes it. The essential vow of Amida Buddha encompasses everyone, including one who utters nembutsu just once or ten times, even though it is said that birth in the Pure Land is impossible for those with shallow virtuous roots. One who has committed the ten transgressions or the five grave offenses can still achieve birth in the Pure Land through nembutsu, even though it is said that the karmically defiled cannot attain birth in the Pure Land.

Amida Buddha's compassionate vow was designed specifically for the mass of common mortals, who perpetually transmigrate in the delusive worlds, although it is said that Amida Buddha's mercy is selective. The mere teaching of nembutsu will be prolific even after the extinction of the teachings of Buddha Śākyamuni following the period of the decline of the Dharma that lasts ten thousand years. This is despite the fact that much time has elapsed since the age of Buddha Śākyamuni. The teaching of nembutsu cannot be separated from the common mortals who seek deliverance, even if someone tries to nullify it.

Nevertheless, there are conditions in which Amida Buddha is unable to extend his compassion toward common mortals. That is, birth in the Pure Land is possible when one sincerely relies upon Amida Buddha with a heart that knows he will certainly embrace anyone, including the karmically defiled. This is irrespective of the time of the decline of the Dharma. Birth in the Pure Land is possible if one, without engaging in independent contemplation, exclusively believes that all common mortals will be able to attain birth in the Pure Land through the great karmic power of the essential vow, without distinction between the virtuous and the nonvirtuous. However, disbelief in Amida Buddha's compassion and doubt of birth in the Pure Land through the essential vow truly become great obstacles to the attainment of birth in the Pure Land.

Nembutsu is the supplication for the happiness of common mortals in the period of the decline of the Dharma, and nothing but nembutsu will allow one to attain birth in the Pure Land in the life to come.

I am not telling you this by my own initiative. I just state exactly what the sacred scriptures describe, as if holding the text up to a mirror. Please look over the scriptures.

3. A Reply to the Lay Priest Kumagai

I was most delighted to receive your letter. I had been concerned about how you were getting on since we last met. What you said in your letter really gratified me. I will now explain the sole practice of nembutsu for birth in the Pure Land. Please read this reply carefully.

Nembutsu is the practice taught in the essential vow of Amida Buddha. Other religious practices, such as observing the precepts, reciting a sutra, chanting *dhāraṇī*, and meditation on the noumenal aspects of reality, are not prescribed in the essential vow. For this reason, one who aspires for birth in the Pure Land must recite nembutsu first. It is acceptable for one to further perform other practices in addition to nembutsu, if one wishes. But, undoubtedly, nembutsu taught in the essential vow is sufficient in itself for birth in the Pure Land.

Master Shan-tao taught that those who only observe practices other than nembutsu while desiring birth in the Pure Land will not achieve birth in the Pure Land. The sole practice of nembutsu is the karmic cause for the certain attainment of birth in the Pure Land. Master Shan-tao was an emanation of Amida Buddha, so his teaching is absolutely right.

Having relations with a woman is a violation from the standpoint of the Buddhist precept that one should refrain from committing adultery. Disowning one's child in anger is also a violation of the precept that one should refrain from being angry. However, observation of the precepts is not part of the essential vow; therefore, you may keep them to the best of your ability. Making efforts toward filial piety is performed in the same manner.

Meditation on the bronze letter *a* in the Sanskrit alphabet is also the same. Using a Buddhist walking staff is not in the essential vow either, but you may hold it if you wish. A pictorial presentation of Amida Buddha, who comes to welcome a nembutsu devotee to the Pure Land at his time of death, is truly precious, yet it is secondary to nembutsu. The single-hearted recitation of nembutsu thirty, fifty, or sixty thousand times a day is indeed the practice for the certain attainment of birth in the Pure Land.

Virtuous deeds other than nembutsu may also be performed if one has spare time between nembutsu. However, if one recites nembutsu sixty thousand times in a single day, what else is one able to do? If one practices nembutsu thirty or fifty times a day with his whole heart, one will certainly attain birth in the Pure Land, even if one commits a few violations of the precepts.

As I mentioned above, attending dutifully to one's parents is not in the practice of the essential vow. Nevertheless, your mother is eighty-nine years old now. Please encourage her to recite nembutsu within her heart so that Amida Buddha may come to welcome her this year.

Sincerely yours,
Genkū
May 2nd

*Dōkō's note: This letter Hōnen-shōnin wrote in his own hand.

4. A Reply on One Occasion

I have no comment to make here on the description of auspicious auguries you [Kumagai] have experienced. They are truly propitious. Experiencing such wonderful omens is indeed virtuous, especially for one who desires birth in the Pure Land.

Besides you, there have been many who have known the time of their death before attaining birth in the Pure Land. However, having such extraordinary omens as you experienced, which surprise the ears and eyes of people, will probably not happen again, especially in this period of the decline of the Dharma. To my knowledge, Master Tao-ch'o in China was the only case on record in the past. It is really incomparable.

Nevertheless, the way of striving for buddhahood is often accompanied by an overall unfavorable condition—this is extremely grave. Please take full precaution against it. I want to hear again if such an augury occurs to you. The reason I tell you these things is that although your experience with the favorable omens is really laudable, I am worried about you. I hope you behave cautiously and pray to Amida Buddha for your protection.

I wonder when you will come up to the capital, Kyōto. Please be sure to come. Most people here in the capital believe in birth in the Pure Land through nembutsu and are encouraged to recite nembutsu with each other.

Therefore, practice nembutsu even more. Do not think badly about what I have said here. Reciting nembutsu for birth in the Pure Land is felicitous indeed.

Sincerely yours,
Genkū
April 3rd

*Dōkō's note: This is the reply from Hōnen-shōnin to the lay priest Kumagai, who experienced auspicious omens through nembutsu and reported them to his master.

32. Admonitions for the Attainment of Birth in the Pure Land

1. It is commendable for one to recite nembutsu sixty thousand times as a daily practice. Ten repetitions or even a single utterance of nembutsu will assure birth in the Pure Land if one does not harbor doubts about the essential vow of Amida Buddha. However, reciting large numbers of nembutsu leads one to the high category of birth in the Pure Land. Master Fa-chao stated, "One who is born in the high category of birth will see the lord of compassion [Amida Buddha] on the lotus platform in the Pure Land. The accomplishment of birth in the Pure Land in this state is due to the merit of a multitude of nembutsu recitations."[451]

2. People say that the attainment of birth in the Pure Land is due to the residue of one's virtuous deeds performed in previous existence. This is correct. What one receives in this fleeting world may turn out favorable or unfavorable depending upon the virtue and vice committed in one's previous state of existence. Sacred texts teach that the crucial matter of birth in the Pure Land presupposes one's residual virtues.

   Nevertheless, birth in the Pure Land through nembutsu does not require one to have residual virtuous deeds. According to the *Meditation Sutra*, even the wicked who murder their own father or mother, or who drew the blood of a buddha, will still achieve birth in the Pure Land through the ten repetitions of nembutsu at the time of death.[452]

The good who have residual virtuous karma, without special instruction, are afraid of committing nonvirtues and strive for the way of a buddha: they never commit the five grave offenses. On the other hand, the wicked, who have committed the five grave offenses, will still achieve birth in the Pure Land by repeating nembutsu ten times even though they have no residual virtues. The *Meditation Sutra* states:

> If individuals are able to hear the six Chinese characters *Na-mo A-mi-t'o-fo*, the flaming chariot, which carries the wretched to hell, will naturally disappear, and Amida Buddha will come to welcome them on the lotus platform, even if they have repeated various unvirtuous karma. In order to attain birth in the Pure Land of Ultimate Bliss, a mortal heavily burdened with grave karmic wrongs has no means of deliverance except recitation of the name of Amida Buddha. One with no karmic cause for being born in the Pure Land due to the obstruction of grave karmic negativity will attain birth in the Pure Land if he entrusts himself to the power of Amida Buddha's essential vow.[453]

This means: (1) upon hearing the name of Amida Buddha, which consists of the six Chinese characters, the flaming chariot departs as a matter of course, and Amida Buddha appears on the lotus pedestal to welcome a nembutsu devotee, even if he has committed the five grave offenses; (2) a wicked one with grave negative karma [normally] has no chance to attain birth in the Pure Land, but such a wicked one still achieves birth in the Pure Land by chanting the name of Amida Buddha; and (3) the total reliance on the power of the essential vow makes birth in the Pure Land possible, even when one has no means to achieve birth in the Pure Land because of one's grave karmic wrongs. Hence, nembutsu is dependable.

Master Shan-tao commented, "Amida Buddha realized buddhahood in order to welcome sentient beings who have sunk to the bottom of the river of the transmigration of the six delusive worlds of saṃsāra and have remained there for countless eons up to the present time, with no karmic condition for escape from the six delusive worlds."[454] Here, the so-called "sentient beings who have sunk to the bottom of the river of transmigration" are the common mortals of the defiled world. They are compared to beings who dwell permanently on the floor of the Ganges River, with bodies too big and long to move.

Kōbō-daishi (774–835)[455] interpreted the two Chinese letters *fan-fu* ("ordinary mortals") as "drunk."[456] It is true that the heart of a common man cannot distinguish between right and wrong, just like a person who is distracted and intoxicated. One hundred worldly passions well up within his heart immediately, and he is easily confused about good and evil. Eventually, he is unable to accomplish any practice through his own power.

In order to detach from the delusive worlds of transmigration, to enter the path leading to buddhahood, and to accomplish buddhahood, one must awaken the heart of enlightenment, renounce all worldly passions, and undergo religious austerities for countless eons. However, common mortals in the nonvirtuous world of the five defilements will continue to transmigrate in the six delusive worlds while repeating the four modes of birth due to their lack of power to establish and practice a vow successfully.

Having seen and lamented on this, Tathāgata Amida, when he was called Bodhisattva Dharmākara in the distant past, underwent penance for an extraordinarily large number of eons, which would be impossible for us to endure. He accumulated various merits and finally realized buddhahood as "Amida Buddha." He was endowed with the merits of the internal realization, such as the four kinds of wisdom, the three phases of the body, the ten powers of wisdom, and the four forms of fearlessness, as well as the merits of his external virtues, such as the special physical attributes, the ray of light, the preaching of the Dharma, and the benefit to other people. All of these virtues are embodied in the three letters of *A-mi-da*.

Master Shan-tao, therefore, stated: "Amida Buddha vowed that those who call his name ten times or just once will definitely be welcomed, and that he will not realize enlightenment if they are not born in the Pure Land. Amida Buddha *did* attain buddhahood and presently resides in the Pure Land. Sentient beings who recite his name should not entertain doubts about their certain attainment of birth in the Pure Land."[457]

One who firmly believes in the teaching of birth in the Pure Land through nembutsu and who diligently recites nembutsu without doubts is referred to as "one who has faith in the power other than self." There are similar concepts in our society. For instance, it is impossible for an individual whose legs are weak and whose back is bent to go a long distance using his own efforts. Knowing this, he rides a boat or some vehicle to reach his destination—this is much easier. This is not done by using his own power but by using the power of a boat or vehicle—that is, by a power other than self. Even a vehicle made by ignorant people with perverted hearts in the defiled world possesses such power. How much clearer is it that one can cross the delusive ocean of saṃsāra in the boat or raft of the essential vow made by Amida Buddha who practiced virtue for five eons? One must not harbor any doubts about this.

Likewise, there exist magical powers in medicinal herbs to cure an illness, in a magnet to attract iron, in musk to emit a fragrance, and in the horn of a rhinoceros to repel water. Although herbs are merely vegetation without hearts and animals never awaken spiritual aspiration, they have magical powers within. The power of the teachings of Buddha Śākyamuni must be even more wondrous.

Each utterance of nembutsu has the power to nullify negative karma accumulated for eight billion eons in the delusive worlds of transmigration.[458] You should bear in mind that Amida Buddha has the power to welcome everyone, including those with grave karmic negativity, and that birth in the Pure Land will be assured to everyone who recites nembutsu, whether or not they have residual virtues and regardless of the gravity of their nonvirtues.

Amida Buddha does not discriminate between one who observes the precepts and one who violates them, nor does he discriminate between the poor and the wealthy and pays no regard to social class. His power changes the karmic nature of man through nembutsu like a stone or tile transformed into gold. He also promised that he would come to welcome all nembutsu devotees without exception. In the *Liturgy for the Rite of the Fivefold Rhythmic Chanting of Nien-fo*, Master Fa-chao thus relates:

> When Amida Buddha was in the state of a bodhisattva, he made the universal vow for saving mortals, saying, "I will come to welcome all those who listen to and meditate on my name. I will not discriminate between the poor and the rich, the ignorant and the educated. I will not choose only the learned observers of the precepts or the errant in breach of the precepts. If they but turn their meritorious hearts toward birth in the Pure Land and recite my name, I will welcome them to the Pure Land of Ultimate Bliss, like broken tiles and pebbles turned into gold."[459]

Merely counting a string of prayer beads without vocalizing nembutsu is being indolent. Master Shan-tao interpreted the intimate relationship, one of the three kinds of karmic relationships between Amida Buddha and a nembutsu devotee, as follows:

> When sentient beings worship Amida Buddha, he sees them. When they recite the name of Amida Buddha, he listens to them. When they are mindful of Amida Buddha, he is also mindful of them. Therefore, the three categories of acts exercised by both Amida Buddha and the nembutsu devotee unite into one. Since this relationship between Amida Buddha and a nembutsu devotee is like that between parents and their children, it is called the "intimate karmic relationship."[460]

In the same way, when a nembutsu devotee holds a string of prayer beads in his hand, Amida Buddha sees him. When he wishes to recite nembutsu, Amida Buddha is also mindful of that desire. Thus, we must strive to be seen and to be within the awareness of Amida Buddha in order to benefit from his benevolence. To accomplish this relationship a practitioner must recite nembutsu continually in order to bring harmony between Amida Buddha and the three categories of acts of a nembutsu practitioner. The three categories are physical, verbal, and mental acts.

The vocalization of nembutsu is significant because the recitation of nembutsu is in accordance with the essential vow. If one can hear one's own recitation, that suffices as reciting nembutsu in an audible voice. It is said that nembutsu in an audible voice is practiced while worshiping a Great Buddha, and that being mindful of Amida Buddha is also a part of nembutsu. Both the recitation and mindfulness become the karmic causes for birth in the Pure Land.

3. It is respectable to recite nembutsu without saying something else. To think that exchanging a word during the recitation has less merit is a misunderstanding. For instance, nembutsu can be compared to gold. The bright color of gold improves even after burning in fire and does not fade in the water. In the same way, nembutsu neither becomes defiled by the illusory thought that

arises in a devotee's heart during practice nor loses its merit by exchanging a word during practice.

Knowing this, you should strive to increase the number of nembutsu without committing to other things, but if you forget these instructions and accidentally verbalize other things during practice, don't think, "What a shameful thing I have done! The nembutsu I have performed is in vain." Do not allow yourself to think this way. No matter how one recites nembutsu, the recitation definitely becomes the cause for birth in the Pure Land.

4. There is no reference to one million recitations of nembutsu in the essential vow of Amida Buddha. It is taught in the *Smaller Sutra* that one who recites nembutsu one day through seven days will be born in the Pure Land.[461] Accordingly, one should strive for the seven-day repetition of nembutsu. The Senior Master Chia-ts'ai[462] determined seven days to be the requisite length of time for one million recitations of nembutsu.[463] So, ideally, one practices one million recitations in seven days. If this is impossible, however, one may take eight days or nine days.

   This should not be construed to mean that birth in the Pure Land is impossible if one does not achieve one million recitations of nembutsu. Birth in the Pure Land is still possible through just a single utterance or ten repetitions of nembutsu. Out of the elation experienced from the knowledge that birth in the Pure Land is possible with one or ten nembutsu grows the joy at the merit of the recitation of one million recitations of nembutsu.

5. I would like to mention the idea that a memorial service for the departed actually brings the seven portions of merit to the observer and only one portion to the departed as it is generally taught. It is right that people observe a service for themselves before they die. Even if there is someone who will perform the service for you, bear these things in mind: without depending upon him, devote yourself to practicing nembutsu, strive to attain birth in

the Pure Land speedily, and be endowed with the three and five transcendent faculties;[464] save all the sentient beings transmigrating through the four modes of birth and the six delusive worlds; find out the world where your parents, teachers, and elders live and welcome them to the Pure Land of Ultimate Bliss.

You should also dedicate the merit of your daily nembutsu to their birth in the Pure Land. If you dedicate the merit of nembutsu to the departed, Amida Buddha will emit rays of light over the three lower realms of hell, starving spirits, and animals. The deceased who are suffering in the three lower realms will be free from their pain, and emancipation will come to pass when their lives in those worlds come to an end.

The *Larger Sutra* states: "If those who suffer indescribable pain in the three lower realms see this light, they will gain relief, pain will be eliminated, and when their lives in those worlds come to an end, they will realize deliverance."[465]

6. It is lamentable to hear one say, "I believe in the essential vow of Amida Buddha and long for birth in the Pure Land, yet even knowing that unshakable faith in Amida Buddha through nembutsu leads to the certain attainment of Amida Buddha, a deep aspiration for birth in the Pure Land does not arise morning and evening in my heart." One who has heard of the teaching of the Pure Land gate but acts like one who has not heard is one who has escaped from the three lower realms and received life as a human being but is still ensnared by unwholesome karma. This is also taught in the *Sutra of Universal Enlightenment*.[466]

   One who does not aspire for birth in the Pure Land has scant desire to forsake this world of suffering. To illustrate, it is as if someone kindly offers a boat to a person who has no intention of going down to the western provinces from the capital. Although the person does not think the boat unseaworthy, he feels no special gratitude for the offer simply because he has no need of the boat. On the contrary, if a person who has been bound in his enemy's castle barely escapes and flees down the road, only to find a wide river or ocean standing in his way, his heart will be unable to contain his great joy if his parents have prepared a boat in order to save him.

Similarly, we have been firmly fettered by the enemy of worldly passions such as greed and anger and have transmigrated in the cage of the delusive three realms. Upon seeing this, Amida Buddha, with deep sympathy like a compassionate mother, cuts our ties of transmigration with the sharp sword of his name, sets the cherished boat of the essential vow afloat on the waves of the ocean of anguish and leads us to the shore of the Pure Land. Upon reflection of this, our joy becomes too much for words; we can wring the tears of joy out of our sleeves, and our heart is overwhelmed in adoration of Amida Buddha.

If I speak of this, one should feel so grateful that one's hair stands on end, but it is the case that some may instead ignore this without consideration. This is what people are like. People naturally known how to commit a karmic wrong without having been taught. This is because they have transmigrated in the six delusive worlds from beginningless time to the present. In each instance, their appearances have changed but their nature remains unchanged. They have performed various nonvirtuous actions repeatedly and are now easily accustomed to committing karmic defilements. They have heard of the teaching of birth in the Pure Land through nembutsu for the very first time in this life; therefore, it may be natural that they cannot believe in the teaching of nembutsu in such a short period of time.

Moreover, hearts may be categorized into two types: the heart for the instantaneous realization of enlightenment and the heart for the gradual realization of enlightenment. The former attains deliverance quickly after listening to the Dharma, and the latter, slowly. For instance, when visiting a Shintō shrine or Buddhist temple, one who is fleet of foot arrives there in a few hours while another who trudges slowly may take more than a day. In any event, those who have the intention to visit will reach there eventually. In the same manner, if one aspires to birth in the Pure Land, faith in one's birth in the Pure Land through nembutsu will deepen with the passage of time.

7. Someone says, "Birth in the Pure Land will be unattainable for one who practices nembutsu daily unless one meets a virtuous teacher in one's last moments. It will also be hard to achieve birth in the Pure Land for one whose heart is disturbed by a severe illness." However, according to Master Shan-tao, Amida Buddha, together with the host of celestial beings, will welcome any nembutsu devotee who desires birth in the Pure Land at his time of death whether he recites nembutsu many times or just a few. Amida Buddha will welcome those who habitually rely on the power of the essential vow and practice nembutsu even without meeting a virtuous teacher at the time of death.

   The attainment of birth in the Pure Land through the helping power of a virtuous teacher applies to people in the three grades of the low category, as described in the *Meditation Sutra*.[467] People in the low grade of the low category in particular do not perform daily nembutsu, have no desire for birth in the Pure Land, and have committed the five grave offenses. They can still attain birth in the Pure Land, however, through meeting with a virtuous teacher for the first time on their deathbed, hearing the teaching of nembutsu, and reciting nembutsu ten times. Conversely, those who always rely upon the power of the essential vow and strive to practice the recitation of the name of Amida Buddha, who contemplated the deliverance of all sentient beings for an enormously long period—their desire for birth in the Pure Land will certainly be welcomed by Amida Buddha without the help of a virtuous teacher.

   It is desirable for one to pray for a respite if one becomes ill during life's final moments. Nevertheless, even one who dies without an illness partakes in the great agonies of death. The severe torment of illness attacks one on the deathbed from the eighty thousand gates of the innumerable dusts of suffering. It is as if one were slashed with hundreds and thousands of spears and swords. As a result, even though one has eyes, it is as though one has no eyes and is unable to see a thing; one's tongue becomes so hardened one cannot speak a single word.

Since this distress is referred to as the *suffering of death*, one of the eight kinds of suffering, even a nembutsu devotee who believes in the essential vow and desires birth in the Pure Land is unable to escape from this agony. Even with pain and fainting in agony at the time of death, the practitioner serenely abides in the rightly settled state of mind for birth in the Pure Land, due to the compassionate power of Amida Buddha, and truly realizes this birth. The moment of death is no longer than the time it takes to cut a hair, and a common mortal cannot predict the moment. Only Amida Buddha and a dying nembutsu devotee appreciate it within their hearts.

In addition, the three kinds of attachment arise within a person during his final moments. Following this, an unwholesome condition disturbs his heart, and eventually he loses the rightly settled state of mind for birth in the Pure Land. It is impossible to remove the three kinds of attachment by means of the helping power of a virtuous teacher. Only the compassionate power of Amida Buddha is able to eradicate them. Master Shan-tao stated, "At the time of death, Amida Buddha himself arrives to welcome the nembutsu devotee, so that the various karmic negativities that tie one to this delusive world cannot be an obstacle to birth in the Pure Land."[468] His words are indeed dependable.

One who seeks birth in the Pure Land in the life to come says that Amida Buddha will come to welcome us when we abide in the rightly settled state of mind for birth in the Pure Land and recite nembutsu. However, the *Smaller Sutra* states, "Amida Buddha, accompanied by his assembly of holy beings, appears before a nembutsu devotee when his life is almost at an end. With his mind free from distraction, he will attain birth in the Pure Land of Ultimate Bliss."[469] In other words, Amida Buddha, together with his celestial attendants, appears before a nembutsu devotee during his final moments. After seeing his arrival, the heart of the devotee becomes composed, and he eventually attains birth in the Pure Land. This should be known.

Accordingly, if you have a light illness, have time to pray, and are meeting with a virtuous teacher at the time of death, utter nembutsu even once while you are healthy. Then resolve to meet Amida Buddha during your final moments, to be free from the three kinds of attachment, to abide in the rightly settled state of mind for birth in the Pure Land, and to be born in the Pure Land.

This does not mean, however, that one does not need the help of a virtuous teacher at all during one's final moments. According to the instruction of senior masters, the manner of dying is described thus: enshrine the image of Amida Buddha on the west wall of the room of the dying, put him in bed facing west before the image, and let a virtuous teacher encourage him to utter nembutsu.[470] This is the desirable way.

Nevertheless, the fact is that no one can predict the time and place of his own death. It may suddenly happen on the road, along a mountain pass, or in a toilet. It is extremely difficult to escape from one's own residual karmic burdens. There are many who may lose their lives by being cut down by a long or short sword; others may die by fire or drowning due to their residual karma, which is impossible to escape. No matter what kind of death one meets, one who has aspiration for birth in the Pure Land through daily nembutsu should believe in the welcoming of Bodhisattva Avalokiteśvara and Bodhisattva Mahāsthāmaprāpta as well as Amida Buddha at the very moment of death.

The *Collection of Essentials on Attaining Birth in the Pure Land* composed by Genshin states, "Without regard for time, place, and various karmic relationships, merely reciting nembutsu makes birth in the Pure Land possible if one desires birth in the Pure Land at the end of one's life."[471] Nembutsu is indeed dependable.

Thus, I (Hōnen) have answered the eight questions[472] you have asked me. Please read them. The following are also replies to the questions posed by you later.

8. Your statement, "It may be more meaningful to perform a small number of daily nembutsu than to set a large number of daily nembutsu and to fail to practice them, because it is taught that birth in the Pure Land of Ultimate Bliss is assured by the utterance of nembutsu just once," is plausible.

In the *Hymns in Praise of Birth in the Pure Land*, Master Shan-tao said: "Birth in the Pure Land, with certainty, will come to pass through ten repetitions of nembutsu or even one. One should not harbor doubt about this teaching even for a moment."[473] His *Commentary on the Meditation Sutra* also instructs, "The vocal nembutsu without cessation for life is called the *rightly established practice*."[474] Therefore, you should firmly believe in the certain attainment of birth in the Pure Land through ten repetitions of nembutsu or just a single utterance and devote yourself to accumulating nembutsu. Master Shan-tao taught, "Recite the name of Amida Buddha without cessation."[475] Hence, you should continuously recite nembutsu without interruption throughout your life.

It is the desirable sequence of nembutsu to think of and recite nembutsu three times during a meal. If you always think of and recite nembutsu, the accumulation of nembutsu becomes possible without counting the number of nembutsu up to sixty thousand or one hundred thousand times. One's mind is easily distracted by the things one sees and hears, and nembutsu becomes difficult to remember and practice. Therefore, setting the number of daily nembutsu and holding a string of prayer beads help the remembrance of nembutsu.

If one neglects one's daily practice due to some inconvenience and regretfully says, "How shameful I am! I did not recite nembutsu today," one is bearing nembutsu in mind. At any rate, if one does not forget nembutsu, it is referred to as the accumulation of nembutsu. In addition, it may happen that one comes to practice nembutsu tomorrow when one cannot perform daily nembutsu today, but it is not desirable to become lax in one's focus and to put off daily practice until the next day. I would like you to think about this carefully.

9. It is proper to perform religious abstinence and refrain from eating fish or poultry for seven days after the death of a close relative, but such a custom is not prescribed in any Buddhist scripture. All living beings we eat today might have been our fathers and mothers in the past; therefore, we should refrain from eating them as much as possible.

Further, since people who have their final moments refrain from impure foods including wine, fish, chicken, garlic, leeks, and onions, those who are mortally ill should also refrain from having them. Nevertheless, those who are not mortally ill or those who have been suffering from unbearable pain in bed for a long time are permitted to eat them for the purpose of recovery. At any rate, please try to get as much rest as possible and concentrate on recuperation in order to practice nembutsu. Blindly holding fast to your life can be an obstacle to the attainment of birth in the Pure Land, to be sure, but you are allowed to have fish and poultry as medical treatment when you are ill.

Thus, I (Hōnen) have written two additional answers to questions you have asked me. Please read them carefully.

Epilogue

THUS, I HAVE COLLECTED and recorded the collected writings of Hōnen-shōnin to the best of my humble knowledge.

However, there are many other works said to be composed by Kurodani, such as the *Collection of Practices for the Certain Attainment of Birth in the Pure Land*, the *Collection Clarifying that Common Mortals Are in Accordance with the Essential Vow*, the *Collection Regarding the Steadfast Heart, Practice, and Exercise*, and the *Reply to the Lady Kujō*.[476] (*Dōkō's note: There are two different replies to the Lady Kujō from Hōnen-shōnin; this is the one in which Hōnen-shōnin mentions the topic of the threefold devotional heart.) These works are different in style and tone from the other Japanese writings of Hōnen-shōnin that I have compiled here. I excluded them from this work because I have grave doubt about their authorship, and the elders said that they were forged.

In addition to these works, I excluded the *Dialogue on Twenty-Two Topics*,[477] which consists of approximately twenty-six or twenty-seven sheets, and the *Manner of Dying*,[478] five or six sheets, because they are also of dubious authenticity and I feel uncertain. There is also the *Merit and Demerit of Nembutsu*,[479] which is said to have been composed by Hōnen-shōnin. This is an apparent forgery, however. Further, there are in addition to these works a few other questionable writings that are unworthy of attention.

For more than twenty years, I searched for the literary remains of

Hōnen-shōnin all over the capital Kyōto and the provinces. I carefully examined their authenticity and have properly selected them. I assume, however, that I may have made many errors in selection; I strongly hope that any errors made will be rectified by junior masters. If someone should find other authentic works of Hōnen-shōnin that I failed to have noticed, he should add these to this supplement to *Collected Teachings of Hōnen: The Japanese Anthology*.

The purpose of this compilation is to encourage all sentient beings to enter the "right path" toward the Pure Land.

Yours truly.
Written respectfully by Monk Bōseirō Ryōe Dōkō.

The Auspicious Dream of the Japanese Anthology

THERE WAS ONCE a court lady in Saga, Kyōto, whose heart had great depth in aspiring for birth in the Pure Land in the life to come. One time she confined herself inside Zendō Shrine within Ōjō-in Temple[480] at Saga and prayed for her attainment of birth in the Pure Land. That night she had a dream that Master Shan-tao appeared with a scroll in his hand and said, "This writing is called the *Literary Light*. If you read it and recite nembutsu, you will, with certainty, attain birth in the Pure Land." Master Shan-tao then gave her the scroll. She received it with great joy, and her dream ended. The court lady marveled at such a dream and asked everyone she could about the writings, but to no avail. No such scroll existed, and she began to feel that the dream was merely an illusion.

The next time she went to Zendō Shrine to confine herself and pray for birth in the Pure Land, a monk who served both Nison-in Temple[481] and Ōjō-in Temple in Saga came to the shrine. His name was Honshin-bō.[482] When the lady asked him about the writings, he replied, "The writing called the *Literary Light* is most likely the *Japanese Anthology*. It is a collection of the literary works of Hōnen-shōnin." Honshin-bō then kindly lent her the *Japanese Anthology*.

The lady read the *Japanese Anthology* with great joy and was convinced that she would unquestionably achieve birth in the Pure Land. She planned to make a copy of the writing and that night had a dream in which two noble men in formal court dress appeared on either side of her. When she asked them from whence they came, one replied, "We came here from Kitano and Hirano in order to protect the *Literary Light*." At the same time a respectable priest stood beside the two noble men and explained, "These two are the gracious deities of Kitano Shrine and Hirano Shrine.[483] I will send thirty deities in turn to protect the holy teachings of the *Literary Light* during that time, and the teachings will deepen faith in birth in the Pure Land through nembutsu for all sentient beings."

The court lady was astounded by this remark. She also felt great appreciation, made a copy of the writing, and read it continuously. To Honshin-bō she said, "I now distinctly understand about the attainment of birth in the Pure Land through nembutsu." Thereafter, she earnestly recited nembutsu.

Three days before August in the first year of Shōwa (1312), the year of the Rat and Water, the court lady had predicted the specific date and hour of her attainment of birth in the Pure Land, saying, "I shall accomplish birth in the Pure Land during the hour of the hare [5:00–7:00 A.M.] on the fourth day of August."

Without the slightest deviation in the day or time, the court lady recited nembutsu 130 times in a loud voice at the beginning of the hour of the hare on the fourth day of August, and together with the sound she passed away. It is said that she was twenty-nine years of age. This description is recorded in detail in the *Examination of Analects*.[484] I [Dōkō] felt grateful that both the instruction of Master Shan-tao and the protection of the deities were given to this *Japanese Anthology*. For this reason, I have dared to give an account of the court lady's dream here.

There are many people who have possessed the steadfast heart and realized birth in the Pure Land through reading this *Japanese Anthology*. It is not necessary to elaborate on this here.

Colophon

IN THE FIRST YEAR of Genkō (1321), the year of the rooster and metal, Enchi[485] printed the block of the *Japanese Anthology*, with gratitude for the benevolence bestowed by Hōnen-shōnin, in order to lead all sentient beings to the "right path" toward birth in the Pure Land.

Written by Monk Enchi, who single-heartedly and exclusively recites *Namu Amida Butsu*.

Monk Ryōe Dōkō, filled with great admiration and rejoicing to excess, wrote the original for the engraving block of the *Japanese Anthology* in seven fascicles while rubbing his seventy-nine-year-old eyes.

Written by Hokkyō Kōgon[486] on the eighth of July of the first year of Genkō, the year of the rooster and metal.

Appendix: The Forty-Eight Vows of Buddha Amitābha

1. If, when I am to attain buddhahood, the realms of hell beings, starving spirits, or animals are in my land, I will not realize enlightenment.

2. If, when I am to attain buddhahood, the humans and heavenly beings who return again to the realms of hell beings, starving spirits, and animals at the end of their lives are in my land, I will not realize enlightenment.

3. If, when I am to attain buddhahood, the humans and heavenly beings in my land are not golden in color, I will not realize enlightenment.

4. If, when I am to attain buddhahood, there is distinction in the personal appearance of the humans and heavenly beings in my land, I will not realize enlightenment.

5. If, when I am to attain buddhahood, the humans and heavenly beings in my land do not acquire the ability to recollect all former existences of themselves and others going back at least a hundred thousand million eons, I will not realize enlightenment.

6. If, when I am to attain buddhahood, the humans and heavenly beings in my land do not possess the divine eyes to see at least

a hundred thousand million buddhalands, I will not realize enlightenment.

7. If, when I am to attain buddhahood, the humans and heavenly beings in my land do not acquire the divine ears to hear at least a hundred thousand million teachings of manifold buddhas, I will not realize enlightenment.

8. If, when I am to attain buddhahood, the humans and heavenly beings in my land do not obtain the ability to read the thoughts of others in at least a hundred thousand million buddhalands' beings, I will not realize enlightenment.

9. If, when I am to attain buddhahood, the humans and heavenly beings in my land do not possess the divine feet to travel, in a single thought moment, to at least a hundred thousand million buddhalands, I will not realize enlightenment.

10. If, when I am to attain buddhahood, the humans and heavenly beings in my land have any thought of delusory attachment to their own lives, I will not realize enlightenment.

11. If, when I am to attain buddhahood, the humans and heavenly beings in my land do not abide in the rightly established state for entering into nirvāṇa, I will not realize enlightenment.

12. If, when I am to attain buddhahood, my light is limited and does not illuminate at least a hundred thousand million buddhalands, I will not realize enlightenment.

13. If, when I am to attain buddhahood, my lifespan is limited and does not last at least a hundred thousand million eons, I will not realize enlightenment.

14. If, when I am to attain buddhahood, the number of practitioners in my land is able to be counted by the pratyekabuddhas and śrāvakas of the three thousand great-thousand worlds within a hundred thousand eons, I will not realize enlightenment.

15. If, when I am to attain buddhahood, the humans and heavenly beings in my land are limited in the length of their lives, I will not realize enlightenment. Excluded are only those who have vowed their limited life span.

16. If, when I am to attain buddhahood, the humans and heavenly beings in my land ever hear the name of the unvirtuous, I will not realize enlightenment.

17. If, when I am to attain buddhahood, all the countless buddhas of the ten directions do not praise my name, I will not realize enlightenment.

18. **If, when I am to attain buddhahood, all sentient beings in the ten directions who hold faith with genuine hearts and who wish to be born in my land are not born there with just ten moments of being mindful of me, I will not realize enlightenment. Excluded only are those who have committed the five grave offenses and those who have abused the true Dharma.**

19. If, when I am to attain buddhahood, all sentient beings in the ten directions awaken the heart of enlightenment, accumulate the various roots of merit, sincerely desire to be born in my land, yet do not receive the welcome of myself surrounded by the host of celestial beings at their time of death, I will not realize enlightenment.

20. If, when I am to attain buddhahood, all sentient beings in the ten directions, upon hearing my name, keep their thoughts fixed on my land, cultivate the various roots of merit, dedicate the merit to birth in my land, but fail this birth, I will not realize enlightenment.

21. If, when I am to attain buddhahood, the humans and heavenly beings in my land are not fully endowed with the thirty-two prominent features a buddha, I will not realize enlightenment.

22. If, when I am to attain buddhahood, all the bodhisattvas in other buddhalands, who are born in my land, are unable to attain the state of nonregression to realize buddhahood, I will not realize enlightenment. Excluded are those bodhisattvas who, due to their own vows designed to save sentient beings, fortify themselves with the armor of the universal vow, accumulate the roots of merit, realize emancipation for sentient beings, visit other buddhalands to observe the bodhisattva perfections, pay homage to various buddhas and tathāgatas in the ten directions, show the path to enlightenment to sentient beings as numerous as the grains of sand in the Ganges, and make them abide in the unsurpassed and true path. Furthermore, excluded are those bodhisattvas who are superior to ordinary bodhisattvas, have attained the final stage of the bodhisattva stages, and have been endowed with the virtues of Buddha Samantabhadra.

23. If, when I am to attain buddhahood, all the bodhisattvas in my land cannot possess the transcendent faculties of a buddha to pay homage to various buddhas, and cannot visit all the countless buddhalands within the time of taking a meal, I will not realize enlightenment.

24. If, when I am to attain buddhahood, all the bodhisattvas in my land cannot present their cultivated merits in the presence of all the buddhas and cannot obtain articles of worship freely whenever they desire to pay homage to other buddhas, I will not realize enlightenment.

25. If, when I am to attain buddhahood, all the bodhisattvas in my land cannot preach the perfect wisdom, I will not realize enlightenment.

26. If, when I am to attain buddhahood, all the bodhisattvas in my land cannot be endowed with the diamond-like body of Nārāyaṇa,[487] I will not realize enlightenment.

27. If, when I am to attain buddhahood, all the things belonging to the humans and heavenly beings in my land are not sublime

and brilliant, are not wondrous in colors and forms, are not extremely exquisite, and also if sentient beings, with their divine eyes, are not able to clearly describe the names and number of those things, I will not realize enlightenment.

28. If, when I am to attain buddhahood, all the bodhisattvas as well as those who have less virtue in my land cannot perceive the most exquisitely colored tree of enlightenment reaching four hundred *yojanas* in height, I will not realize enlightenment.

29. If, when I am to attain buddhahood, all the bodhisattvas in my land cannot acquire wisdom and eloquence through reading, reciting, and preaching the sutras to others, I will not realize enlightenment.

30. If, when I am to attain buddhahood, the wisdom of any of the bodhisattvas in my land has any limitations, I will not realize enlightenment.

31. If, when I am to attain buddhahood, my land is not pure and serene, and cannot reflect all the countless and inconceivable buddhalands in the ten directions as clear as seeing one's own image in a mirror, I will not realize enlightenment.

32. If, when I am to attain buddhahood, all bodhisattvas do not pursue the bodhisattva perfections even after hearing that: all the adornments of the palaces, pavilions, streams, flowers, and trees from the ground up to the sky in my land are made of countless jewels and a hundred thousand kinds of fragrance; the exquisite fragrance of my land is wondrous, surpassing the realms of humans and heavenly beings and spreading throughout the worlds of the ten directions, I will not realize enlightenment.

33. If, when I am to attain buddhahood, all the sentient beings of the countless and inconceivable buddhalands in the ten directions, though bathed in and touched by my light, cannot be gentle in body and mind beyond the reach of humans and heavenly beings, I will not realize enlightenment.

34. If, when I am to attain buddhahood, all the sentient beings of the countless and inconceivable buddhalands in the ten directions, upon hearing my name, do not attain the bodhisattva stage of patience accepting that all things are unborn or profound *dhāraṇī*, I will not realize enlightenment.

35. If, when I am to attain buddhahood, there are women of the countless and inconceivable buddhalands in the ten directions who may be born again in a female form after hearing my name, having joy and faith, awakening aspiration for enlightenment, and detesting femininity, I will not realize enlightenment.

36. If, when I am to attain buddhahood, all the bodhisattvas of the countless and inconceivable buddhalands in the ten directions do not, upon hearing my name, always observe the bodhisattva practice to accomplish the path leading to enlightenment in their lives to come, I will not realize enlightenment.

37. If, when I am to attain buddhahood, all the humans and heavenly beings of the numerous and inconceivable buddhalands in the ten directions do not win reverence from other humans and heavenly beings when they, upon hearing my name, prostrate themselves on the ground to worship me and observe the bodhisattva practice with joy and faith, I will not realize enlightenment.

38. If, when I am to attain buddhahood, all the humans and heavenly beings in my land do not spontaneously obtain garments approved by a buddha upon wishing for them, and if the garments require sewing, bleaching, or cleaning, I will not realize enlightenment.

39. If, when I am to attain buddhahood, all the humans and heavenly beings in my land do not receive the same pleasure and happiness of fully ordained monks who are freed from their worldly passions, I will not realize enlightenment.

40. If, when I am to attain buddhahood, all the bodhisattvas in my land, upon their wish, cannot see the countless sublime and pure buddhalands in the ten directions reflected among the jeweled trees of my land as clear as one sees his own image in a clear mirror, I will not realize enlightenment.

41. If, when I am to attain buddhahood, all the bodhisattvas of other buddhalands, hearing my name, become deformed until they attain buddhahood, I will not realize enlightenment.

42. If, when I am to attain buddhahood, all the bodhisattvas of other buddhalands, hearing my name, do not enter the pure samādhi of emancipation in which they can pay homage to various tathāgata buddhas within a moment of thought, I will not realize enlightenment.

43. If, when I am to attain buddhahood, all the bodhisattvas of other buddhalands, hearing my name, are not reborn as ārya beings, I will not realize enlightenment.

44. If, when I am to attain buddhahood, all the bodhisattvas of other buddhalands, hearing my name, do not become so happy they dance for joy and pursue the bodhisattva practices, and are not endowed with the roots of merit, I will not realize enlightenment.

45. If, when I am to attain buddhahood, all the bodhisattvas of other buddhalands, hearing my name, do not abide in the state of the universal samādhi in which they can see all the countless inconceivable buddhas until they attain buddhahood, I will not realize enlightenment.

46. If, when I am to attain buddhahood, all the bodhisattvas in my land are unable to hear the Dharma according to their wishes, I will not realize enlightenment.

47. If, when I am to attain buddhahood, all the bodhisattvas in my land, hearing my name, do not attain the state of the nonregression, I will not realize enlightenment.

48. If, when I am to attain buddhahood, all the bodhisattvas of other buddhalands, hearing my name, do not acquire the three kinds of wisdom nor attain the state of nonregression through the Dharma, I will not realize enlightenment.

Notes

1. *Sutra of the Samādhi of All Buddhas' Presence*, Taishō 13 (417): 899.
2. *Smaller Sutra*, Jōzen 1: 53–54, Seiten 1: 199–202, Taishō 12 (366): 347.
3. *Meditation Sutra*, Jōzen 1: 13–14, Seiten 1: 186–87, Taishō 12 (365): 345–46.
4. While attributed to Nāgārjuna, no corresponding text is extant in Sanskrit or Tibetan.
5. *Commentary on the Ten Bodhisattva Stages*, Taishō 26 (1521): 42–43.
6. The Chinese term for applying familiar language to unfamiliar concepts is *ko-i*; it often designates the use of Taoist terms to make sense of Buddhism's vast array of concepts during the early years of Buddhism's introduction to China.
7. *Commentary on Treatise on Birth in the Pure Land*, Taishō 40 (1819): 826.
8. Ibid., 843.
9. Ibid., 839.
10. Ibid., 834.
11. *Collection of Passages on the Blissful Land*, Jōzen 1: 674, Taishō 40 (1819): 834. This prophecy of the Dharma's decline, set forth in a number of early Buddhist sources, describes a series of four or five successive five-hundred-year eras in which beings become increasingly unable to realize the teachings of the Buddha, and the possibility of enlightenment therefore becomes more and more remote. This theory is similar to the three-period theory mentioned in note 19 below.
12. *Collection of Passages on the Blissful Land*, Jōzen 1: 675, Taishō 47 (1958): 5.
13. *Further Biographies of Eminent Monks*, Taishō 50 (2060): 684.
14. *Hymns in Praise of Birth in the Pure Land*, Taishō 47 (1980): 439.
15. Wang-ku, *New Biographies of Eminent Monks Who Attained Birth in the Pure Land*, Taishō 83 (2611): 158.
16. *Commentary on the Meditation Sutra*, Jōzen 2: 56, Seiten 2: 121, Taishō 37 (1753): 271.
17. Ibid.
18. Mount Wu-t'ai, located in the northeast area of Shan-hsi Province, is one of the three holy mountains in China. The other two are Mount Ngo-mei in Szechwan Province and Mount P'u-t'o in Che-chiang Province. Bodhisattva Mañjuśrī is said to have expounded on the teachings of Buddha Śākyamuni on this mountain. The

first monasteries were built there in the fourth to fifth centuries, and by the sixth century over two hundred monasteries were in existence. Mount Wu-t'ai is also an important center for Mongolian Buddhism.

19. This three-period declensionist theory of history is similar to the one mentioned in note 11 above. But instead of four or five five-hundred year eras, this one in its various incarnations begins with a period of true Dharma (Jp. *shōbō*) followed by a period of semblance of Dharma (Jp. *zōhō*), each of which may last either five hundred or a thousand years depending on the commentator. These are followed by a third era, which we are in presently, called the era of decline (Jp. *mappō*) that lasts for ten thousand years. It is said that in this degenerate age the Dharma remains, but no one is capable of observing the precepts, practicing, or attaining enlightenment. In general, when wars, natural disasters, famine, environmental destruction, social disorder, and unscrupulous clergy are prevalent, people have nothing to rely upon. Historically, Pure Land Buddhism, teaching the power of Amida's compassion to save people, gained popularity under these conditions.
20. *An Illustrated Biography of Hōnen-shōnin*, Jōzen 16: 116, Seiten 6: 10.
21. These three schools are discussed in notes 98, 99, and 122 below.
22. *Commentary on the Meditation Sutra*, Jōzen 2: 58, Seiten 2: 126, Taishō 37 (1753): 272.
23. This work was published in English translation in 1997 as volume 104-II in the BDK English Tripiṭaka series.
24. *Collection on Nembutsu*, Jōzen 7: 72–73, Seiten 3: 90, Taishō 83 (2608): 19–20.
25. Daigo edition of the *Biography of Hōnen-shōnin*, compiled in the *Hōnen-shōnin Zenshū*: 453.
26. *Collection on Nembutsu*, Jōzen 7: 3, Seiten 3: 5, Taishō 83 (2608): 1.
27. *Collection on Nembutsu*, Jōzen 7: 75, Seiten 3: 91, Taishō 83 (2608): 20.
28. *An Illustrated Biography of Hōnen-shōnin*, Jōzen 16: 384–86, Seiten 6: 486–89.
29. *An Illustrated Biography of Hōnen-shōnin*, Jōzen 16: 426–27, Seiten 6: 542.
30. *An Illustrated Biography of Hōnen-shōnin*, Jōzen 16: 434–35, Seiten 6: 551–52.
31. *An Illustrated Biography of Hōnen-shōnin*, Jōzen 16: 435–36, Seiten 6: 553–54.
32. *Collection on Nembutsu*, Jōzen 7: 69, Seiten 3: 86, Taishō 83 (2608): 19. Textual descriptions regarding Shan-tao's attainment of samādhi appear in Wang-ku's *New Biographies of Eminent Monks who Attained Birth in the Pure Land*, Taishō 83 (2611): 158.
33. Seikan-bō Genchi was a prominent disciple of Hōnen and the second archbishop of Chion-in Temple in Kyōto. Genchi was born the son of Taira no Moromori, the governor of Ecchū Province (presently Toyama Prefecture). At the age of thirteen, after the death of Moromori, Genchi's mother brought him to Hōnen, who sent him to Jichin (1155–1225), the abbot of the Tendai school. At the end of the following year, Genchi returned to Hōnen and devoted himself to serving his master for eighteen years until Hōnen's death. Genchi received special attention from Hōnen, who bestowed upon Genchi the image of Amida Buddha that Hōnen himself had worshiped, the *Record of the Awakening of Samādhi*, copies of the Pure Land scriptures, as well as the *Single-Sheet Covenant*.
34. Shinran was the founder of Jōdo Shin Shū and a disciple of Hōnen. Shinran was born to Hino Arinori in Kyōto. Having lost his parents in childhood, he entered

the priesthood on Mount Hiei. In 1201, he confined himself in Rokkakudō Hall in Kyōto for a hundred days and at dawn on the ninety-fifth day, received the words of inspiration from the bodhisattva Avalokiteśvara. He then went to see Hōnen in order to learn the true way of deliverance. Shinran was permitted to copy his master's major work, the *Collection on Nembutsu*, in 1205. Their time together was not long, however, as Hōnen was exiled to Shikoku in 1207 and Shinran to Echigo Province (the present-day Niigata Prefecture) in the same year. While exiled in Echigo, Shinran married the nun Eshin (1182–1268) and propagated nembutsu in the Kantō region as he would later in Kyōto. Fundamental to Shinran's nembutsu theory was his view that "No pure mind has existed" in humankind, and he became convinced that the prerequisite for birth in the Pure Land was simply absolute faith in the vow of Amida Buddha. He composed many writings based on this concept, including the *True Teaching, Practice, and Realization of the Pure Land Way* (*Kyōgyō Shinshō*), *Gutoku's Notes* (*Gutokushō*), *Hymns of the Dharma-Ages* (*Shōzōmatsu Wasan*), *Hymns in Praise of Prince Shōtoku* (*Kōtaishi Shōoku Hōsan*), *Passages on the Pure Land Way* (*Jōdo Monruijushō*), *Notes on Once-Calling and Many-Calling* (*Ichinen Tanen Mon'i*), and the *Record in Lament of Divergences* (*Tannishō*).

35. Ryōchū, also called Nen'a and posthumously by the title Kishi-zenji given by Emperor Go-Uda (1267–1324), was the founder of Kōmyō-ji Temple in Kamakura. Ryōchū was born in Iwami Province (the present-day Shimane Prefecture) and entered the priesthood under the mentorship of Shinsen, a Tendai monk from Wanibuchi Temple, in 1211. He received the precepts on Mount Hiei in 1214 and studied the doctrines of the Tendai, Kusha, Hossō, Zen, and Ritsu schools. In 1236, Ryōchū visited Shōkō-bō Benchō (see next note) at Tempuku-ji Temple in Chikugo (presently Fukuoka Prefecture), became his disciple, and was given Shōkō's *Personal Seal Attesting to the Transmission of Hōnen's Teaching of Nembutsu for the Future Generations* and the *In-depth Study of the Collection on Nembutsu*. Ryōchū entered the Kantō area in 1249, established Kōmyō-ji Temple in Kamakura, and engaged in extensive propagation of the nembutsu teachings of Hōnen and Shōkō. It is said that Ryōchū wrote over fifty commentaries and manuscripts, including the *Solution to Problems Regarding Shōkō's Jushuin* (*Kettō Jushuin Gimon-shō*), the *Commentary on the Collection on Nembutsu for Resolving Doubts and Spreading Its Teachings* (*Senchaku Dengu Ketsugi-shō*), *Exposition of the Commentary on the Meditation Sutra* (*Kangyō-sho Denzūki*), *Commentary on the Threefold Devotional Heart* (*Sanjin Shiki*), the *Outline of Birth in the Pure Land* (*Jōdo Tai'i-shō*), and the *Collection of the Essentials on Jōdo Shū* (*Jōdo Shū Yōshū*).

36. Shōkō-bō Benchō founded the Chinzei lineage of Jōdo Shū. Benchō is also known as Benna or Chinzei-shōnin. He was born in Katsuki, Fukuoka, in 1162, went to Mount Hiei to study the Tendai doctrine in 1183, became a distinguished disciple of Hōnen in 1197, and extensively propagated the nembutsu teaching of Hōnen, mainly in Kyūshū. It is said that Hōnen bestowed Benchō with the *Collection on Nembutsu* in the spring of 1198 immediately after its compilation. Benchō's major works are the *Collection of the Essentials on Jōdo Shū* (*Jōdo Shū Yōshū*), the *Personal Seal Attesting to the Transmission of Hōnen's Teaching of Nembutsu for Future Generations* (*Matsudai Nembutsu Jushuin*), and the *In-depth Study of the Collection on Nembutsu* (*Tetsu Senchaku-shū*).

37. *Meditation Sutra*, Jōzen 1: 44, Seiten 1: 166, Taishō 12 (365): 343.
38. This is one phase of the three-period theory promulgated by the Chinese T'ien-t'ai monk Hui-szu (514/15–77).
39. *Treatise on the Pure Land* by Chia-ts'ai, Jōzen 6: 659, Taishō 47 (1963): 98.
40. Hōjō Masako was decorated with the second rank in the court of Kamakura in 1218. She became a nun in 1199 after the death of Shōgun Yoritomo, but she continued to wield power through her sons and was, therefore, referred to as the Shōgun nun (Jp. *ama Shōgun*).
41. Tarō Sanehide (d. 1246) lived in the village of Ōgo, which was situated approximately six miles northwest of Maebashi in Kotsuke (presently Gunma Prefecture). He was the son of Ōgo no Shirō Takayoshi, who was in the service of the Minamoto family. While staying in Kyōto, Takayoshi visited Hōnen in Yoshimizu and became an ardent nembutsu devotee thereafter. Sanehide also received the instructions on nembutsu directly from Hōnen in the capital. After returning to Ōgo, Sanehide wrote a letter to Hōnen in order to clarify some points.
42. The lay priest Kumagai no Jirō Naozane, Hōriki-bō Rensei, was a disciple of Hōnen and the feudal lord of Kumagai. Naozane had been a famous warrior in the battle between the Genji and Heike clans, which continued from the end of the eleventh century until the end of the twelfth century. Naozane initially helped to establish the Kamakura government for the Genji clan, but he came to develop ill will toward Minamoto no Yoritomo. In 1192, he fell out with Kuge Naomitsu about the boundary of their domains, entered religious life, and took the name Rensei, becoming an ardent nembutsu practitioner under Hōnen's tutelage. One famous tale says that when he returned to Kumagai from Kyōto, since he had to travel to the east, he would put the saddle on the horse backward and ride facing the west in order to face in the direction of Amida Buddha and his master in the capital.
43. Tsunoto no Saburō Tamemori (1163–1243) was a warrior in Tsunoto, a suburb of Tōkyō. In 1180 at the age of eighteen, Tamemori joined the forces of Minamoto no Yoritomo and took part in a battle at Mount Ishibashi in Sagami (presently Kanagawa Prefecture). When Yoritomo visited Nara to attend the dedication service for the newly built Tōdai-ji Temple in 1196, Tamemori went along with his master. Passing through Kyōto on the way to Nara, Tamemori visited Hōnen, was deeply impressed by his teaching, and became an ardent nembutsu devotee. After the death of Hōnen, Tamemori's earnest desire for birth in the Pure Land increased day by day while at the same time disgust with this defiled world of anguish grew. He committed disembowelment in 1243.
44. Kōmyō-bō's (early thirteenth century) birthplace, birth date, and personal history are unknown. He was from Ecchū Province (presently Toyama Prefecture) and was a devotee of the principle that multiple recitations of nembutsu assured birth in the Pure Land. However, one day in Echigo Province (presently Niigata Prefecture), his nembutsu was criticized by a disciple of Jōkaku-bō Kōsai (1163–1247), also a disciple of Hōnen, who advocated that a mere single utterance sufficed. Kōmyō-bō wrote to Hōnen, who severely refuted the single-utterance view in his reply.
45. Nun Shōnyo-bō (d. 1201) was the daughter of Emperor Go-Shirakawa (1127–92), the seventy-seventh Japanese emperor. Known also as Princess Shokushi, at age seven she apparently served as a Shintō high priestess (Jp. *saiin*) at the Kamo Shrines

in Kyōto. She learned poetry under the guidance of the famous poets Fujiwara no Shunzei and his son Fujiwara no Teika. A large number of her poems were recorded in the *Collection of a Thousand Years* (*Senzai Wakashū*) completed in 1187 and the *New Collection from Ancient and Modern Times* (*Shin Kokin-shū*) printed in 1205. She later became a nun, embraced the nembutsu teaching of Hōnen, and died on January 25 in 1201.

46. Zenshō-bō was a Tendai scholar who lived in Renge-ji Temple in Tōtomi (presently Shizuoka Prefecture). Around the age of twenty-nine, he met the lay priest Kumagai and learned the way to attain birth in the Pure Land through nembutsu. Zenshō-bō then went up to the capital to receive mentorship from Hōnen. Among Hōnen's disciples, Zenshō-bō was renowned as the monk with steadfast faith.
47. Of the three fascicles in this work, only the second and third are extant. The work is attributed to Shinzui (d. 1279), a disciple of Shinkū (1146–1228). This work clarifies the nembutsu theories of eight prominent monks who belonged to the Tendai and Shingon schools and converted to Jōdo Shū due to Hōnen's influence.
48. Myōhen (1142–1224) of Mount Kōya in Wakayama Prefecture; son of Fujiwara no Michinori; the distinguished monk of the Sanron school. Myōhen entered the priesthood in his childhood and studied Sanron under the mentorship of Hōin Binkaku (d. 1181) at Tōdai-ji Temple. When Myōhen was forty-five years old, he was given the second rank title in the Buddhist hierarchy, but he declined the imperial appointment simply because he disliked all worldly fame, and he retired to his hermitage in a thatched hut on Mount Kōya. After reading the *Collection on Nembutsu* and meeting with Hōnen, Myōhen converted to become an earnest nembutsu practitioner and gave himself the name of Kū Amida Butsu. It is said that after the death of Hōnen, he devoted himself to observing the one million recitations of nembutsu with Hōnen's remains hanging around his neck.
49. Jōgan-bō Sōgen (1168–1251) was originally a Shingon priest and studied esoteric Buddhism at Ninna-ji Temple in Kyōto. He later converted to Jōdo Shū under the mentorship of Hōnen. Sōgen detested renown and personal gain and devoted himself to the exclusive practice of nembutsu.
50. Hōren-bō Shinkū (1146–1228), one of Hōnen's most intimate disciples, served Hōnen for fifty-six years, followed in the academic tradition of Hōnen, and secured the foundation of Jōdo Shū after Hōnen's passing. He received the precepts for perfect and instantaneous enlightenment (Jp. *endonkai*) from both Eikū and Hōnen and wrote the *Monition in Seven Articles* (*Shichikajō kishōmon* or *Shichikajō seikai*). The name Hōren-bō was the first among Hōnen's many disciples listed in the *Monition in Seven Articles* presented to the Archbishop Shinshō of the Tendai school in 1204. Shinkū was also known as Shirakawa-shōnin because he lived at his chamber at Shirakawa in the eastern section of the capital.
51. Dōhen (active ca. 1200). Dōhen's name as a layman was Shibuya no Shichirō, and he was also known as Dōben, Ishikawa Zenmon, and Ishikawa Nyūdō. According to the biography, Dōhen was one of Hōnen's disciples that moved his remains from Ōtani to Saga in order to protect them from the Mount Hiei monks who planned to destroy Hōnen's tomb and dispose of his remains in the Kamo River in Kyōto.
52. Shunjō-bō Chōgen helped oversee the reconstruction of Tōdai-ji Temple in Nara, the central Buddhist institution. Chōgen was born in Kyōto, entered Daigo-ji

Temple, studied Shingon Buddhism, and traveled to China three times between 1167–77. In 1180 during the Taira-Minamoto War, Tōdai-ji Temple was burned down. Hōnen proposed to the court that Chōgen be appointed as the head priest to solicit funds for reconstructing it. He received popular contributions as well as great support from Emperor Go-Shirakawa (1127–92), Minamoto no Yoritomo (1137–99), and Regent Kujō Kanezane (1149–1207). The inaugural ceremony, where the eyes on the statue of the Great Buddha were "opened," was performed in 1185, and the reconstruction was completed in 1195. Chōgen composed the *Collection of the Virtues of Chōgen* (*Namu Amida-butsu Sazen-shū*) in 1203.

53. *Ōjō* in Japanese means "birth in the Pure Land of Amida Buddha." Although the term *rebirth* is frequently used to describe birth in the Pure Land, the word *birth* is more appropriate. In Buddhism, *rebirth* is a term technically associated with the notion of transmigration within the six delusive worlds of saṃsāra. Birth in the Pure Land, however, transcends the six delusive worlds.
54. Paekche (ca. 350–663), one of the three kingdoms of early Korean history. The other two kingdoms were Silla (57 B.C.E.–935 C.E.) and Koguryo (37 B.C.E.–668 C.E.).
55. Prince Shōtoku (574–622), son of Emperor Yōmei (d. 587) and Empress Anahobe no Hashibito. In 592, he was crowned as prince. Later he became the prince regent, and in 604 promulgated the *Constitution of Seventeen Articles* (*Jūshichijō Kempō*). He was a staunch supporter of Buddhism, establishing many temples. He composed the *Commentaries on the Three Sutras* (*Sangyō Gisho*), i.e., the commentaries on the *Lotus Sutra*, the *Vimalakīrti Sutra*, and the *Lion's Roar of Queen Śrīmāla Sutra*.
56. Zenkō-ji Temple is a Buddhist temple in Nagano Prefecture affiliated with the Tendai school and Jōdo Shū. Zenkō-ji Temple enshrines the first Buddhist image to arrive in Japan from the Korean kingdom of Paekche in 552, an image of Amida Buddha flanked by his two attendant bodhisattvas.
57. In other words, the image embodied the merit of Amida's name, and the true intent of the teachings of the Two Honored Ones was revealed to the world.
58. Gyōki (668–749), a Hossō monk, was also known as Gyōgi. He was born in Kawachi Province (presently Ōsaka) and studied the Hossō doctrines at Yakushi-ji Temple in Nara. Gyōki undertook various public works, such as building bridges, dams, and many temples, including Tōdai-ji Temple in Nara in 741. Emperor Shōmu (r. 724–49) bestowed on him the title Great Bodhisattva.
59. Jikaku-daishi En'nin (794–864), a Japanese Tendai monk, played an important role in the introduction of Pure Land Buddhism into Japan. In 838, he traveled to China and studied Fa-chao's *Fivefold Rhythmic Chanting of Nien-fo* on Mount Wu-t'ai. After about ten years in China, En'nin returned to Mount Hiei with 559 Chinese manuscripts, including the important works of Tao-ch'o, Fa-chao, and Shan-tao. En'nin built a study center on Mount Hiei for the practices of the constant-walking samādhi and rhythmic chanting of nembutsu. His disciples were the first to observe these practices in Japan.
60. Eshin-sōzu Genshin (942–1017) was a prominent Tendai monk in Japan. He composed the *Contemplation on the White Curl Between the Eyebrows of Amida Buddha* (*Amida-butsu Byakugōkan*), the *Essentials of the Smaller Sutra* (*Amida-kyō Ryakuki*), and the *Collection of Essentials on Attaining Birth in the Pure Land* (*Ōjō Yōshū*), which is his primary work. In this three-fascicle collection Genshin

graphically describes birth in the Pure Land for the deliverance of the common people. This work established the scholastic foundation of Pure Land Buddhism during the Heian period (794–1185) in Japan.

61. Monk Yōkan (1033–1111) was the author of the *Ten Conditions for Attaining Birth in the Pure Land* (*Ōjō Jūin*). A scholarly Pure Land monk in the southern capital of Nara, he originally studied the teachings of the Sanron and Hossō schools. It is said that Yōkan recited nembutsu ten thousand times a day from the time he was eighteen years old and recited nembutsu sixty thousand times a day in his later years.
62. Another name for the *Book of History* (*Shu-ching*) in the *Five Classics* of Confucianism in China. This work describes the politics and religions of ancient Chinese dynasties.
63. The *Larger Sukhāvatīvyūha Sūtra*, translated by Sanghavarman in 252 C.E., two fascicles, Jōzen 1, Seiten 1, Taishō 12 (360). See the introduction, pp. 7–9.
64. *Amitāyurdhyāna Sūtra*, translated by Kālayaśas, a Central Asian monk in the fourth century, one fascicle, Jōzen 1, Seiten 1, Taishō 12 (365). See introduction, pp. 9–11.
65. The *Smaller Sukhāvatīvyūha Sūtra*, trans. Kumārajīva in 402 C.E., one fascicle, Jōzen 1, Seiten 1, Taishō 12 (366). This text has one Sanskrit version, two Chinese translations, and one Tibetan translation. In this scripture, Buddha Śākyamuni gives a discourse to Śāriputra and 1,250 disciples in the garden of Jetavana. It consists of four parts: The first part is a description of the Pure Land. The second part is devoted to the exercise by which one may be born in the Pure Land. In the third part, all buddhas in the ten directions testify to the supremacy of the recitation of nembutsu.
66. Tathāgata Lokeśvararāja is the last of the fifty-three previous buddhas described in the *Larger Sutra* and the mentor of Bodhisattva Dharmākara.
67. *Larger Sutra*, Jōzen 1: 7, Seiten 1: 28, Taishō 12 (360): 268.
68. *Commentary on the Meditation Sutra*, Jōzen 2: 10, Seiten 2: 28, Taishō 37 (1753): 250.
69. It is unclear from which text Hōnen quoted these passages. The description of this concept appears in Genshin's *Collection of Essentials on Attaining Birth in the Pure Land*. See Jōzen 15: 69, Taishō 84 (2682): 48.
70. The Sanskrit term *kalpa* (eon) is the largest Indian unit of time and is a symbolic term referring to an immeasurably long period of time. It is metaphorically explained that every hundred years a silk garment from a celestial woman is rubbed once on a giant rock; when the rock is worn away, one *kalpa* still will not have passed.
71. *Larger Sutra*, Jōzen 1: 11, Seiten 1: 40, Taishō 12 (360): 269.
72. *Larger Sutra*, Jōzen 1: 11, Seiten 1: 41, Taishō 12 (360): 269.
73. Ibid.
74. *Hymns in Praise of Birth in the Pure Land*, Jōzen 4: 376, Taishō 47 (1980): 447.
75. *Larger Sutra*, Jōzen 1: 19–20, Seiten 1: 73, Taishō 12 (360): 272.
76. *Larger Sutra*, Jōzen 1: 19–20, Seiten 1: 71–73, Taishō 12 (360): 272.
77. *Larger Sutra*, Jōzen 1: 7–8, Seiten 1: 28–29, Taishō 12 (360): 268.
78. This means that though there are three different categories in aspirants, Amida, without distinction, will appear in front of all nembutsu devotees at the time of death because of his essential vow to save everyone who recites nembutsu.
79. *Larger Sutra*, Jōzen 1: 21, Seiten 1: 76, Taishō 12 (360): 272.
80. Unknown.

81. *Biographies of Those Who Attained Birth in the Pure Land*, pp. 267–68.
82. *Larger Sutra*, Jōzen 1: 35, Seiten 1: 134, Taishō 12 (360): 279.
83. The "meditative practices with a focused mind" are the first thirteen among the sixteen types of contemplation described in the *Meditation Sutra*; the "meditative practices with a distracted mind" are the remaining three types of meditation. The thirteen objects of meditation with a focused mind are: (1) meditation on the setting sun, (2) meditation on the pure water of the Pure Land, (3) meditation on the ground of the Pure Land, (4) meditation on the jeweled trees of the Pure Land, (5) meditation on the jeweled lakes of the Pure Land, (6) meditation on the jeweled pavilions of the Pure Land, (7) meditation on the flower throne of the Pure Land, (8) meditation on the figures of Buddha Amitābha, (9) meditation on the true physical features of Buddha Amitābha, (10) meditation on the physical features of Bodhisattva Avalokiteśvara, (11) meditation on the physical features of Bodhisattva Mahāsthāmaprāpta, (12) meditation on the state of one's own birth in the Pure Land, and (13) meditation on the figures of Buddha Amitābha, the bodhisattvas, and all beings in the Pure Land. The three types of meditation with a distracted mind are meditations on each of the three categories of aspirants for birth in the Pure Land—high, middle, and low.
84. *Meditation Sutra*, Jōzen 1: 51, Seiten 1: 193, Taishō 12 (365): 346.
85. *Meditation Sutra*, Jōzen 1: 44, Seiten 1: 166, Taishō 12 (365): 343.
86. *Larger Sutra*, Jōzen 1: 7, Seiten 1: 28, Taishō 12 (360): 268.
87. Ibid.
88. *Larger Sutra*, Jōzen 1: 11, Seiten 1: 40, Taishō 12 (360): 269.
89. *Hymns in Praise of Birth in the Pure Land*, Jōzen 4: 356, Taishō 47 (1980): 439.
90. *Commentary on the Meditation Sutra*, Jōzen 2: 49, Seiten 2: 105, Taishō 37 (1753): 268.
91. *Larger Sutra*, Jōzen 1: 7, Seiten 1: 28, Taishō 12 (360): 268.
92. *Meditation Sutra*, Jōzen 1: 44, Seiten 1: 166, Taishō 12 (365): 343.
93. *Meditation Sutra*, Jōzen 1: 46, Seiten 1: 176, Taishō 12 (365): 344.
94. *Commentary on the Meditation Sutra*, Jōzen 2: 55, Seiten 2: 119, Taishō 37 (1753): 270–71.
95. *Commentary on the Meditation Sutra*, Jōzen 2: 56, Seiten 2: 121, Taishō 37 (1753): 271.
96. *Commentary on the Meditation Sutra*, Jōzen 2: 59, Seiten 2: 127, Taishō 37 (1753): 272.
97. Shan-tao summarized the passage from the *Commentary on the Meditation Sutra*. Jōzen 2: 2, Seiten 2: 6–7, Taishō 37 (1753): 246.
98. The Sanron school was one of the six schools of Nara and one of the thirteen schools of China. The Sanron tradition was first transmitted to China by Kumārajīva (344–413) in the early fifth century and then introduced into Japan in 625. Sanron literally means "three treatises," referring to the three texts on which the school was based. The three treatises are Nāgārjuna's *Treatise on the Middle Way* (*Madhyamaka Śāstra*) and *Treatise on the Twelve Gates* (*Dvādaśamukha Śāstra*), and Āryadeva's (third century) *One Hundred Verse Treatise* (*Śata Śāstra*).
99. The Hossō school, a Mahāyāna school, was one of the six schools of Nara and one of the thirteen schools of China. The Hossō school is based on the doctrine

of Mind-Only as advocated by Asaṅga (310–90), Vasubandhu (fifth century), and Dharmapāla (sixth century). The main text of the school is the *Treatise on the Attainment of Consciousness-Only* (*Vijñaptimātratāsiddhi Śāstra*, Jp. *Jō Yuishiki-ron*), compiled by the seventh-century Chinese pilgrim Hsüan-tsang. The Hossō tradition was introduced into Japan in 652.

100. A disciple of Buddha Śākyamuni, Jīvaka (which means "physician") was a skilled physician who lived in Rājagṛha, the capital of the Magadha kingdom. He was renowned for curing the illnesses of King Bimbisāra, Ajātaśatru, Buddha Śākyamuni, and his disciples.
101. A famous physician active sometime during the seventh to third century B.C.E. in China. Since his name often appears in the *Historical Memories* (*Shih-chi*), we can assume that the name P'ien-ch'üeh was also a general word for a distinguished physician.
102. This is a summary of quotations from the *Sutra on the Compassionate Lotus Flower* (Skt. *Karunāpuṇḍarīka Sūtra*, Jp. *Hike-kyō*), translated by Dharmaṣema in ten fascicles. See Taishō 3 (157): 174–220.
103. The true teachings that directly reveal the intent of Buddha Śākyamuni. In the Tendai school, this specifically refers to the teaching of the *Lotus Sutra*. The expedient teachings are designed for those who are not yet to ready to comprehend the true teaching. In the Tendai school, they refer to various teachings other than the *Lotus Sutra*.
104. This is the summary of the passage from the *Smaller Sutra*, Jōzen 1: 52–54, Seiten 1: 196–203, Taishō 12 (366): 345–46.
105. *Smaller Sutra*, Jōzen 1: 55, Seiten 1: 208, Taishō 12 (366): 348.
106. This is the summary of the passage from the *Smaller Sutra*, Jōzen 1: 55, Seiten 1: 208–9, Taishō 12 (366): 348.
107. *Commentary on the Meditation Sutra*, Jōzen 2: 71, Seiten 2: 152, Taishō 37 (1753): 278.
108. *Hymns of the Nien-fo Liturgy*, Jōzen 4: 25, Taishō 47 (1979): 435.
109. *Hymns in Praise of Birth in the Pure Land*, Jōzen 4: 372, Taishō 47 (1980): 442.
110. *Commentary on the Meditation Sutra*, Jozen 2: 10, Seiten 2: 23–24, Taishō 37 (1753): 250.
111. *Larger Sutra*, Jōzen 1: 7, Seiten 1: 28, Taishō 12 (360): 268.
112. *Methods of Contemplation on Buddha Amitābha*, Jōzen 4: 224, Taishō 47 (1959): 23.
113. *Smaller Sutra*, Jōzen 1: 53–54, Seiten 1: 202, Taishō 12 (366): 347.
114. The three thousand great-thousand worlds (Skt. *trisāhasramahāsāhasralokadhātu*) is another name for the universe. Literally, it means one thousand to the third power world realms, or one billion worlds, and is sometimes called a *trichiliocosm*. The physical feature of the long tongue covering the universe alludes to the buddhas "speaking the truth."
115. *Methods of Contemplation on Buddha Amitābha*, Jōzen 4: 235, Taishō 47 (1959): 28.
116. *Hymns of the Nien-fo Liturgy*, Jōzen 4: 22, Taishō 47 (1979): 433.
117. *Hymns in Praise of Birth in the Pure Land*, Jōzen 4: 372, Taishō 47 (1980): 446.
118. *Hymns of the Nien-fo Liturgy*, Jōzen 4: 30, Taishō 47 (1979): 437.

119. *Gudon* in Japanese. This term carries the crucial notion of the Pure Land view of man, how deeply the mind is consumed by unwholesome passions. This type of reflection is an important basis for cultivating the Pure Land faith.
120. See note 33.
121. Genkū is Hōnen's clerical name, given to him by his master Eikū on Mount Hiei. The name Genkū was made using one Chinese character from his first master, Genkō, and another from Eikū.
122. The Kegon school, a Mahāyāna school, is one of the six schools of Nara and one of the thirteen schools of China. The Kegon school was systematized by Fa-tsang (Jp. Hōzō, 643–712) in the T'ang dynasty based on the *Flower Garland Sutra*. The Kegon school classifies the teachings of Buddha Śākyamuni into five groups and regards the *Flower Garland Sutra* as the supreme and highest teaching. Kegon also asserts the idea of mutual penetration of all things (i.e., all things are encompassed in a single thing). The Kegon tradition was introduced into Japan in 736, and Tōdai-ji Temple in Nara is known as its grand head temple.
123. The dragon girl is the daughter of the dragon king, Sāgara. The "Devadatta" chapter from the *Lotus Sutra* narrates the story where she realizes enlightenment under the guidance of Buddha Mañjuśrī. Many monks did not believe she attained enlightenment because she was female, so she appeared before Buddha Śākyamuni and was transformed into a human form, thus proving her attainment of buddhahood. See the *Lotus Sutra*, Taishō 9 (26): 35. The southern buddha-world where she reached enlightenment is called Stainless.
124. These are the four stages of stream-enterer, once-returner, nonreturner, and arhat.
125. The Jōjitsu school is one of the six schools of Nara and one of the thirteen schools of China. The main text of this school is Harivarman's (250–350) *True Attainment Treatise* (*Satyasiddhi Śāstra*), which asserts that everything is provisional existence from the standpoint of the theory of emptiness. The Jōjitsu school was introduced into Japan in 625, where it was practiced in conjunction with the Sanron school.
126. The Kusha school; one of the six schools of Nara. The Kusha school is based on Vasubandhu's Treasury of Abhidharma (*Abhidarmakośa*). The Kusha school teaches that the self is nonsubstantial but dharmas exist as constituents of diverse elements such as sensation, memory, and intelligence. The Kusha tradition was brought to Japan in 658, but it never became an independent school in Japan.
127. The 250 Hīnayāna regulations for a monk are classified into five and seven groups based on the gravity of one's negative karma.
128. The Ritsu school is one of the six schools of Nara and one of the thirteen schools of China. The Ritsu school teaches that observance of the Mahāyāna precepts, such as the threefold pure precepts, is the path leading to enlightenment. The Ritsu tradition was brought from China to Japan in 754 by the Chinese monk, Chien-chen (688–763), who established the ordination platform in Tōdai-ji Temple. He also founded Tōshōdai-ji Temple in Nara as a center for studying the precepts.
129. See pages 16–18 of the introduction.
130. *Collection of Passages on the Blissful Land*, Jōzen 1: 693, Taishō 47 (1958): 13.
131. *The Moon-Matrix Section of the Great Collection Sutra*, Taishō 13 (397). This section, in which the Buddha explained both the concept of emptiness and the esoteric teaching of Buddhism, was translated by Dharmakṣema (385–433) into Chinese.

It contains a detailed description of the theory of nembutsu in the period of the decline of the Dharma. Chinese Pure Land monks including Tao-ch'o referred to it often.

132. *Collection of Passages on the Blissful Land*, Jōzen 1: 693, Taishō 47 (1958): 13.
133. *Hymns in Praise of Birth in the Pure Land*, Jōzen 4: 362, Taishō 47 (1980): 441.
134. These three phases derive from the three-period theory promoted by the Chinese T'ien-t'ai monk Hui-szu (515–77).
135. *Commentary on the Meditation Sutra*, Jōzen 2: 10, Seiten 2: 23, Taishō 37 (1753): 250.
136. Thus *steadfast heart* is a synonym for the threefold devotional heart. *Meditation Sutra*, Jōzen 1: 46, Seiten 1: 176, Taishō 12 (365): 344.
137. *Hymns in Praise of Birth in the Pure Land*, Jōzen 4: 354, Taishō 47 (1980): 438.
138. *Commentary on the Meditation Sutra*, Jōzen 2: 55, Seiten 2: 119, Taishō 37 (1753): 270–71.
139. *Commentary on the Meditation Sutra*, Jōzen 2: 56, Seiten 2: 120–21, Taishō 37 (1753): 271.
140. *Commentary on the Meditation Sutra*, Jōzen 2: 55–56, Seiten 2: 119–121, Taishō 37 (1753): 270–71.
141. See note 60.
142. *Collection of Essentials on Attaining Birth in the Pure Land*, Jōzen 15: 53, Taishō 84 (2682): 58.
143. *Meditation Sutra*, Jōzen 1: 47, Seiten 1: 177, Taishō 12 (365): 344.
144. *Commentary on the Meditation Sutra*, Jōzen 2: 6, Seiten 2: 15–16, Taishō 37 (1753): 248.
145. See chapter 9 of the *Collected Teachings of Hōnen-shōnin: The Chinese Anthology*, Jōzen 9: 431–33, Taishō 83 (2611): 160–61. For the list of ten virtues, see the glossary.
146. *Commentary on the Meditation Sutra*, Jōzen 2: 55, Seiten 2: 119, Taishō 37 (1753): 270–71.
147. A nearly identical passage on these four distinctive qualities of the genuine heart appears in chapter 31 below.
148. The lesser precepts admonish us to refrain from acts that may be criticized by others. These precepts, which include refraining from consuming the five pungent vegetables, from drinking wine, and from accumulating wealth and other valuables, are prescribed to avoid offending the sensibilities of other people and thus bringing ignominy upon the Buddhist order.
149. *Hymns in Praise of Birth in the Pure Land*, Jōzen 4: 354, Taishō 47 (1980): 438.
150. *Commentary on the Meditation Sutra*, Jōzen 2: 56, Seiten 2: 121, Taishō 37 (1753): 271.
151. *Commentary on the Meditation Sutra*, Jōzen 2: 2, Seiten 2: 6, Taishō 37 (1753): 246. The dominant karmic relationship is one of the three kinds of karmic relationships with Amida Buddha. It states, "The third, and dominant karmic relationship is thus explained: 'If sentient beings are mindful of Buddha Amitābha and recite his name, he will eliminate the negative karma that they have accumulated for many eons. Also, when their lives are about to end, Buddha Amitābha, together with his attendant bodhisattvas, will arrive to welcome them into the Pure Land. They cannot

be hindered by the negative karma that ties them to this delusive world. Therefore, this is called the *dominant karmic relationship.*" Also see the *Commentary on the Meditation Sutra,* Jōzen 2: 49, Seiten 2: 105, Taishō 37 (1753): 268. The three kinds of karmic relationships with Amida Buddha are described in the *Commentary on the Meditation Sutra*: (1) the immediate reliance, (2) the familiar reliance, (3) the dominant reliance (Skt. *adhipati-pratyaya*).

152. *Commentary on the Meditation Sutra,* Jōzen 2: 2, Seiten 2: 6, Taishō 37 (1753): 246.
153. *Meditation Sutra,* Jōzen 1: 50, Seiten 1: 190–91, Taishō 12 (365): 346.
154. Ibid.
155. Ibid.
156. *Larger Sutra,* Jōzen 1: 36, Seiten 1: 135, Taishō 12 (360): 279.
157. *Hymns in Praise of Birth in the Pure Land,* Jōzen 4: 362, Taishō 47 (1980): 441.
158. *Hymns in Praise of Birth in the Pure Land,* Jōzen 4: 355, Taishō 47 (1980): 439.
159. *Hymns in Praise of Birth in the Pure Land,* Jōzen 4: 356, Taishō 47 (1980): 439.
160. *Methods of Contemplation on Buddha Amitābha,* Jōzen 4: 224–27, Taishō 47 (1959): 23–24.
161. All quotes in the next three paragraphs come from *Commentary on the Meditation Sutra,* Jōzen 2: 56, Seiten 2: 121, Taishō 37 (1753): 271.
162. This and the extract that follow are summaries of the passage that states "... establishing an unshakable faith in birth in the Pure Land with respect to persons" in *Commentary on the Meditation Sutra,* Jōzen 2: 57, Seiten 2: 122, Taishō 37 (1753): 271.
163. *Larger Sutra,* Jōzen 1: 7, Seiten 1: 28, Taishō 12 (360): 268.
164. These are the four continents lying in four cardinal directions from Mount Meru.
165. *Hymns of the Nien-fo Liturgy,* Jōzen 4: 16, Taishō 47 (1979): 431.
166. *Hymns in Praise of Birth in the Pure Land,* Jōzen 4: 357, Taishō 47 (1980): 439.
167. *Larger Sutra,* Jōzen 1: 7, Seiten 1: 28, Taishō 12 (360): 268.
168. Here, the phrase "ten moments of being mindful of me" written in the first fascicle of the *Larger Sutra* is changed to "recite *Namu Amida Butsu* ten times." Chinese Pure Land forerunners were so deeply concerned with the emancipation of the masses that they developed an appropriate form of nembutsu for the populace. It was Shan-tao who finally negated the practice of meditation simply because it is too difficult for ordinary people to practice and advocated the vocal nembutsu as the sole Pure Land practice for the masses. See Shan-tao's *Methods of Contemplation on Buddha Amitābha,* Jōzen 4: 233, Taishō 47 (1959): 27. Also see the *Hymns in Praise of Birth in the Pure Land,* Jōzen 4: 356, Taishō 47 (1980): 447.
169. *Meditation Sutra,* Jōzen 1: 46, Seiten 1: 176, Taishō 12 (365): 344.
170. *Larger Sutra,* Jōzen 1: 7, Seiten 1: 28, Taishō 12 (360): 268.
171. *Liturgy for the Rite of the Fivefold Rhythmic Chanting of Nien-fo,* Jōzen 6: 686, Taishō 47 (1983): 481.
172. *Meditation Sutra,* Jōzen 1: 46, Seiten 1: 176, Taishō, 12 (365): 344.
173. *Hymns in Praise of Birth in the Pure Land,* Jōzen 4: 354, Taishō 47 (1980): 438.
174. *Smaller Sutra,* Jōzen 1: 54, Seiten 1: 202, Taishō 12 (366): 347.
175. *Commentary on the Meditation Sutra,* Jōzen 2: 58, Seiten 2: 126, Taishō 37 (1753): 272.

176. *Commentary on the Meditation Sutra*, Jōzen 2: 55, Seiten 2: 119, Taishō 37 (1753): 270.
177. Shan-tao's *Methods of Contemplation on Buddha Amitābha*, Jōzen 4: 262, Taishō 47 (1959): 24; and chapter 6 of Eshin's *Collection of Essentials on Attaining Birth in the Pure Land*, Jōzen 15: 108–12, Taishō 84 (2682): 67–71.
178. *Hymns in Praise of Birth in the Pure Land*, Jōzen 4: 360, Taishō 47 (1980): 440.
179. *Commentary on the Meditation Sutra*, Jōzen 2: 62, Seiten 2: 133, Taishō 37 (1753): 274.
180. *Commentary on the Meditation Sutra*, Jōzen 2: 58, Seiten 2: 126, Taishō 37 (1753): 272.
181. Her story is in the "Devadatta" chapter of the *Lotus Sutra*. See note 123.
182. *Larger Sutra*, Jōzen 1: 7, Seiten 1: 28, Taishō 12 (360): 268.
183. *Commentary on the Meditation Sutra*, Jōzen 2: 49, Seiten 2: 105, Taishō 37 (1753): 268.
184. *Hymns in Praise of Birth in the Pure Land*, Jōzen 4: 356, Taishō 47 (1980): 439.
185. See pages 14–16 in the introduction.
186. The four treatises elaborating the theory of "emptiness" are the three treatises of the Sanron, or "Three Treatise," school mentioned in note 98 above with the addition of the *Great Commentary on the Perfection of Wisdom* (*Mahāprajñāpāramitā Śāstra*) attributed to Nāgārjuna. A subschool of the Three Treatise school in China called the Four Treatise school was based on the teachings of these four works.
187. K'uei-chi, one of the greatest disciples of Hsüan-tsang, was the founder of the Fa-hsiang school in China. He was born in Ch'ang-an, became a disciple of Hsüan-tsang at the age of seventeen, studied Sanskrit at Tz'u-en Temple, and engaged himself in translating voluminous sutras, commentaries, and tantras Hsüan-tsang had brought back from India. The most significant work he helped translate with Hsüan-tsang was the *Treatise on the Attainment of Consciousness-Only* (*Vijñaptimātratāsiddhi Śāstra*). It is said that he also composed the *Essentials for Birth in the West*, but this is still debated.
188. *Essentials for Birth in the West*, Jōzen 6: 603, Taishō 47 (1964): 109.
189. *Essentials for Birth in the West*, Jōzen 6: 605, Taishō 47 (1964): 110.
190. *Record of Holy Chu-lin Temple*, by Fa-chao, one fascicle. This text is not extant, but it is described in the biography of Fa-chao in the *Sung Biographies of Eminent Monks*. See Taishō 50 (2061): 844.
191. Fa-chao (eighth century), known as the successor to Shan-tao, produced the *Liturgy for the Rite of the Fivefold Rhythmic Chanting of Nien-fo* in 774. See pages 24–25 in the introduction.
192. *Record of Holy Chu-lin Temple*, Taishō 50 (2061): 844.
193. *Hymns of the Nien-fo Liturgy*, Jōzen 4: 25, Taishō 47 (1979): 435.
194. *Sutra of Universal Enlightenment*, Taishō 12 (361): 299.
195. *Liturgy for the Rite of the Fivefold Rhythmic Chanting of Nien-fo*, comp. Fa-chao (Jp. Hosshō), Jōzen 6: 686, Taishō 47 (1983): 481.
196. *Collection of Passages on the Blissful Land*, Jōzen 1: 693, Taishō 47 (1958): 13.
197. Ibid.
198. *Larger Sutra*, Jōzen 1: 7, Seiten 1: 28, Taishō 12 (360): 268. Also see the *Methods of Contemplation on Buddha Amitābha*, Jōzen 4: 233, Taishō 47 (1959): 27.

199. *Hymns in Praise of Birth in the Pure Land,* Jōzen 4: 376, Taishō 47 (1980): 447.
200. *Meditation Sutra,* Jōzen 1: 46, Seiten 1: 176, Taishō 12 (365): 344.
201. *Commentary on the Meditation Sutra,* Jōzen 2: 55, Seiten 2: 119, Taishō 37 (1753): 270.
202. *Commentary on the Meditation Sutra,* Jōzen 2: 56, Seiten 2: 121, Taishō 37 (1753): 271.
203. *Hymns in Praise of Birth in the Pure Land,* Jōzen 4: 354, Taishō 47 (1980): 438.
204. *Commentary on the Meditation Sutra,* Jōzen 2: 56, Seiten 2: 121, Taishō 37 (1753): 271.
205. *Hymns in Praise of Birth in the Pure Land,* Jōzen 4: 354, Taishō 47 (1980): 438.
206. *Commentary on the Meditation Sutra,* Jōzen 2: 56, Seiten 2: 120, Taishō 37 (1753): 271.
207. Ibid.
208. *Sutra in Praise of the Pure Land,* Jōzen 1:188, Taishō 12 (367): 350.
209. *Meditation Sutra,* Jōzen 1: 49, Seiten 1: 186, Taishō 12 (365): 345.
210. *Commentary on the Meditation Sutra,* Jōzen 2: 57, Seiten 2: 122, Taishō 37 (1753): 271.
211. *Shi* (Skt. *śamatha*) means concentration and *kan* (Skt. *vipaśyanā*) means insight. Accordingly, *shikan*, or *śamatha-vipaśyanā*, refers to the realization of enlightenment through concentration and insight—here, as taught in the Tendai school.
212. *Larger Sutra,* Jōzen 1: 7, Seiten 1: 28, Taishō 12 (360): 268.
213. *Commentary on the Meditation Sutra,* Jōzen 2: 58–59, Seiten 2: 126, Taishō 37 (1753): 272.
214. *Hymns in Praise of Birth in the Pure Land,* Jōzen 4: 354, Taishō 47 (1980): 438.
215. *Commentary on the Meditation Sutra,* Jōzen 2: 58, Seiten 2: 125, Taishō 37 (1753): 272.
216. Ibid.
217. Ibid.
218. *Commentary on the Meditation Sutra,* Jōzen 2: 58, Seiten 2: 126, Taishō 37 (1753): 272.
219. The original text states, "only one or two out of one hundred, and only three or five out of one thousand attain birth in the Pure Land." See the *Hymns in Praise of Birth in the Pure Land,* Jōzen 4: 356–57, Taishō 47 (1980): 439.
220. The author of this text is unknown, but it was probably compiled in China around the sixth century. It is an apocryphal work popular in China and Japan. Tao-ch'o quoted this work in his *Collection of Passages on the Blissful Land.*
221. *Hymns in Praise of Birth in the Pure Land,* Jōzen 4: 375–76, Taishō 47 (1980): 447–48.
222. See note 40.
223. Lady Kujō Kaneko (1152–1201) was the consort of Regent Kujō Kanezane (1149–1207), a strong patron-disciple of Hōnen. She received the Buddhist precepts from Hōnen a year before her death.
224. *Collection of Essentials on Attaining Birth in the Pure Land,* Jōzen 15: 108, Taishō 84 (2682): 67.
225. *Larger Sutra,* Jōzen 1: 19, Seiten 1: 72, Taishō 12 (360): 272.
226. Dengyō-daishi Saichō (767–822) was the founder of the Tendai school in Japan.

227. The instructions on destroying the seven disasters is described in chapter 25 of the *Lotus Sutra*, "Gateway to Every Direction." The seven disasters arise from fire, water, malevolent spirits, an evil king, dead spirits, confinement, and bandits. See the *Lotus Sutra*, Taishō 9 (262): 56.
228. This is addressed to the same figure as chapter 8. See introduction and note 40.
229. See notes 42–43.
230. *Hymns of the Nien-fo Liturgy*, Jōzen 4: 25, Taishō 47 (1979): 435.
231. *Ten Conditions for Attaining Birth in the Pure Land*, Jōzen 15: 219, Taishō 84 (2683): 93.
232. *Collection of Passages on the Blissful Land*, Jōzen 1: 693, Taishō 47 (1958): 13.
233. *Moon-Matrix Section of the Great Collection Sutra*, Taishō 13 (397): 363.
234. This is a summary of quotations from *Collection of Passages on the Blissful Land*, Jōzen 1: 693, Taishō 47 (1958): 13.
235. See note 61.
236. *Ten Conditions for Attaining Birth in the Pure Land*, Jōzen 15: 394, Taishō 84 (2683): 102.
237. This monk is Miao-le-ta-shih Chan-jan (711–82), Myōraku-daishi Tannen in Japanese; the sixth patriarch of the Chinese T'ien-t'ai school. Chan-jan was a scholarly monk in the T'ang dynasty who resided at Miao-le Temple. He studied the T'ien-t'ai doctrines under the mentorship of Hsüan-lang and composed ninety fascicles of commentaries on the three major works of the T'ien-t'ai school.
238. *Detailed Solutions for the Practical Problems in the Attainment of Tranquility through Meditation*, Taishō 46 (1912): 182.
239. *Commentary on the Meditation Sutra*, Jōzen 2: 58, Seiten 2: 125–26, Taishō 37 (1753): 272.
240. *Commentary on the Meditation Sutra*, Jōzen 2: 49, Seiten 2: 105, Taishō 37 (1753): 268.
241. *Larger Sutra*, Jōzen 1: 19, Seiten 1: 71, Taishō 12 (360): 272.
242. *Meditation Sutra*, Jōzen 1: 51, Seiten 1: 193, Taishō 12 (365): 346.
243. *Commentary on the Meditation Sutra*, Jōzen 2: 71, Seiten 2: 153, Taishō 37 (1753): 278.
244. *Meditation Sutra*, Jōzen 1: 44, Seiten 1: 166, Taishō 12 (365): 343.
245. *Methods of Contemplation of Buddha Amitabha*, Jōzen 4: 228, Taishō 47 (1959): 25.
246. *Commentary on the Meditation Sutra*, Jōzen 2: 58, Seiten 2: 126, Taishō 37 (1753): 272.
247. *Collection of Essentials on Attaining Birth in the Pure Land*, Jōzen 15: 37, Taishō 84 (2682): 33.
248. *Commentary on the Meditation Sutra*, Jōzen 2: 3, Seiten 2: 9, Taishō 37 (1753): 247.
249. On Huai-kan, see page 22 of the introduction.
250. Chih-i (538–97), the great Chinese scholar-monk, was the third patriarch of the T'ien-t'ai school. Chih-i systematized Buddhist philosophy and established the practice of concentration and insight based on the teachings of the *Lotus Sutra* and the academic tradition of Nāgārjuna.
251. *Commentary on the Meditation Sutra*, Jōzen 2: 55–56, Seiten 2: 119–21, Taishō 37 (1753): 270–71.

252. This is a summary of quotations from the *Commentary on the Meditation Sutra*, Jōzen 2: 56–58, Seiten 2: 121–26, Taishō 37 (1753): 271–72.
253. This is a summary of quotations from the *Commentary on the Meditation Sutra*, Jōzen 2: 58–59, Seiten 2: 126–27, Taishō 37 (1753): 272.
254. *Commentary on the Meditation Sutra*, Jōzen 2: 56–60, Seiten 2: 125–31, Taishō 37 (1753): 272–73.
255. *Smaller Sutra*, Jōzen 1: 54, Seiten 1: 202, Taishō 12 (366): 347.
256. *Commentary on the Meditation Sutra*, Jōzen 2: 59, Seiten 2: 126, Taishō 37 (1753): 272.
257. *Larger Sutra*, Jōzen 1: 7, Seiten 1: 28, Taishō 12 (360): 268.
258. *Larger Sutra*, Jōzen 1: 24, Seiten 1: 89, Taishō 12 (360): 347.
259. *Larger Sutra*, Jōzen 1: 7, Seiten 1: 28, Taishō 12 (360): 268.
260. *Larger Sutra*, Jōzen 1: 19, Seiten 1: 70, Taishō 12 (360): 272.
261. *Meditation Sutra*, Jōzen 1: 50, Seiten 1: 190, Taishō 12 (365): 346.
262. *Larger Sutra*, Jōzen 1: 36, Seiten 1: 135, Taishō 12 (366): 347.
263. *Smaller Sutra*, Jōzen 1: 54, Seiten 1: 202, Taishō 12 (366): 347.
264. *Smaller Sutra*, Jōzen 1: 54–55, Seiten 1: 202–7, Taishō 12 (366): 347–48.
265. *Commentary on the Meditation Sutra*, Jōzen 2: 58, Seiten 2: 125, Taishō 37 (1753): 272.
266. *Essentials for Birth in the West*, Jōzen 6: 604, Taishō 47 (1964): 109.
267. *Hymns in Praise of Birth in the Pure Land*, Jōzen 4: 355, Taishō 47 (1980): 439.
268. *Collection of Essentials on Attaining Birth in the Pure Land*, Jōzen 15: 88, Taishō 84 (2682): 57.
269. The six periods in a day are sunset from 4:00–6:00 P.M., early evening from 8:00–10:00 P.M., the beginning of night from 12:00–2:00 A.M., the end of night from 4:00–6:00 A.M., morning from 8:00–10:00 A.M., and midday from 12:00–2:00 P.M.
270. Ancient Indian unit of distance. Vasubandhu's *Treasury of Abhidharma* puts it at about four miles. Other commentators say that a *yojana* is equivalent to 16 km, 64 km, or 120 km.
271. *Essentials for Birth in the West*, Jōzen 6: 604–5, Taishō 47 (1964): 109–10.
272. Ibid.
273. Ibid.
274. *Hymns in Praise of Birth in the Pure Land*, Jōzen 4: 356, Taishō 47 (1980): 439.
275. *Treatise Clarifying Doubts Regarding Pure Land Buddhism*, Jōzen 6: 49, Taishō 47 (1960): 50.
276. *Meditation Sutra*, Jōzen 1: 50, Seiten 1: 186, Taishō 12 (365): 346.
277. *Meditation Sutra*, Jōzen 1: 51, Seiten 1: 193, Taishō 12 (365): 346.
278. *Hymns in Praise of Birth in the Pure Land*, Jōzen 4: 356, Taishō 47 (1980): 439.
279. *Hymns in Praise of Birth in the Pure Land*, Jōzen 4: 376, Taishō 47 (1980): 447.
280. *Meditation Sutra*, Jōzen 1: 46, Seiten 1: 176, Taishō 12 (365): 344.
281. *Commentary on the Meditation Sutra*, Jōzen 2: 55, Seiten 2: 119, Taishō 37 (1753): 270.
282. This is a summary of the passage from the *Commentary on the Meditation Sutra*. See Jōzen 2: 57–58, Seiten 2: 123–25, Taishō 37 (1753): 271–72.
283. *Hymns in Praise of Birth in the Pure Land*, Jōzen 4: 354, Taishō 47 (1980): 438.

284. *Sutra in Praise of the Pure Land*, Jōzen 1: 188, Taishō 12 (367): 350.
285. *Meditation Sutra*, Jōzen 1: 49, Seiten 1: 186, Taishō 12 (365): 345.
286. *Commentary on the Meditation Sutra*, Jōzen 2: 58, Seiten 2: 125–26, Taishō 37 (1753): 272.
287. *Commentary on the Meditation Sutra*, Jōzen 2: 58, Seiten 2: 126, Taishō 37 (1753): 272.
288. Ibid.
289. Ibid.
290. *Hymns in Praise of Birth in the Pure Land*, Jōzen 4: 356–57, Taishō 47 (1980): 439.
291. *Larger Sutra*, Jōzen 1: 7, Seiten 1: 28, Taishō 12 (360): 268.
292. *Hymns in Praise of Birth in the Pure Land*, Jōzen 4: 376, Taishō 47 (1980): 447.
293. *Meditation Sutra*, Jōzen 1: 44, Seiten 1: 166, Taishō 12 (365): 343.
294. *Hymns in Praise of Birth in the Pure Land*, Jōzen 4: 372, Taishō 47 (1980): 446.
295. *Meditation Sutra*, Jōzen 1: 51, Seiten 1: 193, Taishō 12 (365): 346.
296. *Commentary on the Meditation Sutra*, Jōzen 2: 71, Seiten 2: 152–53, Taishō 37 (1753): 278.
297. *Methods of Contemplation of Buddha Amitābha*, Jōzen 4: 235, Taishō 47 (1959): 28.
298. *Hymns in Praise of Birth in the Pure Land*, Jōzen 4: 356–57, Taishō 47 (1980): 439.
299. Renjō-bō Sonkaku was most likely a disciple of Hōnen, but his birthplace and personal history are unknown. According to the *Illustrated Biography of Hōnen-shōnin*, Hōjō Masako in Kamakura sent Renjō-bō Sonkaku as her courier to Hōnen to ask about the teaching of nembutsu. See chapter 25 of the *Illustrated Biography of Hōnen-shōnin* 16: 390.
300. *Hymns of the Nien-fo Liturgy*, Jōzen 4: 25, Taishō 47 (1979): 435.
301. Shinkan-bō Kansei or Kansai (d. 1200) was a Pure Land monk. Kansei became a disciple of Hōnen at the age of nineteen and studied Pure Land Buddhism under the mentorship of Hōnen. Kansei was known as a man of letters; he engaged in writing Hōnen's primary work, the *Collection on Nembutsu*. Kansei died at the age of forty-eight when Hōnen was sixty-eight years old. Chapter 48 of the *Illustrated Biography of Hōnen-shōnin* describes Hōnen's grief at the early death of Kansei.
302. A holy monk in Kuroda. Kuroda usually refers to the name of the village of Nabari in Iga Province (presently Mie Prefecture). Here, the monk is unidentified. Itō Yūkō assumed that the monk was Shunjō-bō Chōgen (1121–1206), who traveled about the provinces soliciting contributions for rebuilding Tōdai-ji Temple in Nara in 1185. Sanda Zenshin believed that the monk was Gyōken (twelfth century), a disciple of Chōgen who lived in Nabari. This is still controversial. This letter is commonly known as the *Note on a Single Page* (*Koshōsoku*), which has been as essential to understanding Hōnen's Pure Land thought as his *Single-Sheet Covenant*. In this letter, he examines the attitudes of the nembutsu devotee, focusing on the issue of faith in Pure Land Buddhism. This is compiled in chapter 21 of the *Illustrated Biography of Hōnen-shōnin*.
303. *Hymns in Praise of Birth in the Pure Land*, Jōzen 4: 354, Taishō 47 (1980): 438.
304. *Hymns of the Nien-fo Liturgy*, Jōzen 4: 25, Taishō 47 (1979): 435.
305. *Larger Sutra*, Jōzen 1: 7, Seiten 1: 28, Taishō 12 (360): 268.
306. *Hymns in Praise of Birth in the Pure Land*, Jōzen 4: 376, Taishō 47 (1980): 448.

307. *Larger Sutra*, Jōzen 1: 19, Seiten 1: 70, Taishō 12 (360): 272.
308. *Hymns in Praise of Birth in the Pure Land*, Jōzen 4: 354, Taishō 47 (1980): 438.
309. *Meditation Sutra*, Jōzen 1: 50, Seiten 1: 190, Taishō 12 (365): 346.
310. Ibid.
311. This is a summary of the passage from the *Commentary on the Meditation Sutra*. See Jōzen 2: 57–58, Seiten 2: 123–25, Taishō 37 (1753): 271–72.
312. *Sutra in Praise of the Pure Land*, Jōzen 1: 188, Taishō 12 (367): 350.
313. *Hymns in Praise of Birth in the Pure Land*, Jōzen 4: 356–57, Taishō 47 (1980): 439.
314. See note 60.
315. *Collection of Essentials on Attaining Birth in the Pure Land*, Jōzen 15: 151–53, Taishō 84 (2682): 87–88.
316. *Commentary on the Meditation Sutra*, Jōzen 2: 58, Seiten 2: 126, Taishō 37 (1753): 272.
317. See note 226.
318. *Complete Works of Dengyō-daishi-I* (Jp. *Dengyō-daishi Zenshū*), five vols. (Kyōto: Hieizan tosho kankōsho, 1927), p. 418.
319. *Meditation Sutra*, Jōzen 1: 50, Seiten 1: 190, Taishō 12 (365): 366.
320. *Hymns in Praise of Birth in the Pure Land*, Jōzen 4: 376, Taishō 47 (1980): 448.
321. *Methods of Contemplation of Buddha Amitābha*, Jōzen 4: 226, Taishō 47 (1959): 24.
322. *Hymns in Praise of Birth in the Pure Land*, Jōzen 4: 354, Taishō 47 (1980): 438.
323. *Commentary on the Meditation Sutra*, Jōzen 2: 58, Seiten 2: 126, Taishō 37 (1753): 272.
324. *Commentary on the Meditation Sutra*, Jōzen 2: 62, Seiten 2: 133, Taishō 37 (1753): 274.
325. *Larger Sutra*, Jōzen 1: 20, Seiten 1: 73, Taishō 12 (360): 268.
326. *Commentary on the Meditation Sutra*, Jōzen 2: 10, Seiten 2: 24, Taishō 37 (1753): 250.
327. *Commentary on the Meditation Sutra*, Jōzen 2: 58, Seiten 2: 126, Taishō 37 (1753): 272.
328. *Larger Sutra*, Jōzen 1: 7, Seiten 1: 29, Taishō 12 (360): 268.
329. *Meditation Sutra*, Jōzen 1: 46, Seiten 1: 176, Taishō 12 (365): 344.
330. See note 46.
331. A prominent disciple of Hōnen. Ryūkan (1148–1227) upheld the principle of the multiple recitations of nembutsu for attaining birth in the Pure Land and established the Chōraku-ji lineage, a subschool of Jōdo Shū. Chōraku-ji Temple, established earlier by Saichō, was situated east of Maruyama Park in Kyōto.
332. *Larger Sutra*, Jōzen, 1: 7, Seiten 1: 28, Taishō 12 (360): 268.
333. *Hymns in Praise of Birth in the Pure Land*, Jōzen 4: 356, Taishō 47 (1980): 439.
334. *Commentary on the Meditation Sutra*, Jōzen 2: 58, Seiten 2: 126, Taishō 37 (1753): 272.
335. *Meditation Sutra*, Jōzen 1: 46, Seiten 1: 176, Taishō 12 (365): 344.
336. *Commentary on the Meditation Sutra*, Jōzen 2: 55, Seiten 2: 119, Taishō 37 (1753): 271.
337. *Shin'nyokan* in Japanese. The meditative practice on the ultimate reality was a concept espoused by Genshin. See the *Complete Works of Eshin-sōzu-I* (*Eshin-sōzu Zenshū*), five vols. (Kyōto: Hieizan tosho kankōsho, 1984), p. 451.

338. A religious meal for purification, taken before noon, with abstention from food in the afternoon.
339. Lay followers are encouraged to observe the eight precepts on the eighth, fourteenth, fifteenth, twenty-third, twenty-ninth, and thirtieth days of each month.
340. A strand of five-colored thread, usually made up of blue, yellow, red, white, and black threads, was commonly used during the Heian period (794–1185) by nembutsu devotees on their deathbed. The devotees held one end of the thread in their hands and placed the other end of the thread in the left hand of Amida Buddha, symbolizing their connection to the Pure Land.
341. An eminent monk or master, a master who bestows the precepts, is a title given to officially appointed eminent priests of the Tendai and Shingon schools.
342. Bodhisattva Sadāparibhūta is mentioned in the *Lotus Sutra*, stating, "He was called Bodhisattva Sadāparibhūta because whenever he saw any monk, priestess, layman, or laywoman, he would pay homage to them, saying, 'I deeply respect you and dare not belittle you. Why is this? Because all of you are practicing the path toward becoming buddhas.'" See chapter 10 of the *Lotus Sutra*, Taishō 9 (262): 50.
343. In medieval Japan, this was someone, neither ordained nor lay, who became a professional wandering teacher of Buddhism.
344. The Buddhist walking staff is equipped with metal rings at the top that make sounds each time the staff touches the ground. The sounds are supposed to frighten off any small animals and reptiles that might be injured or killed by the Buddhist pilgrim walking through a forest or meadow. The reference here is to chapter 7 of the *Flower Garland Sutra*, which states, "When using a Buddhist walking staff, you should sincerely recite the words of the scripture in order to show all sentient beings the true path of the Dharma." See Taishō 9 (278): 431.
345. The Chinese and Japanese used to believe that the birth date is impure because birth caused many deaths of mothers and babies. Therefore, they celebrated everyone getting one year old together with the New Year celebration. The sexagenary cycle counts days and years by combining ten stems and twelve branches to arrive at sixty unique combinations. Hōnen here must be referring to performing worship on a day with the same name in the sixty-day cycle.
346. Todai-ji Temple in Nara, the grand head temple of the Kegon school, was founded by Emperor Shōmu (r. 724–49). The Great Buddha Hall burned down in 1180 and was reconstructed by the abbot Shunjō-bō Chōgen (1121–1206), a prominent disciple of Hōnen. Shitennō-ji Temple in Ōsaka is the head temple of the Wa school. It is the oldest temple compound in Japan and was built in the Asuka period (593–710).
347. The collective name for three Shintō shrines in the Kumano district of Wakayama Prefecture. The three shrines are Kumano Hongū Taisha in Hongū, Kumano Hayatama Taisha in Shingū, and Kumano Nachi Taisha in Nachi. From ancient times, Kumano was believed to be a dwelling place of deities and became the center of mountain worship. In the middle of the Heian period, Kumano Hongū Taisha was regarded as the holy place where Amida Buddha resided, and the Kumano district, his Pure Land. Thereafter, the worship of Amida Buddha, the Buddha of Healing, and the Thousand-Armed Bodhisattva became popular in Kumano.
348. See note 331.
349. See also chapter 44 of the *Illustrated Biography of Hōnen-shōnin*.

350. See note 49.
351. *Solution to Problems Regarding Shōkō's Jushuin*, Jōzen 10: 34, Seiten 5: 103.
352. This work is not extant.
353. This *Dialogue on the Next Life* (*Kantei Mondō-shū*) is most likely the *Kantei Gose Monogatari*, in two fascicles, composed by Ryūkan and published in 1692 (Jōzen *zoku* 9). This work articulates Ryūkan's rationale for accumulating recitations of nembutsu for birth in the Pure Land.
354. See note 50.
355. This text describes the contents of the heart that aspires to enlightenment and its later development, but the passage Hōnen cites here is not found in it.
356. A similar passage appears as the final question in chapter 22 above.
357. *Hymns in Praise of Birth in the Pure Land*, Jōzen 4: 376, Taishō 47 (1980): 447.
358. Ibid. See also *Methods of Contemplation of Buddha Amitābha*, Jōzen 4: 233, Taishō 47 (1959): 27.
359. *Larger Sutra*, Jōzen 1: 7, Seiten 1: 29, Taishō 12 (360): 268.
360. *Hymns in Praise of Birth in the Pure Land*, Jōzen 4: 376, Taishō 47 (1980): 447.
361. Jūshin-bō Kakuyu (1158–1233). Jūshin-bō was born in Kyōto and studied the Tendai doctrines under the mentorship of Ryōkei at Onjō-ji Temple in Mii. Jūshin-bō later asked a question of Hōnen regarding birth in the Pure Land through the recitation of nembutsu while he was living in Izumo-ji Temple in Kyōto. He then became an ardent nembutsu practitioner. It is said that Jūshin-bō experienced birth in the Pure Land while still living.
362. Also called Onjō-ji Temple, in Ōtsu, Shiga Prefecture. Founded in 686 by Ōtomo no Yota, this became the head temple of the Tendai Jimon school.
363. This work is not extant.
364. On Shōkō-bō Benchō (1162–1238), the second patriarch of Jōdo Shū, see note 36.
365. The illiterate seer Awanosuke, from Fushimi in Kyōto, had a penchant for negative behavior. Realizing the error of his ways and concerned about the life to come, his heart awoke to enlightenment, and he became a disciple of Hōnen. Awanosuke always carried two-ringed prayer beads with which he counted the number of his recitations of nembutsu. Jōdo Shū nembutsu devotees use this type of prayer beads to this day for their daily nembutsu.
366. This work is not extant.
367. *Personal Seal Attesting to the Transmission of Hōnen's Teaching of Nembutsu for the Future Generations*, composed by Shōkō (1162–1238), Jōzen 10, Seiten 5, Taishō 83 (2613). After Hōnen's death in 1212, various interpretations of his nembutsu came out, which deeply concerned Shōkō. In 1228, Shōkō observed a special nembutsu retreat for forty-eight days at Ōjō-in Temple in Higo Province (presently Kumamoto Prefecture) and composed this work in order to prevent the spread of erroneous views.
368. Hōnen means "spontaneous awakening." I don't quite understand what "with no special reason" is getting at here, since Hōnen renounced the world in response to his father's death. This paragraph may have been a later insertion, but we can't know for sure.

369. *Commentary on the Meditation Sutra*, Jōzen 2: 58, Seiten 2: 126, Taishō 37 (1753): 272.
370. *Collection of Essentials on Attaining Birth in the Pure Land*, Jōzen 15: 108, Taishō 84 (2682): 67.
371. This text is not extant, but this passage also appears in the opening of the *Collection on Nembutsu*.
372. Kakuchō (960–1034), a Tendai monk on Mount Hiei, was born in Izumi Province (present-day Ōsaka). Kakuchō lost his parents at the age of thirteen, and so Genshin took him to Mount Hiei, where he entered the priesthood, learned the Tendai doctrines, and also studied rituals of esoteric Buddhism. Kakuchō later composed various works relating to the esoteric Buddhism of the Tendai school.
373. *In-Depth Study of the Collection on Nembutsu*, Jōzen 7: 95–96, Seiten 3: 284–85.
374. This work is not extant.
375. See note 51.
376. This most likely refers to Shōkō's *Collection of the Essentials on Jōdo Shū* (Jōzen 10), also called the *Chinzei Yōshū* or *Sai Yōshū*. The same passage is not found in this work, however.
377. The following translations are based on Coates and Ishizuka's work. See chapter 30 of the *Illustrated Biography of Hōnen-shōnin*.
378. Skt. *Gṛdhrakūṭa*. This mountain near Rājagṛha is where Buddha Śākyamuni is said to have preached the *Heart Sūtra* among other discourses.
379. These are: (1) Hell of Repeating Torments (Skt. *Saṃjīva*, Jp. *Tōkatsu-jigoku*), (2) Hell of the Black Cable (Skt. *Kālasūtra*, Jp. *Kokujō-jigoku*), (3) Hell of Combined Torments (Skt. *Saṃghāta*, Jp. *Shūgō-jigoku*), (4) Hell of Wailing (Skt. *Raurava*, Jp. *Kyōkan-jigoku*), (5) Hell of Great Wailing (Skt. *Mahāraurava*, Jp. *Daikyōkan-jigoku*), (6) Hell of Scorching Heat (Skt. *Tāpana*, Jp. *Shōnetsu-jigoku*), (7) Hell of Great Scorching Heat (Skt. *Pratāpana*, Jp. *Daishonetsu-jigoku*), and (8) Hell of Continuous Torments (Skt. *Avīci*, Jp. *Muken-jigoku*). Genshin's *Collection of Essentials on Attaining Birth in the Pure Land* gives fearful and detailed descriptions of these hells.
380. The Golden Glen (a famous park in China's Hunan Province) and the Southern Mansion (a famous place for moon-viewing in China) were introduced in Chinese poems in the *Collection of Chinese and Japanese Poems* (*Wakan Roei-shū*) by Fujiwara no Kinto (966–1041) during the Heian period. The idea of the Southern Mansion comes from a poem by General Yu-liang of the ancient Tsin dynasty, who wrote about the beauty of the autumn moon from the southern belvedere of the Wu-ch'ang Castle.
381. *Collection of Passages on the Blissful Land*, Jōzen 1: 706, Taishō 47 (1958): 20, and also see the *Worship and Repentance Through Reciting the Name of Amida Buddha* (*Butsumyōe Raisan-gi*) in the *Collection of the Services of Jōdo Shū*, p. 251.
382. *Meditation Sutra*, Jōzen 1: 50, Seiten 1: 190, Taishō 12 (365): 366.
383. Hsiung-chün was a Chinese monk active during the T'ang dynasty. His secular surname was Chou. An account of Hsiung-chün appears in the *Sung Biographies of Eminent Monks*, Taishō 50 (2061): 865.

384. *Collection of Essentials on Attaining Birth in the Pure Land,* Jōzen 15: 128, Taishō 84 (2682): 76.
385. Queen Vaidehī, whose tragedy is recounted in the *Meditation Sutra*, was the consort of King Bimbisāra of Magadha during the time of Buddha Śākyamuni and the mother of Prince Ajātaśatru. She asked Buddha Śākyamuni for counsel while she was imprisoned by her son.
386. See the glossary.
387. *Commentary on the Meditation Sutra,* Jōzen 2: 2, Seiten 2: 6, Taishō 37 (1753): 246.
388. *Larger Sutra,* Jōzen 1: 7, Seiten 1: 28, Taishō 12 (360): 268.
389. *Hymns in Praise of Birth in the Pure Land,* Jōzen 4: 376, Taishō 47 (1980): 447.
390. *Meditation Sutra,* Jōzen 1: 51, Seiten 1: 193, Taishō 12 (365): 346.
391. *Meditation Sutra,* Jōzen 1: 43, Seiten 1: 164, Taishō 12 (365): 343. Also see the *Hymns in Praise of Birth in the Pure Land,* Jōzen 4: 372, Taishō 47 (1980): 446.
392. *Smaller Sutra,* Jōzen 1: 53–54, Seiten 1: 202, Taishō 12 (366): 347.
393. Ibid.
394. This is a summary of quotations from the *Sutra of the Samādhi of All Buddhas' Presence,* Taishō 13 (417): 899.
395. This text is not extant, but it is described in the biography of Fa-chao in the *Sung Biographies of Eminent Monks,* Taishō 50 (2061): 844.
396. Mononobe no Moriya (d. 587) served as Minister of State under Emperor Bidatsu (r. 572–85) and Emperor Yōmei (r. 585–87). The Mononobe family strongly opposed the spread of Buddhism, while the Soga family supported it. After the death of Emperor Yōmei, a Buddhist convert, the two parties battled, leading to the defeat of the Mononobe family and the murder of Moriya.
397. The two aspects of a *maṇḍala* (a geometric design representing the universe) in esoteric Buddhism. The Diamond Realm (Skt. *vajradhātu*) represents the wisdom of Buddha Mahāvairocana, and the Womb Realm (Skt. *garbhadhātu*) represents the all-encompassing compassion of Buddha Mahāvairocana.
398. *Sutra Resolving Doubts Regarding the Period of the Imitative Dharma,* Taishō 85 (2870): 1337.
399. *Great Commentary on the Perfection of Wisdom,* Taishō 25 (1509): 63.
400. *Hymns of the Nien-fo Liturgy,* Jōzen 4: 25, Taishō 47 (1979): 435.
401. See the glossary.
402. The lesser forty-eight Mahāyāna precepts are prescribed in the *Brahma Net Sutra.*
403. *Meditation Sutra,* Jōzen 1: 50, Seiten 1: 190–91, Taishō 12 (365): 346.
404. *Hymns in Praise of Birth in the Pure Land,* Jōzen 4: 354, Taishō 47 (1980): 438.
405. *Commentary on the Meditation Sutra,* Jōzen 2: 58, Seiten 2: 126, Taishō 37 (1753): 272.
406. "Outstanding bodhisattvas" here are bodhisattvas who have attained the stages from the forty-first through fiftieth in the fifty-two stages of bodhisattva practice.
407. This is a summary of the establishment of the essential vow of Bodhisattva Dharmākara. See the *Larger Sutra,* Jōzen 1: 5–7, Seiten 1: 22–27, Taishō 12 (360): 267–68.
408. *Larger Sutra,* Jōzen 1: 7, Seiten 1: 28, Taishō 12 (360): 268.
409. Ibid.
410. *Smaller Sutra,* Jōzen 1: 54, Seiten 1: 203, Taishō 12 (366): 347.

411. *Methods of Contemplation on Buddha Amitābha,* Jōzen 4: 235, Taishō 47 (1959): 28.
412. *Hymns of the Nien-fo Liturgy,* Jōzen 4: 25, Taishō 47 (1979): 435.
413. *Commentary on the Meditation Sutra,* Jōzen 2: 57, Seiten 2: 124, Taishō 37 (1753): 271.
414. One of the names of Buddha Śākyamuni when he performed the bodhisattva perfections for the attainment of buddhahood. This story appears in the *Great Commentary on the Perfection of Wisdom,* Taishō 25 (1509): 89 and 151; in chapter 40 of the *Sutra of the Wise and the Foolish,* Taishō 4 (202): 404–9; and also in the second fascicle of the *Commentary on T'i-kuan's Fourfold Doctrines of the T'ien-t'ai School.*
415. *Hymns in Praise of Birth in the Pure Land,* Jōzen 4: 376, Taishō 47 (1980): 447.
416. *Hymns in Praise of Birth in the Pure Land,* Jōzen 4: 356, Taishō 47 (1980): 439.
417. His birth place, date of birth, and personal history are unknown.
418. Unknown. This text is not extant.
419. A disciple of Hōnen. His birth date and activities are unknown. Jōshō-bō's name appears in chapter 28 of the *Illustrated Biography of Hōnen-shōnin.* It states, "Tsunoto no Saburō Tamemori invited two disciples of Hōnen, Jōshō-bō and Yuigan-bō, from the capital to his province. Regarding them as senior masters, he engaged in the continuous practice of nembutsu for several days."
420. *Meditation Sutra,* Jōzen 1: 44, Seiten 1: 166, Taishō 12 (365): 343.
421. *Commentary on the Meditation Sutra,* Jōzen 2: 49, Seiten 2: 106, Taishō 37 (1753): 268.
422. Probably, this title refers to chapter 32 below, and the passage in question states, "Blindly holding fast to your life can be an obstacle to the attainment of birth in the Pure Land, but you are allowed to have... medical treatment when you are ill."
423. According to chapter 24 of the *Illustrated Biography of Hōnen-shōnin,* this lady is an aunt of Fujiwara no Nobuzane (1177–1265) of Hosshō-ji Temple, who was the director of the left section of the capital. Nobuzane had two aunts, the wife of Minamoto no Michiyoshi and the wife of Fujiwara no Sanekiyo. It is uncertain which lady is referred to here.
424. *Meditation Sutra,* Jōzen 1: 49, Seiten 1: 185–86, Taishō 12 (365): 345.
425. *Larger Sutra,* Jōzen 1: 7, Seiten 1: 29, Taishō 12 (360): 268.
426. Ibid.
427. *Hymns in Praise of Birth in the Pure Land,* Jōzen 4: 356, Taishō 47 (1980): 439.
428. *Meditation Sutra,* Jōzen 1: 50, Seiten 1: 190, Taishō 12 (365): 346.
429. *Hymns in Praise of Birth in the Pure Land,* Jōzen 4: 375, Taishō 47 (1980): 447.
430. *Hymns in Praise of Birth in the Pure Land,* Jōzen 4: 354, Taishō 47 (1980): 438.
431. *Larger Sutra,* Jōzen 1: 35, Seiten 1: 134, Taishō 12 (360): 279.
432. *Commentary on the Meditation Sutra,* Jōzen 2: 29, Seiten 2: 64, Taishō 37 (1753): 259.
433. *Larger Sutra,* Jōzen 1: 7, Seiten 1: 28, Taishō 12 (360): 268.
434. *Commentary on the Meditation Sutra,* Jōzen 2: 58, Seiten 2: 126, Taishō 37 (1753): 272.
435. *Larger Sutra,* Jōzen 1: 19, Seiten 1: 71, Taishō 12 (360): 272.
436. For these two enumerations, see the glossary.
437. *Larger Sutra,* Jōzen 1: 7, Seiten 1: 28, Taishō 12 (360): 268.
438. *Larger Sutra,* Jōzen 1: 20, Seiten 1: 73, Taishō 12 (360): 272.

439. *Larger Sutra*, Jōzen 1: 6, Seiten 1: 24, Taishō 12 (360): 267.
440. *Commentary on the Meditation Sutra*, Jōzen 2: 62, Seiten 2: 133, Taishō 37 (1753): 274.
441. The statement, "Rely upon the Dharma; do not depend upon a man," appears in the ninth fascicle of the *Great Commentary on the Perfection of Wisdom*, Taishō 25 (1509): 125.
442. *Meditation Sutra*, Jōzen 1: 46, Seiten 1: 176, Taishō 12 (365): 344.
443. *Commentary on the Meditation Sutra*, Jōzen 2: 55–56, Seiten 2: 119–21, Taishō 37 (1753): 270–71.
444. *Commentary on the Meditation Sutra*, Jōzen 2: 56, Seiten 2: 121, Taishō 37 (1753): 271.
445. *Commentary on the Meditation Sutra*, Jōzen 2: 57, Seiten 2: 122, Taishō 37 (1753): 271.
446. *Hymns in Praise of Birth in the Pure Land*, Jōzen 4: 354, Taishō 47 (1980): 438.
447. *Commentary on the Meditation Sutra*, Jōzen 2: 57, Seiten 2: 122, Taishō 37 (1753): 271.
448. *Larger Sutra*, Jōzen 1: 7, Seiten 1: 28, Taishō 12 (360): 268.
449. *Commentary on the Meditation Sutra*, Jōzen 2: 58–59, Seiten 2: 126, Taishō 37 (1753): 272.
450. *Hymns in Praise of Birth in the Pure Land*, Jōzen 4: 354, Taishō 47 (1980): 438.
451. *Liturgy for the Rite of the Fivefold Rhythmic Chanting of Nien-fo*, Jōzen 6: 683, Taishō 47 (1983): 480.
452. *Meditation Sutra*, Jōzen 1: 50, Seiten 1: 190–91, Taishō 12 (365): 346.
453. This is a summary of the description of the middle grade of the low category of birth in the Pure Land. See the *Meditation Sutra*, Jōzen 1: 49–50, Seiten 1: 188–89, Taishō 12 (365): 345–46.
454. *Commentary on the Meditation Sutra*, Jōzen 2: 56, Seiten 2: 121, Taishō 37 (1753): 271.
455. Kōbō-daishi Kūkai (774–835) was the founder of the Shingon school in Japan. Kūkai was born in Sanuki Province (present-day Kagawa Prefecture on Shikoku) during the Heian period and went to Kyōto to study Confucianism at the age of fifteen. When he was twenty-four, Kūkai composed *Indications of the Goals of the Three Teachings* (*Sangō Shiiki*) in order to show the superiority of Buddhism over Confucianism and Taoism. He then took ordination to become a Buddhist monk. In 804, Kūkai left for China, studied esoteric Buddhism under the guidance of Monk Hui-kuo of Ch'ing-lung Temple for three years, and returned to Japan with voluminous sutras and images of esoteric Buddhism. In Japan, Kūkai extensively engaged in the spread of esoteric Buddhism, established Kongōbu-ji Temple on Mount Kōya in Wakayama Prefecture as the center of the Shingon school, and was entrusted with Tō-ji Temple in Kyōto.
456. *Precious Key to the Secret Treasury*, Taishō 77 (2426): 363.
457. *Hymns in Praise of Birth in the Pure Land*, Jōzen 4: 376, Taishō 47 (1980): 447.
458. *Meditation Sutra*, Jōzen, 1: 50, Seiten 1: 189, Taishō 12 (365): 346.
459. *Liturgy for the Rite of the Fivefold Rhythmic Chanting of Nien-fo*, Jōzen 6: 686, Taishō 47 (1983): 481.

460. *Commentary on the Meditation Sutra*, Jōzen 2: 49, Seiten 2: 105, Taishō 37 (1753): 268.
461. *Smaller Sutra*, Jōzen 1: 54, Seiten 1: 202, Taishō 12 (366): 347.
462. Chia-ts'ai (seventh century); his birthplace, date of birth, and personal history are unknown, as he does not appear in any biographical anthology. He lived at Hung-fa Temple in Ch'ang-an and composed his *Treatise on the Pure Land* based on Tao-ch'o's *Collection of Passages on the Blissful Land*.
463. *Treatise on the Pure Land*, Jōzen 6: 647, Taishō 47 (1963): 93.
464. The five transcendent faculties possessed by a buddha and bodhisattva are the first five of the six transcendent faculties. The three transcendent faculties relate to the second, the fifth, and the sixth of the six transcendent faculties. See the glossary.
465. *Larger Sutra*, Jōzen 1: 13, Seiten 1: 48, Taishō 12 (360): 270.
466. *Sutra of Universal Enlightenment*, Taishō 12 (361): 299.
467. *Meditation Sutra*, Jōzen, 1: 49, Seiten 1: 186, Taishō 12 (365): 346.
468. *Commentary on the Meditation Sutra*, Jōzen 2: 49, Seiten 2: 105, Taishō 37 (1753): 268.
469. *Smaller Sutra*, Jōzen 1: 54, Seiten 1: 202, Taishō 12 (366): 347.
470. See Genshin's *Collection of Essentials on Attaining Birth in the Pure Land*, Jōzen 15: 112, Taishō 84 (2682): 69, and also see Yōkan's *Formulas of Birth in the Pure Land*, Jōzen 15: 467, Taishō 84 (2725): 880.
471. See chapter 8 of the *Collection of Essentials on Attaining Birth in the Pure Land*, Jōzen 15: 92, Taishō 84 (2682): 76.
472. Here, it is called the eight questions, but there are actually only seven. It is uncertain if one answer is missing or if the seventh answer is divided into two.
473. *Hymns in Praise of Birth in the Pure Land*, Jōzen 4: 354, Taishō 47 (1980): 438.
474. *Commentary on the Meditation Sutra*, Jōzen 2: 58, Seiten 2: 126, Taishō 37 (1753): 272.
475. *Hymns of the Nien-fo Liturgy*, Jōzen 4: 17, Taishō 47 (1979): 431.
476. Respectively, the *Ketsujō Ōjō Gyōsō-shō*, *Hongan Sōō-shō*, *Anjin Kigyō Sagō-shō*, and *Kujō no kita no mandokoro e mairasu gohenji*. None of these four works are extant.
477. *Nijūni Mondō*. This reply is not extant.
478. *Rinjū Gyōgi*. It is said that this work was composed by Hōnen, but its authorship has been controversial. See the *Shōwa Shinshū Hōnen-shōnin Zenshū* [*Shōwa Edition of the Complete Works of Hōnen-shōnin*], pp. 917–20.
479. The attribution of this work to Hōnen has also been controversial. See the *Shōwa Shinshū*, pp. 983–87.
480. A now ruined temple in Saga, Kyōto, that was established by Nembutsu-bō Ryōchin, a disciple of Hōnen.
481. Nison-in Temple is a Tendai temple in Saga, Kyōto. Emperor Saga (766–842) first established the temple, and Hōnen restored the temple and stayed there for a short period. Hōnen's *Monition in Seven Articles* is preserved in Nison-in Temple today.
482. Unknown.
483. Kitano Shrine in Kamigyō Ward, Kyōto, is dedicated to the spirit of Sugawara no Michizane (845–903), a scholar and court official. Hirano Shrine, a former national shrine in Kita Ward, Kyōto, was transferred from Yamato no kuni (presently Nara

Prefecture) when Emperor Kanmu (737–806) moved the capital from Nara to Kyōto.

484. *Goroku Genki.* Unknown.

485. Enchi (d. 1357) was a Jōdo Shū priest and the eleventh archbishop of Chion-in Temple in Kyōto, but it is not certain that this Enchi is the same one whose name appears here.

486. Unknown.

487. Originally a Hindu god, the same as Viṣṇu. A divinity who is extremely strong and protects the Buddha.

Glossary

ācārya. An eminent monk or master, a master who bestows the precepts, a title given to officially appointed eminent priests of the Tendai and Shingon schools.

Ānanda. The most erudite of Buddha Śākyamuni's disciples, Ānanda was a cousin of Buddha Śākyamuni and served as his attendant for the last twenty-five years of the Buddha's life. Ānanda was known for his unequalled memory, and after the passing of Buddha Śākyamuni, Ānanda recited the Dharma at the first Buddhist assembly.

arhat. One who reached the highest religious stage in Hīnayāna Buddhism. One who attains this stage has eliminated defilements and is free from all delusive attachments.

Bodhisattva Avalokiteśvara (Jp. *Kannon-bosatsu*). The bodhisattva of great compassion is one of the two attendant bodhisattvas of Amida Buddha. He is also called the "bodhisattva who freely perceives the worlds of the ten directions" (Jp. *Kanjizai-bosatsu*).

Bodhisattva Mahāsthāmaprāpta (Jp. *Seishi-bosatsu*). The bodhisattva of great wisdom is one of the two attendant bodhisattvas of Amida Buddha. He usually stands on the righthand side of Amida Buddha.

Bodhisattva Maitreya. Maitreya is believed to be the buddha to come. He is said to reside in Tuṣita Heaven at the moment and is to appear in this world 5,670 million years after the death of Buddha Śākyamuni in order to save future sentient beings.

defilement (Skt. *kaṣāyāḥ*). *See* five defilements

delusive. Characterized by the delusions or afflictions (Skt. *kleśa*), such as attachment, anger, ignorance, and pride. Along with karma, the afflictions keep sentient beings locked in the cycle of suffering transmigration.

delusive triple realms (Skt. *trayodhātavaḥ*). Unenlightened beings cycle through three worlds: (1) the realm of desire, comprising the world of hell beings, starving spirits, animals, fighting spirits, human beings, and heavenly beings; (2) the realm of form, in which inhabitants have neither sexual desire nor other appetites; (3) the realm of the formless, in which there are no material elements and entities enjoy only meditative states.

dependent reward. The circumstantial or environmental aspect of residual karma from previous lives.

Dharma body (Skt. dharmakāya). *See under* rewarded buddha

eight and nine traditional schools of Japanese Buddhism. The Kusha, Jōjitsu, Ritsu, Hossō, Sanron, and Kegon schools were practiced in the southern capital, Nara, during the Nara period and the Tendai and Shingon schools were established during the Heian period (794–1185). During the Kamakura period (1192–1333), the Dharma (Zen) school with the Heart of the Buddha was founded. These nine schools were referred to as the nine traditional schools (Jp. *kushū*).

eight difficult conditions. (Skt. *aṣṭākṣāṇāḥ*). These are the life circumstances in which one can neither see a buddha nor hear his teachings due to (1) staying in hell, (2) existing as a starving spirit, (3) existing as a beast, (4) staying in heaven for a long time, (5) being in Uttarakuru (which has too much pleasure), (6) being deficient in the sensory organs, (7) being consumed by worldly affairs, and (8) living in an age when Buddha Śākyamuni does not exist.

eight kinds of deities who protect Buddhism. Described in the *Lotus Sutra*, these are: (1) *deva*, heavenly beings who have supernatural powers, (2) *nāga*, dragons or sea serpents, (3) *yakṣa*, demons with supernatural powers who can fly, (4) *gandharva*, celestial musicians and the attendants of Indra, (5) *asura*, warring spirits who always fight with Indra, (6) *garuḍa*, supernatural birds that feed on dragons, (7) *kiṃnara*, heavenly musicians whose appearance is part human and part animal, (8) *mahoraga*, supernatural beings with human bodies and snake heads.

eight kinds of suffering. The first four kinds of suffering are: (1) the suffering of birth (Jp. *shō-ku*), (2) the suffering of old age (Jp. *rō-ku*), (3) the suffering of illness (Jp. *byō-ku*), and (4) the suffering of death (Jp. *shi-ku*). In addition to these four kinds of suffering, the following four are added: (5) the suffering of separation from beloved ones (Jp. *aibetsuri-ku*), (6) the suffering of meeting those whom one dislikes (Jp. *onzōe-ku*), (7) the suffering of the not getting what one desires (Jp. *gufutoku-ku*), and (8) the suffering of pain from the five aggregates (Jp. *goonjō-ku*).

eight major aspects. The eight major events in the life of Buddha Śākyamuni. Although there are different interpretations regarding the eight aspects, the most common is: (1) descent from Tuṣita Heaven, (2) entering his mother's womb, (3) birth, (4) leaving his household, (5) conquering all evil spirits, (6) attaining enlightenment, (7) expounding the Dharma, and (8) entering parinirvāṇa.

eight precepts (Skt. *aṣṭaśīla*). These eight are vows taken by lay people for a day at a time: (1) to refrain from taking any form of life, (2) to refrain from stealing, (3) to refrain from sexual activity, (4) to refrain from telling a lie, (5) to refrain from taking intoxicants, (6) to refrain from adorning oneself with perfumes and from enjoying dancing and singing, (7) to refrain from lying down on high and comfortable beds, and (8) to refrain from eating after noon.

eightfold negation. These are (1) no birth, (2) no extinction, (3) no cessation, (4) no permanence, (5) no uniformity, (6) no diversity, (7) no going, and (8) no coming. This negation is meant to illustrate that all phenomena exist not in and of themselves but only as dependently arisen entities. Their actual aspect emerges only when fixed conceptions of them have been negated.

fifty-two stages of bodhisattva practice. These stages outlining a bodhisattva's complete journey to enlightenment are presented in the *Flower Garland Sutra*. The first fifty are broken into five groups of ten. The first ten, the ten stages of faith, are a precursor to direct realization of reality and entrance into the bodhisattva path proper. For stages 11–40, see the entry on threefold wisdom below. Stages 41–50 are the well-known ten bodhisattva stages (*bhūmis*). And the final two stages are stages of enlightenment.

five aggregates (Skt. *pañcaskandhāḥ*). The elements constituting a person: material form, sensation of pain or pleasure, conception or discrimination, other mental formations, and basic consciousness or awareness.

five aspects of meditation. This is a theory by which one may be born in the Pure Land. Cited by Vasubandhu in his *Treatise on Birth in the Pure Land*, these five are: (1) worshiping Amida Buddha (Jp. *raihai-mon*); (2) praising his virtues by invoking his name (Jp. *sandan-mon*); (3) aspiring for birth in the Pure Land (Jp. *sagan-mon*); (4) meditating on Amida Buddha, his attendant bodhisattvas, and the majestic adornments of the Pure Land (Jp. *kanzatsu-mon*); (5) dedicating merit to save other sentient beings (Jp. *ekō-mon*). The second aspect appears to mean the recitation of nembutsu, but it actually refers to the practice of "reciting the name of Amida Buddha in order to praise twelve different designations of Amida Buddha" as presented in the *Larger Sutra*. Shan-tao established his theory of the five right practices by interpreting Vasubandhu's idea of the five aspects of meditation.

five defiled worlds. These are the six delusive worlds minus the world of fighting spirits, or *asuras*.

five defilements (Skt. *pañcakaṣāyāḥ*). The five marks of corruption in the defiled age, which are: (1) a period of social ills, such as famines, war, and plagues; (2) a period of harmful views; (3) a period of unwholesome passions; (4) a period of decline in potential; (5) a period of short lifespans.

five distinct natures of sentient beings. Based on their capabilities, these are: (1) one who is determined to become a bodhisattva, (2) one who is determined to become a pratyekabuddha, (3) one who is determined to become a śrāvaka, (4) one who is not determined to become one of the above three, and (5) one who will never be free from suffering. This theory was established by the Hossō school.

five fundamental precepts (Skt. *pañcaśīlāni*). These are the everyday vows designed for the lay Buddhist: (1) to refrain from taking any form of life, (2) to refrain from stealing, (3) to refrain from committing adultery, (4) to refrain from telling a lie, and (5) to refrain from taking intoxicants.

five grave offenses (Skt. *pañcānantarīyāṇi*). These are: (1) killing one's mother, (2) killing one's father, (3) killing an arhat, (4) causing blood to come out of the body of the Buddha, and (5) causing a schism in the Sangha.

five hindrances for a woman (Skt. *pañcāvaraṇāni*). In ancient India, it was believed that the female body was polluted and that there were five obstructions to women realizing enlightenment. According to the *Lotus Sutra*, the five hindrances for a woman are the inability to become the god kings Brahmā, Śakra, or Māra, a chakravatin king, or a buddha.

five pungent vegetables. These are leeks, onions, garlic, scallions, and ginger. Buddhist monks in Japan were prohibited from eating these vegetables as well as from eating meat.

five religious stages. Preceding the first ten of the fifty-two stages of bodhisattva practice, designed by the Tendai school, these are: (1) rejoicing upon hearing the teachings of the *Lotus Sutra*, (2) reciting the *Lotus Sutra*, (3) expounding on the teachings of the *Lotus Sutra* to others, (4) the right contemplation while practicing the six bodhisattva perfections, and (5) practicing perfectly the six bodhisattva perfections.

five right practices. *See* right practices

five transcendent faculties. Possessed by a buddha, bodhisattva, or arhat, these are the first five of the six transcendent faculties. They are: (1) the ability to go anywhere at will in a single thought-moment, (2) the ability to see countless buddhalands, (3) the ability to hear the teachings of countless buddhas, (4) the ability to read the thoughts of others, and (5) the ability to know all former existences of self and others.

five vehicles (Skt. *pancayāna*). Five divisions of the teachings of the Buddha that lead practitioners to enlightenment according to their needs as a: human being, heavenly being, śrāvaka, pratyekabuddha, or bodhisattva.

five wisdoms (Skt. *pañcajñānāni*, Jp. *gochi*). In esoteric Buddhism, the five wisdoms are attributed specifically to Buddha Mahāvairocana. They are (1) the wisdom of perceiving the quintessence of the realm of ultimate reality (Skt. *dharmadhātusvabhāvajñāna*, Jp. *hokkaitai shōchi*), (2) the wisdom that reflects all phenomena as clearly as a mirror (Skt. *ādarśajñāna*, Jp. *daien kyōchi*), (3) the wisdom of knowing that all phenomena are equally the same (Skt. *samatājñāna*, Jp. *byōdō shōchi*), (4) the wisdom of observing the distinctions among all phenomena (Skt. *pratyavekṣaṇājñāna*, Jp. *myōkan zacchi*), and (5) the wisdom of accomplishing what is to be done for oneself and others (Skt. *kṛtyānuṣṭhānajñāna*, Jp. *jōsho sacchi*).

four buddhas residing in the four quarters. As taught in esoteric Buddhism, these are: Buddha Akṣobhya (Jp. *Ashuku-butsu*) in the east, Buddha Amitābha in the west, Buddha Ratnasaṃbhava (Jp. *Hōshō-butsu*) in the south, and Buddha Amoghasiddhi (Jp. *Fukūjōju-butsu*) in the north.

four forms of fearlessness (Skt. *catvārivaiśāradyāni*). These are the four kinds of wisdom possessed by a buddha in preaching the Dharma. They are: (1) fearlessness in asserting that one has realized the perfect enlightenment (Jp. *shōtōgaku-mui*), (2) fearlessness in remarking that one has repudiated all worldly passions that hinder the realization of the Dharma (Jp. *royōjin-mui*), (3) fearlessness in explaining the matter of worldly passions (Jp. *sesshōhō-mui*), and (4) fearlessness in teaching the way to extricate oneself from worldly passions (Jp. *setsushutsudō-mui*).

four grave offenses (Skt. *pārājika*). The transgressions of monastic rules that may result in expulsion from the Buddhist Sangha: (1) taking any form of life, (2) stealing, (3) engaging in sexual intercourse, and (4) lying about one's spiritual attainments.

four great elements (Skt. *catvārimahābhūtāni*). These are the four constituent elements of the material world: earth, water, fire, and air.

four kinds of wisdom of a buddha (Skt. *catvārijñānāni*). Taught by the Yogācāra or Hossō school, these are: (1) the perfect mirror-wisdom (Skt. *ādarśajñāna*, Jp. *daien kyōchi*), (2) the wisdom of equality (Skt. *samatajñāna*, Jp. *byōdō shōchi*), (3) the wisdom of wondrous perception (Skt. *pratyaveksaṇajñāna*, Jp. *myōkan zacchi*), and (4) the wisdom of accomplishing all that is to be done (Skt. *kṛtyānuṣṭhānajñāna*, Jp. *jōsho sacchi*).

four modes of birth. All beings in the delusive triple realms are born by one of four modes of birth: (1) birth from a womb, (2) birth from an egg, (3) birth from moisture, or (4) spontaneous birth.

four modes of exercise. These exercises for a nembutsu devotee to attain birth in the Pure Land are explained in Shan-tao's *Hymns in Praise of*

Birth in the Pure Land. They are to practice nembutsu: (1) with reverence, (2) with purity, (3) with continuity, and (4) infinitely.

four noble truths (Skt. *āryasatyānicatvāri*). One of the most fundamental Buddhist teachings, said to have been the Buddha's first teaching upon reaching enlightenment: (1) there is suffering (the truth of suffering), (2) the cause of suffering is worldly passions and deluded attachments (the truth of cause), (3) suffering can be eliminated (the truth of cessation), and (4) nirvāṇa is achieved by the eightfold noble path (the truth of the path).

four paths to achieve nirvāṇa. The four stages of practice needed to attain enlightenment are (1) the stage in which a practitioner observes the threefold discipline in order to eliminate worldly passions (Jp. *kegyō-dō*), (2) the stage in which a practitioner has eliminated his worldly passions (Jp. *muken-dō*), (3) the stage in which a practitioner properly realizes the Dharma (Jp. *gedatsu-dō*), and (4) the stage in which the threefold discipline of a practitioner further develops to produce enlightenment (Jp. *shōshin-dō*).

four stages and four fruits (Skt. *catvāripramkhāni, phalāni*). To realize the religious goal of Hīnayāna Buddhism. The first stage of the path is *srotāpanna* (Jp. *yoru*, entering the stream), in which one enters the stream of the Buddhadharma and nearly eliminates one's intellectual defilements. The second stage of the path is *sakṛdāgāmin* (Jp. *ichirai*, once-returning), in which one returns only once to this world before attaining enlightenment and one nearly eliminates the volitional defilements. The third stage of the path is *anāgāmin* (Jp. *fugen*, nonreturning), in which one has exhausted all defilements of the realm of desire and is destined to realize enlightenment. The fourth stage of the path is an *arhat*, in which one attains nirvāṇa and is free from all worldly passions.

four universal vows. These are made by all bodhisattvas. They are, according to this passage from Chih-i's (538–97) *Great Concentration and Insight* (Taishō 46–1911, p. 56): "Sentient beings are numberless; I earnestly aspire to enlighten them all. The worldly passions are inexhaustible; I earnestly aspire to eradicate them all. The teachings of the Buddha are immeasurable; I earnestly aspire to comprehend them all. Enlightenment is unsurpassable; I earnestly aspire to realize it by all means."

four vehicles. The four ways to attain one's religious goal in Buddhism. They are: (1) *śrāvakayāna*, the path to become an arhat by listening to the teachings of a buddha, (2) *pratyekabuddhayāna*, the path to arhatship through solitary effort, (3) *bodhisattvayāna*, the path to attain buddhahood in order to save every suffering being, (4) *buddhayāna*, the path to attain buddhahood in this very life, sometimes associated with esoteric Buddhism.

heart of enlightenment (Skt. *bodhicitta*). To "awaken the heart of enlightenment" is to realize the bodhisattva attitude, which aspires to become a buddha so as to liberate all sentient beings from suffering. Shan-tao and Hōnen taught that ordinary beings are unable to genuinely awaken the heart of enlightenment and should focus instead on the attaining birth in the Pure Land through the power of nembutsu and then pursue the bodhisattva perfections there.

heavenly demons (Skt. *paranirmitavaśavartinodevāḥ*). The "masters of others' creations," beings of the sixth and highest heaven in the realm of desire. Hōnen suspects that buddhas who may appear to reject the nembutsu teaching are not actually buddhas but are instead this kind of being.

house on fire (Skt. *ādiptāgāra*). Refers to *saṃsāra*, the state of transmigration within the delusive triple realms of birth and death filled with worldly passions and suffering. This metaphorical expression is often employed in Buddhist texts such the *Lotus Sutra*.

Jōdo Shū. Literally "Pure Land school," the school founded by Hōnen in 1175.

Kāśyapa (Jp. *Kashō*). One of the ten great disciples of Buddha Śākyamuni. He was foremost in ascetic practices and presided over the first council after the death of Buddha Śākyamuni.

King Māra (Jp. *Maō*). The king of the heavenly demons, who rules the sixth and highest heaven within the realm of desire and deceives sentient beings.

Maudgalyāyana (Jp. *Mokuren*). One of the ten great disciples of Buddha Śākyamuni. He was born the son of a brahman and later converted to Buddhism through the persuasion of his friend Śāriputra. He was known for his supernormal abilities (*abhijñā*).

middle path (Skt. *madhyamāpratipad*). The path that leads to enlightenment and avoids two extremes: the extreme of indulgence in desire and the extreme of ascetic deprivation. This path consists of the noble eightfold path.

miscellaneous practices. Buddhist practices other than the five right practices for attaining birth in the Pure Land advocated by Shan-tao. The practices of Buddhist schools other than the Pure Land school.

Mount K'un-lun (Jp. *Konron*). The name of a fictitious mountain in Western China believed to produce precious gems. In general, it referred to the area around the Himalāyas and the Pamirs as well as the K'un-lun Mountains.

Mount Meru. According to ancient Indian cosmology, Mount Meru is the highest mountain and constitutes the center of the world. Mount Meru is surrounded by the four continents, one in each of the four cardinal directions. Jumbudvīpa (Jp. Enbudai), the southern continent, is where we are said to live.

Nāgārjuna (ca. 150–250 C.E.). The systematizer of the Madhyamaka school, which was based on the theory of emptiness (Skt. *śūnyatā*). Nāgārjuna is believed to have lived in southern India. He is accredited with composing the *Commentary on the Ten Bodhisattva Stages*, in which is introduced the notion of the "easy practice" of relying on the power of Amida Buddha so as to reach the state of *avinivartanīya* (nonregression). However, in that text, the easy practice is cast as an inferior practice.

nine grades of aspirants for birth in the Pure Land. These, explained in the *Meditation Sutra*, are categories of practitioners arranged by their potential and depth of practice. There are three major categories: (1) the high category, (2) the middle category, and (3) the low category, and each category is in turn divided into three grades—high, middle, and low.

nine kinds of worldly passions. These are: (1) desire, (2) anger, (3) arrogance, (4) ignorance, (5) aberrant views, (6) grasping at what one desires, (7) doubt, (8) envy, and (9) attachment.

nine objects of contemplation. The Tendai school expounds on the ten objects of contemplation as the proper way to observe this phenomenal world. The ten objects are: (1) the realm of phenomenal objects recognized through one's sensory organs (Jp. *in-kyō*), (2) the realm of worldly passions (Jp. *bonnō-kyō*), (3) the realm of illness (Jp. *byōgen-kyō*), (4) the realm of karmic phenomena (Jp. *gōsō-kyō*), (5) the realm of unfavorable conditions (Jp. *maji-kyō*), (6) the realm of the ultimate state of meditation (Jp. *zenjō-kyō*), (7) the realm of various views (Jp. *shoken-kyō*), (8) the realm of conceit (Jp. *zōjōman-kyō*), (9) the realm of a *śrāvakayāna* and a *pratyekabuddhayāna* (Jp. *nijō-kyō*), and (10) the realm of a bodhisattva (Jp. *bosatsu-kyō*). The nine objects of contemplation apply to the second through the tenth objects.

nonregression. *See* state of nonregression for attaining buddhahood

one vehicle (Skt. *ekayāna*). The Tendai concept that all sentient beings are able to attain enlightenment without distinguishing between Hīnayāna Buddhism and Mahāyāna Buddhism.

one who has no intrinsic goodness (Skt. *icchantika*). In early Buddhism, this referred to one who could never attain enlightenment. In Mahāyāna Buddhism, it came to refer to one who could ultimately attain enlightenment but only with great difficulty.

precept master. A Buddhist master who understands, recites, and is deeply versed in the precepts. The third rank in the Buddhist hierarchy.

pratyekabuddha. A "solitary realizer" is a Hīnayāna sage who strives to attain the state of an arhat without recourse to a teacher.

primary reward. The body received as the result of residual karma in previous lives.

realm of desire. *See* delusive triple realms

residual karma. The ripening in the present life of karmic seeds planted by actions performed in past lives with one's body, speech, or mind. These can be residual virtues leading to positive experiences or residual karmic burdens, which create obstacles along the Buddhist path as well as other kinds of misfortune.

rewarded buddha (Skt. *saṃbhogakāya*). One of the three facets of the body of a buddha (Skt. *trayokāyāḥ*). The three ways that a buddha may manifest are: (1) the *dharmakāya*, or Dharma body, the ultimate reality of a buddha in which the body transcends any physical form and is in itself absolute (can refer to the realizations in a buddha's mind); (2) the *saṃbhogakāya*, or rewarded body, is the richly adorned pure aspect of a buddha in his exalted form, his reward for having completed the bodhisattva perfections; (3) the *nirmāṇakāya*, or transformed body, the normal human body a buddha manifests so that ordinary human beings can perceive him.

right practices. These five are (1) the recitation of the three sutras of Pure Land Buddhism, (2) the contemplation of both Amida Buddha and the majestic adornments of the Land of Ultimate Bliss, (3) the worship of Amida Buddha, (4) the recitation of the name of Amida Buddha, (5) the praise of Amida Buddha and the making of offerings to him. Sometimes the final practice is divided into two, making six practices in all.

saṃsāra. The cycle of birth and death in the delusive six worlds through which ordinary beings transmigrate due to the force of their ignorance, attachment, and contaminated karma.

Śāriputra (Jp. *Sharihotsu*). One of the ten outstanding disciples of Buddha Śākyamuni. Born the son of a brahman in Magadha, he first followed Saṃjaya, along with his friend Maudgalyāyana (Jp. *Mokuren*), but later he converted to Buddhism. He was known for his brilliant intelligence and commonly referred to as the "most knowledgeable disciple." He died before Buddha Śākyamuni's entrance into parinirvāṇa.

seven kinds of precious jewels (Skt. *saptaratna*). Although these seven are variously enumerated in the Buddhist scriptures, they usually refer to gold, silver, lapis lazuli, crystal, sapphire, red pearls, and emerald. Amber, coral, and diamond are also sometimes included in this group of precious jewels.

seven past buddhas who appeared in succession in this world. They were (1) Buddha Vipaśyin, (2) Buddha Śikhin, (3) Buddha Viśvabhū, (4) Buddha Krakucchanda, (5) Buddha Kanakamuni, (6) Buddha Kāśyapa, and (7) Buddha Śākyamuni.

Shan-tao (Jp. Zendō, 613–81). The systematizer of Chinese Pure Land Buddhism in the T'ang Dynasty. Shan-tao followed the Pure Land tradition of both T'an-luan and Tao-ch'o and advocated the recitation of nembutsu for attaining birth in the Pure Land. It is said that he copied the *Smaller Sutra* more than one hundred thousand times and painted more than three hundred works of art depicting the Pure Land. Hōnen's Pure Land theory is based on Shan-tao's academic tradition of Pure Land Buddhism.

Shinran (1173–1262). The founder of Jōdo Shin Shū and a disciple of Hōnen.

six bodhisattva perfections (Skt. *ṣaḍpāramitā*). In Mahāyāna Buddhism, the six fundamental meritorious practices by which a bodhisattva attains buddhahood (1) giving (Jp. *fuse*), (2) observing the precepts (Jp. *jikai*), (3) forebearance (Jp. *nin'niku*), (4) endeavor (Jp. *shōjin*), (5) concentration (Jp. *zenjō*), and (6) wisdom (Jp. *chie*). Giving consists of three categories: (1) giving material things (Jp. *zaise*), (2) expounding on the Dharma (Jp. *hōse*), and (3) relieving fears and giving peace to other people (Jp. *muise*).

six delusive worlds of saṃsāra. The desire-realm worlds of (1) hell beings; (2) starving spirits (Skt. *preta*); (3) animals, including creatures crawling on the ground, birds, and fishes; (4) fighting spirits (Skt. *asura*); (5) human beings; (6) heavenly beings (Skt. *deva*).

six elements (Skt. *ṣaḍdhātavaḥ*). The constituents of all existence: earth, water, fire, wind, space, and consciousness.

six requirements observed by a female Buddhist novice. Those who aspire to be a nun are to refrain from (1) touching a man affectionately, (2) stealing even a small amount of money, (3) taking the lives of animals, (4) telling a lie, (5) eating after noon, and (6) taking intoxicants.

six sensory organs (Skt. *ṣaḍindriyāṇi*). These render the senses of sight, hearing, smell, taste, touch, and the mental faculty.

six stages to enlightenment. Taught by the Tendai school, these are (1) the stage in which one has not yet realized that all beings possess buddha nature, (2) the stage in which one has realized that all beings possess buddha nature, (3) the stage in which one observes the Tendai meditation and the six bodhisattva perfections, (4) the stage in which one has attained wisdom similar to that of Buddha Śākyamuni, (5) the stage in which one has attained partial enlightenment, and (6) the stage in which one has realized complete enlightenment.

six transcendent faculties (Skt. *ṣaḍabhijñāḥ*). These are attained by a buddha, bodhisattva, or arhat: (1) the ability to go anywhere at will (Jp. *jinsoku-tsū*), (2) the ability to see everything, including countless buddhalands (Jp. *tengen-tsū*), (3) the ability to hear anything, including the teachings of countless buddhas (Jp. *tenni-tsū*), (4) the ability to read the thoughts of others (Jp. *tashin-tsū*), (5) the ability to recollect all former existences of the self and others (Jp. *shukumyō-tsū*), and (6) the ability to extinguish worldly passions (Jp. *rojin-tsū*). *See also* five transcendent faculties

six types of consciousness (Skt. *ṣaḍvijñānāni*). These are: visual consciousness, auditory consciousness, olfactory consciousness, gustatory consciousness, tactile consciousness, and mental consciousness.

six varieties of dust (or defilement) (Skt. *ṣaḍviṣayāḥ*). The six objects corresponding to the six sensory organs: that is, the colors, sounds, odors, tastes, tactile objects, and mental objects that pollute one's mind.

śrāvaka. A sage who strives to become an arhat through listening to the teachings of a buddha. In this sense, all disciples of Hīnayāna Buddhism are referred to as *śrāvakas*.

state of nonregression for attaining buddhahood (Skt. *avinivartanīya*). In Hīnayāna Buddhism, this refers to the stage in which a practitioner no longer falls back into the delusive worlds of transmigration. However, in Mahāyāna Buddhism, it indicates the stage in which a bodhisattva no longer falls back to the status of a pratyekabuddha or śrāvaka. According to Jōdo Shū, it applies to the state of one who has attained birth in the Pure Land.

Tao-ch'o (Jp. *Dōshaku*) (562–645). A Chinese monk who was regarded by Hōnen as the second of the five Chinese Pure Land patriarchs. Tao-ch'o came to recite the name of Buddha Amitābha as many as seventy thousand times daily and lectured on the *Meditation Sutra* two hundred times before his death at the age of eighty-four. He composed the *Collection of Passages on the Blissful Land*. It is also said that everyone older than seven living in Chin-yang, T'ai-yüan, and Wen-shui of Shan-hsi Province, where he lived, came to understand the teachings of Buddha Amitābha and to recite nembutsu.

tathāgata. This means "thus come" or "thus gone." Mahāyāna Buddhism interprets it as "one who has come to suchness (the ultimate reality)." It generally refers to a buddha.

ten bodhisattva perfections (Skt. *daśapāramitā*). These are the practices by which a bodhisattva attains buddhahood: (1) giving, (2) observing the precepts, (3) forbearance, (4) endeavor, (5) meditation, (6) wisdom, (7) skillful means, (8) vows, (9) power, and (10) the perfect wisdom.

ten bodhisattva stages (Skt. *daśabhūmi*). These are the stages by which a bodhisattva actualizes enlightenment after becoming a noble one (Skt. *ārya*). Among what are called the fifty-two stages of bodhisattva practice, these ten correspond to stages 41 through 50. The Tendai school lists them as the stages called (41) joy, (42) freedom from all defilements, (43) emitting the light of wisdom, (44) growing wisdom, (45) overcoming all difficulties, (46) manifestation of ultimate reality, (47) proceeding far, (48) attainment of mental immobility, (49) attainment of supreme wisdom, (50) the Dharma-cloud.

ten cardinal Mahāyāna precepts. As prescribed in the *Brahma Net Sutra*, these instruct us to refrain from: (1) taking any form of life, (2) stealing, (3) engaging in sexual misconduct, (4) telling a lie, (5) ingesting or selling intoxicants, (6) speaking of the faults of others, (7) praising oneself and reviling others, (8) begrudging others, (9) harboring or inciting anger, and (10) slandering the Three Jewels. Bodhisattvas must observe these precepts and encourage others not to violate them.

ten directions. These are east, west, north, south, northeast, northwest, southeast, southwest, upward, and downward—that is, all directions. It refers to the whole universe.

ten powers of wisdom (Skt. *daśabalāni*). Attributed to a buddha, these are: (1) the power to distinguish right from wrong; (2) the power to know the karmic life of each sentient being in the three periods of past, present, and future; (3) the power to know all forms of meditation; (4) the power to know the superior and inferior capabilities of all sentient beings; (5) the power to know the desires of all sentient beings; (6) the power to know the nature of all things; (7) the power to know the ultimate goal of all sentient beings; (8) the power to know each man's previous state of existence; (9) the power to know the states of saṃsāra of all sentient beings; (10) the power to know the state and means to attain nirvāṇa.

ten regulations for Buddhist novices. A novice monk (Skt. *śrāmaṇera*) is to refrain from: (1) taking any form of life, (2) stealing, (3) sexual activity, (4) telling a lie, (5) taking intoxicants, (6) adorning oneself with perfumes, (7) singing and dancing, (8) sleeping on high and luxurious beds, (9) eating after noon, and (10) obtaining wealth and jewels.

ten transgressions. Taught in the *Meditation Sutra* these are: (1) taking life, (2) stealing, (3) engaging in sexual misconduct, (4) telling a lie, (5) abusive speech, (6) slander, (7) frivolous talk, (8) covetousness, (9) malice, and (10) perverted views.

ten virtues of Master Shan-tao. In order to praise Master Shan-tao, Hōnen presented Shan-tao's ten virtues based on the model of Chih-i. They are (1) the virtue of nembutsu with sincerity, (2) the virtue of the realization of samādhi, (3) the virtue of emitting light from his mouth, (4) the virtue of solving questions for his master, (5) the virtue of having inspired dreams during the compilation of his work, (6) the virtue of the extensive propagation of Pure Land Buddhism, (7) the virtue of the self-immolation of his followers, (8) the virtue of the emperor's devotion to Master Shan-tao, (9) the virtue of radiance from his writings, and (10) the virtue of the transcendent power of his image.

ten virtuous acts. These are refraining from the ten transgressions.

theory of the five levels of contemplation on the principles of Mind-only. Taught by the Hossō school, the five levels are: (1) rejecting the delusory existences produced by one's imagination while holding on to the actual existence; (2) abandoning the objective aspect of consciousness while retaining the subjective aspect; (3) encompassing the objective aspect of consciousness and realizing perception in the basis of consciousness; (4) concealing the inferior function (mental attributes) of consciousness while retaining the superior function of consciousness; (5) rejecting the phenomenal aspects of consciousness while realizing the true nature of consciousness.

three aspects of emptiness. A practitioner realizes these three through meditation: (1) the nonsubstantiality of the self, (2) the nonsubstantiality of existence, and (3) the nonsubstantiality of the self and existence.

three categories of acts. Physical, verbal, and mental deeds.

three categories of aspirants for birth in the Pure Land. According to the *Larger Sutra*, the people who attain birth in the Pure Land are divided into three categories: (1) the high category, (2) the middle category, and (3) the low category. The high category is further divided into these individuals: (1) one who leaves one's home, renounces one's desires, and becomes a monk; (2) one who awakens the heart of enlightenment; (3) one who is single-heartedly and exclusively mindful of Amida Buddha; (4) one who performs various meritorious deeds; and (5) one who desires to be born in the Pure Land. These are the middle category of individuals: (1) one who awakens the heart of enlightenment; (2) one who is single-heartedly and exclusively mindful of Amida Buddha; (3) one who observes the precepts; (4) one who builds a temple and makes an image of a Buddha; (5) one who offers food to monks; (6) one who adorns a ceremonial site with banners, lights lamps, scatters flowers, and burns incense; and (7) one who desires to be born in the Pure Land. These are the low category individuals: (1) one who awakens the heart of enlightenment; (2) one who wholeheartedly and exclusively desires to be born in the Pure Land with just ten moments of being mindful of Amida Buddha; (3) one who desires to be born in the Pure Land.

three lower realms. The first three of the six delusive worlds of saṃsāra, that is, the worlds of hell beings, starving spirits, and animals.

three fairy mountains. Mount P'eng-lai (Jp. *Hōrai-san*), Mount Fan-chang (Jp. *Hōjō-san*), and Mount Ying-chou (Jp. *Eishū-san*), where, according to Chinese mythology, an elixir of life exists. It is said that the mountains are somewhere in the eastern sea where a long-lived hermit resides. According to the *Historical Memoirs* (*Shih-chi*), the mountains are in the Gulf of Po-hai, where all beings are white in color and the palaces are made of gold and silver. From a far distance, the mountains look like clouds, and from a short distance, they appear to be located under the sea; however, no one can reach them.

three great innumerable eons. An extraordinarily large unit of time. It is traditionally said that it takes three incalculable eons for a bodhisattva to complete the bodhisattva perfections in order to become a buddha.

three insights. These are the second, the fifth, and sixth of the six transcendent faculties.

three kinds of attachment. Arising at the time of one's death, cited in Genshin's *Collection of Essentials on Attaining Birth in the Pure Land*, they are: (1) attachment to one's family, relatives, and material possessions (Jp. *kyōgai-ai*); (2) attachment to one's own life (Jp. *jitai-ai*); (3) attachment to one's rebirth in a particular world in the next life (Jp. *tōjō-ai*).

three kinds of wisdom. This term appears in the forty-eighth vow. The three are (1) the wisdom to recognize the truth (Jp. *hōnin*), (2) the wisdom possessed by cultivating faith (Jp. *shinnin*), and (3) the wisdom in accordance with the truth (Jp. *junnin*).

three meritorious acts. According to the *Meditation Sutra*, these are (1) worldly meritorious acts, such as filial piety and service to one's teachers and elders, (2) meritorious acts performed by way of observing the Buddhist precepts, such as never taking any form of life and treating all with kindness, and (3) meritorious acts performed by way of awakening the heart of enlightenment, such as conviction in the principle of cause and effect and reading Mahāyāna texts.

three mystic practices. Taught in esoteric Buddhism, these are: (1) the physical mystic practice, (2) the verbal mystic practice, and (3) the mental mystic practice by which one seeks to attain unity with the deity.

three vehicles (Skt. *triyāna*). The first three of the four vehicles.

threefold contemplation. The three are contemplation of (1) emptiness, (2) momentariness, and (3) the truth of the middle path.

threefold devotional heart. The three aspects of faith indispensable for attaining birth in the Pure Land of Ultimate Bliss. These three are: the genuine heart, the profound heart, and the heart that seeks birth in the Pure Land through the dedication of merit.

threefold discipline (Skt. *triṇiśikṣāṇi*). The primary Buddhist discipline, which embraces all the aspects of Buddhist teachings and practices: training in (1) ethical conduct (Jp. *kai*), (2) meditation (Jp. *jō*), and (3) wisdom (Jp. *e*).

threefold pure precepts to be observed by a bodhisattva. These are the fundamental Mahāyāna precepts. They are (1) observing the ten cardinal Mahāyāna precepts (Jp. *shōritsugikai*), (2) practicing all Buddhist teachings and cultivating virtuous deeds (Jp. *shōzenbōkai*), and (3) embracing all sentient beings and seeking compassion for them (Jp. *shōshujōkai*). The precepts are introduced in the second fascicle of the *Sutra of Bodhisattva Ornament.*

threefold wisdom. According to the Tendai and Kegon schools, the threefold wisdom refers to the three groups of ten stages each among the fifty-two stages of bodhisattva practice outlined in the *Flower Garland Sutra*. The first group applies to the ten stages of the knowledge of the Dharma, which corresponds to stages 11–20 among the fifty-two stages. The second group is the ten stages of the practice of the Dharma, which corresponds to stages 21–30. The third group is the ten stages of the dedication of merits, which corresponds to stages 31–40.

three-period theory. Promoted by Chinese T'ien-t'ai monk Hui-szu (Jp. Eshi, 514/15–77), the three periods are: (1) the period of the true Dharma (Jp. *shōbō*), (2) the period of the semblance of the Dharma (Jp. *zōhō*), and (3) the period of the decline of the Dharma (Jp. *mappō*). The first period began immediately after the death of Buddha Śākyamuni and lasted for five hundred years, during which time his teachings were rightly observed and a practitioner was able to achieve enlightenment. The second period lasted for the next thousand years. Although both the teachings and practices remained, no one was able to attain enlightenment. The third period will extend for the next ten thousand years, during which time the teachings of Buddha Śākyamuni remain but no one practices them. This concept of the period of the decline of the Dharma considerably influenced the development of Pure Land Buddhism in China and Japan. In Japanese Buddhism, it was generally taught that the period of the true Dharma lasted for a thousand years.

transformed body/buddha (Skt. *nirmāṇakāya*). A buddha's mundane human form that is visible to ordinary beings with sufficient merit. *See* rewarded buddha

Trāyastriṃśa Heaven (Jp. *Tōri-ten*). The second of the six heavens in the realm of desire, the home of Indra, is located on the top of Mount Meru.

Tripiṭaka. The three "baskets" (that is, divisions or collections) of the Buddhist scriptures: i.e., Sutra (discourses), Vinaya (monastic regulation), and Abhidharma (commentary).

Tuṣita Heaven. The pure buddhaland where Buddha Maitreya resides; also the fourth of the six heavens in the realm of desire.

twelve links of dependent origination (Skt. *dvādasāṅgapratīyasamutpāda*). One of the central teachings of Buddha Śākyamuni, the twelve links describe how the suffering of *saṃsāra* arises from ignorance. They are (1) *avidyā* (ignorance), (2) *saṃskāra* (actions produced by ignorance), (3) *vijñāna* (consciousness), (4) *nāmarūpa* (mental functions and physical elements), (5) *ṣaḍāyatana* (the six sensory organs), (6) *śparsa* (contact), (7) *vedanā* (perception), (8) *tṛṣnā* (desires), (9) *upādāna* (grasping what one desires), (10) *bhava* (existence), (11) *jāti* (birth), and (12) *jāramaraṇa* (aging and death). It is also interpreted that 1 and 2 belong to the previous life and become the causes of the present life; 3–7 are the results of the present; 8–10 are the present causes for the future; and 11 and 12 are the results in the future. Any of the twelve stages can come first, and like a wheel, there is no beginning nor end.

two vehicles. The first two of the four vehicles.

universal sovereign (Skt. *cakravartin*). The fictitious and ideal king in India who governs the entire world by turning a wheel bestowed from the sky. In Buddhism, it is thought that the king, who has the thirty-two prominent features of Buddha Śākyamuni and the seven treasures (the wheel, elephants, horses, gems, attendants, ladies, and generals), rules the four quarters with righteousness.

Vulture Peak (Skt. *Gṛdhrakūṭa*). This mountain near Rājagṛha is where Buddha Śākyamuni frequently preached.

Selected Bibliography

I. Primary Sources

Biography of Hōnen-shōnin (*Hōnen-shōnin Denki*), nine fascicles. Jōzen 17.

Biographies of Those Who Attained Birth in the Pure Land (*Ōjō Jōdo-den*). Compiled in vol. 6 of the *Tsukamoto Zenryū Chosakushū*, 7 vols. Tōkyō: Daitō shuppansha, 1976.

Brahma Net Sutra (Skt. *Brahmajāla Sūtra*, Ch. *Fa-wang-ching*, Jp. *Bommō-kyō*). Taishō 24 (1484).

Clarifying the Essentials and Promoting Wholesome Conduct (*Myōgi Shingyō-shū*), three fascicles. Attributed to Shinzui (d. 1279).

Collected Teachings of Kurodani-shōnin [Honen] (*Kurodani-shōnin Gotō-roku*). Ed. Ryōe Dōkō. Jōzen 9, Seiten 4, Taishō 83 (2611–12). This consists of the *Chinese Anthology* (*Kango Tōroku*) and the *Japanese Anthology* (*Wago Tōroku*) along with their supplements.

Collection of Essentials on Attaining Birth in the Pure Land (*Ōjō Yōshū*) by Genshin. Jōzen 15, Taishō 84 (2682).

Collection of Dialogues on Nembutsu (*Nembutsu Mondō-shū*). Not extant.

Collection of the Essentials on Jōdo Shū (*Jōdo Shū Yōshū*) by Ryōchū. Jōzen 11.

Collection of the Essentials on Jōdo Shū (*Jōdo Shū Yōshū*) by Shōkō. Jōzen 10. Also called the *Chinzei Yōshū* or *Sai Yōshū*.

Collection of Passages on the Blissful Land (Ch. *An-lo-chi*, Jp. *Anraku-shū*) by Tao-ch'o. Jōzen 1, Taishō 47 (1958).

Collection of Passages on Nembutsu Chosen in the Essential Vow (*Senchaku Hongan Nembutsu-shū*) by Hōnen. Jōzen 7, Seiten 3, Taishō 83 (2608). See also English translation below.

Collection of Stories (*Monogatari Shū*). Not extant.

Collection on Nembutsu. See *Collection of Passages on Nembutsu Chosen in the Essential Vow*

Commentary on the Meditation Sutra (Ch. *Kuan-ching-shu*, Jp. *Kangyō-sho*) by Shan-tao. Jōzen 2, Seiten 2, Taishō 37 (1753).

Commentary on the Ten Bodhisattva Stages (Skt. *Daśabhūmivibhāṣa Śāstra*, Ch. *Shih-chu-p'i-p'o-sha-lun*, Jp. *Jūjū Bibasha-ron*) by Nāgārjuna (ca. 150–250). Taishō 26 (1521).

Commentary on the Treatise on Birth in the Pure Land (Ch. *Wu-liang-shou-ching-lung-chu*, Jp. *Muryōju-kyō Ronchū*) by T'an-luan. Jōzen 1, Taishō 40 (1819).

Commentary on T'i-kuan's Fourfold Doctrines of the T'ien-t'ai School (Ch. *T'ien-t'ai-szu-chiao-i-chi-chu*, Jp. *Tendai Shikyōgi Shucchū*).

Commentary on Vasubandhu's Treatise on Birth in the Pure Land (Ch. *Wang-sheng-lun-chu*, Jp. *Ōjō Ronchū*) by T'an-luan. Jōzen 1, Taishō 40 (1819).

Compendium of the Mahāyāna (Skt. *Mahāyānasaṃgraha Śāstra*, Jp. *Shō Daijō-ron*) by Asaṅga. Taishō 31 (1593).

Complete Works of Dengyō-daishi-I (*Dengyō-daishi Zenshū*), 5 vols. Kyōto: Hieizan tosho kankōsho, 1927.

Complete Works of Eshin-sōzu-I (*Eshin-sōzu Zenshū*), 5 vols. Kyōto: Hieizan tosho kankōsho, 1984.

Detailed Solutions for the Practical Problems in the Attainment of Tranquility through Meditation (Ch. *Chih-kuan-ju-hsing-ch'uan-hung-chüeh*, Jp. *Shikan Bugyōden Guketsu*), forty fascicles, by Chan-jan. Taishō 46 (1912).

Dialogue on the Next Life (*Kantei Mondō-shū*), two fascicles, by Ryūkan. Jōzen *zoku* 9.

Discourse on Ten Issues Regarding Birth in the Pure Land (Ch. *Ching-t'u-shih-i-lun*, Jp. *Jōdo Jūgi-ron*) by Chih-i. Jōzen 6, Taishō 47 (1961).

Discourses Treating Enumerations (*Zōichi Agongyō*). Taishō 2 (125).

Dialogue on Twenty-Eight Topics (*Nijūhachi Mondō*). Not extant.

Essentials for Birth in the West (Ch. *Hsi-fang-yao-chüeh*, Jp. *Saihō Yōketsu*) by K'uei-chi. Jōzen 6, Taishō 47 (1964).

Flower Garland Sutra (Skt. *Avataṃsaka Sūtra*, Ch. *Hua-yen-ching*, Jp. *Kegon-kyō*). Taishō 9 (278, 279, and 293).

Formulas of Birth in the Pure Land (Jp. *Ōjō Kōshiki*) by Yōkan. Jōzen 15: 467, Taishō 84 (2725).

Further Biographies of Eminent Monks (Ch. *Hsi-kao-seng-ch'uan*, Jp. *Zoku Kōsō-den*) by Tao-hsüan. Taishō 50 (2060).

Great Commentary on the Perfection of Wisdom (Skt. *Mahāprajñāpāramitā*

Śāstra, Ch. *Ta-chih-tu-lun*, Jp. *Daichido-ron*) by Nāgārjuna. Taishō 25 (1509).

Great Concentration and Insight (Ch. *Mo-ho-chih-kuan*, Jp. *Maka Shikan*) by Chih-i. Taishō 46 (1911).

Guide to the Western Pure Land (*Saihō Shinan-sho*). Taishō 83 (2674).

Heart Sutra (Skt. *Prajñāpāramitāhṛdaya Sūtra*, Jp. *Hannya Shin-gyō*). Taishō 8 (251).

Hymns in Praise of Birth in the Pure Land in the Six Periods of a Day (Ch. *Wang-sheng-li-tsan*, Jp. *Ōjō Raisan*) by Shan-tao. Jōzen 4, Taishō 47 (1980).

Hymns of the Nien-fo Liturgy (Ch. *Fa-shih-tsan*, Jp. *Hōjisan*) by Shan-tao. Jōzen 4, Taishō 47 (1979).

Hymns on the Samādhi of All Buddhas' Presence (Ch. *Pan-chao-tsan*, Jp. *Han-jusan*) by Shan-tao. Jōzen 4, Taishō 47 (1981).

Illustrated Biography of Hōnen-shōnin (*Hōnen-shōnin Gyōjō-ezu*) by Shunjō. Jōzen 16, Seiten 6. English translation in Coates and Ishizuka below.

In-depth Study of the Collection on Nembutsu (*Tetsu Senchaku-shū*) by Shōkō. Jōzen 7, Seiten 3, Taishō 83 (2609).

Larger Sutra [Also called *Two-Fascicle Sutra* or *Infinite Life Sutra*] (Skt. *Sukhāvatīvyūha Sūtra*, Ch. *Wu-liang-shou-ching*, Jp. *Muryōju-kyō*). Jōzen 1, Seiten 1, Taishō 12 (360).

Letters of Shirakawa (*Shirakawa Shōsoku*). Not extant.

Lion's Roar of Queen Śrīmāla Sutra (*Śrīmālādevīsiṃhanāda Sūtra*, Ch. *Sheng-man-ching*, Jp. *Shōman-gyō*). Taishō 12 (353).

Liturgy for the Rite of the Fivefold Rhythmic Chanting of Nien-fo (Ch. *Wu-hui-fa-shih-tsan*, Jp. *Goe Hōjisan*) by Fa-chao. Jōzen 6, Taishō 47 (1983).

Lotus Sutra (Skt. *Saddharmapuṇḍarīka Sūtra*, Ch. *Fa-hua-ching*, Jp. *Hoke-kyō*). Taishō 9 (262).

Meditation Sutra [or *Amitāyus Meditation Sutra*] (Skt. *Amitāyurdhyāna-sūtra*, Ch. *Kuan-wu-liang-shou-ching*, Jp. *Kan Muryōju-kyō*). Jōzen 1, Seiten 1, Taishō 12 (365).

Methods of Contemplation on Buddha Amitābha (Ch. *Kuan-nien-fa-men*, Jp. *Kannen Hōmon*) by Shan-tao. Jōzen 4, Taishō 47 (1959).

Moon-Matrix Section of the Great Collection Sutra (Skt. *Mahāsaṃnipāta Sūtra*, Ch. *Ta-chi-yüeh-ts'ang-ching*, Jp. *Daijikkyō Gatsuzō-bun*). Taishō 13 (397).

New Edition of the Biographies of Those Who Attained Birth in the Pure Land (Ch. *Hsin-hsiu-wang-sheng-ch'uan*, Jp. *Shinshū Ōjōden*) by Wang-ku. Taishō 83 (2611).

Nirvāṇa Sutra (Skt. *Mahāparinirvāṇa Sūtra*, Ch. *Nieh-p'an-ching*, Jp. *Nehan-gyō*). Taishō 12 (374).

Personal Seal Attesting to the Transmission of Hōnen's Teaching of Nembutsu for the Future Generations (*Matsudai Nembutsu Jushuin*) by Shōkō. Jōzen 10, Seiten 5, Taishō 83 (2613).

Precious Key to the Secret Treasury (*Hizō Hōyaku*) by Kūkai. Taishō 77 (2426).

Record of Holy Chu-lin Temple (Ch. *Ta-sheng-chu-lin-szu-chi*, Jp. *Daishō Chikurinji-ki*) by Fa-chao. Appears in the *Sung Biographies of Eminent Monks* (Ch. *Sung Kao-seng-ch'uan*, Jp. *Sō Kōsō-den*). Taishō 50 (2061).

Records of Western Regions (Ch. *Ta-t'ang-hsi-yü-chi*, Jp. *Daitō Saiiki-ki*) by Pien-chi. Taishō 51 (2087).

Smaller Sutra [also called the *Amitābha Sutra*] (Skt. *Sukhāvatīvyūha Sūtra*, Ch. *A-mi-t'o-ching*, Jp. *Amida-kyō*). Jōzen 1, Seiten 1, Taishō 12 (366).

Solution to Problems Regarding Shōkō's Jushuin (*Kettō Jushuin Gimon-shō*) by Ryōchū. Jōzen 10, Seiten 5.

Sung Biographies of Eminent Monks (Ch. *Sung-kao-seng-ch'uan*, Jp. *Sō Kōsō-den*) by Tsan-ning and Chih-lun. Taishō 50 (2061).

Sutra in Praise of the Pure Land (Skt. *Sukhāvatīvyūha Sūtra*, Ch. *Ch'eng-tsan-ching-t'u-ching*, Jp. *Shōsan Jōdo-kyō*). An alternate translation by Hsüan-tsang of the *Smaller Sutra*. Jōzen 1, Taishō 12 (367).

Sutra of Bodhisattva Ornament (Ch. *P'u-sa-ying-lo-pen-yeh-ching*, Jp. *Bosatsu Yōraku Hongō-kyō*). Taishō 24 (1485).

Sutra of the Samādhi of All Buddhas' Presence (Skt. *Pratyutpannasamādhi Sūtra*, Ch. *Pan-chao-san-mei-ching*, Jp. *Hanju Zammai-kyō*). Taishō 13 (418), and also one fascicle, Taishō 13 (417).

Sutra of Universal Enlightenment (Skt. *Sukhāvatīvyūha Sūtra*, Ch. *P'ing-teng-chüeh-ching*, Jp. *Byōdōkakkyō*). Taishō 12 (361). An alternate translation of the *Larger Sutra*.

Sutra of the Wise and the Foolish (Skt. *Damamūkanidāna Sūtra*, Ch. *Hsien-yu-ching*, Jp. *Gengu Innengyō*). Taishō 4 (202).

Sutra on the Compassionate Lotus Flower (Skt. *Karuṇāpuṇḍarīka Sūtra*, Ch. *Pei-hua-ching*, Jp. *Hike-kyō*) ten fascicles. Trans. by Dharmakṣema. Taishō 3 (157).

Sutra Resolving Doubts Regarding the Period of the Imitative Dharma (Ch. *Hsian-fa-chüeh-i-ching*, Jp. *Zōbō Ketsugi-kyō*). No Sanskrit. Taishō 85 (2870).

Taishō Edition of the Chinese and Japanese Buddhist Canons (*Taishō Shinshū Daizō-kyō*). Ed. Takakusu Junjirō and Watanabe Kaigyoku. Tōkyō: Taishō Shinshū Daizō-kyō kankōkai, 1960–64 (reprint).

Ten Conditions for Attaining Birth in the Pure Land (*Ōjō Jūin*) by Yōkan. Jōzen 15, Taishō 84 (2683).

Treatise on the Awakening of Faith in the Mahāyāna (Skt. *Mahāyāna-śraddhotpāda Śāstra*, Ch. *Ta-ch'eng-ch'i-hsin-lun*, Jp. *Daijō Kishin-ron*) by Aśvaghoṣa. Taishō 32 (1666).

Treatise on Birth in the Pure Land (Skt. *Sukhāvatīvyūha Upadeśa*, Ch. *Wang-sheng-lun*, Jp. *Ōjōron*) by Vasubandhu. Jōzen 1, Seiten 1, Taishō 26 (1524).

Treatise Clarifying Doubts Regarding Pure Land Buddhism (Ch. *Shih-ching-t'u-ch'ün-i-lun*, Jp. *Shaku Jōdo Gungi-ron*) by Huai-kan. Jōzen 6, Taishō 47 (1960).

Treatise on the Pure Land (Ch. *Ching-t'u-lun*, Jp. *Jōdo-ron*) by Chia-ts'ai. Jōzen 6, Taishō 47 (1963).

Vimalakīrti Sutra (Skt. *Vimalakīrtinirdeśa Sūtra*, Ch. *Wei-mo-ching*, Jp. *Yuima-gyō*). Taishō 14 (475).

II. Books in English

Andrews, Allan A. *The Teachings Essential for Rebirth: A Study of Genshin's Ōjōyōshū*. Tōkyō: Sophia University, 1973.

Anesaki, Masaharu. *History of Japanese Religion*. Rutland, VT: Charles E. Tuttle, 1963.

Atone, Jōji. *Shan-tao: His Life and Thought*. Doctoral dissertation, University of Wisconsin, 1988.

Bloom, Alfred. *The Life of Shinran Shōnin: The Journey to Self-Acceptance*. Leiden: E. J. Brill, 1968.

———. *Shinran's Gospel of Pure Grace*. Tucson: University of Arizona Press, 1965.

Bowring, Richard. *The Religious Traditions of Japan, 500–1600*. Cambridge: Cambridge University Press, 2005.

Chappell, David, ed. *Buddhist and Taoist Practice in Medieval Chinese Society*. Honolulu: University of Hawai'i Press, 1987.

———. *Tao-ch'o: A Pioneer of Chinese Pure Land Buddhism*. Doctoral dissertation, Yale University, 1976.

Ch'en, Kenneth. *Buddhism in China: A Historical Survey*. Princeton: Princeton University Press, 1964.

———. *Chinese Transformation of Buddhism*. Princeton: Princeton University Press, 1973.

Coates, Harper H., and Ryōgaku Ishizuka. *Hōnen the Buddhist Saint: His Life and Teaching*. Kyōto: Chion-in, 1964 (reprint of original 1925 edition). Includes a translation of the *Illustrated Biography of Hōnen-shōnin* (*Hōnen-shōnin Gyōjō-ezu*). Abridged and re-edited in Fitzgerald 2006.

The Collected Works of Shinran, 2 vols. Kyōto: Jōdo Shinshū Hongwanjiha, 1997.

A Comprehensive Review of the Pure Land Buddhism of Hōnen, ed. Bukkyo University–Los Angeles Extension. Los Angeles: BULA, 1998.

Conze, Edward. *Buddhism: Its Essence and Development*. New York: Harper Torchbooks, 1964.

———. *Buddhist Thought in India*. Ann Arbor: University of Michigan Press, 1967.

Corless, Roger J. *T'an-luan's Commentary of the Pure Land Discourse: An Annotated Translation and Soteriological Analysis of the Wang-sheng-lun-chu*. Doctoral dissertation. University of Wisconsin, 1973.

Davis, Winston. *Japanese Religion and Society: Paradigms of Structure and Change*. Albany: State University of New York Press, 1992.

de Bary, William Theodore, ed. *The Buddhist Tradition in India, China, and Japan*. New York: Random House, 1969.

———. *Sources of Chinese Tradition*. New York: Columbia University Press, 1960.

———. *Sources of Japanese Tradition*. New York: Columbia University Press, 1964.

Dobbins, James C. *Jōdo Shinshū: Shin Buddhism in Medieval Japan*. Indianapolis: Indiana University Press, 1989.

Earhart, Byron H. *Japanese Religion: Unity and Diversity*. Belmont, CA: Wadsworth Publishing Company, 1970 (third edition).

Eliot, Sir Charles. *Japanese Buddhism*. London: Routledge and Kegan Paul, 1964.

Fitzgerald, Joseph A., ed. *Hōnen the Buddhist Saint: Essential Writings and Official Biography*. Bloomington, IN: World Wisdom, 2006. This volume is an abridgment and re-editing of the work by Coates and Ishizuka.

Foard, James, Michael Solomon, and Richard Payne, eds. *The Pure Land Tradition: History and Development*. Berkeley: Regents of the University of California & Institute of Buddhist Studies, 1996.

Footsteps to Enlightenment: Zen, Nembutsu and the Dharma. Ed. Bukkyo University–Los Angeles Extension. Los Angeles: BULA, 2000.

Fozdar, Shirin. *Buddha and Amitābha*. New Delhi: Arcee Press, 1978.

Fujiwara, Ryōsetsu. *The Development of the Practice of Nembutsu*. San Francisco: Buddhist Churches of America, 1962.

———. *The Way to Nirvāṇa: The Concept of the Nembutsu in Shan-tao's Pure Land Buddhism*. Tōkyō: Kyōiku shinchōsha, 1974.

Gomez, Luis O. trans. *The Land of Bliss: The Paradise of the Buddha of Measureless Light. Sanskrit and Chinese Versions of the Sukhāvatīvyūha Sūtras*. Honolulu: University of Hawai'i Press, 1996.

Hakeda, Yoshio, trans. *The Awakening of Faith Attributed to Aśvaghoṣa*. New York: Columbia University Press, 1967.

Hanayama, Shinshō. *Biography on Buddhism*. Tōkyō: Hokuseidō Press, 1961.

Haneda, Nobuo. *The Development of the Concept of Pṛthagjana, Culminating in Shan-tao's Pure Land Thought: The Pure Land Theory of Salvation of the Inferior*. Doctoral dissertation, University of Wisconsin–Madison, 1979.

Harrison, Paul, trans. *The Samādhi of Direct Encounter with the Buddhas of the Present*. Tōkyō: International Institute for Buddhist Studies, 1990.

———, trans. *The Tibetan Version of the Pratyutpanna-Buddha-Saṃmukhā-vasthita-Samādhi-Sūtra*. Tōkyō: Reiyūkai Library, 1978.

Harvey, Peter. *An Introduction of Buddhism: Teachings, History, and Practices*. New York: Cambridge University Press, 1990.

Hattori, Shō-on. *Hōnen Shōnin and Buddhism*. Tōkyō: Jōdo Shū Press, 1992.

———. *A Raft from the Other Shore: Hōnen and the Way of Pure Land Buddhism*. Tōkyō: Jōdo Shū Press, 2001.

Hirota, Dennis, trans. *Tannishō: A Primer*. Kyōto: Ryūkoku University Translation Center, 1982.

Hōnen. *Senchaku Hongan Nembutsu Shū: A Collection of Passages on Nembutsu Chosen in the Original Vow*. Trans. by Morris J. Augustine and Kondō Tesshō. BDK English Tripiṭaka 104-II. Berkeley: Numata Center for Buddhist Translation and Research, 1997. Also released with additional apparatus as *Hōnen's Senchakushū* (Honolulu: University of Hawai'i Press, 1998).

Hsiao, Ching-fen. *The Life and Teachings of T'an-luan*. Doctoral dissertation, Princeton Theological Seminary, 1967.

Inagaki, Hisao, trans. *The Three Pure Land Sūtras: A Study and Translation from Chinese*. Kyōto: Nagata bunshōdo, 1994.

Ishii, Shinpō. *The Teachings of Saint Hōnen*. Kamakura: Tōyōbunka shuppan, 1982.
Kashiwahara, Yūsen, and Kōyū Sonoda, eds. *Shapers of Japanese Buddhism*. Tōkyō: Kōsei Publishing Company, 1994.
Kawamura, Leslie, ed. *The Bodhisattva Doctrine in Buddhism*. Ontario, Canada: Wilfrid Laurier University Press, 1981.
Kitagawa, Joseph M. *On Understanding Japanese Religion*. Princeton: Princeton University Press, 1987.
______. *Religion in Japanese History*. New York: Columbia University Press, 1966.
Kiyota, Minoru. *Mahāyāna Buddhist Meditation: Theory and Practice*. Honolulu: University of Hawai'i Press, 1978.
Kyōjo, Ananda Vergara, trans. *Buddha Tells of the Infinite: Amida Kyō*. New York: American Buddhist Academy, 1973.
Ling, Trevor Oswald, ed. *A Dictionary of Buddhism*. New York: Scribner, 1972.
Machida, Sōhō. *Renegade Monk: Hōnen and Japanese Pure Land Buddhism*. Berkeley: University of California Press, 1999.
Matsunaga, Alicia. *Foundation of Japanese Buddhism I: The Aristocratic Age*. Los Angeles and Tōkyo: Buddhist Books International, 1974.
______. *Foundation of Japanese Buddhism II: The Mass Movement*. Los Angeles and Tōkyo: Buddhist Books International, 1976.
Matsunami, Kōdō. *Essentials of Buddhism*. Tōkyō: Omega-Com, 2005.
______. *Essentials of Buddhist Images*. Tōkyō: Omega-Com, 2005.
______. *Essentials of Buddhist Manners and Rituals*. Tōkyo: Omega-Com, 2007.
______. *Essentials of Buddhist Scriptures*. Tōkyō: Omega-Com, 2006.
McMullin, Neil. *Buddhism and the State in Sixteenth-Century Japan*. Princeton: Princeton University Press, 1984.
Morrel, Robert E. *Early Kamakura Buddhism: A Minority Report*. Berkeley: Asian Humanities Press, 1987.
______. *Sand Pebbles: The Tale of Muju Ichinen, A Voice for Pluralism in Kamakura Buddhism*. Albany: State University of New York Press, 1982.
Nakamura, Hajime. *Ways of Thinking of Eastern People: India, China, Tibet, Japan*. Honolulu: University of Hawai'i Press, 1964.
Nakamura Ryōkan, trans. *Words of Dharma*. Tōkyō: Jodo Shū Press, 1994.
Ogiwara, Unrai, ed. *Bodhisattvabhūmi: A Statement of the Whole Course of the Bodhisattva*. Tōkyo: Sankibō, 1971.

Okazaki, Jōji. *Pure Land Buddhist Painting*. Trans. Elizabeth Ten Grotenhuis. Tōkyo: Kōdansha, 1977.

Pas, Julian F. *Shan-tao's Commentary on the Amitāyur-buddhanusmṛti-sūtra*. Doctoral dissertation, McMaster University, 1973.

Prebisch, Charles S., ed. *Buddhism: A Modern Perspective*. University Park: The Pennsylvania State University Press, 1975.

Pye, Michael. *Skillful Means: A Concept in Mahāyāna Buddhism*. London and New York: Routledge, 2003.

Robinson, Richard, and Willard Johnson. *The Buddhist Religion: A Historical Introduction*. Belmont, CA: Wadsworth Publishing Company, 1982.

Saso, Michael, and David W. Chappell, eds. *Buddhist and Taoist Studies* I. Honolulu: University of Hawai'i Press, 1977.

Seah, Ingram Samuel. *Shan-tao: His Life and Teachings*. Doctoral dissertation, Princeton Theological Seminary, 1975.

Shibata, George Elshin. *A Study and Translation of Anrakushū*. M.A. thesis, Ryūkoku University, 1969.

Sponberg, Alan, and Helen Hardacre, eds. *Maitreya, the Future Buddha*. Cambridge: Cambridge University Press, 1988.

The Sūtra of Contemplation on the Buddha of Immeasurable Life, ed. Ryūkoku University. Kyōto: Ryūkoku University, 1984.

Suzuki, D. T. *Buddha of Infinite Light*. Boston: Shambhala Publications, 1997.

———. *Shin Buddhism*. New York: Harper and Row, 1970.

Takasaki, Jikidō. *An Introduction to Buddhism*. Trans. Rolf W. Biebel. Tōkyō: Tōhō gakkai, 1987.

Tanabe, George Jr. *Myōe the Dreamkeeper: Fantasy and Knowledge in Early Kamakura Buddhism*. Cambridge, MA: Harvard University Press, 1992.

Tanaka, Kenneth K. *The Dawn of Chinese Pure Land Buddhist Doctrine*. Albany: State University of New York Press, 1990.

Teaching of Hōnen. Los Angeles: Bukkyo University–Los Angeles Extension, 2007 (revised).

Unno, Taitetsu. *River of Fire, River of Water: An Introduction to the Pure Land Tradition of Shin Buddhism*. New York: Doubleday, 1998.

Urakami, Kenjō. *Amida Buddha and His Pure Land: Three Sūtras and One Treatise*. Italy: Kenjō S. Urakami, 1997.

Watts, Jonathan, and Yoshiharu Tomatsu, eds. *Never Die Alone: Death as Birth in Pure Land Buddhism*. Tōkyō: Jōdo Shū Press, 2008.

———. *Traversing the Pure Land Path*. Tōkyō: Jōdo Shū Press, 2005.

Williams, Paul. *Mahāyāna Buddhism: The Doctrinal Foundations.* London: Routledge, 1989.

Wright, Arthur F. *Buddhism in Chinese History.* Stanford, CA: Stanford University Press, 1959.

Zurcher, Erich. *The Buddhist Conquest of China.* 2 vols. Leiden: E. J. Brill, 1959.

III. Reference Materials

Bonwa Daijiten (Sanskrit-Japanese Dictionary). Comp. Ogiwara Unrai. Suzuki Research Foundation. Tōkyō: Kōdansha, 1991 (sixth print).

Buddhist Hybrid Sanskrit Grammar and Dictionary, 2 vols. Comp. Franklin Edgerton. India: Motilal Banarsidass, 1972 (third print).

Bukkyō Daijii. Ed. Ryūkoku University. Tōkyō: Fuzanbō, 1978 (reprint).

Bukkyōgo Daijiten. Ed. Nakamura Hajime. Tōkyō: Tōkyōshoseki, 1981 (second print).

Bussho Kaisetsu Daijiten, 14 vols. Ed. Ono Genmyō. Tōkyō: Daitō shuppansha, 1978 (reprint).

Butten Kaidaijiten. Ed. Mizuno Kōgen. Tōkyō: Shunjūsha, 1980 (third print).

A Dictionary of Chinese Buddhist Terms. Comp. William Edward Soothill and Lewis Hodous. London: Kegan Paul, Trench, Trubner, 1937. Reprints: Taipei: Ch'eng Wen Publishing Company, 1976. Delhi: Motilal Banarsidass, 1977.

Dictionary of Japanese Buddhist Terms. Inagaki Hisao. Kyōto: Nagata bunshodō, 1984.

Hōnen-shōninden Zenshū. Comp. Ikawa Jōkei. Kyōto: Naigai insatsu, 1978 (third print).

Hōnen-shōnin no Gohōgo, 3 vols. Ed. Jōdo Shū sōgō kenkyūsho. Tōkyō: Jōdo Shū Press, 2001.

Hōnen Zenshū, 3 vols. Comp. Ōhashi Shunnō. Tōkyō: Shunjūsha, 1989.

Japan: An Illustrated Encyclopedia. Tōkyō: Kōdansha International, 1993.

Japanese-English Buddhist Dictionary. Tōkyō: Daitō shuppansha, 1965.

Jōdo Shū Daijiten, 4 vols. Ed. Jōdo Shū daijiten hensan iinkai. Tōkyō: Sankibō, 1982.

Jōdo Shū Seiten, 6 vols. Ed. Jōdo Shū seiten kankō iinkai. Kyōto: Dōhōsha, 1999.

Jōdo Shū Zensho, 23 vols. Ed. Jōdo Shū shūten kankōkai. Tōkyō: Sankibō, 1970.

Mochizuki Bukkyō Daijiten, 10 vols. Comp. Mochizuki Shinkō. Tōkyō: Sekai seiten kankō kyōkai, 1967 (reprint).

Nihon Bukkyōgo Jiten. Comp. Iwamoto Yutaka. Tōkyō: Heibonsha, 1990 (second print).

Nihon Bukkyō Jinmei Jiten. Ed. Nihon Bukkyō jinmei jiten hensai iinkai. Kyōto: Hōzōkan, 1992.

Sanskrit-English Dictionary. Ed. Monier Monier-Williams. London: Oxford University Press, 1979 (reprint).

Shōwa Shinshū Hōnen-shōnin Zenshū [*Shōwa Edition of the Complete Works of Hōnen-shōnin*]. Comp. Ishii Kyōdō. Kyōto: Heirakuji shoten, 1991 (fourth print).

Index of Selected Terms

A

Āgama Sūtras (Jp. *Agon-gyō*), 93
Amida-kyō. See *Smaller Sutra*
A-mi-t'o-ching. See *Smaller Sutra*
Amitāyurdhyānasūtra. See *Meditation Sutra*
Ānanda (Jp. Anan)
  Buddha Sakyamuni's entrustment of nembutsu to, 32, 85, 117, 175, 229–30
  and recitation of the name Amida Buddha, 75, 332, 335
Anjin Kigyō Sagō-sho (*Collection Regarding the Steadfast Heart, Practice, and Exercise*), 403, 441n476
An-lo-chi. See *Collection of Passages on the Blissful Land*
Araṇemi, King, 84
arhats, 1, 16, 95, 156, 426n124
auxiliary practices
  as enhancements to the recitation of nembutsu, 169, 222
  and the four right practices, 132–33, 191, 351
  Shan-tao on meditation, 306
Avalokiteśvara, Bodhisattva (Jp. Kannon-bosatsu)
  embodiment of, during the reign of Ōi no Tennō, 68
  as inspiration of Shinran, 418n34
  as mentor, 213
  at the moment of death, 400
  and the nembutsu practitioner, 211
  as object of meditation, 328, 424n83
  protection from, 172, 173
  response to prayers, 299
  Thousand-Armed, 291
Avataṃsaka Sūtra. See *Flower Garland Sutra*
Awanosuke, 311, 436n365

B

Benchō, Shōko-bō (1162–1238), 40, 51, 62, 419n36
Bhaiṣajya-guru-buddha, (Jp. Yakushibutsu), 153, 291
Biography of Hōnen-shōnin, 39
Bodhiruci (Jp. Bodairushi), 12, 14, 327
Book of Documents, 70, 423n62
Buddha Śākyamuni. *See* Great Sage; Śākyamuni, Buddha
buddha nature, 16, 82, 325
Buddha of Healing (Jp. Yakushi-nyorai), 153, 291

C

Cakravartin (Jp. Rinnō), 120
Chan-jan (Jp. Tannen, 711–82), 189, 431n237
Ch'eng-tsan-ching-t'u-ching (Jp. *Shōsan Jōdo-kyō, Sutra in Praise of the Pure Land*), 163, 220

Chia-ts'ai (Jp. Kazai, seventh century), 395, 441n462
Chih-i (Jp. Chigi, 528–597), 195, 431n250
Ching-t'u-lun (Jp. *Jōdo-ron, Treatise on the Pure Land*), 441n462
Ching-t'u-shih-i-lun (Jp. *Jōdo Jūgi-ron, Discourse on Ten Issues*), 195
Chōgen, Shunjō-bō (1121–1206), 54–55, 62, 367–74, 421n52, 433n302, 435n346
Chuan-hsiu-ching-yeh-wen (Jp. *Senju Shōgō-mon, Treatise of the Exclusive and Right Practices*), 351
Chu-lin Temple (Jp. Chikurin-ji), 149, 333, 429n190
Clarifying the Essentials and Promoting Wholesome Conduct, 50, 51, 262, 304, 310, 421n47
Collection Clarifying that Common Mortals Are in Accordance with the Essential Vow, 403
Collection of Dialogues on Nembutsu, 52, 315–19, 437n374
Collection of Essentials on Attaining Birth in the Pure Land (Jp. *Ōjō Yōshū*), 26–27, 176, 189, 193, 255–56, 314, 400–401, 422n60
Collection of Essentials on Jōdo Shū, 319, 437n376
Collection of Passages on the Blissful Land (*An-lo-chi*, Jp. *Anraku-shū*)
  on the decline of the Dharma, 417n11
  En'nin's return to Japan with, 26
  the holy gate and the Pure Land gate, 17–18, 187–88, 327
Collection of Practices for the Certain Attainment of Birth in the Pure Land, 403, 441n476
Collection of Stories, 51
Collection on Nembutsu, 33, 38, 40, 62–63, 418n32
Commentary on the Meditation Sutra (Ch. *Kuan-ching-shu*, Jp. *Kangyō-sho*)
  birth, categories of, 101
  on the essential vow, 109, 427n151
  faith, meanings of, 112
  Hōnen on, 28–29, 32, 314
  on the name Amida Buddha, 81
  on nembutsu practice, 176
  on the profound heart, 105
  on rebirth in the Pure Land, 79–80
  on the rightly established practice, 401
  the threefold devotional heart, 99–100
concentration and insight (*śamatha-vipaśyanā*), 430n211
Crane Forest, 323

D

Daichido-ron. See *Great Commentary on the Perfection of Wisdom*
delusive triple realms
  Hōnen on, 52
  liberation from, 149, 227
  and negative karmas, 80
  and the practice of nembutsu, 281
  and the profound heart, 21, 160
  transmigration through, 105, 327, 379
dependent rewards, 196
dhāraṇī (mystic phrases), 55, 276, 386, 414
Dharma, the decline of, 27, 418n19. *See also* period of the decline of the Dharma
Dharma (Zen) school with the heart of Buddha Śākyamuni, 94, 96
Dharmākara, Bodhisattva (Jp. Hōzō-bosatsu)
  attainment of buddhahood, 342, 391–92
  Jōdo Shū on, 301
  in the *Larger Sutra*, 8, 71–73
  vow of, 125, 138, 226
dharmakāya (Dharma body), 227, 370
Dialogue on the Next Life, 305, 436n353
Dialogue on Twenty-Eight Topics, 305, 403, 436n352
Dialogue on Twenty-Two Topics, 403, 441n477
difficult path, 98, 157

Discourse on Ten Issues, 195
Dōhen (twelfth century), 51, 319, 421n51
Dōkō, Ryōe (1243–1330)
  colophon of the *Japanese Anthology*, 407
  on a court lady's dream, 405–6
  Hōnen's literary remains, compilation of, 39, 40–42, 56
  notes by, included in the *Japanese Anthology*, 92, 117, 174, 233, 239, 262, 299, 300, 303–5, 310–13, 315–19, 356, 374, 384, 387, 388, 403–4
dragon girl (Skt. *nāga-kanyā*), 94, 143, 426n123, 429n181

E

easy path, 98, 157, 175, 204, 306
eight difficult conditions, 120, 122
eight hot hells, 323, 437n379
eight kinds of suffering, 399
eight major aspects, 84
eight precepts, 288, 435n339
eighteenth vow, 19–20, 42, 53, 71–72, 74, 76, 80, 98, 158, 340–42
eightfold negation, 82, 94
Enchi (d. 1357), 40, 407, 442n485
En'nin, Jikaku-daishi (794–864), 26, 69, 422n59
essential vow
  for all beings, 178–79, 235, 354, 363, 385–86
  of Amida Buddha, 72, 73–75, 77–79, 157–58, 203, 204, 263, 339–40, 381
  belief in, 107–12, 247, 301
  and birth in the Pure Land, 86, 234, 241, 254, 264
  Bodhisattva Mañjuśrī on, 150
  and the decline of the Dharma, 119
  Dōkō on, 41
  doubts about, 123–25, 215–16, 218
  the eighteenth vow, 8
  faith in, 147, 160–62, 228, 268
  and false buddhas, 165–66
  Hōnen on, 3, 28, 31, 36, 55, 69, 256, 257, 259–61, 302, 309, 316–17, 386–87
  Master Shan-tao on, 9, 158, 213, 216–17, 249–50, 342, 347–48, 379–80
  and the miscellaneous practices, 231–32, 368
  Nāgārjuna on, 11–12
  and nembutsu, 43, 47, 223, 226–28, 229–30, 345, 350
  power of, 137, 141, 211, 330, 338, 364
  and proponents of other practices, 248
  requirements of, 123, 126–27
  and the rightly established practice, 124, 169, 222, 259–60, 314
  salvation for all, 271–73
  T'an-luan on, 14
  at the time of death, 163–64, 220–21, 251, 399
Essentials for Birth in the West. See *Hsi-fang-yao-chüeh*
estranged miscellaneous practices, 132, 170, 193, 289
Examination of Analects, 406
expedient teachings, 84, 325, 367, 425n103

F

Fa-chao (Jp. Hosshō, eighth century)
  life and practice of, 24–25
  from the *Liturgy for the Rite of the Fivefold Rhythmic Chanting of Nien-fo*, 153, 393, 429n191
  on nembutsu recitation, 389
  questioning of Bodhisattva Mañjuśrī, 149, 333
  Record of Holy Chu-lin Temple, 429n190
Fa-hua-ching. See *Lotus Sutra*
falsity and fickleness
  and the genuine heart, 134, 196, 364, 377
  and the lesser precepts, 104
  Master Shan-tao on, 78, 159
  practitioners with, 378
  vs. sincerity and constancy, 102
Fa-shih-tsan (Jp. *Hōjisan*, *Hymns of the Nien-fo Liturgy*), 26, 150
five aspects of meditation, 12, 313, 369

five defilements, 115, 188, 391
five fundamental precepts, 95
five grave offenses
and birth in the Pure Land, 111, 118, 127, 228, 240, 241, 269
and the essential vow of Amida Buddha, 79–80
and the low category of birth, 88, 110, 398
and negative karma, 286–87, 293, 336, 385
and nembutsu recitation, 97, 244, 252, 329, 348, 390
five hindrances for a woman, 3, 127–28, 263–64
five pungent vegetables, 123, 296
five right practices, 132, 168, 221, 351
five transcendent faculties, 72, 441n464
fivefold rhythmic chanting of nien-fo, 24, 26
See also *Liturgy for the Rite of the Fivefold Rhythmic Chanting of Nien-fo*
Flower Garland Sutra (*Avataṃsaka Sūtra*, Jp. *Kegon-kyō*)
Buddhist walking staffs, reference to, 435n344
doctrines of, 11, 80–81
as holy gate teaching, 93
in the Kegon school, 426n122
forty-eight vows, 8, 15, 21, 105
of Amida Buddha, 228, 341–42, 409–16
and the eighteenth vow, 42, 98, 135, 143, 157
and faith, 160, 197
in the *Larger Sutra*, 71–72, 112, 145
four forms of fearlessness, 391
four grave offenses, 80, 110, 336, 337
four kinds of wisdom, 391
four modes of birth, 391, 396
four modes of exercise, 32, 37, 92, 211, 313
four noble truths, 95
four stages, 95, 426n124
Four Treatises, 148, 429n186
four universal vows, 94–95
four vehicles, 43, 93, 95, 156

G
Genchi, Seikan-bō (1183–1238), 37, 39, 62, 418n33
Genkū, Hōnen-bō (1133–1212), 1
name given by Eikū, 27, 60, 426n121
on the Pure Land gate, 30
See also Hōnen
Genshin, Eshin-sōzu (942–1017), 26–27, 193, 330, 400–401, 422n60, 434n337
genuine heart
as aspect of the threefold devotional heart, 100, 129–30, 134, 146, 158–60, 196, 203, 215, 218
and birth in the Pure Land, 357, 364
and the burning heart, 100
in the essential vow, 411
in the first fascicle of the *Larger Sutra*, 226, 308
four aspects of, 378
Hōnen on, 101–5
Master Shan-tao on, 78, 99, 377, 382
Golden Glen, 324, 437n380
Goroku Genki (*Examination of Analects*), 406
Great Collection of the Moon-Matrix Sutra, 96, 188, 426n131
Great Commentary on the Perfection of Wisdom (*Mahāprajñāpāramitā Śāstra*), 335, 440n441
Great Concentration and Insight, 60
Great Sage (Buddha Śākyamuni), 20, 188, 212. *See also* Śākyamuni, Buddha; World-Honored One
Guide to the Western Pure Land, 39, 45–50
Gyōki (668–749), 69, 422n58

H
Hanju Zammai-kyō. See *Sutra of the Samādhi of All Buddhas' Presence*
Hannyakyō. See *Perfection of Wisdom Sutra*

heart aspiring birth in the Pure Land through the dedication of merit
as dedication of virtues, 198, 364–65
faith and, 382
Master Shan-tao on, 166, 383
as third aspect of the threefold devotional heart, 20, 78, 87, 99, 129, 133, 134, 196, 268, 369
Hīnayāna Buddhism
and the holy gate, 88, 131, 156, 367
Hōnen-shōnin on, 313
practitioners of, 88
regulations for monks, 426n127
stages of, 95
and the teachings of Buddha Śākyamuni, 325
Hirano Shrine, 406, 441n483
Hoke-kyō. See *Lotus Sutra*
holy gate
as compared to the Pure Land gate, 130–31, 156–58, 187, 367
different understandings and practices of, 113–14, 164, 381
difficulty of, 96, 98, 143, 152, 188
Hōnen on, 30, 31, 93, 310, 373
and nembutsu practice, 154
Tao-ch'o on, 327
Hōnen (1133–1212)
after his death, 39–41
biographical information, 27–30, 33–37
chronology of events during his lifetime, 59–63
longing for birth in the Pure Land, 131
Monk Ryōe Dōkō on, 69–70
poems of, 319–20
sayings of, 304–19
See also Genkū, Hōnen-bō
Hōnen-shōnin Denki (*Biography of Hōnen-shōnin*), 39
Hongan Sōō-shō (*Collection Clarifying that Common Mortals Are in Accordance with the Essential Vow*), 403
Honshin-bō, 405, 406
Hossō school, 82, 94–95, 148, 189, 334, 381, 424n99
house on fire, 105, 107, 200
Hsian-fa-chüeh-i-ching (Jp. *Zōbō Ketsugi-kyō*, *Sutra Resolving Doubts Regarding the Period of the Imitative Dharma*), 335
Hsi-fang-yao-chüeh (Jp. *Saihō Yōketsu*, *Essentials for Birth in the West*), 148–49, 195, 206–7, 209–11
Hsin-chung (Jp. Shinchū), 351, 439n417
Hsiung-chün (Jp. Ōshun), 329–30, 437n383
Huai-kan (Jp. Ekan, seventh to eighth century), 22, 211, 306, 327
Huai-yün (639–701), 22–23
Hüan-t'ung (Jp. Gentsū), 74–75
Hui-yüan (334–416), 13, 14, 23, 24
Hymns in Praise of Birth in the Pure Land, 19, 99, 129, 171–73, 231, 258, 401
Hymns of the Nien-fo Liturgy, 26, 150

I

Instructions of Destroying the Seven Disasters, 176, 431n227

J

Jīvaka (Jp. Giba), 83, 425n100
Jōdo Shū (Pure Land school)
on Amida Buddha, 301
and Buddha Śākyamuni's teachings, 367–68
essence of, 82, 134
essentials, an outline of, 156–74
Hōnen's establishment of, 1, 28, 31, 255
Master Shan-tao on, 221–23
meditative practice, 328–29
nembutsu recitation, 373
patriarchs of, 40–41
persecution, 52–53
the *Single-Sheet Covenant* of, 43
and the threefold devotional heart, 136
worldly passions and, 135
See also Pure Land gate
Jōdo Shū Yōshū (*Collection of Essentials on Jōdo Shū*), 319, 437n376

Jōjitsu school, 95, 426n125
Jōshō-bō, 351, 439n419

K

Kakuchō (960–1034), 314–15, 437n372
Kakuyu, Jūshin-bō (1158–1233), 310–11, 436n361
Kan Muryōju-kyō. See *Meditation Sutra*
Kangyō-sho. See *Commentary on the Meditation Sutra*
Kansei, Shinkan-bō (1153–1200), 61, 433n301
Kantei Mondō-shū (*Dialogue on the Next Life*), 305, 436n353
Kāśyapa (Jp. Kashō), 94
Kegon school, 27, 93, 94, 426n122, 435n346
Ketsujō Ōjō Gyōsō-shō (*Collection of Practices for the Certain Attainment of Birth in the Pure Land*), 403, 441n476
Kinmei (509–71), Emperor, 67, 68, 324
Kintano Shrine, 406, 441n483
Kōfuku-ji Temple, 59, 60, 61, 63
Kōmyō-bō (thirteenth century), 49, 63, 243–45, 420n44
Kṣitigarbha, Bodhisattva (Jp. Jizō-bosatsu), 82
Kuan-ching-shu (Jp. *Kangyō-sho*). See *Commentary on the Meditation Sutra*
Kuan-wu-liang-shou-ching. See *Meditation Sutra*
Kuan-nien-fa-men (Jp. *Kannen Hōmon*, *Methods of Contemplation on Buddha Amitābha*), 9
K'uei-chi (Jp. Kiki, 632–82), 148–49, 429n187
Kujō Kaneko (1152–1201), 45–46, 430n223
Kujō Kanezane (1149–1207), 30, 45, 62
Kūkai, Kōbō-daishi (774–835), 391, 440n455
Kumagai no Jirō Naozane, Hōriki-bō Rensei (1141–1207), 48, 55–56, 62, 235, 420n42
Kumano shrines, 297, 435n347
Kurodani, 27, 28, 39, 60, 61, 69
Kusha school, 95, 426n126

L

lady of Tarō Sanehide, 47, 420n41
  replies to, 214–25, 226–33
Lamp for the Period of the Decline of the Dharma, 27, 257
Larger Sutra (*Two Fascicle Sutra*; Skt. *Sukhāvatīvyūha Sūtra*)
  belief in, 112
  on the essential vow of Amida Buddha, 74–75, 308, 330–31
  on the forty-eight vows of Amida Buddha, 71
  listening to the teachings of, 97
  meditation on the Buddha of Immeasurable Light (Amida Buddha), 176, 192
  on mindfulness of Amida Buddha, 73, 204–5, 428n168
  on nembutsu recitation, 110, 243, 362, 372–74
  the three categories of aspirants, 31, 74
  and the three lower realms, 396
  translations of, 7–8
lesser forty-eight Mahāyāna precepts, 336, 438n402
lesser precepts, 104, 427n148
Letters of Shirakawa, 51, 311
Literary Light, 405–6
Liturgy for the Rite of the Fivefold Rhythmic Chanting of Nien-fo, 26, 126–27, 153, 393, 429n191
Lokeśvararāja (Jp. Sejizai-ō), Buddha, 121, 226, 423n66
Lotus Sutra (*Saddharmapuṇḍarīka Sūtra*)
  capacity to embrace the teachings of, 118–19
  concepts of, 81, 213
  as holy gate teaching, 93, 187
  Hōnen's study of, 60
  the "miscellaneous practices," 255–56
  mystic phrases of, 276

practice of the recitation of, 171, 194–95, 221, 222, 224, 289
on the seven disasters, 431n227
as a true teaching, 425n103
worship of, 191

M

Mahāprajñāpāramitā Śāstra. See *Great Commentary on the Perfection of Wisdom*
Mahāsthāmaprāpta Bodhisattva (Jp. Seishi-bosatsu), 41, 69, 144, 172, 173, 328, 400
Mahāvairocana, Buddha (Jp. Dainichi-nyorai), 93, 274
Mahāyāna Buddhism
attaining buddhahood, 118
and the bodhisattva tradition, 1, 12, 15
and the holy gate, 93, 156, 367
precepts of *vs.* reciting nembutsu, 302
receiving the precepts of, 60, 61, 62
and the schools of Buddhism, 325
Maitreya, Bodhisattva (Jp. Miroku-bosatsu), 8, 75, 94, 151, 186–87, 189
Mañjuśrī, Bodhisattva (Jp. Monju-bosatsu), 24, 82, 149–50, 333
Manner of Dying, 403, 441n478
Mappō Tōmyōki (*Lamp for the Period of the Decline of the Dharma*), 27, 257
Masako, Hōjō, 45, 46, 174, 420n40
Matsudai Nembutsu Jushuin (*Personal Seal Attesting to the Transmission of Hōnen's Teachings of Nembutsu for the Future Generations*), 313, 436n367
Maudgalyāyana (Jp. Mokuren), 85–86
Meditation Sutra
aspirants for birth in the Pure Land, 88, 110, 328–29, 377, 389–90, 398
Buddha Śākyamuni on, 75–76, 106
entrusted to T'an-luan, 327
faith in, 112
Hōnen on, 42, 54, 336–37
Master Shan-tao on, 330–31, 362
meditative practices with a focused mind, 424n83
on nembutsu at the time of death, 163–64, 220, 247
and the practice of nembutsu, 32, 192–93, 228–29
recitation of, 221
the steadfast heart, 98–99
as the *Sutra of Protection*, 172–73
teachings of, 9–11
and the threefold devotional heart, 21, 78, 126, 129, 158, 203–4, 214–15, 267, 358
translations of, 13–14
See also *Commentary on the Meditation Sutra*
Merit and Demerit of Nembutsu, 403
Meru, Mount, 120
Methods of Contemplation on Buddha Amitābha, 9
Miao-yün (Jp. Myōun), 346–47
middle path, 82
miscellaneous practices
and Amida Buddha, 112, 113, 132–33
and birth in the Pure Land, 168, 190–91, 210, 231–32, 367, 374
description of, 222–25
and the essential vow, 107, 368
and the exclusive practice, 349–51
practitioners of, 169–70, 181
vs. recitation of nembutsu, 32–33, 47, 69, 145, 148, 154
Mo-ho-chih-kuan (Jp. *Maka Shikan*, *Great Concentration and Insight*), 60
Monogatari-shū (*Collection of Stories*), 51
Mononobe no Moriya, 334, 438n396
Muryōju-kyō. See *Larger Sutra*
Myōgi Shingyō-shū (*Clarifying the Essentials and Promoting Wholesome Conduct*), 50, 51, 262, 304, 310, 421n47
Myōgyōgō-ki (*Wondrous Biography*), 314
Myōhen (1142–1224), 51, 302–3, 421n48

N

Nāgārjuna (Jp. Ryūjyu, ca. 150–250), 6, 11–12, 14–15

Namu Amida Butsu
and birth in the Pure Land, 36, 37, 92, 109, 119, 247, 312–13, 380
Chinese characters for, 68
in *Commentary on the Meditation Sutra*, 30
in the essential vow, 125
faith in, 161
as the fourth right practice, 221
Hōnen on, 302
as nembutsu, 2, 4
and the profound heart, 218
Shan-tao on, 428n168
See also nembutsu gate
nembutsu. See *Namu Amida Butsu*
nembutsu gate, 45, 142, 144, 152–54, 194
Nembutsu Mondō-shū (*Collection of Dialogues on Nembutsu*), 52, 315–19, 437n374
Nembutsu Tokushitsugi (*Merit and Demerit of Nembutsu*), 403
Nijūhachi Mondō (*Dialogue on Twenty-Eight Topics*), 305, 436n352
Nijūni Mondō (*Dialogue on Twenty-Two Topics*), 403, 441n477
nine grades of aspirants
and the Amida Buddha's welcome, 358
Buddha Śākyamuni on, 256–57
condition of aspirants, 88–89
Hōnen on, 43
Master Shan-tao on, 87
from the *Meditation Sutra*, 10, 106, 328
and the threefold devotional heart, 100–101
Nirvāṇa Sutra, 14, 16, 81, 94, 148
Nison-in Temple, 35, 405, 441n481

O

Ōgo no Tarō Sanehide (d. 1246). *See* lady of Tarō Sanehide
Ōjō Jūin (*Ten Conditions for Attaining Birth in the Pure Land*), 69, 186
Ōjō Yōshū. See *Collection of Essentials on Attaining Birth in the Pure Land*
one millions recitations of nembutsu, 56, 277, 395
Onjō-ji Temple, 59, 60, 436n362

P

Perfection of Wisdom Sutra (Skt. *Prajñāpāramitā Sūtra*), 81, 194, 206, 323
period of the decline of the Dharma
and becoming a Buddhist itinerant preacher, 284
and the essential vow, 73
Hōnen on, 45, 307
from the *Lamp for the Period of the Decline of the Dharma*, 257
from the *Larger Sutra*, 205
length of, 235
Master Shan-tao on, 110, 111
and the miscellaneous practices, 148
and the Pure Land gate, 188
and recitation of nembutsu, 28, 44, 118, 142–44, 179, 333, 362, 385, 386
and respect for priests, 300
period of the semblance of the Dharma, 97
period of the true Dharma, 97
Personal Seal Attesting to the Transmission of Hōnen's Teachings of Nembutsu for the Future Generations, 313, 436n367
P'ien-ch'üeh (Jp. Henjaku), 83, 425n101
Ping-chou (Jp. Hei-shū), 148, 353
P'ing-teng-chüeh-ching (Jp. *Byōdōkakkyō, Sutra of Universal Enlightenment*), 150–51, 396
power other than self
and birth in the Pure Land, 169, 264
and the essential vow of Amida Buddha, 193, 211, 358
faith in, 392
Genkū on, 119–20, 260–61
Hōnen on, 44, 50
T'an-luan on, 15
Tao-ch'o's belief in, 16–17
Prajñāpāramitā Sūtra. See *Perfection of Wisdom Sutra*

Prabhūtaratna, Buddha (Jp. Tahō-butsu), 206
pratyekabuddhas
  and the attainment of birth in the Pure Land, 217, 249, 382
  bodhisattva practice of, 198
  as disciples of the three vehicles, 370
  Vehicle of, 93, 95, 156
Pratyutpannasamādhi Sūtra. See *Sutra of the Samādhi of All Buddhas' Presence*
prayer beads. *See* string of prayer beads
Prince Great Giver, 342–45
profound heart
  as aspect of the threefold devotional heart, 78, 79, 99, 105, 129, 130, 134, 146, 158, 196, 364, 377
  and belief in nembutsu, 135
  as faith in the essential vow of Amida Buddha, 147, 160, 162
  Hōnen on, 43
  as profound faith, 106, 215, 218, 268, 337, 380
  Shan-tao on, 21, 196–97, 198, 379
Pure Land gate
  Buddha Śākyamuni's teaching on, 114
  commentaries on, 195–96
  and "different understandings and practices," 113, 164
  vs. the holy gate, 130–31, 156–58, 187–89, 327, 367
  Hōnen on, 30, 31, 43, 96–99, 310, 376–77
P'u-t'i-hsin-ching (Jp. *Bodai Shingyō, Sutra of the Aspiration for Enlightenment*), 307

R

Record of Holy Chu-lin Temple, 149, 333, 429n190
religious meal for purification, 278, 279, 289, 290, 291–92, 297, 307, 435n338
right practices
  the five right practices, 132–33, 351
  Master Shan-tao on, 168–69, 221–23
  and the miscellaneous practices, 31, 117, 190–91, 224–25, 367–68
rightly established practice
  vs. the auxiliary practices, 191, 351
  and the essential vow of Buddha Amitābha, 28, 132, 140, 168–69, 314, 338
  Hōnen on, 31, 367
  Master Shan-tao on, 170, 222, 259
  as nembutsu recitation, 258
rightly settled state of mind for birth in the Pure Land
  faith in the essential vow, 163–64, 170, 265
  and karmic conditions, 223, 231
  and nembutsu recitation, 273
  and the suffering of death, 399–400
  at the time of death, 44, 138, 139–40
  and the welcome of the Amida Buddha, 220, 250–51
  vs. the worldly passions, 134
Rinjū Gyōgi (*Manner of Dying*), 403, 441n478
Ritsu school, 95, 426n128
Ryōchū (1199–1287), 40, 419n35
Ryōgon-in Temple, 69, 330
Ryūkan, Chōraku-ji (1148–1227), 50, 51, 63, 304, 434n331

S

Sadāparibhūta, Bodhisattva (Jp. Jō Fugyō-bosatsu), 435n342
Saddharmapuṇḍarīka Sūtra. See *Lotus Sutra*
Sahasra-bhuja-sahasra-netra (Jp. Senju-kannon). *See* Thousand-Armed Bodhisattva
Saichō, Dengyō-daishi (767–822), 27, 257, 430n226
Saihō Shinan-shō (*Guide to the Western Pure Land*), 39, 45–50
Śākyamuni, Buddha
  belief in the teachings of, 90, 112
  on birth in the Pure Land, 6, 67, 84–85, 192, 227, 256–57, 354
  and the emancipation of sentient beings, 84

and the essential vow, 165, 216–17, 249, 381
extinction of the teachings of, 97, 385
Hōnen on, 32, 33
on the *Larger Sutra*, 8, 75
Master Shan-tao on, 114
in the *Meditation Sutra*, 229–30, 332
on men and women practitioners, 3
on nembutsu recitation, 178
parinirvāṇa of, 85
as Prince Great Giver, 342, 439n414
teachings of, 94, 143–44, 334, 354
See also Great Sage; World-Honored One

Samantabhadra (Jp. Fugen), Bodhisattva, 149, 276, 333, 412

Sanron school, 82, 94, 334, 424n98

Śāriputra (Jp. Sharihotsu), 6, 33, 96, 150, 178, 423n65

self-power
and birth in the Pure Land, 123, 169
meaning of, 120–21
and nembutsu recitation, 119, 137
vs. power other than self, 15, 44, 50, 260

Senchaku-shū (*Collection on Nembutsu*), 33, 38, 40, 62–63, 418n32

Shang-shu (Jp. *Shōsho, Book of Documents*), 70, 423n62

Shan-tao (Jp. Zendō, 613–81)
on Amida Buddha, 391, 393–94
on birth in the Pure Land, 98, 108, 140, 217–18, 221, 226–27, 243, 248–50, 252, 340, 382, 386
on buddhalands, 121
his confession of worldly passions, 240
on criticizing other schools of practice, 335
and the development of vocal nembutsu, 12–25
on *entrance with distance*, 97
on the essential vow, 76–77, 108–9, 213, 229, 308, 332, 342, 347, 363
on the forty-eight vows, 72
on the genuine heart, 78, 99, 134, 267
Hōnen's reliance on, 29, 38, 230
as manifestation of Amida Buddha, 179, 352
on meditation, 306, 428n168
and nembutsu practice, 4, 9, 87, 89, 145–46, 207, 210, 212, 216, 231, 235–36, 362
his practice of nembutsu, 101, 148
on practitioners with different views, 381
on profound faith, 107, 114–15, 174
on the profound heart, 337, 379
his Pure Land tradition, 1–2
on recitation of the *Smaller Sutra*, 278
on the right practices, 168–70, 190–91, 222–24
on the rightly established practice, 259
on the three ways of teaching, 331
on the threefold devotional heart, 100, 159, 160–62, 166, 196, 203, 377, 384
on the time of death, 399
See also *Commentary on the Meditation Sutra*

Shao-k'ang (Jp. Shōkō, d. 805), 23, 25, 327

Shichinan shōmetsu no hō (*Instructions of Destroying the Seven Disasters*), 176, 431n227

Shih-wang-sheng-ching (Jp. *Jū Ōjō-kyō, Sutra of the Ten Right Practices for Birth in the Pure Land*), 172, 430n220

Shingon school, 59, 82, 93, 213, 301, 373

Shinkū, Hōren-bō (1146–1228), 35, 51, 60, 305–11, 421n50

Shirakawa Shōsoku (*Letters of Shirakawa*), 51, 311

Shitennō-ji Temple, 290, 435n346

Shōnyo-bō (d. 1201), 49, 246–52, 420n45

Shōtoku (574–622), Prince, 68, 422n55

six bodhisattva perfections, 94, 96, 339

six days of observance of the precepts, 278, 279, 291

six delusive worlds
the bondage of thoughts, 120–21

and the essential vow of Amida Buddha, 368
extrication from, 85, 87
life as a human being, 270
and the nembutsu devotee, 209, 211
and the profound heart, 130, 147
rebirth in, 2, 422n53
transmigration in, 79, 83, 105, 151, 185, 197, 391, 396, 397
six stages of enlightenment, 96
six transcendent faculties, 187
Smaller Sutra (Skt. *Sukhāvatīvyūha Sūtra*)
belief in the teachings of, 112
on the end of life, 399–400
Hōnen on, 43, 304
on nembutsu, 145, 205–6, 332
recitation of, 277, 278
teachings of, 89–90
of the three sutras of Pure Land Buddhism, 6, 71, 195
Sōgen, Jogen-bo (1168–1251), 51, 421n49
Southern Mansion, 324, 437n380
śrāvakas
disclaiming of nembutsu practice, 382
holy gate teachings and, 118–19, 143
reverence for, 209, 370
Śrāvaka Vehicle, 93, 95, 156
Śrāvastī, 323
steadfast heart (Jp. anjin)
for birth in the Pure Land, 57, 166, 168, 384
as faith, 158, 376, 382
Hōnen on, 55
Master Shan-tao on, 98–99
as the threefold devotional heart, 427n136
See also threefold devotional heart
strand of five-colored thread, 278–79, 280, 292, 435n340
string of prayer beads, 124, 182, 266, 291, 298, 300–301, 369–70, 393–94, 401
Sukhāvatīvyūha Sūtra. See *Larger Sutra*; *Smaller Sutra*
Sutra in Praise of the Pure Land, 163, 220
Sutra of Protection, 172–73. See also *Meditation Sutra*
Sutra of the Aspiration for Enlightenment, 307
Sutra of the Samādhi of All Buddhas' Presence (*Pratyutpannasamādhi Sūtra*) 5, 6, 333, 438n394
Sutra of the Ten Right Practices for Birth in the Pure Land, 172, 430n220
Sutra of Universal Enlightenment, 150–51, 396
Sutra Resolving Doubts Regarding the Period of the Imitative Dharma, 335

T

Ta-chi-yüeh-ts'ang-ching (Jp. *Daiju no Gatsuzō-kyō, Great Collection of the Moon-Matrix Sutra*), 96, 188, 426n131
T'an-luan (Jp. Donran, 476–542), 8–9, 14–17, 18, 148, 327
Tao-ch'o (Jp. Dōshaku, 562–645), 16–19, 97, 148, 156–57, 327
Ta-sheng-chu-lin-szu-chi (Jp. *Daishō Chikurinji-ki, A Record of Holy Chu-lin Temple*), 149, 333, 429n190
ten bodhisattva perfections, 297
ten bodhisattva stages, 149, 339
ten cardinal Mahāyāna precepts, 96, 336
Ten Conditions for Attaining Birth in the Pure Land, 69, 186, 423n61
ten powers of wisdom, 391
ten transgressions, 110, 118, 151, 240, 244, 269, 336–37, 362
ten virtues of Master Shan-tao, 101
ten virtuous acts, 151
Tendai school, 27, 52, 60, 82, 94, 194–95, 430n226
thirteen types of contemplation with a focused mind, 75, 192, 229, 328–29, 330, 424n83
Thousand-Armed Bodhisattva (Jp. Senju-kannon), 291. *See also* Avalokiteśvara
thread. *See* strand of five-colored thread
three categories of acts, 99, 211, 394

three categories of aspirants, 31, 192
Three Jewels, 5, 38, 110, 209, 260, 370–71
three kinds of attachment, 77, 399, 400
three lower realms, 71, 150–51, 179–80, 237, 318, 324–25, 341, 396
three meritorious acts, 106, 229, 328
three mystic practices, 187
three poisons, 120
three sutras of Pure Land Buddhism, 9, 13, 15, 31, 71, 98, 135, 195, 348, 367
three transcendent faculties, 187, 441n464
threefold contemplation, 96
threefold devotional heart
  and birth in the Pure Land, 147, 158, 167–68, 196, 216, 219, 357
  Hōnen on, 32, 43, 44, 45, 54, 305, 312, 315, 365
  Master Shan-tao on, 89, 203, 214, 218, 358, 384
  in the *Meditation Sutra*, 11, 20–21, 267
  and nembutsu practitioners, 126, 136, 138, 146
  the significance of, 129–33
  the steadfast heart, 427n136
  the three aspects of, 78–79, 87, 99–101, 120
  the two types of, 368–69
  See also steadfast heart (Jp. anjin)
threefold discipline, 260–61, 313, 314, 335
threefold pure precepts, 96
threefold wisdom, 331, 339
Tōdai-ji Temple, 54, 59, 61, 62, 367, 435n346
Treatise of the Exclusive and Right Practices, 351
Treatise on the Pure Land, 441n462
Tsunoto no Saburō Tamemori (1163–1243), 48, 420n43, 439n419
Tuṣita Heaven, 151, 189–90, 195, 383
Two Fascicle Sutra. See *Larger Sutra*
Two Honored Ones, 67–68, 69, 92, 113

V

Vaidehī, Queen, 9, 330, 438n385
Vairocana, Buddha (Jp. Birushana-butsu), 19
Vimalakīrtinirdeśa Sutra (Jp. Yuimagyō), 14, 194, 195
virtuous teacher, 10, 88, 110, 208, 220, 250, 269, 287, 329, 398, 399, 400
Vulture Peak, 323, 437n378

W

Wang-sheng-li-tsan (Jp. *Ōjō Raisan, Hymns in Praise of Birth in the Pure Land*), 19, 99, 129, 171–73, 231, 258, 401
white path between two rivers, 199–202
women practitioners. *See* five hindrances for a woman
Wondrous Biography, 314
World-Honored One, 85, 150, 335. *See also* Great Sage; Śākyamuni, Buddha
worldly passions
  the ancients on, 122
  arising out of greed and anger, 134–35, 136, 201
  the *Commentary on the Meditation Sutra* on, 105
  as grave illnesses, 83
  the holy gate *vs.* the Pure Land gate, 130, 327
  Hōnen on, 313–14
  human fallibility, as theme of Pure Land Buddhism, 2, 147, 160, 215–16, 391
  the *Meditation Sutra* on, 110
  and nembutsu practice, 85, 161, 165
  and the power of the essential vow, 141
  and self-power, 120–21
  Shan-tao on, 79, 87, 107–8, 111, 379, 380, 381
  Shan-tao's confession of, 20, 240
  the Tendai school on, 94
Wu-hui-fa-shih-tsan (Jp. *Goe Hōjisan, Liturgy for the Rite of the Fivefold Rhythmic Chanting of Nien-fo*), 26, 126–27, 153, 393

Wu-liang-shou-ching. See *Larger Sutra*
Wu-t'ai, Mount, 417n18

Y
Yama (Jp. Enma), 74–75, 325, 329
Yōkan (1033–1111), 69, 189, 423n61

Z
Zendō Shrine, 405
Zenkō-ji Temple, 68, 422n56
Zenrin-ji Temple, 69
Zenshō-bō (1174–1258), 49, 50, 253–54, 315–20, 421n46

About the Translators

Born in Fukuoka, Japan, in 1951, JOJI ATONE received a B.A. from Taishō University in Tōkyō and a Ph.D. from the University of Wisconsin–Madison in 1988. He served as a lecturer at Bukkyō University in Kyōto and Taishō University from 1988–91 and has been an administrator at Bukkyō University–Los Angeles Extension since 1992. He lives in Los Angeles.

YŌKO HAYASHI HORIUCHI was born in Hilo, Hawaii, where her father was a Jōdo Shū missionary priest. She earned a B.A. in Education and a Professional Administrator's certificate from the University of Hawaii and an M.A. in Education from the University of LaVerne in California. Her career as teacher and administrator in the State of Hawaii Department of Education spanned thirty years. She has two daughters, a grandson, and a granddaughter and now makes her home in Los Angeles.

About Wisdom Publications

WISDOM PUBLICATIONS, a nonprofit publisher, is dedicated to making available authentic works relating to Buddhism for the benefit of all. We publish books by ancient and modern masters in all traditions of Buddhism, translations of important texts, and original scholarship. Additionally, we offer books that explore East-West themes unfolding as traditional Buddhism encounters our modern culture in all its aspects. Our titles are published with the appreciation of Buddhism as a living philosophy, and with the special commitment to preserve and transmit important works from Buddhism's many traditions.

To learn more about Wisdom, or to browse books online, visit our website at www.wisdompubs.org.

You may request a copy of our catalog online or by writing to this address:

Wisdom Publications
199 Elm Street
Somerville, Massachusetts 02144 USA
Telephone: 617-776-7416
Fax: 617-776-7841
Email: info@wisdompubs.org
www.wisdompubs.org

Wisdom is a nonprofit, charitable 501(c)(3) organization affiliated with the Foundation for the Preservation of the Mahayana Tradition (FPMT).